Network Models
in Finance

The Frank J. Fabozzi Series

Network Models in Finance

Expanding the Tools for Portfolio and Risk Management

GUEORGUI S. KONSTANTINOV
FRANK J. FABOZZI

WILEY

Published by John Wiley & Sons, Inc., Hoboken, New Jersey.
Published simultaneously in Canada.

For general information on our other products and services or for technical support, please contact our Customer Care Department within the United States at (800) 762-2974, outside the United States at (317) 572-3993 or fax (317) 572-4002.

Wiley also publishes its books in a variety of electronic formats. Some content that appears in print may not be available in electronic formats. For more information about Wiley products, visit our web site at www.wiley.com.

Library of Congress Cataloging-in-Publication Data
Names: Fabozzi, Frank J., author. | Konstantinov, Gueorgui S., author.
Title: Network models in finance: expanding the tools for portfolio and risk management / Gueorgui S. Konstantinov, Frank J. Fabozzi.
Description: Hoboken, New Jersey: John Wiley & Sons Inc., [2025] | Series: The Frank J. Fabozzi series | Includes bibliographical references and index. | Summary: "*Network Models in Finance: Expanding the Tools for Portfolio and Risk Management* explores the application of network theory to asset management, emphasizing how network-based methodologies can enhance portfolio and risk management. The book integrates quantitative modeling, causal relationships, and optimization within a network framework, extending beyond traditional asset management tools. It provides a comprehensive overview of graph-theoretical approaches and practical implementations using R, bridging classical methods with modern financial data science. By offering both theoretical insights and practical applications, the book aims to address complex challenges in finance, making it a valuable resource for practitioners and academics seeking advanced network-based solutions in asset management"– Provided by publisher.
Identifiers: LCCN 2024041153 (print) | LCCN 2024041154 (ebook) | ISBN 9781394279685 (hardback) | ISBN 9781394279708 (ebook) | ISBN 9781394279692 (epub)
Subjects: LCSH: Portfolio management–Mathematical models. | Financial risk management–Mathematical models. | System analysis.
Classification: LCC HG4529.5.F33455 2025 (print) | LCC HG4529.5 (ebook) | DDC 332.6–dc23/eng/20241107
LC record available at https://lccn.loc.gov/2024041153
LC ebook record available at https://lccn.loc.gov/2024041154

Cover Image: Courtesy of Frank J. Fabozzi
Cover Design: Wiley

SKY10093319_120924

To my family.
– Gueorgui S. Konstantinov

*To the memory of the 13 courageous soldiers who gave their lives during
the Afghanistan evacuation.*
– Frank J. Fabozzi

Contents

PART THREE

Preface

N*etwork Models in Finance: Expanding the Tools for Portfolio and Risk Management* integrates network theory with asset management, delving into quantitative modeling and the simulation approaches of networks and their applications to two aspects of aspect management: portfolio and risk management. Drawing on practitioner and academic research on network theory and the theories associated with asset management, we provide a timely and comprehensive overview of innovative network-based tools and methodologies applied to asset management. The approaches discussed in this book are not necessarily novel but extend beyond traditional models and tools in asset management by incorporating causal relationships, inference, association, probabilistic structures, and optimization within a new network-based framework using time-series data.

In this book, we showcase the broad and deep knowledge of network theory and its applications. Networks provide new perspectives for asset managers, offering insights into investment management topics highly relevant for institutional investors, family offices, researchers, academics, and industry practitioners. This book stands out by providing insights that extend current knowledge in network theory to address specific needs in portfolio and risk management. It offers a unique contribution compared to the existing literature, making it a valuable resource for understanding and applying network-based methodologies in asset management.

The motivation for this book comes from our proven track record and practical experience with network models in asset management. We have successfully implemented network-based asset allocation across a broad set of portfolios. Scientifically, our motivation and background are influenced by numerous seminal works reported in the literature that highlight the connectedness in various organizational, biological, informational, financial, social, economic, technological, and physical fields. These works suggest that traditional reductionist approaches in science may benefit from more holistic methods that preserve and explain complexity. This foundational perspective drives our exploration of network theory in the context of asset management.

In this line of thought, the underlying assumption in the book is that there is a relationship between the interacting entities in financial markets. In finance, several studies have embraced these themes, where researchers have argued that economics is a science of relations and finance needs new tools to investigate financial market complexity. These works gave birth to this book.

This book distinguishes itself by implementing several graph-theoretical frameworks in asset management. Specifically, it provides an overview of various types of networks that can be investigated, implemented, and validated in practice. The techniques covered are the product of rigorous theoretical research and development by many experts and researchers in network theory, graph theory, economics, finance, mathematics, and the physical sciences. Concepts borrowed from diverse scientific research are adapted to fit the asset management framework, representing a unified approach to quantitative portfolio and risk management that extends traditional models to modern financial data science and analytics.

In addition to offering a solid theoretical foundation for network science, we emphasize the practical implementation of network modeling approaches that can be successfully applied in real-world multi-asset, bond, equity, and alternative asset allocation. This book bridges traditional investment methods, such as optimization approaches and variance-covariance frameworks, with modern financial data science applications, integrating the domain of networks into asset management.

Covering a wide range of applications relevant to both practitioners and academics, we guide the reader by first developing a robust theoretical framework, and then providing practical illustrations and codes in the programming language R for actual portfolios comprising traditional and alternative asset classes, factors, and other economic variables like payments and transaction data. A major objective is to shed light on the problems faced by practitioners in portfolio management and risk management, considering that asset classes and factors are integrated into a holistic framework. Potential solutions to these problems are provided.

The primary distinction of *Network Models in Finance*, compared to other books on network modeling, lies in its comprehensive coverage of the visualization, analysis, research, estimation, and computation of a wide range of networks applied in asset management. This book focuses specifically on evaluating portfolio networks and investigating their properties.

Related literature has been published that explore various aspects of networks in finance and economics. For instance, some books provide network analysis and models applied to economics, finance, corporate governance, and investments, focusing on analytical modeling and the econometric and statistical analysis of properties emerging from individual-level interactions. These authors combine observational and theoretical insights in networks and agent-based models, which are valuable for understanding nonlinear and evolving complex systems.

Other works explicitly focus on networks' risk management advantages, discussing the risk propagation, contagion, and spillover effects that networks provide to different asset classes. Additionally, while some books offer a broad and detailed analysis of networks and their relation to markets, they often need a more focused view of asset management.

In contrast, our book integrates these various approaches to provide a detailed and specific examination of network-based methods in asset management, which makes it a unique and valuable resource in the field.

CENTRAL BOOK THEMES

A network consists of nodes and links between them. The nodes and links are the central fields of investigation. The chapters of this book cover different topics related to nodes and links and describe, explain, and apply various tools used to model and analyze financial networks in asset management. The datasets include a broad set of asset classes and factor time series. Additionally, we use datasets from country payments and other transaction data.

Network Models in Finance contains 12 chapters, which are divided into three parts. Part One comprises Chapters 1–4.

- Chapter 1 introduces the basic concepts of real networks, network science, and different network types. The importance of understanding the interactions among economic variables, individuals, and financial institutions to capture and explain complex market behaviors is explained. The chapter's focus then shifts to data, detailing the types of datasets used in network analysis within finance.
- Chapter 2 covers network structure and description, network representation, types, and visualization. The chapter begins with an overview of both basic and complex network types and the definition of connectedness. Specific topics include metrics that explain, describe, and capture the complex relationships underlying graphs, as well as importance scores and specific node and edge properties that

describe networks. The chapter features numerous examples of networks across different asset classes and topics in asset management, providing a broad overview of modeling networks at both the node and edge levels.

■ Chapter 3 investigates descriptive network metrics and their application in asset management, offering descriptive statistics that characterize networks. These metrics refer to a network's overall properties and aim to describe its underlying structure.

■ Chapter 4 focuses on centrality and other importance scores, which are among the most critical nodal characteristics of networks.

Part Two comprises Chapters 5–10, focusing on the network construction for portfolio management.

■ Chapter 5 provides an overview of networks and how they are constructed using mathematical models. It explains the various approaches to modeling real networks, including topics such as the Erdös–Renyi random graph model, the Albert–Barabasi preferential attachment model, and the small-world model.

■ Chapter 6 covers the most widely used networks in finance, focusing on association network models constructed using statistical tests. The chapter's primary focus is on link prediction models, which aim to use existing data and observations to generate scores that indicate the likelihood of links between vertices. While these links are not directly observable, observable market data can be leveraged to model these relationships effectively.

■ Chapter 7 discusses statistical and econometric models, focusing on network construction used in portfolio allocation models based on different types of regression models. The regression models applied are both linear and nonlinear. These models may consist of multifactor or single-factor structures, incorporating one or multiple explanatory variables and possibly interaction terms governing cross-relationships between these variables.

■ Chapter 8 describes probability models used to construct portfolio networks. Probability theory offers a straightforward approach to implement mathematical and statistical tools for edge prediction and simulation. The probabilistic models discussed in this chapter include Markov chain network models and Bayesian networks, which enable model generation without requiring prior information about the underlying network structure.

■ Chapter 9, one of the most advanced chapters in this book, covers model selection and network manipulation using three statistical models: the Exponential Random Growth model, the Latent Network Model, and the Laplacian Spectral Partitioning model. This chapter also includes discussions and visual examples of causal network interference models, which estimate the network impact of preselected nodes under treatment. Key topics include network inference, mathematical models for network simulation using unobserved and observed data, and their implementation within nonoptimization and optimization algorithms. Additionally, it discusses data science models that help evaluate the goodness-of-fit of networks.

■ Chapter 10 summarizes how different networks can be applied to asset management. This chapter, which is central to the book, focuses on portfolio construction using networks. It uses concrete asset class and factor networks to demonstrate the advantages and versatility of networks in asset management, providing tools and practical examples for simulating, estimating, and applying networks to asset allocation. It also discusses the role of networks in financial markets and their advantages for the asset management industry, including examples of portfolio allocation using networks with both nonoptimization and optimization approaches.

Part Three of the book comprises Chapters 11 and 12, focusing on risk management with networks.

- Chapter 11 discusses various frameworks for risk management, differentiating between spillover, contagion, and financial stress. A major topic in this chapter is the impact of risk on nodes and edges.
- Chapter 12 is dedicated to portfolio risk management, providing readers with an advanced framework for implementing networks in risk management. The chapter begins with a detailed description of spillover and contagion risks and how these risks can be modeled using networks. Key themes include the computation of risk, fragility, and other metrics that help manage portfolio risk using a graph-theoretical framework. This chapter also features network-based risk indicators for modeling and predicting spillover and contagion risks in global asset markets. Using a broad set of examples, the advantages of novel time-varying metrics such as entropy, Ricci curvature, and spillover indices are demonstrated.

THE AUDIENCE FOR THIS BOOK

This book's intended audience includes portfolio managers, risk managers, chief investment officers, consultants, researchers/analysts, investors (i.e., beneficial owners), sales managers, and academic researchers.

- For portfolio managers, the book provides insights into a holistic approach to quantitative network-based portfolio management, including risk analysis, monitoring and control, portfolio optimization, and asset allocation. Portfolio managers can utilize networks to simulate and validate asset networks, capture asset interconnectedness in portfolios and benchmarks, and apply methods from financial data science like cross-validation, goodness-of-fit estimation, statistical inference, optimizations, allocation, and backtesting.
- Risk managers within the portfolio management team will benefit from tools designed to investigate the risks associated with interconnected asset classes and factors in the market rather than isolated risk drivers of risk. These tools can actively monitor, predict, and identify time-varying spillover and contagion associated with portfolio assets, helping to identify risk scores using different metrics to explain interconnectedness, fragility, risk increment, and the criticality of asset classes and portfolios.
- Chief investment officers (CIOs) seeking to expand the role of networks in portfolio and risk analysis, allocation, and management within their organizations will gain a deeper understanding of interconnectedness risks and how portfolio managers apply network theory to quantitative asset management. The book provides valuable insights beyond traditional allocation methods and analysis, offering CIOs a new perspective on asset management.
- Consultants will find the book useful for analyzing and investigating managers' investment processes applying network theory to quantitative portfolios. It helps consultants evaluate the merits of network-based and traditional portfolio managers and their investment processes, broadening their knowledge of network and financial data science-based portfolio management tools that are less familiar to asset owners and prospective clients. Researchers and analysts seeking to expand their and understanding of the risks associated with networks and interconnected asset classes and factors will benefit from the book's coverage. It provides insightful information on constructing networks in portfolio and risk management.
- Investors (i.e., beneficial owners) should understand the construction process of network-based portfolios and the resulting risk attributes for fund selection, holistic analysis, and interconnectedness. The book covers the functionality and relationships of the network constituents and risks, demonstrating how portfolio managers apply analytical tools to generate alpha.

- Sales managers (i.e., "asset gathers") must explain to clients how their firm's asset manager performed and added value using novel and alternative capital allocation and investing techniques. This requires a deep understanding of network science, how network-based portfolios are managed, along with the benefits of incorporating network analysis into investors' portfolios.
- Academic researchers need to understand network theory and the application of network-based portfolio models, recognize the potential for added value, limitations of theoretical frameworks, and how practitioners address the challenges of network theory applied to portfolios. The book provides practical examples and codes, offering insightful information for asset allocation and risk management, which may differ from mainstream approaches in investment textbooks that treat asset risk more as separable and isolated rather than holistic, integrated, and interconnected.

Acknowledgments

This book was inspired by Professor Otto Loistl of the Vienna University of Economics and Business, whose insights, vision, and work on the analysis and applications of interactions in financial markets have been profoundly influential.

We are deeply grateful for the feedback, suggestions, constructive criticism, and shared experiences of our colleagues who collaborated with us on previous projects. Their invaluable insights, inspiration, and encouragement were instrumental in the development of this book. In particular, we would like to thank:

- Irene Aldridge of AbleMarkets
- Atanas Angelov of ResTec
- Eduard Baitinger of FERI Trust
- Jennifer Bender of State Street Global Advisors
- Andreas Chorus of LBBW Asset Management
- Alexander Denev of Turnleaf Analytics
- Alexander Fleiss of Rebellion Research
- Daniel Giamouridis of Qube Research & Technologies and Bayes Business School
- Petia Zeiringer of Union Invest Real Estate Austria
- Frank Hagenstein of Hagenstein Real Estate
- Hossein Kazemi of CISDM/Isenberg School of Management and the University of Massachusetts at Amherst
- William Kinlaw of State Street Global Markets
- Panagiotis Patzartzis of LBBW Asset Management
- Momtchil Pojarliev of Wellington
- David Primik of Wiener Städtische Versicherung
- Jonas Rebman of LBBW Asset Management
- Mario Rusev of d-fine
- Axel Sima of Generali
- Joseph Simonian of Autonomous Investment Technologies
- Andreas Otto St. Vogelsinger of Astro-Pharma
- Ronny Weise of Societe Generale
- Christoph Witzke of Deka Investments

We extend our special thanks to Marcos Lòpez de Prado for his insights and for pushing financial data science forward.

We also thank AQR Capital Management, LLC, and Professor Kenneth French for providing their data libraries, which were invaluable to our research.

Gueorgui S. Konstantinov is senior portfolio manager FX and Fixed Income at DekaBank in Frankfurt, Germany. For more than 18 years, he held senior portfolio manager roles at several asset management companies where he managed global bond portfolios and currencies for institutional investors and pension funds. He is an advisory board member of *The Journal of Portfolio Management, The Journal of Alternative Investments*, and *The Journal of Financial Data Science*. He has authored articles in both academic and practitioner journals and is a coauthor of *Quantitative Global Bond Portfolio Management*. He earned the Chartered Alternative Investments Analyst (CAIA) and Financial Data Professional (FDP) designations. He received his MA in economics in 2005 and a doctoral degree in 2008 from the Vienna University of Economics and Business Administration (WU).

Frank J. Fabozzi is a Professor of Practice in the Carey Business School at Johns Hopkins University. He is the editor of *The Journal of Portfolio Management*, co-editor/ co-founder of *The Journal of Financial Data Science*, and an editor of *Annals of Operations Research*. Over the past 50 years, he has held professorial positions at MIT, Yale, Princeton, EDHEC Business School, New York University, Carnegie Mellon, and Rutgers. From 1988 to 2023, he was a trustee of the BlackRock closed-end fund complex. Dr. Fabozzi is the CFA Institute's 2007 recipient of the C. Stewart Sheppard Award and the CFA Institute's 2015 recipient of the James R. Vertin Award. He was inducted into the Fixed Income Analysts Society Hall of Fame in November 2002. He has earned the designations of Chartered Financial Analyst (CFA) and Certified Public Accountant (CPA). He received his bachelor's and master's degrees in economics in 1970 from the City College of New York, where he was elected to Phi Beta Kappa. He received his doctorate degree in economics in 1972 from the City University of New York. In 1994, he was awarded an Honorary Doctorate of Humane Letters from Nova Southwestern.

PART
One

Introduction

Contents

The main purpose of this book is to provide a broad overview of how to build financial networks used in investment management. In general, finance is a discipline in which all aspects of real-life networks can be found. Collaboration and exchange of services, financial transactions, and contractual obligations represent connections. These connections and the interacting entities can be considered as networks. Finance is not a system that resides in a state of chaos but is characterized by organized complexity. These networks represent the underlying structures and organization. Applying statistical, econometric, and mathematical models when building financial networks helps reveal the often-hidden underlying architecture of financial markets.

In this chapter, we provide a comprehensive introduction to the various types of networks and their relevance to financial markets. We begin with a general overview of networks, covering technological and infrastructure, in addition to information, social, and biological networks. The chapter emphasizes the unique characteristics of financial networks, particularly their proprietary nature, which necessitates specific modeling and estimation techniques.

The chapter further describes how different network properties, such as dyads and triads, apply to financial markets. It explains the importance of understanding the interactions among economic variables, individuals, and financial institutions to capture and explain complex market behaviors. The chapter focus then shifts to data, detailing the types of datasets used in network analysis within finance, including assets and factor returns, hedge fund and mutual fund returns, global equity market returns, and country bond market index returns.

Finally, the chapter delves into the application of network theory in asset management. It discusses how networks can be used for risk and portfolio management, data analysis, trading, risk management, and performance evaluation. The chapter concludes with a discussion on the design of financial networks and the key takeaways from understanding and applying network theory to finance.

NETWORK THEORY, GRAPH THEORY, AND TOPOLOGY

Network theory is a field of mathematics with roots tracing back to the works of some of the world's most famous mathematicians, such as Leonhard Euler, Bernhard Riemann, and Henri Poincaré. It offers a framework for understanding and analyzing the relationships and interactions among interconnected entities. This theory extends the graph theory principles, founded by Euler's solution to the Königsberg bridge problem.[1] Graph theory involves studying graphs (or mathematical structures) used to model pairwise relations between objects. In graph theory, graphs consist of vertices (or nodes) and edges (or links) that connect pairs of vertices. Euler's work laid the groundwork for network theory by introducing these basic components and demonstrating the connection between topology and network theory.

Network theory builds on these concepts to study more complex and large-scale networks, which can be found in various fields that will be discussed later in this chapter. It looks at how nodes (which can represent anything from people in a social network to computers in a technological network) are interconnected and how these connections affect the behavior and properties of the entire network.

Topology, another branch of mathematics, studies how shapes and spaces can change by stretching or bending without breaking apart or sticking together. At its core, topology is a study of how objects are connected, shaped, and arranged in space. Topology shares similarities with network analysis, especially in understanding how different elements are connected and how these connections affect the overall structure (i.e., the arrangement and organization of the elements) and behavior (i.e., how the system operates, reacts, or changes based on these connections).

WHAT IS A NETWORK?

According to Wasserman and Faust (1994), nodes often represent actors in social sciences. The term nodes and actors can be used interchangeably in network science because actors represent social (investors, individuals, corporate or institutional units, countries, and economic entities) that interact. Interaction might be a transfer of goods and services, physical connection, relation, association, or any type of material or non-material movement. When interacting, actors are linked by ties, edges, or links. The basic properties of a network, denoted by $G = (n,m) \equiv G(V,E)$, include the number of nodes (or vertices) $n(V)$ and the number

---

[1]The Königsberg bridge problem asked if it was possible to walk through the city of Königsberg and only cross each of its seven bridges exactly once. Euler's clever solution introduced the idea of using points, called vertices, to represent landmasses, and lines, called edges, to represent bridges. See Newman (2010).

of links (or edges) (E), where $n \in \mathbb{R}^n$ and $m \in \mathbb{R}^{n \times n}$ $(m_{i,j} \neq m_{j,i})$. Throughout this book, we will use the terms "nodes" and "vertices" interchangeably.

In an *undirected network*, $G^* = (n^*, m^*)$ represents the number of nodes n and links or edges (connections) m, where $n^* \in \mathbb{R}^n$ and $m^* \in \mathbb{R}^{n \times n}$ $(m_{i,j}{}^* = m_{j,i}{}^*)$. The nodes or actors in a network are connected by relational ties, links, or edges, which we also use interchangeably. The edges between the nodes govern the relations, which might be directional or unidirectional. These relations can arise from social connections, information exchange, biological ties, transportation, financial transactions, economic intermediation, social interactions, physical laws, or other forms of interaction. The term "catallactics," meaning exchange, can be used to describe networks in general. In this book, we will explore various types of relationships within networks, summarized into several major categories.

Increased computer power and data processing capabilities have enhanced personal and collective data recording. For example, data collection by smartphones and apps extends the datasets available for analysis. Data gathering using satellites, web scraping, text analysis, social networks, transactions, market data, and the like has grown tremendously. The term "alternative data" refers to novel methods of gathering data. Financial market research is evolving by applying not only traditional methods of analysis, but also tools capable of analyzing and describing a huge amount of data and possible relationships within the data. A shift from traditional methods of analysis like calculus, differential equations, and regression models to new techniques is inevitable and desirable for investigating underlying economic relationships, as stressed by Focardi and Fabozzi (2012).[2]

While traditional methods and procedures rely broadly on statistical correlations, the era of Big Data and significant computing power necessitates new pragmatic tools grounded in both mathematics and economics to enable efficient financial research. Modern finance is evolving, with financial markets, individual actions, and investor behavior and sentiment continually changing, leading to the emergence of new structures. As new data emerges, patterns, transmission channels, and causality also shift. Graph theory aids in identifying and exploring the underlying structure in the data, revealing relationships and connections between economic players and their interactions.

Network theory is dedicated to the science of connections between objects, and as Focardi and Fabozzi (2012) argued, economics is the science of relations. Therefore, network theory is an essential tool for analyzing relationships among actors, institutions, and instruments in financial markets. Within this framework, the nodes in a graph, applied to financial markets, represent various entities such as asset classes, individual security (i.e., stocks, bonds, and funds), countries, factors, financial institutions, trading partners, derivative contracts, or similar financial entities or instruments. The primary focus of graph theory is to identify relationships between these nodes and model the edges based on robust statistical, economic, and mathematical principles. This book aims to model financial networks and the edges between the nodes, which are typically known, but the links between them are often not observable.

Real-world networks might be observed, but networks in financial markets are mostly model-based as opposed to being sample-based. Having said that, it is worth discussing the common characteristics of the major types of real networks, how their properties relate to financial networks used in portfolio and risk

---

[2]Shannon (1948), Simon (1962), Haken (1978), Kauffman (1993), Loistl and Landes (1989), Watts (1999, 2003), Wasserman and Faust (1994), Mandelbrot and Hudson (2004), Watts (1999a, 1999b, 2003), Laughlin (2005), Klir (2006), Holland (2012), and Newman (2010), among others, highlighted the idea that there is connectedness in various organizational, biological, informational, financial, social, economic, technological, and physical fields. Their work suggests that reductionist approaches in science should be replaced by more holistic methods that preserve and explain complexity.

management, and what the necessary model specifications are to model such networks. The most interesting and decisive property of real-world networks like biological, informational, technological, or social networks is the underlying flow process of transmitting information between the nodes.[3] In the upcoming sections, we provide details of some of the existing and well-known real networks, highlighting the principles that apply to financial markets and asset management.

Technological and Infrastructure Networks

Technological networks include power grids, infrastructure, industrial, and water supply networks.[4] The most interesting property of such networks is the existence of numerous Micro-Nets, which are locally autonomous networks yet form part of an entire global network. According to Newman (2010), examples of technological networks include the Internet, power grids, telephone networks, and other networks underlying physical infrastructure.

Technological networks, such as subway systems in cities, connect stations of other transport routes. Package delivery networks exemplify networks using the shortest path between nodes for efficient delivery. In these networks, information is not duplicated. Rather, each package or delivery is fixed, with a known receiver, which ensures that the goods arrive at the correct node. Additionally, the information or goods are indivisible. Borgatti (2005) illustrates that the delivery of goods follows the shortest possible path between two points within a given space or network, which minimizes the number of edges transversed (referred to as a geodesic path), ensuring the most efficient route is taken. This is a critical concept for optimizing routes and efficiently connecting points in various types of networks, including transportation, communication, and logistics systems. Minimizing distance is the goal, thereby reducing the time and resources needed to move from one node to another. A similarity in financial markets can be observed in transactions.

Although physical delivery no longer applies to all financial market transactions as it did in the early twentieth century when physical delivery was customary, the financial assets bought by an investor still follow a direct path, arriving from the seller to the buyer. Additionally, financial markets might contain local networks that are part of the entire financial landscape. Consider, for example, a network comprising highly connected private equity managers who build a local network. They might be part of a global network of limited and general partners within their private equity network.

Information Networks and Financial Markets

Many types of information networks exist.[5] The most important and well-known are citation networks and the World-Wide Web (WWW). Whereas the citation network links all available bibliographic works already published and there is a specific order when establishing the links between the nodes, the WWW is a network linking the pages available on the Internet. Newman (2010) stresses that the WWW is different from the Internet, which is a physical network connecting computers. The WWW connects pages, enabling information to travel without any specific order. Among the most interesting examples of information networks are email communications and the spread of electronic information. Emails, for example, can reach

---

[3]Several of the important works on networks include Milgram (1967), Merton (1968), Rapoport (1968) Freeman (1996), Albert and Barabási (2000, 2002), and Newman (2000, 2002).

[4]Seminal works among others are Watts (2002, 2003), Watts and Strogatz (1998), Amaral et al. (2000), and Almaas (2002).

[5]Some of the important papers on information networks, including citation networks, are Price (1965), Seglen (1992), and Redner (1998). Key papers dedicated to the World-Wide Web are Bornholdt and Ebel (2001); Kleinberg and Lawrence (2001); Albert, Jeong, and Barabási (1999); and Krapivsky and Redner (2002).

numerous places and numerous receivers both simultaneously and concurrently. The information is spread through replication.

The relationship of such networks to financial markets highlights two important aspects of modern social and economic life: information processing and information efficiency as well as the exchange of goods, services, or financial instruments. While information processes refer to how information is processed, the transmission or movement of financial assets involves a different dynamic. As we shall see, information can be copied or replicated, but financial assets are indivisible.

Grossman and Stiglitz (1980) investigated the information process in financial markets and discussed the impossibility of achieving information efficiency. They demonstrated that markets cannot be fully efficient because new information is constantly arriving. As a result, equilibrium can only be momentarily achieved until new information arrives or the decision-making context changes.[6]

Importantly, information travels by replication, functioning as a "copy" mechanism, in contrast to a "move" mechanism. The move mechanism applies to money transfers, where the money transfer or payments have a fixed receiver – the buyer of the goods or services.

Social Networks and Financial Markets

Social networks are perhaps the most compelling types of networks that attract interest due to the rise of social platforms that connect individuals.[7] The nodes in these social networks are called actors and are connected by ties, or links. Where the actors are connected or the basic property of social networks, is the dyad, which represents the connection between two actors establishing a social relationship.

An important characteristic of social relations is the existence of triads, which involve the relationships among three actors. A triad consists of three dyads – one between each pair of actors. Unlike dyads, which are simply connections that either exist or do not exist between two actors, triads are more complex due to their potential directions of connections. With 16 possible configurations, triads enable the modeling of intricate social interactions, revealing patterns and local structures.

Wasserman and Faust (1994), Robins et al. (2007), and Robins et al. (2005) emphasized that in social sciences, local structures shape the global structure. The knowledge of these local structures provided by analyzing triads helps to understand the overall network dynamics. Thus, triads represent the global structure of an actor network.[8] A real-life example of a triad this would be the social interactions between individuals on social media platforms.

Facebook, X (formerly Twitter), LinkedIn, and Instagram are not only social network platforms but also successful companies. However, the underlying mechanism is for two actors to be connected. The major principle is that "friends of my friends are also my friends." Social networks are central to how people are influenced by others. An essential property is that connections coincide simultaneously rather than sequentially from individual to individual. However, social networks also possess the distinctive property of directedness, meaning that the links between nodes have specific directions. This directedness implies that an edge between two nodes does not always translate into an edge between a third node and the other

---

[6]See Monk et al. (2019).

[7]Newman (2010) argues that social networks are among the most studied networks. Notable examples of network studies refer to corporate business, social, sexual, and individual relationships on social networks including those discussed by Mariolis (1975), Mizruchi (1982), Merton (1968), Wasserman and Faust (1994), Glaskiewicz and Marsden (1978), Newman (2001), Girvan and Newman (2002), and Bramoulle et al. (2009).

[8]The triads are directly related to the clustering coefficient or transitivity of a graph. Transitivity of node connectedness means that when there is an edge between node i and j, and there is also an edge between node i and h, then there is an edge between j and h. See Newman (2010) and Robins et al. (2005).

two nodes. In other words, the principle "friends of my friends are also my friends" is often violated, and a direct connection between nodes may not necessarily exist.

A simple example provided by Konstantinov, Aldridge, and Kazemi (2023) illustrates the difference. Consider the social network Facebook. Once two people are connected, the link is symmetrical in any direction; if person A connects to person B, then the link is symmetrical, and individual B is a connected "friend" of individual A. Alternatively, consider the social networks X or Instagram. An individual might be linked to or following another, but that does not mean the latter person is linked to the former. This principle is not limited to social networks but also applies to financial markets where transactions, orders, and money flows follow a certain direction because of causal principles within a market framework.

Of essential interest are the flow processes in social networks and their application to financial markets. Unfortunately, the principle "friends of my friends are also my friends" does not work in financial markets. To model financial markets influenced by social networks, it is necessary to use a statistical approach that employs probability models. The reason for this is that in financial markets with heteroscedastic volatility, the edge connectivity is associated rather with large degree of uncertainty than depending on trajectories or steady-state conditions. While the set of nodes is fixed, the connections are modeled probabilistically. In this context, the edges in social networks applied to financial markets arise from realizing probabilities related to the "social aspect" of a network. In other words, the interaction between nodes is governed by probabilities rather than specific node and edge properties, known as covariates, trajectories, or attributes.[9]

A flow principle from social networks that might apply to financial markets is information replication, which underlies the influence approach. Influencing financial markets and investors is a phenomenon that can be traced back to the early years of investment history. The result of social influence observed in financial markets is the phenomenon of crowdedness, as documented by Charles Mackay (1980).[10] Convincing investors has a long tradition in financial markets and can significantly influence investment behavior.[11]

Biological Networks and Financial Markets

Biological networks are among the most interesting and widely studied types of networks.[12] Many examples have attracted research, including food networks, ecology, protein–protein interaction networks, metabolic networks, signaling networks, and intraspecies and interspecies networks. The most widely used

---

[9]The topic of node and edge properties is extensively analyzed in Chapter 9 where the Exponential Random Graph model is introduced and node and edge covariates (i.e., attributes) are discussed and modeled.

[10]The crowdedness results when a mass exhibits the same behavior. Three expressions are used in both the academic and practitioner literature to describe the same phenomenon: crowdedness and herding. Whereas crowdedness and herding apply to the same phenomenon, the origin of crowdedness can be traced back to behavioral economics. An overview of the literature provides an informative picture of this important phenomenon. Holland (2012) defined crowded effects as the decreasing payoff for individuals in the case of an increasing number of players in a strategy. An increasing number of players in a strategy is the consequence of increasing payoff. In such a case, the players are crowding the strategy. The concept of crowding itself is not restricted to specialists.

[11]The literature on the negative impact of crowdedness in financial markets is extensive. Several studies measured the effect of common exposure to the same investment vehicle – fund, style, factor, or asset classes – for equities, for example, Nofsinger and Sias (1999); in trading Cahan and Luo (2013); for volatility Marmer (2010); for alternative risk premia Baltas (2019); for currencies Pojarliev and Levich (2011); and for hedge funds Bussiere, Hoerova, and Klaus (2014); Bayraktar, Doole, Kassam, and Radchenko (2015); and Konstantinov and Rebmann (2020), among others. A positive view of crowdedness is provided by Surowiecki (2005).

[12]Some of the important works include works on protein interactions, biological systems, food webs, and the spread of viruses and diseases. Important works include Jeong et al. (2000), Fell and Wagner (2000), Ito et al. (2001),

biological networks in finance are neural networks. However, the primary purpose of discussing biological networks in the context of the topological structure of financial markets in this book is to understand the underlying information transmission process between the nodes.

According to Borgatti (2005), the process of spreading an infection in biological networks is characterized by duplication. Consider, for example, an infection impacting a specific population. The infection spreads by duplication but does not immediately reinfect the initial nodes because they might have developed immunity. The relevance of infection spread in a biological context to financial markets can be seen in the example of duplication of information such as gossip. Specifically, negative information about a company with an elevated risk of default can be transmitted through the network via news, gossip, company announcements and press releases, negatively impacting holders of that risky asset or company. Consider a portfolio initially impacted and then fully hedged against, say, the depreciation of a specific exchange rate. In this case, the spread of negative information cannot affect that portfolio, to how an infection cannot reinfect immunized nodes.

FINANCIAL MARKETS AND FINANCIAL NETWORKS

After a brief overview of the general types of networks that exist and are detectable in nature, it is logical to focus on the primary type of networks covered in this book: financial networks that model, explain, model, and simulate financial market interactions using time series data. Perhaps the major difference between all other networks and financial markets is that financial networks are often not observable. Structures emerge to stay persistent or transitory based on intrinsic and external conditions. The dynamics of the financial market and financial networks are not governed by nodes in isolation but by the interactions that never cease. Financial markets are an unstable system operating by interactions coined by the arrow of time, whose dynamics operates at the statistical level. Therefore, probabilistic thinking applies to edge formation in financial networks. They must be specified, estimated, or simulated because financial markets generate substantial amounts of hidden or proprietary data. Consider, for example, a stock exchange that generates enormous transaction data in milliseconds, but these data are not available to the public because asset prices are formed by the transactions that occur. In contrast, data availability estimates a bipartite network – a type of network in which the set of nodes can be divided into two distinct groups – possible for scientific publications, citation networks, or actor–movie records.

Once data are gathered, a network can be observed. Financial networks can be easily estimated using various data, such as payments between countries. Generally, the availability of data and directional exchange of information between the nodes makes network construction possible. However, financial market data become increasingly proprietary, and the availability of time series data are one of the most common sources of information.

Financial networks share many properties with biological, technological, informational, social, and industrial networks. Yet, modern finance uses returns derived from asset price data for analytical purposes. This is not surprising, as financial models are applied using time series data. With the rise of computing power, large storage processes, and the ability to analyze large data sets, alternative data are becoming more prevalent in asset management. However, economic variables and portfolio management still use traditional data formats. To remain grounded in traditional financial models that use time series data, in this book we primarily use datasets that comprise time series returns and prices. Consequently, while the

---

Jeaong et al. (2001), Maslov and Sneppen (2002), Sole and Pastor–Satorras (2003), Huxham et al. (1996), Fath et al. (2007), Dorogovtsev and Mendes (2002), and the seminal work of Kauffman (1993) dedicated to the interaction of individuals and the adapting landscape.

models used and applied in this book are not necessarily restricted to time series data, time series models are central to the analysis.

Nevertheless, networks can be constructed using traditional datasets as well as proprietary data, including the exchange of money flows (e.g., loans), market transaction data (e.g., order flow data), or any datasets reflecting interactions between market participants (see Chakrabarti, Pichl, and Kaizoji [2019] and Lee, Liu, and Lin [2010]). Interaction is the key concept and building principle and block of networks. Therefore, networks can be built using any data form measuring interactions between entities.

In finance, the connections among economic variables, individuals, financial institutions, and their relationships are what matter (see Easley and Kleinberg [2010] and Kalyagin, Pardalos, and Rassias [2014]). However, the collective sum might differ from the pure sum of individual parts. Stated differently, the interconnectedness among all hedge funds – based on their risk factor bets, return and risk exposure, stock holdings, etc. – is greater than the sum of all hedge funds active in the market, as merely accounted for by their assets under management and the number of active and dissolved funds. The interactions among economic variables and entities are essential as market complexity increases. Financial research requires techniques that can capture and explain complex behavior and relationships by focusing on the underlying structure rather than design. The most basic property of networks, including financial networks, is the definition of dyads. As explained earlier, dyads are simply the links or connections between two nodes. Dyadic relationships must be modeled and present a challenging task in financial markets. These node relationships can be directional. For example, they can involve the transfer of money or securities from the buyer to the seller or vice versa. Dyadic relationships can also be bidirectional if they are mutual.[13] For instance, the connectivity might be more abstract, such as the contractual obligation between two banks to settle transactions, which is unidirectional. The specific value and amount of the transaction determine the nature of directionality.

DATA

Behind every network, there is underlying data. Data are the central assets in financial data science, which might belong to financial networks. The purpose of this section is to provide an explanation of the data used in this book and why such data – funds, country indices, local markets, currencies, equities, bonds, alternative investments, and other asset classes and data sources –are used. The main idea is to use data that are representative of a wide range of financial analytical allocation processes. Data should provide more insights into how different networks can be modeled and used in asset management. Whereas data in most real networks are directly interpretable to build a network, in finance data are the backbone of almost all types of analytical undertakings. Time series data are the most widely used in finance, and in this book, we will primarily focus on time series data to estimate networks.

Datasets are necessary to illustrate the versatility of networks for portfolio and risk management. Like other books on networks and asset management, we use broad data to provide a better picture regarding the application of graph theory to asset management. For this purpose, we use datasets comprising stocks, assets, factors, country indices, fund returns, and other data used in financial analysis. This intuition behind using different datasets is versatile. For example, an asset network might be of particular interest to portfolio managers. Similarly, a network constructed from index data, such as the S&P 500 Index – a major equity market index – becomes important.

---

[13]The following intuition applies consider two points (nodes) in space. They can be connected by a line with an arrow pointing a direction from one point to another. The two nodes can be connected by two arrows, pointing to bidirectional connectedness.

On the other hand, a fund network is of primary interest to fund-of-fund managers, performance analysts, investment officers, and investors. Analyzing the fund network enables decision-makers to visualize and investigate the risk and return-based connectedness of specific funds in which they might be interested in investing. More central funds, or funds in the network periphery, provide different risk factor characteristics that might explain performance behavior. Elements such as risk, returns, fund size, capital transition, and other properties can be used to represent a fund network. Dynamically representing funds as a network can be particularly beneficial to database users, as the databanks change continuously. With funds representing nodes, data vendors can gain insights into where a liquidated, delisted, or newly added fund might appear in the database with its connections.[14]

The use of equity market data serves many purposes. Equity markets are among the most important markets in asset management with mutual funds, pension funds, hedge funds, and other entities heavily invested in them. These markets are perhaps the most dynamically changing markets. Equity market networks might be built from index data, representing the nodes as the individual stocks comprising an index or as country-specific equity markets (i.e., indices) representing global markets, such as the US, German, Japanese, and French stock markets, to name a few.

The data used in this book comprise datasets used in several publications. The motivation behind using different datasets is to provide more detailed and multidimensional examples of assets to which network analysis applies.[15]

In the upcoming sections, we provide details about the different datasets and briefly highlight their importance in representing networks.

Assets and Factor Returns

The dataset used for factors and asset returns is the sample set from the study by Konstantinov, Chorus, and Rebmann (2020). Similar dataset has also been utilized in factor research by Blitz (2018); Aked, Arnott, Bouchey, Li, and Shakernia (2019); and by Konstantinov and Rebman (2020), who investigated the hedge fund market.

It is worth briefly describing the asset and factor dataset in detail. Assets and factors constitute two broad datasets representing different economic and financial frameworks, each comprising 15 factors and 16 assets, spanning from January 2001 to March 2021. While Kritzman (2021) regards assets as primary economic units and factors as portfolio enhancements, the rise of factor investing has empowered portfolio management and the construction of factor portfolios.[16]

Factors have gained traction in asset management, with Harvey, Liu, and Zhu (2016) identifying over 300 factors available in financial research. However, both their statistical and economic significance can be questioned. When explaining equity returns using a multifactor regression model, Fama and French (1992, 1993) found the most prominent factors in the equity space to be market, value, and size. Carhart (1997)

---

[14]Note that a newly added fund in a database does not represent a newly set up and launched fund, because data providers often have criteria to adda a new fund like minimum track record and other statistics like assets under management. To maintain the backfill bias, which arises when adding previous performance, database providers allow for a newly added fund to a database to add up to certain number of past returns. Another issue with database providers is the survivorship bias, which centers that defunct funds should be considered with their past performance. In a dynamical network context this can be challenging, as funds are the nodes and a node ceasing to exist no longer appears in a network. However, because networks might represent the current stage of a fund network, the survivorship bias is not an issue when considering funds in a network.

[15]Sample datasets used in this book can be downloaded from https://finance-resolution.com/

[16]See Fama and French (1992, 1993, 2005), Jagadeesh and Titman (1993), Moskowitz et al. (2012), Asness et al. (2013), Frazzini and Pedersen (2014), and Ilmanen et al. (2021), among others.

added momentum as an explanatory factor for stock returns, while Fama and French (2015) discovered profitability and investment factors in equities.

We extend these traditional equity factors to include other asset classes available in financial research, such as fixed income, commodities, and currencies. To introduce the concept of categorization, which we will use in chapters in this book to construct networks, the monthly data can be divided into two subsets. The first subset is a pure factor set, widely considered in both academic and practitioner research, and consisting of the following factors:

- The equity premium is the US equity market excess return, denoted by Fama and French (1992, 1993) as Mkt.RF.
- The standard Fama and French (1992, 1993, 2015) factors for value (High minus Low), size (Small minus Big), profitability (Robust minus Weak), and investment (Conservative minus Aggressive) denoted by HML, SMB, RMW, and CMA, respectively. Data are obtained from Kenneth French's data library.[17]
- The one-month–lagged equity premium, denoted by MV(t–1), is the total market value of equity. This metric serves as an illiquidity factor and is relevant in various domains such as equity, credit, and duration.
- Asness et al. (2013) and Moskowitz et al. (2012) stressed that value and momentum are everywhere. For this reason, we use the return of time series value and momentum strategies on commodities, currencies, bonds, and equities provided by AQR Capital Management, LLC. The fixed-income long-short value and momentum are denoted as VALLS_VME_FI, MOMLS_VME_FI, respectively. The FX value and momentum factors are denoted as VALLS_VME_FX, and MOMLS_VME_FX. The commodity factors for value and momentum are denoted as VALLS_VME_COM, and MOMLS_VME_COM, respectively.
- The excess returns of long/short equity Betting-Against-Beta factor (BAB) factor, which consists of portfolios that are long low-beta securities and short high-beta securities, as developed by Frazzini and Pedersen (2014) and obtained from AQR Capital Management, LLC.

The second subset comprises assets and is closely related to asset datasets widely used in financial research to explain fund returns and construct multiasset portfolios.[18] We suggest that investors are interested in broad diversification, encompassing traditional and alternative assets. This dataset includes emerging markets, international equities, corporate bonds, private equity, commodity returns, currency, and hedge fund returns. More specifically, this dataset includes:

- The S&P 500 returns, denoted as S&P500
- MSCI Emerging Markets Index, denoted as EM
- The ICE BofAML U.S. Corporates Index, denoted as US.Corp.
- ICE BofAML U.S. High Yield Corporate Bond Index, denoted as US.HY
- J.P. Morgan U.S. Treasuries Index, as UST
- ICE BofAML U.S. Inflation-linked Index, denoted as INF.L
- Russell 2000 Index for the U.S. Small Cap Equities, denoted as Russell.2000
- HFRX Hedge Fund Global Index, denoted as HFRX
- Gold Index, denoted as Golds

---

[17]https://mba.tuck.dartmouth.edu/pages/faculty/ken.french/data_library.html
[18]For example, see Bender et al. (2019), Nystrup et al. (2018), Aked et al. (2019), Rafinot (2018), and Martellini and Milhau (2018).

- Thomson Reuters Private Equity Index, denoted as PE
- GS Commodity Index, denoted as Comdty
- U.S. Dollar Spot Index, denoted as the average international exchange rate (DXY)
- DJ Euro Stoxx 50 Index for European equities, denoted as EStoxx50
- Nikkei 225 Index for Japanese equities, denoted as Nikkei225
- ICE BofAML Euro Corporate Bond Index, denoted as EU.Corp
- ICE BofAML U.S. Treasury Bills Index, denoted as UST.Bills)

Hedge Fund and Mutual Fund Returns

Funds are significant financial assets whose managers actively engage in trading to implement trading strategies and adjusting their portfolio, interacting extensively with counterparties in the market. From a financial market microstructure perspective, funds are interconnected entities. Their interactions manifest through trading activities, and their exposure to specific asset classes links them with other funds sharing similar market exposures. This exposure creates a network of interconnected funds, often identified through crowdedness analysis. Understanding fund interactions is crucial for investors, portfolio managers, and risk managers, as it helps in assessing systemic risk, identifying market trends, and making informed investment decisions. To provide a comprehensive overview of network analysis, we utilize monthly fund returns from several published studies. Specifically, we incorporate 239 single hedge fund returns from January 2006 to December 2016, and 442 single hedge funds in the period from April 2011 to December 2016, as analyzed by Konstantinov and Simonian (2020). The study covers with the following hedge fund categories: Global Macro (GM), Alternative Risk Premia (ARP), Active Currency (FX), Commodities (C), Credit Long Short (CLS), Managed Futures (MF), Event-Driven (ED), Liquid Alternatives (LA), and Multi-strategy (MS), Equity Long Short (ELS), Equity Market Neutral (EN), Distressed Debt (DD) and Tail Risk Hedge (TH). Additionally, we include 193 bond and equity fund returns from September 2006 to September 2016, as studied by Konstantinov and Rusev (2020).

Applying various network algorithms to fund returns enables us to compute descriptive statistics and other network measures, visualize fund networks, and investigate their properties. This analysis is particularly valuable for fund managers, fund-of-fund managers, investors, chief investment officers, and regulators, as it enhances understanding of fund interactions, risk exposure, and market dynamics.

Global Equity Market Returns

Research on multi-asset portfolios inherently involves equity markets. Leibowitz (2011) stressed that every asset class contains an equity component. Equity markets are a fundamental part of portfolios, and global asset allocation decisions are impossible without them. For this purpose, we use 24 country-specific equity market returns based on the study of Frazzini and Pedersen (2014), provided by AQR Capital Management, LLC. The networks estimated for this dataset cover the period from June 2000 to October 2023.

The countries included in this dataset are

Australia (AUS)

Austria (AUT)

Belgium (BEL)

Canada (CAN)

Chile (CHL)

Germany (DEU)

Denmark (DNK)

Spain (ESP)

Finland (FIN)

France (FRA)

United Kingdom (GBR)

Greece (GRC)

Hong Kong (HKG)

Ireland (IRL)

Israel (ISR)

Italy (ITA)

Japan (JPN)

Netherlands (NLD)

Norway (NOR)

New Zealand (NZL)

Portugal (PRT)

Singapore (SGP)

Sweden (SWE)

United States (USA)

Using these country-specific equity market returns, we apply network estimation techniques to analyze and visualize the interconnectedness and interactions within global equity markets. This comprehensive analysis supports portfolio management and global asset allocation strategies.

European Multi-Asset and Bond Market Data

European markets represent a distinct subset of assets whose development can be traced back to the establishment of the European Monetary Union (EMU) in 2000, which mitigated currency risk within member countries. Despite this unified currency risk, EMU markets exhibit specific dynamics driven significantly by internal monetary policies set by the European Central Bank (ECB), domestic demand, and other macroeconomic factors. These dynamics highlight the interconnectedness of EMU markets and offer insights into how intra-EMU markets are interconnected or diverge over time.

The European bond and multi-asset market data used in this book draw from studies conducted by Konstantinov (2021) with data comprising monthly total return indices denominated in Euro in the period from January 2000 to December 2020, and Konstantinov and Fabozzi (2021), focusing on European bond market dynamics, manager performance, and portfolio allocation strategies. The sample comprises monthly returns for the period from January 2001 to December 2019. The dataset includes bond yields and spreads from core countries such as Germany, Netherlands, Finland, France, Austria, and Belgium, as well as peripheral countries including Spain, Italy, Portugal, and Ireland.[19] Additionally, the dataset encompasses time series data from major European bond and equity markets from January 2000 to December 2020.

---

[19]Konstantinov and Fabozzi (2021) highlighted that the separation between core and periphery countries has been the result of the macroeconomic deterioration of economic fundamentals – debt level, fiscal deficits, growth rates, and current account deficits – and European market structure. EMU's launch shaped the economic and financial dynamics and even more transformed during the 2007 to 2008 Global Financial and the European debt crises. The government bond

This comprehensive dataset provides valuable insights into the behavior and performance of European markets, aiding in the analysis of portfolio management and investment strategies within the EMU framework.

Country Bond Market Index Returns

Asset allocation decisions often underscore the significance of country risk, which can extend to include geopolitical risk.[20] Global bond markets constitute a dedicated asset class in asset management. They reflect the interplay among currencies, interest rates, and liquidity. Bond index data facilitate understanding these dynamics.

Bond markets globally encompass both developed and emerging markets. Country-specific bond indices serve a dual purpose: they act as proxies for country risk, encapsulating risks such as interest rate fluctuations, political instability, currency volatility, macroeconomic conditions, and default risks. Simultaneously, these indices represent the fixed-income market's liquidity and integration into the global financial landscape, highlighting substantial connectivity in both dimensions.

Emerging market bonds are particularly appealing to investors due to their potential for high returns, albeit accompanied by heightened risks during global market crises, liquidity challenges, geopolitical uncertainties, and other factors specific to emerging markets. The exploration of emerging market bond portfolios as a distinct asset class traces back to seminal works by Erb, Harvey, and Viskanta (1999) and Chiang, Wisen, and Zhou (2007). Systematic investment strategies in local currency bonds, focusing on styles and factors, have been investigated by Brooks, Richardson, and Xu (2020), with factor investing gaining attention in emerging market bond research (Brooks et al., 2018). Konstantinov (2022) has proposed a network approach to systematic investing in emerging market fixed income.

In financial literature, indices often represent emerging markets due to limitations in investigating individual securities that are sufficiently liquid and tradable. The dataset used includes bond market country index returns, allowing for the analysis of investable performance from risk and return perspectives. Konstantinov (2022) utilized monthly data for emerging market bond indexes denominated in USD from January 2000 to July 2021. Notably, the J.P. Morgan EMBI Global Diversified Index, which consists of USD-denominated bonds, operates as a total return index.

This index encompasses several countries and includes high-yielding government bonds from emerging markets. Given the prevalence of country risk in emerging market hard-currency bonds, empirical analyses focus on the countries constituting the core of the J.P. Morgan EMBI Global Diversified Investment Grade (IG) Index. Specifically, the analysis includes only those emerging markets with investment grade bonds. The 18 country bond indexes covered are

- Brazil (BR)
- Chile (CL)
- China (CN)
- Colombia (CO)

---

yield widening, which began after the former crisis, has marked the definition of core and peripheral countries. The core category comprises the countries of Germany, Austria, Netherlands, France, Belgium, and Finland. The peripheral category refers to the countries with weak economic fundamentals, including Italy, Greece, Spain, Portugal, and Ireland. Beirne and Fratscher (2013) argued that there are substantial and sustained differences in the pricing of fundamentals for sovereign risk among European countries. De Haan et al. (2014) argued that bond yield fluctuations in the Eurozone are less driven by macroeconomic fundamentals, which inadequately explain the bond dynamics of peripheral countries.
[20]For a detailed explanation of geopolitical risk and an investment management approach to addressing such risks and incorporating them into asset allocation, refer to Simonian (2024).

- Hungary (HN)
- Indonesia (ID)
- Malaysia (MY)
- Mexico (MX)
- Philippines (PH)
- Poland (PL)
- Panama (PA)
- Peru (PE)
- Russia (RU)
- South Africa (ZA)
- Turkey (TR)
- Uruguay (UY)
- Ukraine (UA)
- Vietnam (VN)

Payments and Transaction Data

As emphasized in earlier sections, most financial networks used in asset management are model based. By utilizing specific country-flow data, we can generate a sampling-based network derived from exchanging country flows. This approach employs straightforward payment and transaction data to directly represent a financial network, thereby minimizing the need for extensive modeling.

However, the use of such data in asset management is quite limited and typically restricted to hedge funds, brokerage houses, and other entities with privileged access to large databases. Constructing networks directly applicable to asset management necessitates access to appropriate data obtained through direct observation of market transactions, such as data sourced from stock exchanges. This direct data approach enhances the accuracy and applicability of the networks in reflecting real-world financial interactions and transactions.

APPLICATION OF NETWORKS IN FINANCE

Networks in finance encompass a broad spectrum of applications integrating various types of networks discussed in the preceding sections. The application of networks in finance extends well beyond the scope covered in this book, spanning disciplines such as economics, accounting, insurance, finance, geopolitics, and market microstructure. However, several key aspects related to asset management deserve particular emphasis. Future-oriented quantitative asset management focuses prominently on the following topics:

- *Data analysis and processing*: Leveraging advanced techniques to analyze and process vast amounts of financial data
- *Portfolio construction*: Using quantitative graph-based methods to construct portfolios that optimize risk and return profiles based on investor objectives
- *Portfolio management*: Actively managing network-based portfolios to meet investment goals while considering interrelated market conditions and changing interconnected risk factors
- *Trading*: Executing trades efficiently to capitalize on market opportunities while managing transaction costs involving the strategic use of notional sizes and microstructure data

- *Risk management*: Employing strategies to identify, assess, and mitigate risks associated with investment portfolios in interconnected financial markets
- *Performance and strategy evaluation*: Evaluating the performance of investment strategies using quantitative graph-based metrics and benchmarks to inform future decisions

These aspects highlight the critical role of networks and quantitative methods in modern asset management, driving decision-making processes and enhancing investment outcomes.

Network Application in Investment Management

The application of networks in asset management can be broadly categorized into two major areas. First, networks play a crucial role in the following ways:

- *Risk* and *portfolio management, research, and data analytics*: These are integral parts of the investment process within asset management organizations. Networks are used to model relationships between individual securities, assets, factors, countries, or any financial entities considered as nodes. The links between these nodes are modeled to understand dependencies and optimize portfolios for risk and return profiles.
- *Visualization, representation, and structuring*: Networks provide powerful tools to simplify and visualize the complex underlying structures of financial data. By graphically representing relationships between nodes, networks make it easier to interpret and analyze data dependencies, thus enhancing the understanding of intricate financial connections.

Persistent homology, a mathematical discipline applied to networks discussed in Chapter 6, plays a central role in identifying and measuring network structures that persist over time.[21] It utilizes Betti numbers, which are simple numerical values that count the number of distinct features in data (e.g., clusters or holes) that remain consistent across different time periods to measure the data features that remain consistent across various time periods.

In trading, the application of networks dates to the mid-twentieth century with the works of Weaver (1948), Shannon (1948), and Simon (1962), and Loistl and Landes (1989) followed by Lo (2010, 2017). With advancements in quantitative finance and computing power, modern approaches leverage graph theory to analyze market microstructure. For instance, analyzing bid-ask spreads, notional amounts traded, and distances between trades using network concepts provides insights into market dynamics and trading opportunities.[22]

In the asset management industry, evaluating strategy performance is critical to determining success. Fabozzi and Lopez de Prado (2018) advocate for honest reporting of backtest results, suggesting that networks can enhance this evaluation. Networks of backtest results enable visualization of strategy relationships and centrality scores, helping to identify strategies with diverse performance characteristics.

---

[21] See Cohen–Steiner et al. (2007); Edelsbrunner, Kirkpatrick, and Seidel (1983); Perea and Harer (2015); Aktas, Akbas, and Fatmaoui (2019); Baitinger and Flegel (2021); Otter et al. (2017); and Patania et al. (2017); and Edelsbrunner and Morozovy (2014) for technical details on the persistent homology.

[22] In fixed-income analysis, the distance measures have been successfully applied by Howell (2018) to measure curvature of bonds, and Heckel et al. (2020) who measured the distances between bonds. However, the authors do not apply network analysis to measure mutual distance of all bonds in the investment universe. Mizruchi (1982), Chakrabarti, Pichl, and Kaizoji (2019), König (2014), and Krautz and Fuerst (2015) for modeling market interactions.

This approach complements traditional statistical adjustments of p-values and t-statistics used in strategy evaluation, as discussed by Harvey and Liu (2014, 2015), Lopez de Prado and Fabozzi (2018), and Lopez de Prado (2019).

Moreover, networks can quantify the success of strategies using established performance metrics like the Probabilistic Sharpe Ratio. Figure 1.1 illustrates a network of backtest results, demonstrating how

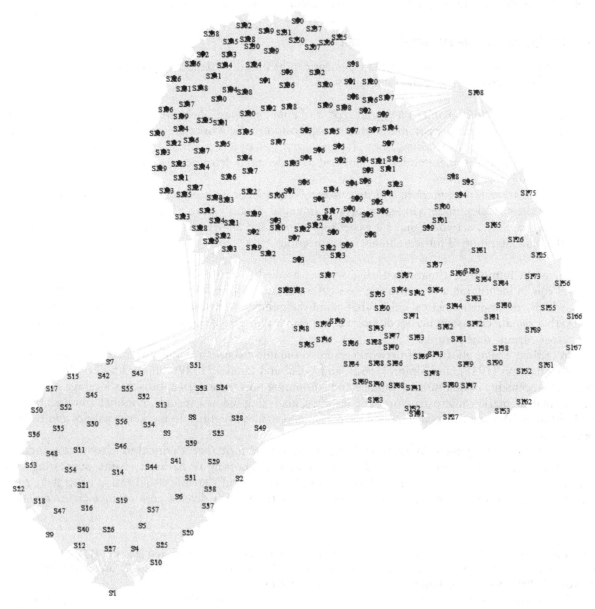

FIGURE 1.1   A Network of Tested Strategies.
Note: In Chapter 6, we explain how to estimate such networks based on the Wasserstein distance. In Chapter 10, we provide information on how to evaluate different networks. The nodes are weighted according to their importance score, which is described in Chapter 4.

strategies can be visualized and evaluated based on their performance characteristics within a network framework. This visualization helps in identifying strategies with diverse and robust performance profiles, providing a more comprehensive evaluation than traditional methods alone.

The application of networks extends beyond strategy evaluation. Another field where networks are applied is risk management, where nodal and edge risks can be considered separately. For example, nodal risk pertains to the risk of default by a financial institution. In contrast, focusing on edge risk identifies the channels through which risk spreads across the network, helping investigate potential paths of risk transmission.

Additionally, networks play a significant role in security selection and asset allocation. In this context, nodes represent financial assets or individual securities, and edges are modeled to represent the links between these financial instruments. Utilizing the tools provided by network theory, it is possible to maintain the entire interconnectedness and construct portfolios that are diversified and capable of risk management, considering the assets in their holistic interconnectedness.

Inference, Structure, Process, Implementation, and Visualization

Network analysis finds application as an asset allocation tool and a risk analysis instrument. Several investment banks apply network theory to asset pricing, specifically in order book and liquidity analysis for electronic trading, order settlement, and order matching. This approach focuses not only on asset price interconnectedness but also on the risks and returns at the industry and macroeconomic levels. Important works in these fields are Vandewalle, Brisbois, and Tordoir (2001); Bonanno et al. (2004); Tumminello et al. (2006); Battistone et al. (2012); Kalyagin et al. (2014); Glasserman and Young (2015); Peralta and Zareei (2016); and Mayoral, Moreno, and Zareei (2022), among others.

The major advantage of network theory in finance is its ability to explain complex interactions and handle large data amounts. The relationship between the three major functions of networks in asset management – implementation, inference, and structure – can be effectively summarized and visualized. Figure 1.2 illustrates this relationship, highlighting how these functions interconnect to support comprehensive financial analysis and decision-making.[23]

Network Modeling   Within the inference stage, network analysis applies to raw data by mapping information on various economic variables, fund networks, private equity investors, and similar entities. Graph-theoretical algorithms can identify relationships within this data. In the structure stage, specific network metrics are used to determine the underlying data structure. Understanding how nodes are interconnected is essential in network theory, unlike traditional analytical tools that isolate a variable to analyze its impact. Networks analyze the entire structure to determine the importance of individual entities, such as nodes or links.

However, financial networks are not directly observable, necessitating modeling as a central task for researchers. While nodes may be considered fixed in the short term, links are dynamic and require explicit modeling efforts. The essential task in network modeling is to uncover these mechanisms that connect disparate data points systematically. Inference aims to uncover these mechanisms, while structure identifies how data points are related to each other.

Network modeling employs four groups of models, broadly categorized into mathematical and statistical models. Mathematical models describe the theoretical nature of network theory, while statistical models and tests have a broader application scope. Models such as link prediction, association models, and probabilistic models serve the purpose of network modeling, with statistical models particularly used for

---

[23]Shearer (2000).

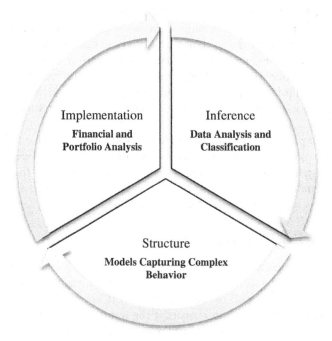

FIGURE 1.2 Network Analysis Applications in Inference, Structure, and Implementation.
Note: The three stages are related to the six-stage Cross Industry Standard Process for Data Mining (CRISP) Investment Process using alternative data.

estimating the probability of edge formation between nodes. These models are central to constructing network structures based on estimates rather than sampling.[24] In other words, other networks underlie different statistical inferences. Statistical inference refers only to the underlying, estimated network structure. Chapter 9 extensively discusses the role of statistical models in network inference.

For instance, in the analysis involving supervised machine learning on a large hedge fund database, techniques may reevaluate data clustering due to strategy shifts.[25] Baitinger and Maier (2019) demonstrated that network analysis effectively identifies hedge fund style shifts based on returns, holdings, or additional attributes, adjusting strategy affiliations or risk factor exposures accordingly. Clustering provides insights into relationships between funds within specific sectors, revealing nonobservable information at first glance. Refer to Figure 1.1 for a comprehensive overview of network analysis in financial data analysis.

---

[24]See Frank and Strauss (1986), Handcock (2003), Snijders (2002), Snijders et al. (2006), Robins et al. (2005), Robins et al. (2007), and Robins and Morris (2007) for a detailed treatment of statistical models and the exponential random graph model, which we discuss in Chapter 9.
[25]A hedge fund style is a critical property of a hedge fund, which states the focus and exposure of a particular strategy. For example, the equity market-neutral strategy postulates that the exposure of a hedge fund should be market, beta, or currency neutral to a market index. Strategy shift is one of the major issues in hedge fund investing and associated with the (unexpected) change in the style exposure of a hedge fund to common factors that drive its returns closely related to that strategy. Equity market-neutral funds have a beta to common equity and bond indices close to zero. In the current example, a strategy shift might be if the hedge fund shifts to a long-equity style. In this case, the beta of that fund might become significantly positive (e.g., 0.5) to the S&P500 index.

Analyzing the inference and structure of financial markets aims to identify the systemic importance of investors, institutions, and assets. Kinlaw et al. (2012) examined the systemic importance of assets within portfolio structures, emphasizing the critical role of interconnectedness between assets and their utilization in asset management. Network statistical measures and the construction of networks effectively serve these purposes.

Fundamentally, the primary application of networks in asset management lies in estimating and constructing portfolio networks for asset allocation and risk management. However, these networks extend beyond portfolio construction and serve well in performance measurement, market analysis, trading, and strategy evaluation.

Processes and Implementation Networks exhibit natural dynamics. Although plotting a network may appear static, networks possess an intrinsic dynamic nature as edges can change with new information and both exogenous and endogenous processes. The network process centers on the evolution of edges over time. The emergence and disappearance of network structures are fundamental to network science and the mathematical framework of persistent homology, which measures the persistence of network structures in space.[26] The role of network processes is to determine how nodes and edges emerge and develop over time. More precisely, the interactions are the essential property of interest in network analysis in financial markets.

Network formation and evolution are continuous processes. These processes can be modeled using either stochastic or deterministic tools, which modern econometric analysis frequently applies in finance. The need to model network processes stems from the desire to identify specific properties that help explore, investigate, and model the network under specific regimes.

For example, consider a portfolio or risk manager who wants to investigate graph-based asset allocation influenced by projections of asset class volatility. The effects change the network structure, and the information might capture specific properties usually not observed under normal conditions.

In implementation, the selected model for network estimation can be used to leverage the interconnectedness underlying a graph. This underlying network might be used to predict network metrics based on the changing number of links and nodes and their interactions. Specifically, in the implementation phase of network analysis in portfolio management, the most compelling statistical measures that explain and gauge relationships can be computed and monitored. These measures and metrics are explained in detail in Chapters 2 and 3. This application pertains to both risk management analysis and investment management decisions. For example, investigating hedge fund exposure might reveal increased factor risks in the equity market (e.g., the S&P 500 Index) or specific risk factor bets.

Visualization Visualizing data is a natural property of understanding inherent in human cognition. Just as a picture can convey more than a thousand words, network visualization provides an insightful overview of the underlying data. Consider a subway map in an underground station: it captures all relevant information about the stations, cross-stations, lines, and endpoints within a public transport system. Network theory's nature enables modeling relationships as edges and nodes, making visualization a central aspect. Visualization can convey complex interactions while also simplifying less relevant data.

Graph theoretical research has identified numerous algorithms to draw and effectively visualize networks, which we discuss in Chapter 2. The main idea of this section is to provide several clues about the proper visualization of networks, including proper edge and node design, size, structure, and groupings. Node size and edge width, along with the use of corresponding colors identifying node and edge properties

---

[26]Baitinger and Flegel (2021) and Baitinger (2021) provide a detailed analysis of the persistent homology in financial markets. In an advanced reading, Do Carmo provides a detailed explanations about the geometry of curves, arcs, surfaces and connectedness in general.

like community affiliation, are among the basic properties that help to visualize a network effectively. It is convenient to use color schemes when plotting networks that highlight the specific attributes. Depending on the network size, which is determined by the number of nodes, some algorithms for network drawing might be more suitable than others.

Figures 1.3a and 1.3b captures the visualization of hedge funds' interconnectedness using the dataset of Konstantinov and Simonian (2020), and in Figure 1.4, we provide a simple network identifying highly connected nodes.

In Panel A of Figure 1.4, simulated weighted networks are shown as interacting securities funds. The most important securities (i.e., nodes) are highlighted as larger dots. Panel A differs from Panel B only in layout.

Programming Codes and Implementation

Throughout this book, we use many codes written in the R programming language. Several packages have been used and found applications. Note that the codes are provided within dedicated boxes throughout the text. However, the responsible package is not explicitly mentioned within every box; thus, it is the researcher's responsibility to install and eventually detach any package that is not needed for a specific code.

FIGURE 1.3A A Single Hedge Funds Network with 442 Nodes and Optimized Edge Structure.
Note: A weighted single hedge fund network with 442 nodes and 194,918 edges minimized by a minimum spanning tree and the Kamada–Kawai graph layout algorithm. The edges result from an unsupervised Wasserstein distance algorithm, as detailed by Konstantinov and Simonian (2020).

FIGURE 1.3B   A Sample Network.

This section describes the packages used in the book. A brief overview of the packages is given. It is crucial for the reader to be familiar with these packages and their descriptions to effectively implement and understand the provided codes:

- The main package used in this book is the "igraph" developed by several graph-theoretical experts, notably Gabor Csardi. The igraph package is a powerful tool for conducting all relevant information and visualization of networks with the corresponding algorithms. It serves as the backbone of the book, supporting the statistical analysis and programming needed to estimate and draw networks.
- The package "glmnet" is used for conducting LASSO and other regularization models like linear, logistic and multinomial regression.
- The package "foreach" is used for looping structures, enabling efficient execution of competitive tasks.
- The package "transport" computes optimal transport plans and Wasserstein distances, which are needed for network construction and evaluation.
- The package "vars," developed by Bernhard Pfaff (2008), is used to estimate Vector Autoregression (VAR) models and perform diagnostics. It assists in estimation, lag selection, diagnostic testing, forecasting, causality analysis, and forecast error variance decomposition models.
- The R package "lmtest" is used for conducting Granger causality tests and additional statistical tests.

- The package "entropy" is used to compute the network nodal-based entropy. Note that the network entropy is based on the Shannon entropy, providing a measure of the unpredictability or information content within the network.
- The package "huge" is used to model high-dimensional undirected networks, enabling for the analysis of complex, large-scale network data.
- The "bnlearn" package is used to model Bayesian networks. It requires the inclusion of the "network" package, which models relational data. Note that attaching the "network" package requires the detachment of the "igraph" package due to compatibility issues.
- One of the widely used packages is "eigenmodel", which enables Monte Carlo Markov Chain simulations for networks developed by Hoff (2007). This package provides the background for implementing statistical models for network processes, which we cover in Chapter 9. The "eigenmodel" provides semiparametric factor and regression models for symmetric relational data.
- The package "ppcor" serves to estimate partial and semi-partial correlations used in the undirected networks.
- The package "ROCR" is used to evaluate the performance of scoring classifiers for network estimation. It plots two-dimensional performance curves using cross-validation, which is crucial for assessing model accuracy.
- The "ergm" package is dedicated to estimating the exponential random graph model, which uses node and edge attributes of existing (observed) networks to model new features of simulated networks. This enables for the sophisticated modeling of network structures based on observed data.

Panel A

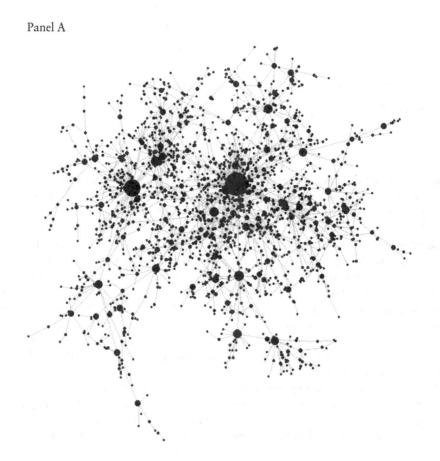

Panel B

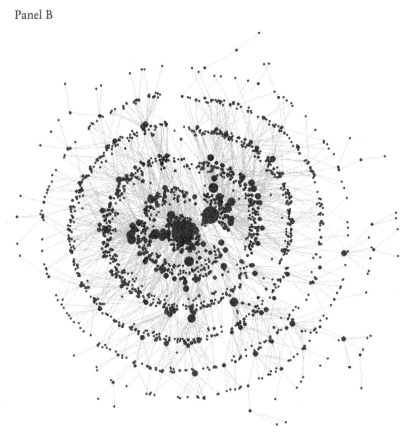

FIGURE 1.4 A Different Network Design with Identification of Highly Connected Nodes and Probabilistic Modelling of Edge Structures.
Note: This is an example of a network that comprises 2,000 nodes simulated using the Barabási –Albert algorithm. See Chapters 4 and 5 for more details on the identification of the node properties (i.e., degree score) and the simulation model defined as "Preferential Attachment."

The book's main idea is to highlight the role of network science in finance and to provide practical examples of network application in asset management. The codes provided can be directly applied to different datasets; however, specifications and adjustments are subject to the specific dataset. Moreover, experienced coders with advanced programming skills might optimize these codes for better performance. As our book's objective is to educate quantitative experts in network science, optimizing the code serves to enhance understanding and proficiency in this area.

NETWORK DESIGN

Nodes and edges are the building blocks of networks. The relationship between nodes is represented by edges, with the adjacency matrix, edge list, and incidence matrix being the most widely used representations to gauge these relationships. The adjacency matrix is a symmetric matrix where the rows and columns represent the nodes, and the elements represent the edges. Usually, the adjacency matrix is the most widely applied matrix that captures relationships, with elements being zero if two neighboring nodes are not connected and one if the two nodes are connected.

The design of a financial network for portfolio and risk management purposes, with data in a time series form, requires careful specification. This design involves modeling the entries of the adjacency matrix, which is the focus of the models presented in this book. The adjacency matrix is the basic unit used in network algorithms to visualize the relationships between nodes. Direct application of the adjacency matrix is provided in Chapter 2.

In Table 1.1, we show an example of a financial network that comprises assets and factors. There are 31 nodes in this network, and the mutual links are represented as 1 if a link between any two nodes exists, and zero otherwise. The purpose of the network models presented in this book is to specify the design experiments for estimating edges between the nodes in financial networks. In the present example, the design experiment is discussed in detail in Chapter 6.

The inclusion of node and edge attributes is not just a design choice but an essential property of complex networks. Node attributes are often assigned based on network model specification and the network statistics that measure node interconnectedness. However, node properties can also originate from external

TABLE 1.1 An Adjacency Matrix for the Undirected Asset and Factor Network.

MktRF	0	0	0	1	1	0	0	0	0	0	1	0	0	1	0	1	0	1	0	0	1	0	0	0	1	0	0	0	0	0	1	1
SMB	0	0	1	0	0	0	0	0	0	0	0	0	0	0	0	0	0	0	0	0	0	0	0	1	0	0	0	0	0	0	0	0
HML	0	1	0	0	1	0	0	0	0	0	0	0	0	0	0	0	0	0	0	0	0	0	0	1	0	0	0	0	0	0	0	0
RMW	1	0	0	0	0	0	0	0	0	0	0	0	0	0	0	0	0	0	0	0	0	0	0	0	0	0	0	0	0	0	1	1
CMA	1	0	1	0	0	0	0	0	0	1	0	0	0	0	0	1	0	0	0	0	0	0	0	0	1	0	0	0	0	1	1	
RF	0	0	0	0	0	0	0	0	0	0	0	0	0	0	0	0	0	0	0	0	0	1	0	0	0	0	0	0	0	0	0	
EuroStoxx50	0	0	0	0	0	0	0	1	1	1	1	0	0	1	1	1	0	1	1	1	0	1	1	0	0	0	0	0	0	0	0	
SPX	0	0	0	0	0	0	1	0	1	1	1	1	0	1	1	1	1	1	1	1	1	1	1	0	0	0	0	0	0	0	0	
RTY	0	0	0	0	0	0	1	1	0	1	1	1	0	1	1	1	1	1	1	1	1	1	0	0	0	0	0	0	0	0	0	
EM	0	0	0	0	1	0	1	1	1	0	1	1	1	1	1	1	1	1	1	1	0	1	0	0	0	0	0	0	0	0	0	
HF	1	0	0	0	0	0	1	1	1	1	0	1	1	1	1	1	1	1	1	1	0	1	1	1	0	0	0	0	0	1	0	
DXY	0	0	0	0	0	0	1	1	1	1	0	1	0	1	1	1	1	1	0	0	1	0	0	0	0	0	0	0	0	0	0	
Golds	0	0	0	0	0	0	0	0	0	1	1	1	0	1	1	1	1	1	1	0	0	0	1	0	0	0	1	0	0	0	0	
UST	1	0	0	0	0	0	1	1	1	1	0	1	0	1	0	1	0	1	1	1	1	1	0	0	0	1	1	0	0	1	0	
USCorp	0	0	0	0	0	0	1	1	1	1	1	1	1	1	0	1	1	1	1	1	0	1	1	0	0	1	1	0	0	0	0	
USHY	1	0	0	0	1	0	1	1	1	1	1	1	1	0	1	0	1	1	1	1	1	0	0	0	0	0	0	0	1	1		
InfLinked	0	0	0	0	0	0	0	1	1	1	1	1	1	1	1	1	1	0	1	1	1	0	0	1	0	0	1	1	0	0	0	
EUCorp	0	0	0	0	0	0	1	1	1	1	1	1	1	1	1	1	1	1	0	1	1	0	1	1	0	0	1	0	0	0	0	
Commodity	1	0	0	0	0	0	1	1	1	1	1	1	1	1	1	1	1	1	1	0	1	0	1	1	0	0	0	0	1	0	1	
PE	0	0	0	0	0	0	1	1	1	1	1	1	0	1	1	1	1	1	1	0	1	1	0	1	1	0	0	0	0	0	0	
USTBills	0	0	0	0	0	1	0	1	1	0	0	0	0	1	0	1	0	0	0	1	0	1	0	1	0	0	0	0	0	0	0	
NKY	0	0	0	0	0	0	1	1	1	1	1	0	0	1	1	1	0	1	1	1	1	0	0	0	0	0	0	0	0	0	0	
BAB	1	1	1	0	0	0	1	1	1	0	1	1	1	0	1	0	1	1	1	0	0	0	0	0	0	0	1	0	1	0		
FXValue	0	0	0	0	0	0	0	0	0	0	0	1	0	0	0	0	0	0	0	0	0	0	0	0	1	0	1	0	0	0	0	
FXMOM	0	0	0	0	1	0	0	0	0	0	0	0	0	0	0	0	0	0	0	0	0	0	0	1	0	0	1	0	0	0	0	
FIValue	0	0	0	0	0	0	0	0	0	0	0	0	0	1	1	0	1	1	0	0	0	0	0	0	0	1	0	0	0	0	0	
FIMOM	0	0	0	0	0	0	0	0	0	0	0	0	0	1	1	0	1	0	0	0	0	0	0	1	1	1	0	0	0	0	0	
COMValue	0	0	0	0	0	0	0	0	0	0	0	0	1	0	0	0	0	0	1	0	0	0	1	0	0	0	0	0	1	0	0	
COMMOM	0	0	0	0	0	0	0	0	0	0	0	0	0	0	0	0	0	0	0	0	0	0	0	0	0	0	0	1	0	0	0	
Liquidity	1	0	0	1	1	0	0	0	0	0	1	0	0	1	0	1	0	0	1	0	0	0	1	0	0	0	0	0	0	0	1	
MOM	1	0	0	1	1	0	0	0	0	0	0	0	0	0	0	1	0	0	0	0	0	0	0	0	0	0	0	0	0	1	0	

sources, incorporating additional information into the network design. This means that network design might involve network process formation or inputs from external factors. Researchers must decide how to model the network to incorporate these attributes.

The network design helps evaluate local structures and identify sectors of particular interest, such as clusters, communities, groups of specific nodes, or the relative importance of nodes with systemic relevance. The statistical processes used in network design are then applied to the specific networks designed by financial researchers. This approach enables a detailed analysis of the network's structure and dynamics, providing valuable insights for portfolio and risk management.

KEY TAKEAWAYS

- The basic properties of networks are nodes and the links between them. Real-world networks gauge social interactions, infrastructure, technological complexity, power grids, water supply systems, transportation systems, and biological chains, among others.
- Financial networks consist of properties found in several other types of networks. They are characterized by the interactions of nodes, which can be individuals, enterprises, institutions, and their contractual, monetary, informational, technological, and organizational relationships.
- The use of financial networks in asset management is versatile. They are used in portfolio management for asset allocation, security selection, strategy evaluation, fund selection, and manager evaluation, among other uses.
- The broad application in investment management extends beyond traditional fields to include risk management, risk evaluation, enterprise risk analysis, and the transmission of risk through interacting entities within a financial network.
- Different data types, such as time series data, are crucial for constructing and analyzing financial networks.
- Persistent homology is applied in identifying and measuring network structures that persist over time, using Betti numbers to quantify these features. Stochastic and deterministic tools are used in modeling network processes, which are relevant to financial network analysis.
- Networks possess an intrinsic dynamic nature, with edges changing due to new information and various processes. Carefully specifying network designs is significant for portfolio and risk management, focusing on the modeling of adjacency matrix entries.

The Basic Structure of a Network

Contents

A network, or graph, is a system of nodes or vertices. The connections between them are represented by links, ties or edges. In practice, the terms "network" and "graph" are used interchangeably. Because financial markets are real systems, the terms "nodes," "links," and "networks" are widely used in finance and economics. On the other hand, "graph," "vertex," and "edges" are mathematical expressions commonly used in mathematics. Networks represent complex systems, and their purpose is to illustrate the interactions between the nodes. Representing these interactions requires defining tools that capture the relationships between the nodes and the links.

Academic research has investigated financial institution networks built using balance sheet information.[1] However, asset networks are based on estimated dependency structures and financial market data. These data are not limited to asset returns but might also comprise 13F holdings,[2] transactions, money flows, and notional amounts exchanged. Moreover, different types of networks apply to specific types of relationships between the nodes. For example, social networks are different from technological networks or power grids. Similarly, biological networks vary from networks of authors who share coauthorship and citations. In this context, the Internet differs from the network that describes the public transportation system.

In this chapter, we will focus on the toolkit needed to define and evaluate the relationships within a network as well as the different types of networks.

---

[1] See, for example, Baitinger and Papenbrock (2017a, 2017b), Acemoglu et al. (2015), and Elliot et al. (2014).

[2] 13F filings are quarterly reports that must be filed by institutional asset managers with the US Securities and Exchange Commission that shows their holdings at the end of the quarter.

NETWORK REPRESENTATIONS

The data used to construct networks are stored in specific formats and data frames. Graph theory requires specific data storage forms to gauge interconnectedness and represent additional node and edge properties. Among the most widely used data files to represent networks are the following:

- *Edge list*: This format presents the nodes as edges in a two-column representation.
- *Adjacency list*: This is an ordered representation of the nodes.
- *Adjacency matrix*: This representation is central in network analysis. It displays the connections between nodes in a matrix format.

In this book, we will focus on adjacency matrices for network representation and analysis.

The Adjacency Matrix

Wasserman and Faust (1994) describe various methods for analyzing social networks, including the concept of the adjacency matrix, which they refer to as the sociomatrix. Note that actors and ties between them define sociomatrices. According to Wasserman and Faust, the adjacency matrix successfully captures the mutual links between the nodes. In other words, the *adjacency matrix* measures the pairwise relationships between nodes. Formally, the links and nodes in a network are represented by an adjacency matrix, which captures their mutual connectedness.[3]

The adjacency matrix is a square matrix whose row and column numbers are equal to the number of nodes in the network. If two nodes are connected, the corresponding element in the matrix is 1. Conversely, if two nodes are not connected, the corresponding matrix element is 0. The entries in the adjacency matrix represent the presence or absence of links between the nodes.

In graph theory, the general notation for a graph is $G(V,E)$ where V is the number of vertices or nodes and E is the number of edges. For a graph with n vertices and m edges, $G = (n,m)$, the entries a_{ij} in the $n \times n$ adjacency matrix is denoted by $[A]_{ij}$ and is estimated using following rule:

$$a_{ij} = \begin{cases} 1, & \text{if node } i \text{ and } j \text{ are connected, or } \{i,j\} \in m \\ 0, & \text{otherwise} \end{cases} \tag{2.1}$$

where a_{ij} are the entries of the adjacency matrix $[A]_{ij}$. In words, if node i does not have a connection to node j, the value in the matrix is set at zero. Put differently, the entry of the adjacency matrix is $a_{ij} = 1$ if an edge between nodes i and j exists, or $a_{ij} = 1$ if no edge between the nodes exists.

The following example demonstrates the adjacency matrix $[A]_{ij}$ for a directed graph with entries a_{ij}.

$$[A]_{ij} = \begin{pmatrix} a_{11} & a_{12} & a_{13} & a_{14} \\ a_{21} & a_{22} & a_{23} & a_{24} \\ a_{31} & a_{32} & a_{33} & a_{34} \\ a_{41} & a_{42} & a_{43} & a_{44} \end{pmatrix} = [A]'_{ij} \begin{pmatrix} 0 & 1 & 0 & 0 \\ 0 & 0 & 0 & 1 \\ 1 & 1 & 0 & 0 \\ 1 & 0 & 1 & 0 \end{pmatrix} \tag{2.2}$$

---

[3] See Wasserman and Faust (1994), Newman (2010), Barabási (2016), and Borgatti et al. (2022).

For example, a_{14} represents the link between node 1 and node 4. If $a_{14} = 0$, no link between node 1 and node 4 exists. Similarly, a_{41} captures the link between node 4 and node 1. In this case, the adjacency matrix (A') denotes that a link exists because $a_{41} = 1$.

The adjacency matrix is quadratic, meaning that the number of rows is equal to the number of columns. However, it is not necessarily symmetric. In an undirected network, which we describe in the upcoming section, the adjacency matrix is symmetric because the connection between node i and node j is the same as between node j and node i. For a directed network, described in the upcoming section, the adjacency matrix is still quadratic but not symmetric. This is because the connection from node i to node j may not be the same as the connection from node j to node i.[4] The main diagonal of the adjacency matrix reflects self-edges, indicating the self-connectedness of a node. Self-edges, or self-loops, are common in many networks, including financial networks. For instance, a financial institution may have leveraged financial instruments with itself. In portfolio management, the covariance matrix is often used to capture the risk between assets in a portfolio. Similarly, the self-edges of the adjacency matrix represent the inherent connectedness of a node or asset. However, in network analysis, the main diagonal of the adjacency matrix is typically set to zero to avoid self-loops, focusing instead on how nodes interact with each other.

Financial networks used in portfolio and risk management can have various types of nodes in the adjacency matrix, such as assets, factors, funds, countries, sectors, indices, and individual securities. The entries in the adjacency matrix represent the connections between these nodes. Computing an adjacency matrix is essential for network analysis, but it can also be challenging, requiring reliance on data and models to represent the elements of the matrix accurately.

One challenge is that the adjacency matrix distinguishes between outgoing and incoming links of a node, which are represented as row or column sums. This distinction is crucial for understanding directed networks, where the links to other nodes may differ depending on whether the network is directed or undirected. We will explore this further in the next section when discussing directed and undirected networks.

The Incidence Matrix

Like the adjacency matrix, the *incidence matrix* captures relationships in the form of a *logical matrix*. However, while the adjacency matrix represents node–node relationships, the incidence matrix captures relationships between two classes of objects. Specifically, the incidence matrix gauges the relation between two types of objects, typically nodes and edges.

In the incidence matrix, each row corresponds to an element of the first object (e.g., nodes), and each column corresponds to an element of the second object (e.g., edges). An entry in the matrix is set to 1 if the corresponding objects are related, indicating a connection between a node and an edge, for example.

For an undirected graph $G = (n,m)$ the incidence matrix is a $n \times m$ matrix, denoted by $[B]_{ij}$, and estimated using the following rule:[5]

$$b_{ij} = \begin{cases} 1, & \text{if node } i \text{ is incident with edge } j \\ 0, & \text{otherwise} \end{cases} \tag{2.3}$$

where b are the entries of the incidence matrix $[B]_{ij}$.

---

[4]We discuss the difference between directed and undirected graph in the upcoming section.
[5]This matrix is referred to as "unoriented." The oriented incidence matrix for undirected graphs is like the incidence matrix for a directed network.

The incidence matrix for a directed graph differs from that of an undirected graph and takes the following form:

$$b_j = \begin{cases} -1, & \text{if edge } j \text{ leaves node } i \\ 1, & \text{if edge } j \text{ enters node } i \\ 0, & \text{otherwise} \end{cases} \tag{2.4}$$

The incidence matrix for an undirected network has a similar structure to the adjacency matrix but with some differences. In the case of an undirected network, each row of the incidence matrix represents a vertex (i.e., node), and each column corresponds to an edge.

If we consider a network with four vertices and four edges, the incidence matrix would have four rows and four columns. Each row would correspond to one of the vertices, and each column would correspond to one of the edges. The entries in the matrix would indicate whether a vertex is incident to an edge, typically with a value of 1 if the vertex is connected to the edge, and 0 otherwise. The following matrix is an example of the incidence matrix, whose rows correspond to the vertices and its columns represent edges.

$$\begin{bmatrix} 1 & 0 & 1 & 0 \\ 0 & 0 & 1 & 1 \\ 1 & 1 & 0 & 0 \\ 0 & 1 & 0 & 1 \end{bmatrix}$$

In an undirected network, each edge connects two vertices. Therefore, each edge in the network is incident to exactly two vertices. Consequently, in the incidence matrix for an undirected network, each column sum would be equal to 2, indicating that each edge is incident to two vertices.

TYPES OF NETWORKS

The major network types can be summarized as directed, undirected, complete, weighted, unweighted networks, multigraphs, as well as trees. These are the most common networks used in portfolio and risk management. In the upcoming sections, we provide information about their structures and differences, which are essential when building portfolios or estimating risk propagation through a network. Each type of network has distinctive properties, which we will discuss next.

Undirected Networks

Perhaps the most widely known networks are *undirected networks*. The most basic properties of an undirected network $G^* = (n^*, m^*)$ are the number of *nodes*, or *vertices* n and *links*, or *edges* (connections) m, where $n^* \in \mathbb{R}^n$ and $m^* \in \mathbb{R}^{n \times n}$ $(m_{i,j}^* = m_{j,i}^*)$. In the case of undirected networks, the transfer of information between nodes is equal. If node i is linked to node j, it implies that node j is connected to node i, rendering the connectedness symmetric.

Newman (2010) argued that most networks are undirected. Consider the social network Facebook: if an individual is linked to another person, the latter is automatically connected to the former. Undirected networks are prevalent in various domains such as infrastructure, biology, and the Internet. Due to their symmetric relationships, undirected networks are straightforward to interpret and model, especially regarding the main diagonal of the adjacency matrix.

Undirected networks exhibit symmetry concerning the main diagonal of the adjacency matrix, although not all links may be fully utilized. The adjacency matrix for an undirected graph is always quadratic and symmetric. The transpose of the adjacency matrix of an undirected graph resembles the regular matrix, as the connectivity of $a_{ij} = a_{ji}$ is symmetric. In an undirected graph's adjacency matrix, the links below the main diagonal mirror the links above it, reflecting the symmetric nature of the relationships between nodes. This symmetry indicates that the relationship between node i and node j is equivalent to the relationship between node j and node i, ensuring that the graph's representation is consistent and symmetric.

For example, the adjacency matrix entries of the undirected matrix are equal with respect to the main diagonal: $a_{24} = a_{42}$.

$$\begin{bmatrix} 0 & 0 & 1 & 0 \\ 0 & 0 & 1 & 1 \\ 1 & 1 & 0 & 0 \\ 0 & 1 & 0 & 0 \end{bmatrix}$$

Directed Networks

The most basic properties of a directed network $G = (n,m)$ are the number of *nodes*, or *vertices* n (assets) and *links*, or *edges* (connections) m, where $n \in \mathbb{R}^n$ and $m \in \mathbb{R}^{n \times n}$ $(m_{i,j} \neq m_{j,i})$. The distinction between undirected and directed networks lies in the definition of edges. In directed networks, edges have an inherent orientation that indicates a directional relationship between nodes that is one way. This means that the connection flows in a single direction from one node to another, which emphasizes the impact or dependency of one node on the other, rather than a mutual or reciprocal connection. For example, using our notation, if node i is connected to node j, there is a directed edge from i to j, typically represented with an arrow pointing from i to j.

Here is an example of a simple, directed, four-node graph, illustrating a quadratic but nonsymmetric adjacency matrix:

$$\begin{bmatrix} 0 & 0 & 1 & 0 \\ 0 & 0 & 1 & 1 \\ 1 & 1 & 0 & 0 \\ 0 & 0 & 0 & 0 \end{bmatrix}$$

The main difference between the adjacency matrix of an undirected and directed network can be seen in the elements of the third row, the second column, and the fourth row of the adjacency matrix. For example, the elements $a_{24} \neq a_{42}$. As a result, the transpose of the adjacency matrix of a directed network is not equal to the regular adjacency matrix $\left([A]_{ij} \neq [A]^T_{ij} \right)$. The reason is that a directed network has a flow direction from node i to node j $(i \rightarrow j)$. The transpose of the adjacency matrix of a directed network changes the flow direction.

Unlike most real-life networks, which are undirected, directed networks are particularly significant in finance due to their ability to represent causal relationships. In finance, understanding causation is often crucial for investigating phenomena or assessing the impact of one variable on another. For instance, determining the cause of inflation might involve analyzing the effect of rising interest rates. Therefore, directed networks play a vital role in financial markets, and their application has been at the forefront of financial research. The rise of factor investing, coupled with the adoption of machine-learning techniques, has significantly bolstered the investigation of directed causal networks, offering valuable insights into the foundational principles and scientific underpinnings of financial factors.[6]

Acyclic Directed Networks

According to Newman (2010), certain directed networks exhibit a distinctive characteristic known as cycles. A cycle manifests as a closed loop of links, where all arrows point consistently in the same direction around the loop. Conversely, directed networks lacking such loops are termed acyclic-directed networks. The practical application of such networks in finance has been demonstrated by Rebonato and Denev (2013), and Laudy, Denev, and Ginsberg (2022). The main intuition behind these graphs is that there is always at least one node with incoming links but no outgoing links. For example, a causal relationship may exist in financial markets between energy prices (e.g., oil price), interest rates, and inflation. In such a causal network, one variable causes a change in the others. Specifically, an increase in oil prices, accompanied by a decrease in interest rates, may cause inflation to rise. In this case, the node representing inflation has no outgoing directional links to other nodes. Usually, in such networks, all vertices are reached before the path arrives at the last node, or if the path never reaches the last node, it is reversed back to the previous node. In other words, acyclic networks always have an end node. The adjacency matrix of an acyclic graph has several properties: the main diagonal contains only zeros, and all eigenvalues are zero.

Completed Networks

A special case of undirected networks is the *completed network*, also known as a *clique*. In the social network context, we experience cliques in everyday life when observing close societies into which we cannot enter. Completed networks are widely used in finance, especially when researchers compute networks using correlation coefficients. Without applying a threshold to the correlation coefficients (e.g., only considering coefficients larger than 0.2), completed networks resemble undirected networks. The following two examples illustrate a clique.

A clique is a term often used to describe closed communities of individuals. An important property of a clique is that it represents a fully connected network, meaning there are links between all pairs of nodes. Consider the following two adjacency matrices:

$$\begin{bmatrix} 0 & 1 & 1 & 1 \\ 1 & 0 & 1 & 1 \\ 1 & 1 & 0 & 1 \\ 1 & 1 & 1 & 0 \end{bmatrix} \begin{bmatrix} 0 & 0.7 & 0.3 & 0.1 \\ 0.7 & 0 & 0.2 & 0.5 \\ 0.3 & 0.2 & 0 & 0.9 \\ 0.1 & 0.5 & 0.9 & 0 \end{bmatrix}$$

In the first matrix, all elements of the adjacency matrix, except those on the main diagonal, are 1, and the matrix is symmetric. The second matrix is an example of a correlation matrix, where the entries are symmetric relative to the main diagonal, which is set to zero.

---

[6] Factors are fundamental elements in asset pricing models that help explain the behavior of asset returns. Essentially, asset pricing can be attributed to a few key factors, which are components in factor models. These models simplify the construction and analysis of portfolios by identifying a parsimonious set of return drivers. Factors serve as the building blocks in factor models, helping to capture the underlying sources of risk and return in financial markets. The primary attraction of factor models lies in their ability to explain asset return behavior through these key drivers, making them essential tools in portfolio management. See, for example, Lopez de Prado (2023) and his analysis of factor investing and causality in finance.

The key distinction between undirected networks and cliques is that cliques typically exhaust the maximum number of possible links, resulting in a complete network where all nodes are connected to each other. A clique might be formed as a subgraph in a larger network.

Weighted vs. Unweighted Networks

In the previous sections, we discussed unweighted networks where the adjacency matrix consists of 1s and 0s. However, in some networks, the connections between nodes are weighted, meaning that a specific weight w_{ij} is assigned to the link between node i and j. Formally, we can express this as

$$a_{ij} = w_{ij} \tag{2.5}$$

where a_{ij} are the components of the adjacency matrix A, and the weights w_{ij} are the elements of the adjacency matrix A.

Consider, for example, a network where two banks are connected. The weight of their mutual link could represent the amount of lending and borrowing exchanged between them. In a portfolio management context, the link between two assets might be associated with a specific amount of systematic risk (i.e., common risk). In such weighted networks, the adjacency matrix does not consist solely of 1s and 0s; instead, the mutual links are weighted by specific information, such as transaction volumes, contract sizes, probabilities, or risk measures.

While most networks are weighted, it is worth noting that assigning weights to nodes in finance is not always feasible. Therefore, a common approach is to assume that networks are unweighted, where the elements of the adjacency matrix take a value of 1 if a link exists between nodes and 0 otherwise.

However, in networks representing interactions between assets, weights can be metrics representing systematic risk. For instance, in networks of funds, node weights might represent assets under management, fund factor exposure, a manager's degree of popularity, or other unique metrics that can be quantified. Throughout this book, we will explore various ways to assign weights to nodes in financial networks for applications in portfolio and risk management, such as risk scores, asset weights, risk factor loadings, or monetary amounts.

There is an ongoing debate as to whether weights should be positive or negative, underscoring the various relationships existing in real-world systems. Typically, in network analysis, positive weights are used to represent various kinds of relationships or interactions between nodes. In social networks, for example, positive weights might represent the intensity of friendships, the strength of collaboration, or the frequency of communication. Negative weights might indicate dislike in social networks. In the case of a financial system network, a positive weight might indicate the volume or the number of transactions between two financial institutions, while a negative weight might indicate negative beta coefficients in a beta-weighted network. The possibility of assigning negative weights represents a valuable advantage when modeling weighted financial networks. For example, using the beta coefficients as indicators of systematic risk, we can show two networks – one with the negative beta coefficients and one with the positive beta coefficients. Another example for negative weights might be the balance of payments between countries or other money flows. These weights might be negative or positive numbers.

Multigraphs

Multigraphs are indeed among the most complex types of networks, as they can incorporate various features, such as weights, self-edges, and both directed and undirected connections. Importantly, the main diagonal of the adjacency matrix is nonzero and usually contains node weights in the form of self-edges.

Multigraphs are crucial in portfolio and risk management as they closely resemble covariance matrices. The key distinction lies in how the adjacency matrix captures the relationships between nodes in a connected manner.

Figure 2.1 represents the most important and widely used networks in investment management as shown by Konstantinov, Aldridge, and Kazemi (2023). Network A represents an undirected, unweighted network. The graph in B represents a weighted, undirected network. The example in C is a directed, unweighted graph. A directed, weighted graph is plotted in D, and E is an example of a completed network. The example in F is an undirected, unweighted network with self-loops. The graph in G is an undirected, weighted multigraph. A directed, weighted multigraph is shown in H, and in I we show a bipartite graph.

Box 2.1 provides the code in programming language R for estimating the different graphs in Figure 2.1. The example graphs are generated from the adjacency matrices specified in the code. Once setting the edge arrow size, the networks are plotted with a random layout.

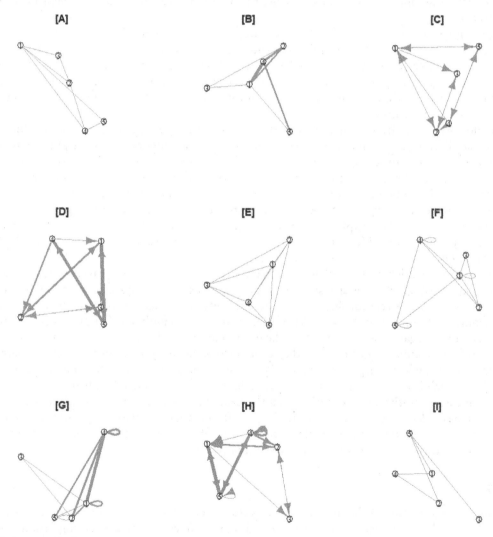

FIGURE 2.1 Network Types.
Note: An example of similar networks is provided in Konstantinov et al. (2023).

BOX 2.1: CODE FOR ESTIMATING THE DIFFERENT GRAPHS.

```
par(mfrow=c(3,3))
#1 undirected unweighted 5-node Network
C<- matrix(c(0,1,1,1,1,
        1,0,1,1,0,
        1,1,0,0,0,
        1,1,0,0,1,
        1,0,0,1,0), ncol = 5, byrow = TRUE)
c<-graph_from_adjacency_matrix(C)
E(c)$arrow.size<-0
plot(c, layout=layout_randomly, main="[A]", vertex.color="white")


#2 undirected weighted 4-node Network
C<- matrix(c(0,2,1,4,1,
        2,0,1,3,0,
        1,1,0,0,0,
        4,3,0,0,2,
        1,0,0,2,0), ncol = 5, byrow = TRUE)
c<-graph_from_adjacency_matrix(C, weighted=TRUE)
E(c)$arrow.size<-0
plot(c, edge.width=E(c)$weight,layout=layout_randomly, main="[B]", vertex.color="white")

#3 directed unweighted 5-node Network
C<- matrix(c(0,1,1,0,1,
        1,0,1,0,0,
        0,1,0,0,0,
        1,1,0,0,1,
        1,0,0,1,0), ncol = 5, byrow = TRUE)
c<-graph_from_adjacency_matrix(C)
E(c)$arrow.size<-0.8
plot(c,layout=layout_randomly, main="[C]", vertex.color="white")

#4 directed weighted 5-node Network
C<- matrix(c(0,2,1,0,5,
        2,0,1,0,0,
        0,1,0,0,0,
        1,2,0,0,4,
        1,0,0,3,0), ncol = 5, byrow = TRUE)
c<-graph_from_adjacency_matrix(C, weighted=TRUE)
E(c)$arrow.size<-0.8
plot(c, edge.width=E(c)$weight,layout=layout_randomly, main="[D]", vertex.color="white")

#5 completed 5-node Network
C<- matrix(c(0,1,1,1,1,
        1,0,1,1,1,
        1,1,0,1,1,
        1,1,1,0,1,
        1,1,1,1,0), ncol = 5, byrow = TRUE)
c<-graph_from_adjacency_matrix(C)
E(c)$arrow.size<-0
plot(c, layout=layout_randomly, main="[E]", vertex.color="white")
```

(Continued)

(Continued)

```
#6 undirected unweighted with Self-loops 5-node Network
C<- matrix(c(1,1,1,1,1,
       1,0,1,1,0,
       1,1,0,0,0,
       1,1,0,1,1,
       1,0,0,1,1), ncol = 5, byrow = TRUE)
c<-graph_from_adjacency_matrix(C)
E(c)$arrow.size<-0
plot(c,layout=layout_randomly, main="[F]", vertex.color="white")

#7 Undirected weighted Multigraph 5-node Network
C<- matrix(c(2,2,1,4,1,
       2,0,1,3,0,
       1,1,0,0,0,
       4,3,0,3,2,
       1,0,0,2,1), ncol = 5, byrow = TRUE)
c<-graph_from_adjacency_matrix(C,weighted=TRUE)
E(c)$arrow.size<-0.0
plot(c, edge.width=E(c)$weight,layout=layout_randomly, main="[G]", vertex.color="white")

#8 Directed weighted Multigraph 5-node Network
C<- matrix(c(2,2,1,0,5,
       2,0,1,0,0,
       0,1,0,0,0,
       1,2,0,3,4,
       1,0,0,3,1), ncol = 5, byrow = TRUE)
c<-graph_from_adjacency_matrix(C,weighted=TRUE)
E(c)$arrow.size<-0.8
plot(c, edge.width=E(c[[[()$weight,layout=layout_randomly, main="[H]", vertex.
color="white")

# 9 Bipartite 4-node Network
#bipartite 4-node Network
C<- matrix(c(1,1,1,1,0), ncol = 2, byrow = TRUE)
c<-graph_from_incidence_matrix(C)
E(c)$arrow.size<-0
plot(c,layout=layout_randomly, main="[I]", vertex.color="white")
```

NETWORK VISUALIZATION

Visualization is a natural method for presenting and understanding complex interactions. Network visualization combines mathematical algorithms, aesthetic design, and intuitive thinking to depict the relationships between connected elements using geometric objects, lines, and curves.[7]

Graphs can be drawn in two or three dimensions, each offering distinct advantages. Two-dimensional graphs are straightforward to draw and comprehend, while three-dimensional visualizations are more

---

[7]Comprehensive overviews on graph visualization are provided by Kaufmann and Wagner (1998), di Battista et al. (1999), and Cleveland (1993).

abstract and complex, potentially offering better visualization of intricate relationships. Drawing a graph is more complex than simply drawing a picture; it requires mathematical models and algorithms to accurately represent nodes' properties, links, and connectedness.

Network attributes play a crucial role in visualization, enabling the presentation of node and link structure based on various attributes, such as classifications, node properties, classes, groups, or other characteristics. In finance, these attributes may originate from various sources.[8] For instance, node size might represent a node's importance score in a network, which could be associated with the size of a financial institution, the number of employees or accounts. Similarly, edge attributes could include money flows, the number of transactions, or other specific information.

When drawing a graph, edge characteristics can describe specific connections. For example, different edge widths might represent varying levels of connectedness. For instance, in a scenario where two banks exchange funds, the size of the nodes could be associated with the market capitalization of the banks, while the edge structure might reflect the different amounts of money exchanged. A bank with higher money flows might be represented by a thicker edge line compared to one with lower amounts of funds transferred.

Researchers have developed several powerful algorithms for drawing networks, each suitable for different graph sizes. The choice of algorithm depends on the size of the network, measured by the number of nodes. Some algorithms are more suitable for large graphs, while others are better suited for small graphs.

To illustrate, consider a simple graph depicting payments sent between European countries sourced from the Trade Reporting and Compliance Engine (TRACE) database.[9] Figure 2.2 provides an overview of the network with different edge and node design. Panel A shows the simple form of network. We use the edge weights in Panel B and set the edge width to be proportional to the edge weights. Panel C sets the edge width to reflect the edge weights, whose graphs are curved. This type of visualization is suitable for directed networks, in which the flow between the nodes is different.

Figure 2.3 shows eight of the most widely used algorithms for graph visualization. For simplicity, we use a small network. Some of the algorithms are more suitable for large networks; others are easily applied to small graphs with fewer nodes. The code provided in Box 2.2 pertains to the visualization of a simple graph. This code includes analytical steps such as community detection, which are discussed in detail in Chapters 3 and 4. By utilizing both node and edge attributes, we simulate different layouts that are useful for network representation.

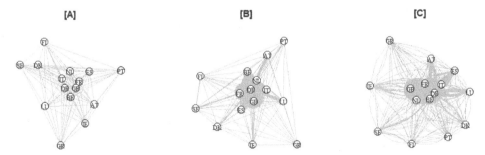

[A] **[B]** **[C]**

FIGURE 2.2 Graphs with Different Types of Edge and Node Design.

---

[8]We discuss importance score and network properties in Chapters 3 and 4.
[9]*Source*: https://www.finra.org/filing-reporting/trace/content-licensing/monthly-volume-report/2019

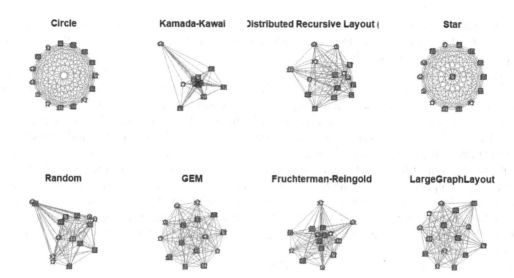

FIGURE 2.3   Graph Plots with Different Design and Graph Algorithms.
Note: The data are obtained by the authors from the TRACE website at https://www.finra.org/filing-reporting/trace/content-licensing/monthly-volume-report/2019.

BOX 2.2:   A GRAPH VISUALIZATION.

```
#A simple visualization code
pay.sent<-as.matrix(Payments.Sent[,2:16])
diag(pay.sent)<-0
pays<-graph_from_adjacency_matrix(pay.sent, weighted = TRUE)
E(pays)$arrow.size<-0
n.w<-t(apply(pay.sent,1, function(x) sum(x))) #


par(mfrow=c(1,3))
#plain graph
plot(pays, vertex.size=15, layout=layout_with_fr, edge.color="grey85", vertex.
shape="circle", vertex.color="white",vertex.label.cex=.8, main="[A]")

#plain graph with edge weights
plot(pays, vertex.size=15, layout=layout_with_fr, edge.color="grey80", vertex.
shape="circle", vertex.color="white",vertex.label.cex=.8, edge.width=E(pays)$weight/1000,
main="[B]")

#plain with curved edges
plot(pays, vertex.size=15, layout=layout_with_fr, edge.color="grey80", vertex.
shape="circle", vertex.color="white",vertex.label.cex=.8, edge.width=E(pays)$weight/1000,
edge.curved=.3, main="[C]")

par(mfrow=c(1,3))
#Adding community structure
csg<-cluster_spinglass(pays)
E(pays)$arrow.size<-0
```

```
plot(csg, pays, vertex.size=log(n.w), vertex.color=csg$membership, edge.color=E(pays)$csg,
edge.width=E(pays)$weight/1000)

plot(pays, vertex.color=csg$membership, edge.width=E(pays)$weight/1000, layout=layout_
with_lgl, edge.curved=.3)


#adding Node attributes - geographic properties of the countries - "P" for peripheral, "C"
for core countries
pays<-set.vertex.attribute(pays, "geography", value=c("C","C", "C", "C", "C", "P", "C",
"P", "P", "P", "P", "C", "C", "P", "C"))

V(pays)$color <- V(pays)$geography
V(pays)$color <- gsub("P","white",V(pays)$color)
V(pays)$color <- gsub("C","grey",V(pays)$color)


V(pays)$shape <- V(pays)$geography
V(pays)$shape <- gsub("P","circle",V(pays)$shape)
V(pays)$shape <- gsub("C","square",V(pays)$shape)


#PLotting the graph with community association and edge weights
plot(pays, vertex.color=csg$membership, edge.width=E(pays)$weight/1000,
layout=layout_as_star)


#simple Designs
par(mfrow=c(2,4))
plot(pays, layout=layout_in_circle, vertex.label.cex=0.7, main="Circle")
plot(pays, layout=layout_with_kk, vertex.label.cex=0.7, main="Kamada-Kawai")
plot(pays, layout=layout.drl, vertex.label.cex=0.7, main="Distributed Recursive
Layout (DrL)")
plot(pays, layout=layout_as_star, vertex.label.cex=0.7, main="Star")
plot(pays, layout=layout_randomly, vertex.label.cex=0.7, main="Random")
plot(pays, layout=layout_with_gem, vertex.label.cex=0.7,main="GEM")
plot(pays, layout=layout_with_fr, vertex.label.cex=0.7, main="Fruchterman-Reingold")
plot(pays, layout=layout_with_lgl, vertex.label.cex=0.7, main="Large Graph Layout (LGL)")
```

The Deep Reinforcement Learning (DrL) and Gray-Level Grouping (GLG) algorithms are the most widely used algorithms for large networks. Additionally, the Fruchterman–Reingold (FR) and Kamada–Kawai (KK) algorithms are also highly popular for their effectiveness in visualizing complex networks.[10].

In finance, the preference for network layouts varies according to network size. For financial institutions, researchers like Diebold and Yilmaz (2009, 2012), Merton et al. (2013), and Lo and Stein (2016) have applied star and circle algorithms. Konstantinov (2022b) used these algorithms for hedge funds. On the other hand, Papenbrock and Schwendner (2015) and Baitinger and Maier (2019) utilized minimum spanning trees (MSTs) for financial networks. MSTs simplify correlation structures by removing unnecessary or redundant edges, creating a more interpretable network.

Reducing the dimension using an MST creates a simplified network with clearer and more visible information. Figure 2.4 illustrates the application of random and MST algorithms for a single hedge fund network with 239 nodes, based on the study in Konstantinov and Simonian (2020).

---

[10]See Kamada and Kawai (1989), Martin et al. (2008), and Fruchterman and Reingold (1991).

However, real-world networks are often large, which is particularly true in finance. Benchmark indices used in investment management comprise many individual securities, which are represented as nodes in a graph. For example, the S&P500 Index comprises the 500 largest stocks, and a global government bond index represents the global government bond market with more than 2,000 individual bonds (i.e., nodes). Global aggregate bond indices, which comprise bonds of different sectors, industries, and currencies among others, comprise even more than 20,000 bonds. Such networks are deemed large, and there are specific algorithms suitable for visualizing them. Several widely applied algorithms for large network visualization are the DrL, MDS, LGL, and KK algorithms.

Figure 2.5 summarizes several graph plots for the same hedge fund network, each using different attributes. Specifically, they are

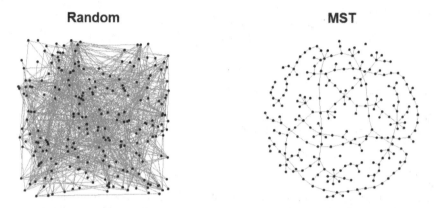

FIGURE 2.4   An Example for a Random and MST Network Design.

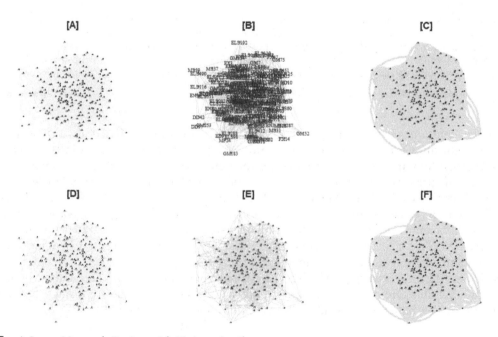

FIGURE 2.5   A Large Network Design with Various Attributes.
Note: This is a partial correlation single hedge fund network with 239 nodes and 2,718 edges.

- *Panel A*: A simple graph with no specific attributes.
- *Panel B*: A network that includes node names and edge weights.
- *Panel C*: A network displaying edged curves and edge weights, without node names or properties.
- *Panel D*: An example highlighting node attributes, specifically annualized node volatility, with no edge weights used.
- *Panel E*: A graph demonstrating community associations, where node colors represent specific community structures.
- *Panel F*: A comprehensive graph incorporating both node and edge attributes – node size reflects volatility, edge width corresponds to edge weight, and node color indicates community structure.

Figure 2.5 demonstrates that various edge and node attributes can be applied to enhance the visualization and interpretation of complex networks.

The construction of such networks is discussed in detail in Chapters 6, 7, and 8. The code for these graphs is shown in Box 2.3. Specifically, the code for constructing the single hedge fund network and the computational details are covered extensively in these chapters, where the network construction models are presented. In these networks, edge attributes are the weights. In contrast, the node attributes are the community affiliation or the volatility of each node, which are computed using the time series returns.

BOX 2.3: A GRAPH VISUALIZATION FOR LARGE NETWORKS – HEDGE FUNDS.

```
#Code for single hedge fund network using partial correlation coefficients
netz_pcor_shf<-graph_from_adjacency_matrix(mat_pcor_shf, weighted=TRUE)
par(mfrow=c(1,3))
E(netz_pcor_shf)$arrow.size<-0
#plain graph
plot(netz_pcor_shf, vertex.size=3, layout=layout_with_mds, edge.color="grey95", vertex.
shape="circle", vertex.color="black",vertex.label.cex=.1, main="[A]")

#plain graph with edge weights
plot(netz_pcor_shf, vertex.size=3, layout=layout_with_mds, edge.color="grey90", vertex.
shape="circle", vertex.color="white",vertex.label.cex=.6, edge.width=E(netz_pcor_
shf)$weight/10, main="[B]")

#plain with curved edges
plot(netz_pcor_shf, vertex.size=3, layout=layout_with_mds, edge.color="grey90", vertex.
shape="circle", vertex.color="black",vertex.label.cex=.1, edge.width=E(netz_pcor_
shf)$weight*3, edge.curved=.3, main="[C]")


#Networks with edge and node attributes
par(mfrow=c(1,3))
n.w<-t(apply(shf,2, function(x) sd(x))) #node volatility estimation using return
time-series
csg<-cluster_spinglass(netz_pcor_shf) #detect community structure
V(netz_pcor_shf)$com<-csg$membership
Csg #show communities
colrs <- adjustcolor(c("black","gray20", "gray30","gray40", "gray50", "gray70","gray90",
"white"), alpha=.6)
```

(Continued)

(*Continued*)

```
#plot(netz_pcor_shf, vertex.color=colrs[V(netz_pcor_shf)$com], layout=layout_with_mds,
vertex.label.cex=0.5, vertex.size=5,edge.color="grey85")

#Node-weights represented by volatilites
plot(netz_pcor_shf, vertex.size=n.w*sqrt(12)*10, layout=layout_with_mds, edge.
color="grey95", vertex.shape="circle", vertex.color="black",vertex.label.cex=.1,
main="[D]")

#plain graph with edge weights and community structure
plot(netz_pcor_shf, vertex.size=3, layout=layout_with_mds, edge.color="grey90", vertex.
shape="circle", vertex.color=colrs[V(netz_pcor_shf)$com],vertex.label.cex=.1, edge.
width=E(netz_pcor_shf)$weight/10, main="[E]")

#plain with curved edges
plot(netz_pcor_shf, vertex.size=3, layout=layout_with_mds, edge.color="grey90", vertex.
shape="circle", vertex.color="black",vertex.label.cex=.1, edge.width=E(netz_pcor_
shf)$weight*3, edge.curved=.3, main="[F]")
```

KEY TAKEAWAYS

- Defined as a sociomatrix, the adjacency matrix captures the mutual links between nodes. In other words, the adjacency matrix measures the pairwise relationships between nodes.
- Formally, the links and nodes in a network are represented by an adjacency matrix, which captures their mutual connectedness.
- The adjacency matrix is a square matrix where the number of rows and columns equals the number of nodes in the network. If two nodes are connected, the corresponding element in the matrix is 1. Conversely, if two nodes are not connected, the corresponding matrix element is 0.
- The entries in the adjacency matrix represent the presence or absence of links between the nodes.
- The major types of networks include directed networks, undirected networks, complete networks, weighted networks, unweighted networks, multigraphs, and trees.
- The degree of a node serves as a critical metric in network analysis, offering direct insight into the number of links associated with that node. It can be compared to the number of connections an individual has within a social network or the number of relationships an asset maintains with other assets.
- Various algorithms and models, such as the Kamada–Kawai layout algorithm and minimum spanning tree, are used in network analysis for effective visualization and analysis.

Network Properties

Contents

Like descriptive statistics used to represent financial time series, networks are characterized by specific metrics. These metrics vary, depending on the type of network and its characteristics. A deep understanding of these metrics is essential for comprehending network dynamics and interconnectedness. Common properties of a network include:

- Assortativity
- Clustering coefficients
- Community structure
- Connectivity
- Degree
- Density
- Diameter
- Geodesic distance
- Reciprocity
- Size

These metrics refer to the overall properties of a network and aim to describe its underlying structure. The structure of a network's connectedness depends on the underlying information flow process, or how nodes interact over the edges. Transfer of information between the nodes is carried out based on a specific way, defined as paths, trails, or walks. That is, whether a node is visited once (or many times) has major implications for the interaction and exchange of information. Similarly, the way that an edge is used once (or multiple times) has an enormous impact on the whole information transmission and the node properties in the network. Understanding the difference between these processes is essential because the information flow in the various network types determines the node and edge connectivity.

Our objective in this chapter is to discuss these network properties.

CONNECTEDNESS

While metrics like network size, diameter, and distance are general descriptive measures, average degree, density, and compactness gauge interconnectedness. Reciprocity and transitivity assess the network balance, while centrality scores and centralization measure the dominance of specific nodes. Before delving into network metrics in Chapter 4, it's crucial to define what connectedness entails.

Connectedness of a network is indicated by the presence of an edge or link between two nodes. If an edge exists between two vertices, the graph is considered connected. This link is represented by a path, walk, or trail, which is essential as it influences the definition and properties of the flow process, thereby determining the network metrics needed to analyze node and link behavior.[1] Das and Sisk (2005) define connectedness between nodes as the presence of a nonzero edge weight between them. A graph is deemed connected if any node can be reached from every other node. Consequently, a node in a network is reachable from another node if a walk exists between them.

Mendelson (1990) delineates three main types of connectedness:

- Intermediate Value Theorem
- Path-connectedness
- Simple connectedness

Understanding these types of connectedness is pertinent in economics and finance, where linear and nonlinear real-value models that incorporate connectedness are often employed. Some understanding of mathematics is necessary to grasp the intuition behind connectedness and the methods used to capture and model it such as linear polynomials, as it is commonly measured in financial research. Central is the definition of a function that connects elements of metric spaces. If A and B are metric spaces, and each element a ($a \in A$) matches each element b ($b \in B$), then a function $a = f(b)$ exists. In words, a is a function of b. In this case, the metric space A is a domain and B is the range. Because mathematical models are used in financial economics, we can say that the elements $a \in A$ are independent variables, and $b \in B$ are the dependent variables. However, if the elements of a metric space A correspond to other elements of the metric space B, then the inverse function maps the elements of the range set (B) back to the domain set (A). In other words, the inverse function of $a = f(b)$ is given by $b = f^{-1}(a)$.

The *Intermediate Value Theorem* states that in a continuous function Y in a fixed interval [a,b], the function Y takes any given value within $f[a]$, and $f[b]$ and $f: Y \to \mathbb{R}$. If x is a real number, so that min

---

[1]These terms are highly relevant for the network flow process, and we define and discuss them extensively later in this chapter.

$(f[a], f[b]) < x < \max(f[a], f[b])$, then there exists a real number y in the interval between a and b $(y \in (a,b))$ so that $f[y] = x$.

Let us define connectedness differently. The Intermediate Value Theorem is closely related to the topological spaces and the notion of connectedness for real numbers $\mathbb{R}$. If A and B are metric spaces, and two elements a $(a \in A)$ and b $(b \in B)$ exist, and E is a subset of A $(E \subset A)$, then $f(E)$ is connected. The set, E is connected only and only if when $a,b \in E$, and x lies between a, and b $(a < x < b)$, then it follows that $x \in E$. Simply applying this to graphs means that connecting two nodes can be done only using a continuous function.

Path-connectedness asserts that any two points are linked by a path or arc. Notably, path-connectedness represents a stronger form of connectedness compared to intermediate-value connectedness, as it guarantees that all nodes are interconnected with paths between them. In financial markets, completed networks (such as correlation networks) can be viewed as path connected. However, alternative network models may permit nodes or assets to not be directly connected. The existence of a walk between nodes in a network establishes the notion of reachability for a node.

Consequently, a *simple connectedness* between two nodes exists if the two nodes are path connected. In the case of simple connectedness, every path between two nodes can be continuously transformed so that the two nodes are preserved. In financial network analysis, the path might be modeled by a mathematical function or polynomial.[2] As we shall see later in this book, statistical tests, factor models, and econometric analysis among others might be applied to model financial market connectedness. Figure 3.1 shows the intermediate value connectedness represented by a function.

Once connectedness is established, we can explore the metrics that characterize graphs. These metrics provide insights into various aspects of the network's structure and behavior, aiding in its analysis and interpretation.

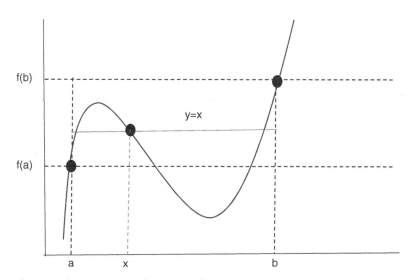

FIGURE 3.1   The Mathematical Expression of Connectedness.

---

[2]Several studies use a simple linear function that models the connectedness, or relation between two nodes (points).

Walks, Trails, and Paths

The most important tasks when investigating networks are to find the mechanisms by which nodes are connected and discover how information travels through the links between them. This knowledge is essential for understanding how various entities, such as information, news, gossip, money, goods, services, and packages, move within a network. In a network context, the movement from node to node follows a sequence. Understanding the node-to-node transmission and the possible trajectories that characterize the flow process between nodes is essential. Centrality metrics, applied to determine importance scores, depend on the process of transferring items in the network and their trajectories. The three most essential types of sequences are walks, trails, and paths. Barabási (2016) argued that paths are fundamental for understanding networks and connectedness.

Walks   Walks represent unrestricted sequences where there is no limit to how often a node and an edge might be visited. According to Wassermann and Faust (1994), in a walk the traversal in a network always starts and ends with a node, but some nodes might be included multiple times. However, not all nodes in the network need to be included in a walk. Therefore, walks are the most unrestricted type of sequence in a network.

Figure 3.2, adopted from Wasserman and Faust (1994), illustrates a possible walk would be W = N5E4N2E1N1E1N2. Note that in the case of a walk, both the edges and nodes are used more than once (E1 and N2). Because the length of a walk is described as the number of nodes occurring in the sequence, a walk is simply a node sequence: W = N5N2N1N2. Borgatti (2005) and Borgatti et al. (2022)

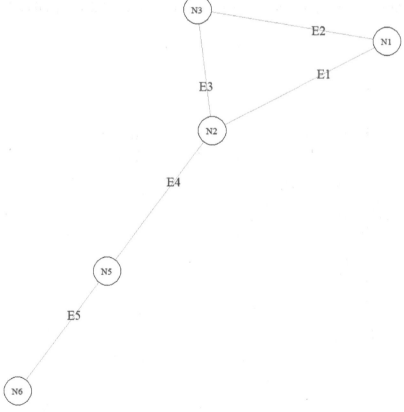

FIGURE 3.2   Edges and Nodes of a Simple Graph.
Note: For more details, see Wasserman and Faust (1994).

BOX 3.1:   A SIMPLE GRAPH WITH EDGE AND VERTEX NAMES.

```
# compute a simple graph with edge and vertex description
wtp = graph_from_literal(N1-N2,N1-N3,N5-N6,N2-N3,N3-N2,N2-N5)
E(wtp)$label <- paste0("E", seq_len(ecount(wtp)))
plot(wtp, vertex.label.cex=0.7)
```

---

illustrated that money flow might move from node i to node j, and then back from node j to node i. The code for this graph is provided in Box 3.1.

Let's consider a simplified example from the mutual fund industry to illustrate the concept of walks in a network. Imagine that we have a network representing connections between different mutual funds, based on their investment strategies of factor exposure and holdings. Each node in the network represents a mutual fund, and the edges between them signify some level of similarity or interaction between the funds.

Now, say we have two mutual funds, Fund i and Fund j, connected in this network. Fund i primarily invests in value stocks, while Fund j focuses on momentum strategy. Here's how a walk between Fund i and Fund j might occur, which is the underlying assumption of the fund interconnectedness analysis of Konstantinov and Rebmann (2019), Konstantinov and Simonian (2020), and Konstantinov and Rusev (2020).

Fund i starts with a high-value exposure but decides to diversify its exposure. Fund i begins to reduce some of its value exposure (i.e., selling value stocks) and starts increasing exposure to momentum (i.e., purchasing shares of companies with strong momentum characteristics) to diversify its portfolio. Suppose Fund i is mimicking (unintentionally) the strategy of Fund j. Fund i increases its momentum exposure, so it becomes more like Fund j, which already specializes in momentum stocks and has significant momentum exposure. Fund j notices the increasing similarity with Fund i and might adjust its portfolio accordingly, potentially reinforcing the connections between the two funds in the network over value and momentum exposure. In this example, the walk between Fund i and Fund j represents the flow of investment decisions and adjustments, highlighting how nodes in a network can influence each other's strategies and holdings over time. In a walk, the information might affect all possible nodes many times simultaneously because, as Asness et al. (2013) found, value and momentum exposure can be found in all asset classes. The existence of a direct walk between any two nodes means that the graph is strongly connected.

Trails   According to Borgatti (2005), a trail is a sequence in which no link is repeated, but the nodes can be included multiple times. The main distinction from a path is that while nodes might be revisited, edges are not. In other words, in a trail a node may be visited several times through different edges connected to neighboring nodes.

For example, consider fixed income as an asset class represented by a bond index node within an asset network. This bond index node might be traversed through various edges connecting it to other nodes, such as commodities, currencies, and equities. These links could represent different types of connections such as carry trades in currencies and bonds.[3]

---

[3]A carry trade is a trade that uses the difference in interest rates. Borrowing in a low interest rate and lending in the higher interest rate is widely used in currency investing. The intuition behind the concept of uncovered interest parity (UIP) is based on the relationship between the current spot rate and the unknown, expected future spot rate of a currency using the corresponding interest rates. One of the early investigations regarding UIP in currency investing goes back to the work of Froot and Thaler (1990). The authors found that contrary to the expectations of the UIP, currencies with higher interest rates were observed to appreciate against the currencies with lower interest rates. Consequently, borrowing in low-interest rate currencies and investing in high-interest rate currencies can be a profitable but risky strategy.

Trails are particularly exemplified in information networks, where information travels only once through a link but might reach the same node via different channels (i.e., links). It's important to note that every trail is a walk, and its length is determined by the number of links between the nodes. For example, in Figure 3.2, a trail could have the following sequence: T = N2N1N3N2.

Paths   A path represents a sequence of connections (i.e., edges) between nodes within a network, and the path length is a network metric that measures the distance between two nodes. The path length can be determined by the value associated with the edges or by counting the number of connections (i.e., links) between nodes. The shortest path between two nodes, i and j, is the one with the fewest number of links.

In economic and financial networks, the path value represents the minimum cost or effort required for two nodes to interact, such as through communication or transactions. These path values can be associated with metrics like transaction volumes or other relevant factors. When using correlation coefficients as distance metrics, a threshold can be applied to reflect path values, ensuring that only correlations above a certain level are considered in the path calculation.

Paths, or path-connectedness, represent a type of connectedness where all pairs of nodes are linked by a path, ensuring that there is always a connection between any two nodes in a network. Paths exhibit a strong form of connectedness compared to walks, where a link between two nodes may or may not exist.

For instance, in Figure 3.2, a path might have the sequence P = N5N2N1. It's important to note that multiple paths can exist within a network. In the example network shown in Figure 3.2, two possible paths are $P1$ = N5N2N1 and $P2\ A$ = N5N2N3N1. Paths ensure that nodes cannot remain disconnected, a crucial property for correlation-based networks, as discussed in Chapter 6. The fundamental characteristic of paths is that both nodes and links are used only once.

Consider a financial market comprising assets. If path-connectedness exists, no asset can remain isolated from the others because there is always a path connecting all the assets in the network. Paths are often associated with directedness in connectivity, resembling the specific sequence that capital follows during a transaction: from the buyer's ledger to the seller's ledger. In paths, neither nodes nor links are repeated in the sequence, ensuring that information travels through each node and link only once. Consequently, paths are vital properties of a network. As Harary (1953) and Wassermann and Faust (1994) point out, if there exists a path between nodes in a network, the graph is considered connected.

Two special cases that merit attention are geodesic paths and Hamiltonian and Eulerian paths. The primary distinction lies in the concept of self-avoiding lines. In a self-avoiding regime, a node sequence is visited only once, thus preventing intersections. This property is significant in financial markets, akin to a financial institution facing a risk that might impact it multiple times. A Hamiltonian path includes each node of a network only once, while a Eulerian path traverses each link exactly once.

Geodesic Distance and Diameter   Geodesic paths represent the shortest distance between two nodes within a network. As Barabási (2016) highlights, paths or distances in networks differ from those in physics. In network science, distances are determined by path lengths or the number of edges required to connect nodes.

The analogy of package delivery can aptly illustrate Geodesics. Historically, physical delivery of stocks, bonds, and futures contracts on commodities involved, following the shortest possible path to reach a fixed destination, akin to geodesics. However, in financial markets, the exchange of securities and payments may not necessarily adhere to the shortest paths.

The link to bonds results in taking short position in short-term bonds and taking a long position in long-term bonds. For carry strategies in global bonds and currencies, see Konstantinov and Fabozzi (2021).

The distance between nodes, often used in finance, refers to the path with the fewest number of links between them. Evaluating the shortest path between two nodes is a fundamental property that requires examination. In a directed network, the distance between nodes i and j may differ from that between nodes j and i, reflecting the one-way directionality within the network $d_{ij} \neq d_{ji}$. For undirected networks, the distance between two nodes is equal, regardless of the direction of information flow $d_{ij} = d_{ji}$. If two nodes are disconnected within a network, the distance between them is infinity $d_{ij} = \infty$.

Measuring the distance between nodes is crucial when analyzing portfolio networks. Hage and Harary (1995) showed that the eccentricity of a network provides the scores of each node as the shortest path to other nodes. Kaya (2015) stressed the application of eccentricity in asset management. The intuition behind it resembles that of the diversification to build portfolios whose nodes show large average path lengths. In general, understanding the spread of risk involves recognizing that it can co-occur, but is often transferred and replicated. To distinguish between paths, trails, and walks, it's crucial to grasp how things move across nodes and the nature of node-to-node transmission. The key distinction lies in whether information is transferred (i.e., moved) or replicated (i.e., copied). For instance, money flows are transferred, while information is often replicated because it can exist in multiple places simultaneously. In a trail, information may pass through the same node multiple times but does not travel through the same link repeatedly. Similarly, infections spread through replication and affect nodes once, after which the nodes (e.g., individuals) become immune.

Applying this concept to financial markets requires some economic context. In financial markets, assets do not become automatically immune to systematic risk after a financial turmoil; the negative impact persists. For example, the October 2008 default of Lehman Brothers was a consequence of the financial turmoil stemming from the subprime mortgage crisis, which emerged in 2007 and intensified in early 2008. The transmission of these adverse effects, related to the market valuation of financial instruments, affected the Lehman Brothers node multiple times. Financial markets share similar properties with information processing, money transfer, infections, goods and services distribution, and social phenomena such as gossip, attitudes, and affections. Therefore, transfer and replication are fundamental attributes of networks and their various dimensions – paths, trails, and walks.

The distance of a network explains the length of the shortest directed path from a node i to node j in the network. In other words, it measures the direct distance between any two nodes of the network. If no path exists between the nodes i and j, the distance is set to infinity $\left(d_{ij} = \infty \right)$. The average path length is equal to the mean of the distances between all pairs of nodes:

$$\bar{l} = \frac{\sum_{i \neq j} d_{ij}}{n(n-1)} \tag{3.1}$$

where d_{ij} is the distance between nodes i and j, and n is the number of nodes.

Whereas the distance represents the shortest path between nodes, the diameter of a network measures the longest distance between any two nodes in a network. Thus, the diameter represents the worst-case scenario for sending information across the network. The importance of the diameter and distance is highlighted in the concept of the "six degrees of separation" or the "small-world" phenomenon, discovered by Watts and Strogatz (1998) based on the empirical work of Milgram (1967). This phenomenon suggests that there are only a few steps are needed to reach every node in a network. Because distance is a measure of path length, it quantifies the number of steps required to reach all nodes in a network. Mathematically, the average path distance, or the small-world property between any two nodes in a network, is a function of the number of nodes and the mean degree. According to Newman, Strogatz, and Watts (2001), Newman (2010), and Barabási (2016), the small-world property of a network depends on the average node degree and the number of nodes, and varies with the size of the network. As a result, the diameter of a network is a function of the network size, and the nodes' average connectedness indicated by the average node degree:

$$d \approx \frac{\ln(n)}{\ln(k)} \tag{3.2}$$

where n is the number of nodes, and k is the mean degree averaged over all node pairs.

Certainly, the mean degree of a network inversely affects its diameter, or the number of steps needed to reach a node within the network. When the number of nodes remains relatively constant, the average node connectivity, or degree, plays a pivotal role in estimating the diameter. Moreover, networks with high density tend to have smaller diameters. For instance, Barabási (2016) reported that the diameter of the social collaboration network is 4.8, meaning that, on average, any two randomly selected nodes in the social network are 4.8 steps away from each other. Similarly, Barabási found that the average path length of the World-Wide Web is approximately 25.

According to Diebold and Yilmaz (2015), economic networks typically have low diameters. For example, the diameter of a single hedge fund network, as studied by Konstantinov and Simonian (2020), is 4, while the diameter of the equity and bond fund network, as investigated by Konstantinov and Rusev (2020), is 2. Bech and Atalay (2011) reported a diameter of 7 for the federal funds market.

In a financial network context, the diameter represents the distance between one asset or financial institution and another. This metric has significant implications for risk management and understanding the contagion effects of systemic risk, as it indicates the shortest path through which two assets might be affected during a financial crisis. For instance, one could consider the network distance between a defaulting financial institution (e.g., Lehman Brothers during the 2007 to 2008 Global Financial Crisis) and another specific institution such as Deutsche Bank.

The distance matrix is a variation of the adjacency matrix. While the adjacency matrix provides information about the connectedness between two vertices, the distance matrix additionally offers pairwise distance information between them. For instance, in an asset network where the distance is 1.67, and the diameter is 3, it means that it takes three steps to connect every two nodes situated in the outermost part of the network. However, the distance of 1.6 signifies the best-case scenario for transmitting information across the network, indicating the shortest path between the vertices of a graph.

Network Size and Connections

The two fundamental components of a network are its nodes and the links between them, which essentially define the network. The size of a network is determined by the number of nodes it contains. According to Yang, Algesheimer, and Tessone (2016), networks with more than 500 nodes are considered large – a common characteristic of many real-world social, information, biological, and technological networks. In finance, network size can vary, depending on the context. For instance, an investment universe comprising 20 assets would constitute a smaller network, while an index like the Russell 2000 with 2,000 individual constituents or the S&P 500 with 500 constituents represents a larger network. A portfolio consisting of 50 to 80 individual securities would be considered a network of small size.

The number of links between the assets (or other entities) in a network indicates its completeness or connectivity. Network connectivity is quantified by the likelihood of nodes sharing a link. Greater connectivity is reflected in a higher number of links within the network.

Drawing from mathematical theory concerning interconnected systems, a network or graph is characterized as a collection of nodes interconnected by edges or links. The most basic properties of a network $G = (n,m)$ are the number of *nodes,* or *vertices* n (i.e., assets) and *links,* or *edges* (i.e., connections) m, where

$n \in \mathbb{R}^n$ and $m \in \mathbb{R}^{n \times n}$ $(m_{i,j} \neq m_{j,i})$. The maximum number of links in a network given the fixed number of nodes would be:

$$m_{max} = \frac{n(n-1)}{2} \tag{3.3}$$

where m_{max} is the maximum number of links in the network, and n are the number of nodes.

Equation (3.3) calculates the maximum number of links in every network, given the network size (i.e., number of nodes). A simple example illustrates the logic behind finding the maximum number of links in a network. For instance, in an S&P 500 network comprising all 500 stocks or 500 nodes, the maximum number of links it can have is calculated as $(500 \times 499)/2 = 124{,}750$ links.

Node and Edge Attributes

Graphs enable the addition of various attributes or properties to both nodes and edges, providing essential information for network analysis. Researchers can leverage existing attributes or introduce new ones to enhance the analysis. These attributes can encompass static or continuous variables that may vary over time.

Node attributes may include categorical variables like gender in social networks or node identifiers. For example, node size could represent a company's market capitalization, as seen in major equity indices like the S&P 500. Nodes within a graph may belong to different sectors, such as industrials, information technology, financials, or consumer staples, providing insights into node properties based on attributes like "type" or "industry."

Edge attributes, on the other hand, could denote notional amounts of transactions between financial institutions. The width of edges in a graph is commonly used as an attribute to represent the strength or weight of connections between nodes.

Degree   The degree of a node serves as a crucial metric in network analysis, offering direct insight into the number of links associated with that node. It can be likened to the number of connections that an individual has within a social network or the number of relationships an asset maintains with other assets. Notably, the degree is considered a node property.

The adjacency matrix serves as a fundamental source of information regarding the connections between nodes. The degree of a node can be determined by summing the values in the corresponding row or column of the adjacency matrix. For instance, let's consider an undirected network consisting of four nodes.

$$\begin{bmatrix} 0 & 0 & 1 & 0 \\ 0 & 0 & 1 & 1 \\ 1 & 1 & 0 & 0 \\ 0 & 1 & 0 & 0 \end{bmatrix}$$

The second node of an undirected (4×4) network has a degree of 3, or $k_{2j} = 4$, which is equal the degree of the $k_{i2} = 4$. The degree number varies based on the network type, and the average degree represents the average number of links per node within a network. In undirected networks, which are symmetric, the average degree of a node is calculated as twice the total number of links divided by the number of nodes. Essentially, the average degrees are determined using the elements of the adjacency matrix a_{ij}.

For undirected networks, the degree of a node (representing incoming links) and the average degree of a node (representing outgoing links) are equal.

$$\hat{k}_i = \hat{k}_j = \sum_i a_{ij} = \sum_j a_{ji} = \frac{2m}{n} \tag{3.4}$$

where m represents the number of links in wthe network, n is the number of nodes, and a_{ij} are the elements of the adjacency matrix.

Directed networks differ from undirected ones because they involve a directionality in the links. In a directed network, the number of links pointing to a node from other nodes can differ from the number of links that point from the node to other nodes. This results in distinct measures referred to as the "in-degree" and "out-degree." The total degree of a node in a directed network is the sum of its in-degree and out-degree.

$$\hat{k}_i^{total} = \hat{k}_i^{in} + \hat{k}_i^{out} \tag{3.5}$$

The adjacency matrix provides the necessary information to compute the in-degrees of a node:

$$\hat{k}_i^{in} = \frac{1}{n}\sum_j a_{ij} = \hat{k}_i^{in} = \frac{1}{n}\sum_j a_{ji} = \frac{m}{n} \tag{3.6}$$

where m represents the number of links in the network, n the number of nodes, and a_{ij} are the elements of the adjacency matrix. The following adjacency matrix represents a directed network:

$$\begin{bmatrix} 0 & 0 & 1 & 0 \\ 0 & 0 & 1 & 1 \\ 1 & 1 & 0 & 0 \\ 0 & 0 & 0 & 0 \end{bmatrix}$$

The second node, whose connectedness is represented by the second row of the adjacency matrix of a directed 4×4 network, has an in-degree of 3, or $k_{i2}^{in} = 1$, which is not equal the out-degree of the $k_{j2}^{out} = 2$.

The degree matrix is a matrix representation of the connectedness on the node level. The main diagonal of the degree matrix $[D]_{ij}$ contains the node degrees representing the number of edges attached to each node and the other entries in the matrix are zeros. The degree matrix $[D]_{ij}$ with entries $\hat{k}_i$ for an undirected and a directed network, respectively is given:

$$\begin{bmatrix} 2 & 0 & 0 & 0 \\ 0 & 4 & 0 & 0 \\ 0 & 0 & 4 & 0 \\ 0 & 0 & 0 & 2 \end{bmatrix} \begin{bmatrix} 2 & 0 & 0 & 0 \\ 0 & 3 & 0 & 0 \\ 0 & 0 & 4 & 0 \\ 0 & 0 & 0 & 1 \end{bmatrix}$$

The code shown in Box 3.2 estimates the degree matrix for the undirected network. Note that the degrees of an undirected network are counted twice ($k = 2m/n$).

The average degree of a network is determined by the total number of links in the network divided by the number of nodes it contains. Degree distributions in networks capture the statistical properties of node degrees, which differ from the return distributions observed in financial markets. However, they share the common characteristic of having fat tail distributions of node degree. In the case of such distributions, the node degree exhibits large skewness or kurtosis. In real networks, the degree distribution often follows a power-law, meaning that some nodes have significantly higher degree scores than others. Power-law distributions exhibit log-linear behavior in their tails. For instance, consider the degree distribution of a single hedge fund network based on correlation coefficients, which is likely to demonstrate a power-law distribution (see Figure 3.3).[4]

---

[4]See Newman (2010), Barabási (2016), and Diebold and Yilmaz (2015).

BOX 3.2: CODE TO ESTIMATE THE DEGREE MATRIX FOR AN UNDIRECTED NETWORK.

```
C<- matrix(c(0,0,1,0,
       0,0,1,1,
       1,1,0,0,
       0,1,0,0), ncol = 4, byrow = TRUE)
c<-graph_from_adjacency_matrix(C)
plot(c, layout=layout_randomly, main="[A]")
degree(c)
deg.matrix<-matrix(0,4,4)
diag(deg.matrix)<-degree(c)
deg.matrix
```

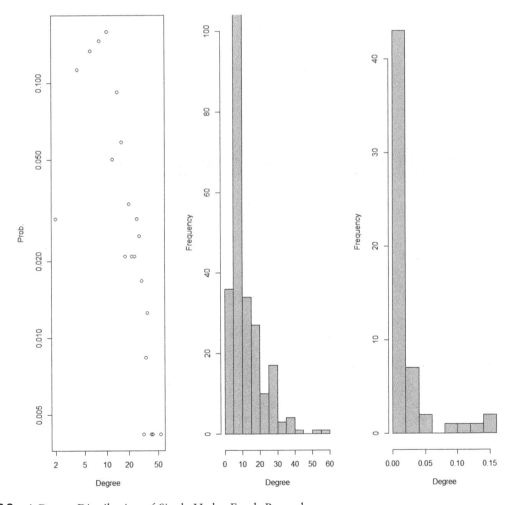

FIGURE 3.3   A Degree Distribution of Single Hedge Funds Power-law.
Note: The data used in this sample are the ones used by Konstantinov and Simonian (2020) for 239 single hedge funds.

The code in Box 3.3 calculates the power-law distribution of node degree of a single hedge fund network, estimated using the correlation coefficients and the Fischer transformation. The code comprises both the network estimation code and the computation of the node degree distribution. (In Chapters 6, 7, and 8, we provide an extensive discussion on how to construct asset and factor networks using time series data.) In the code shown in Box 3.3, we use only one of the presented algorithms based on correlation coefficients, which differs from the directed network estimated for single hedge funds by Konstantinov and Simonian (2020).

Density The metric used to describe the completeness of a network is known as density. Density, denoted by the Greek letter rho (ρ), quantifies the completeness of a network by comparing the number of existing links to the total number of possible links between nodes. This ratio provides insight into the extent of connections within the network relative to its size. In network science, density serves as a measure akin to the concept of density in physics but applied to networks. It follows a binomial process, reflecting the probability of link formation among nodes $\binom{n}{2}$. In this case:

$$\rho = \frac{m}{n\,(n-1)} \approx \frac{m}{n^2} \tag{3.7}$$

were m represents the number of links in the network and n the number of nodes.

The density of a network is a measure that ranges from 0 to 1, indicating the extent of connections within the network. A density value of 0 signifies the absence of connections between nodes. In contrast, a

---

BOX 3.3:   CODE FOR THE POWER-LAW DISTRIBUTION OF A SINGLE HEDGE FUND NETWORK.

```
#Power Law and Fat Tail Distribution of SHF
#Unirected Correlation Network with Fischer Transformation Volatility as Compromise
set.seed(3211)
returns<-shf
heatmap(data.matrix(cor(shf))) #identifies the cluster of the correlation matrix
mtx_corf<-data.frame()
mtx_corf<-matrix(nrow=ncol(shf),ncol=ncol(shf))
mtx_corf<-as.matrix(mtx_corf)
mat_corf=0.5*log((1+cor(returns))/(1-cor(returns)))
mat_corf=abs(mat_corf)
p.tres<-0.05/6 #identified already
mat_corf<-ifelse(mat_corf[,]<p.tres,1,0)
diag(mat_corf)<-0
colnames(mat_corf)<-colnames(shf)
print(mat_corf)
netz_corf<-as.matrix(mat_corf)
netz_corf<-graph_from_adjacency_matrix(netz_corf, weighted=TRUE)
#once estimating the network, the following code generates the node degree distribution
par(mfrow=c(1,3))
d.shf.corf<-degree(netz_corf)
dd.shf.corf<-degree.distribution(netz_corf)
d<-1:max(d.shf.corf)-1
ind<-(dd.shf.corf!=0)
plot(d[ind],dd.shf.corf[ind],log="xy",main="", xlab="Degree", ylab="Prob.")
hist(d.shf.corf, ylim=c(0,100), xlim=c(0,300), main="", xlab="Degree")
hist(dd.shf.corf, main="", xlab="Degree")
```

value of 1 indicates that all possible links between nodes are present, resulting in a fully connected or completed network. Networks with density values close to 0 are termed "sparse networks," indicating a scarcity of links relative to the total possible links.

Understanding density is crucial in financial network analysis. Research by Newman (2010) and Barabási (2016) has demonstrated that real-world networks tend to be sparse, meaning that not all potential links between nodes are realized. Das (2016) has argued that sparse financial networks may be more fragile than highly connected ones. It's important to note that correlation networks, which exhaust the maximum number of possible links, have a density close to 1, indicating dense connectivity. In Chapter 12, we explore the implications of sparse and dense networks on asset management fragility.

Reciprocity   *Reciprocity* in financial networks refers to the possibility of an asset being linked to another asset and vice versa, implying a causal relationship. If an asset is linked to another but not vice versa, it suggests a potential causal link between the two assets or economic variables. Reciprocity is a property observed in directed networks. In correlation or completed networks, where connections are symmetrical, every pair of assets is equally linked.

A node pair (i, j) is considered reciprocal if there are connections between both nodes in both directions. Das (2016) emphasized that reciprocity measures mutual connectedness at a network level. Reciprocity values range between 0 and 1, with 1 indicating a fully reciprocal network where every link has a corresponding reciprocal link. The reciprocity coefficient, adjusted for the parameters of the regression model and the entries in the adjacency matrices, can be calculated as follows:

$$\omega = \frac{\sum_{ij} a_{ij} \, a_{ji}}{m} \tag{3.8}$$

where m represents the number of links in the network and a_{ij}'s are the elements of the adjacency matrix.

The reciprocity of directed networks is an important property and can be associated with the crowdedness of assets in a portfolio. *Crowdedness* is observed when multiple funds have similar exposures to an asset or a factor. For instance, portfolios or fund returns, whose factor exposure is measured using factor models, may experience simultaneous risk-factor information flow or money flow between funds, leading to dynamic changes in fund exposures. However, how can common underlying factors interconnect funds?

Based on various studies on currency funds (Pojarliev and Levich, 2011; and Konstantinov and Rebmann, 2019), bond and equity funds (Konstantinov and Rusev, 2020), and hedge funds (Konstantinov and Simonian, 2020), it has been argued that funds modeled as a directed network demonstrate a direct relation between crowdedness and connectivity. Reciprocity in a network is akin to a measure of crowdedness because it identifies links between assets that may exhibit similar factor exposures. The critical difference is that, in a network context, reciprocity measures the mutual links without isolating the factor loadings in each asset. The relation between pairs of funds in a network is determined by the value of reciprocity, indicating whether asset i is linked to asset j and vice versa.

Assortativity   Exploring social networks often prompts the question of whether similar nodes are drawn together and connected or if opposites attract. Newman, Barabási, and Watts (2006) argue that *assortativity* measures the homophily[5] of a graph and is network-specific phenomenon, and applies to a specific types

---

[5]Homophily refers to the tendency of individuals within a social network to associate and form connections with others who are like themselves in some way. Homophily can be based on various characteristics (e.g., age, gender, education, and social status) and suggests that individuals are more likely to bond with others who share common traits, beliefs, or experiences. This phenomenon plays a significant role in shaping social relationships, group formation, and the overall structure of social networks.

of networks, including social, internet, and biological networks, among others. The most widely empirically tested phenomenon is that high-degree nodes tend to connect to other high-degree nodes.

Newman (2010) offers an in-depth overview of the methodology and computation of the assortativity mixing or the network correlation coefficient. The assortativity metric indicates node behavior, assigning negative values to the correlation coefficient, when there is a negative association between a node and that of its neighbor. Conversely, it assigns positive values when there is a positive relationship between the degrees of a node and its neighbor.

Assortativity represents the degree of correlation of the network, which takes positive values if similar nodes tend to connect to each other and take negative values otherwise. The values of the assortativity degree are often thought-provoking. Soramäki et al. (2006) discussed that networks characterized by negative assortativity coefficients are considered disassortative. In simpler terms, this means that nodes with lower degrees of connectivity are more likely to be linked to nodes with higher degrees of connectivity, rather than being connected to other nodes with similar low connectivity. Newman (2002a) found that biological and technological networks are disassortative. However, Bech and Atalay (2011) contested this finding, asserting that the federal funds network displays disassortative characteristics. Similarly, disassortativity has been observed in the mutual fund industry concerning equity and bond funds, as reported by Konstantinov and Rusev (2020), and in individual hedge funds, as observed by Konstantinov and Simonian (2020).

The question arises whether the nodes are connected based on endogenous or exogenous factors. According to Newman (2002a, 2002b, 2003, 2010) and Barabási (2016), this coefficient is negative if dissimilar nodes tend to connect to each other, based on external factors and vice versa. In other words, this is a metric for node similarity based on some external properties. And in disassortative networks, high-degree nodes build hubs with lower-degree nodes. In networks with positive-degree correlations, hubs connect to other hubs. Graphs with positive-assortativity degree have often distinctive core/periphery structures. The most interesting property of core-periphery structures is that the nodes in the periphery structure are rather strongly connected to the core nodes rather than to other periphery nodes.

An example from financial markets provides an explanation of the difference between core and peripheral structures. Specifically, the mechanism of core and periphery structures in financial assets was observed during the European debt crisis from 2011 to 2015, as documented by Konstantinov and Fabozzi (2021) and shown in Figure 3.4. The bond yield spreads of the periphery countries (i.e., Spain, Italy, Portugal, and Ireland) detached from the core bond yields of Germany, but their dynamics and connectivity to the same

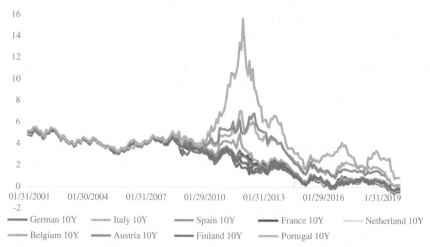

FIGURE 3.4   Historical 10-year Bond Yields in the European Monetary Union (EMU).
Source: For data obtained from Bloomberg, LLC, see Konstantinov and Fabozzi (2021).

cluster of periphery countries remained weak. The heterogeneous bond yield dynamics were a consequence of the fiscal imbalances and deteriorating macroeconomic conditions. The government bond yield widening marked the definition of core and peripheral European Monetary Union (EMU) countries. Beirne and Fratscher (2013) argued that macroeconomic fundamentals explain very little of bond yields of the peripheral countries. Debt pricing and spreads are major determinants of bond market dynamics before the European sovereign debt crisis in 2010. Nevertheless, these economic effects can be captured using networks and used in portfolio management.

Using the notional amounts of payments exchanged by European countries as a directed, weighted network illustrates the formation of core and peripheral structures within the network. Analyzing European bond yields as a directed network reveals the core-periphery connectedness of Portugal's 10-year bond yields, which are heavily linked to the core country yields of France, the Netherlands, and Belgium. Additionally, as shown in Figure 3.5, peripheral links to Italy and Spain are also evident.

Extending assortativity to assets and factors follows the same principle of identifying core and periphery structures. Negative assortativity values are preferred over positive ones because hubs tend to connect with low-degree nodes. This principle finds direct applications in portfolio management. Analyzing directed networks of bonds and equities (with bond and equity funds), Konstantinov and Rusev (2020) demonstrated that core-periphery structures, where hubs connect other asset hubs, are common in normal market conditions, while negative coefficients are observed during market stress. Ricca and Scozzari (2024) utilized assortative mixing in portfolio allocation and optimization to identify disassortative portfolios with a negative node degree correlation. However, visual inspection alone is insufficient for assessing network assortativity, necessitating the computation of assortativity degree. In Figure 3.6, a directed asset and factor network exhibits a degree correlation of 0.38, while another

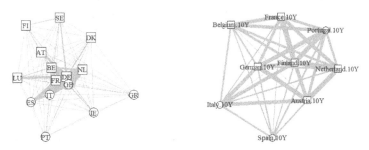

FIGURE 3.5 A Directed Weighted Network for the European Monetary Union (EMU) Government Bonds with Assortativity.

FIGURE 3.6 Examples of Assortative and Disassortative Asset and Factor Networks.
Note: The networks used in this figure are estimated using the algorithms provided in Chapters 6 and 7. We use netz_dir for a assortative network, netz_dir_dist for a disassortative network, and netz_dir_gct for nonassortative networks in this plot. The correlation coefficients are computed using the assortatitive.degree function in igraph in R.

network comprising assets and factors has a degree correlation of –0.36. The third network's correlation coefficient is close to zero (0.03). Figure 3.6 offers an overview of assortative and disassortative asset and factor networks.

COMPONENTS, CLUSTERING, AND COMMUNITIES

The approach often applied in graph theory is to evaluate the possible groups that vertices form in a network. This is widely practiced in finance where these groups of nodes are referred to as "communities" or "clusters." The rationale behind this lies in the natural tendency of vertices to cluster together based on certain underlying properties. For example, equities and high-yield bonds may share similar properties, while private equity might remain separate from other asset classes like equities, bonds, or alternative investments, such as commodities or real estate.

The process of separating vertices into groups is referred to as "graph partitioning," which involves identifying communities and clusters within a network. While communities and clusters are occasionally used interchangeably, they represent distinct concepts and should not be considered equivalent. Specifically, "clustering" is a term used to describe simple groups in financial data science, while community structures are directly associated with networks. Components of a graph represent the basic groups of vertices linked by edges.

Components

A network is often divided into subgroups, with one fundamental inquiry revolving around identifying the most connected components within a graph. These components typically comprise nodes that are directly or indirectly connected. However, the informativeness of these components may vary, depending on the size of the network. In small networks with few nodes, the components may be less informative than those in a larger network.

To illustrate the identification of components, let's consider a network comprising 239 hedge funds, as investigated in a study by Konstantinov and Simonian (2020). The minimum spanning tree (MST) algorithm is commonly used to provide the basic underlying structure or skeleton of such networks and is particularly effective in representing complex relationships. Figure 3.7 provides an overview of the components of the single hedge fund network.

The code provided in Box 3.4 pertains to the components of a single hedge fund network. The network is estimated using the partial correlations of the single hedge fund returns. The number of clusters of hedge funds is used to determine the threshold level of the Bonferroni p-value adjustment.

Clustering

The analysis of common relationships in data often involves clustering, where nodes that share specific properties are grouped into clusters. Hierarchical clustering is a common analytical tool applied to time series data such as asset returns. In this context, clustering requires a process separating data using a distance metric, which we will discuss in detail when applying them to portfolio management in Chapter 10.[6]

---

[6]Provost and Faucett (2013) show that Euclidean, Manhattan, cosine, or binary distance metrics help identify the distance between the data points, represented by nodes. The identification of clusters depends on the underlying distance mechanism applied to identify how close the nodes of a network are.

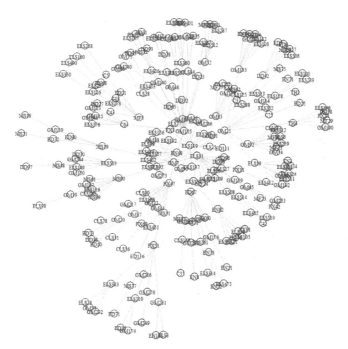

FIGURE 3.7 A Partial Correlation Single Hedge Fund Network with Bonferroni Adjustment.
Note: This is a Bonferroni *p*-value-adjusted partial correlation network of 239 single hedge funds belonging to a single component. The grey-palette colors of the nodes correspond to the coreness scores of the nodes in the network.

BOX 3.4: COMPONENTS OF A SINGLE HEDGE FUND NETWORK.

```
set.seed(122)
returns<-shf
mtx_pcor_shf<-data.frame()
mtx_pcor_shf<-matrix(nrow=ncol(shf),ncol=ncol(shf))
mtx_pcor_shf<-as.matrix(mtx_pcor_shf)
mat_pcor_shf=0.5*log((1+pcor(returns)$estimate)/(1-pcor(returns)$estimate))
mat_pcor_shf=abs(mat_pcor_shf)
p.threshold=0.05/6
mat_pcor_shf<-ifelse(mat_pcor_shf[,]<p.threshold,1,0)
diag(mat_pcor_shf)<-0
colnames(mat_pcor_shf)<-colnames(shf)
print(mat_pcor_shf)
netz_pcor_shf<-as.matrix(mat_pcor_shf)
netz_pcor_shf<-graph_from_adjacency_matrix(netz_pcor_shf)
hist(degree_distribution(netz_pcor_shf))
E(netz_pcor_shf)$arrow.size<-0

#Show the components of the SHF
components(netz_pcor_shf)$csize
#Plot SHF network with components in a MST with GEM-Algorithm
plot(mst(netz_pcor_shf), vertex.color=coreness(netz_pcor_shf), layout=layout_with_gem,
vertex.label.cex=0.5, vertex.size=5,edge.color="grey85")
```

Graph theory has developed specific metrics to measure the clustering of nodes. The probability that the adjacent local vertices of a node i are connected is captured by the *clustering coefficient $\widetilde{C}_i$* given by:[7]

$$\widetilde{C}_i = \frac{2m}{k_i(k_i - 1)} \tag{3.9}$$

where k_{ij} are the average degrees of a node and m represents the number of links.

Fagiolo (2007) provides a comprehensive method for computing the average clustering coefficient across all nodes in directed networks using the graph's adjacency matrix. It's important to note that directed networks possess different properties than undirected networks, such as in-degree and out-degree distributions. Moreover, the degree matrix is symmetric, with the degree entries located on the main diagonal. Therefore, computing the overall clustering coefficients for each vertex requires considering the diagonal elements of the adjacency matrix. The total degree of a directed network is the sum of the in-degree and the out-degree. Following Kolaczyk and Csardi (2020), the clustering coefficient is:

$$\widetilde{C}_n^d = \frac{(A + A^T)^3}{2\left[\hat{k}_i^{total}\left(\hat{k}_i^{total} - 1\right) - 2A^2\right]} \tag{3.10}$$

where $\hat{k}_i^{total}$ is the total (in-degree and out-degree) of a network, A is the adjacency matrix, A^T is the transposed adjacency matrix.

The clustering coefficient measures the tendency of nodes to cluster into local communities within a network. It ranges between 0 and 1, with positive values indicating an increased probability of interconnectedness between nodes. The clustering of a network is heavily influenced by its average node degree. Networks with large average degrees often form a single giant component with strong interconnectedness among nodes. Barabási (2016) demonstrates that real networks typically consist of several components and clusters.

The code for the clustering coefficient is provided in Box 3.5.[8] Note that the clustering coefficient is a function that uses the adjacency matrix and the node degrees to estimate the clustering coefficient.

BOX 3.5:   COMPONENTS OF A SINGLE HEDGE FUND NETWORK.

```
clustering_coefficient<-function(graph){
  AM<-as.matrix(as_adjacency_matrix(graph)) #extract the adjacency matrix
  N<-AM+t(AM)
  deg<-degree(graph, mode=c("total")) #use the node degree
  clustering_coefficient<-mean(diag(N%*%N%*%N)/(2*(deg*(deg-1)-2*diag(AM%*%AM))))
  return(clustering_coefficient)
}
```

---

[7] See, for example, Barrat et al. (2004), Bech and Atalay (2011), and Barabási (2016).
[8] See Borgatti et al. (2022).

Empirical results for networks involving nodes, assets, and other financial variables suggest that node degrees are generally large and clustered despite real networks being sparse. For instance, Konstantinov and Simonian (2020) examined directed single hedge fund networks and found an average degree of 94 with around 700 nodes, yet the networks remained sparse and clustered. Similarly, Konstantinov and Rusev (2020) observed that bond-equity fund networks, averaging 450 nodes, exhibited sparsity with an average degree of 46 and a highly clustered structure.

Community Structure

The identification of clusters or communities in finance is often applied to identify assets belonging to the same group and share common properties. In recent years, several studies have applied clustering algorithms using financial time series data, often utilizing correlation coefficients to estimate clusters and community structures.[9] For example, Suhonen and Vatanen (2024) applied hierarchical clustering to identify alternative risk premia and assign them into groups.

However, community structure in networks differs from applying community structure to correlation coefficients of time series data. This difference arises from a graph's connectedness and its nodes' properties. Community detection is a direct way to investigate the underlying communities of a network using mathematical algorithms. Yang et al. (2016) offer an extensive overview of various network community detection algorithms and recommend choosing the appropriate algorithm based on the size and connectedness of the network.

Some of the most widely used algorithms in network science include:

- cluster_leading_eigen suggested by Newman (2006)
- walktrap suggested by Pons and Latapy (2005)
- fast_greedy developed by Clauset, Newman, and Moore (2004)
- Louvain algorithm investigated by Blondel, Guillaume, Lambiotte, and Lefebvre (2008)
- spinglass suggested by Reichardt and Bornholdt (2006)
- infomap algorithm suggested by Rosvall, Axelsson, and Bergstrom (2009), and
- cluster label_propensity researched by Raghavan, Albert, and Kumara (2007).

While some algorithms are limited to undirected graphs, spinglass and walktrap are suited for large, directed networks. The size of a network is typically determined by the number of nodes, with large networks usually comprising more than 500 nodes.

In general, the choice of clustering algorithm for investigating a graph is determined by the *modularity score*. A larger modularity score indicates less network partitioning and less information loss when detecting network communities. According to the study by Konstantinov and Simonian (2020), Figure 3.8 illustrates the community structure of a single hedge fund network with 239 nodes.

Box 3.6 provides the code for estimating the modularity for the partial correlation network of single hedge funds. The modularity is computed for seven algorithms, and the one with the highest modularity score is selected.

---

[9]See, for example, the various application of clustering in the studies of Bacidore, Berkow, and Polidore (2012); Raffinot (2017); Garvey and Madhavan (2019); Bonne, Lo, Prabhakaran, Siah, Singh, Wang, Zangari, and Zhang (2022); and Elkamhi, Lee, and Salerno (2024).

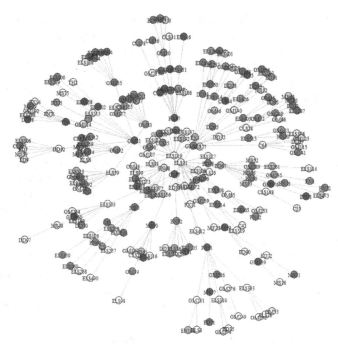

FIGURE 3.8 The Community Structure of a Single Hedge Fund Network.
Note: This is a Bonferroni *p*-value-adjusted partial correlation network of 239 single hedge funds. The graph is computed using a partial-correlation algorithm. The algorithms for network computation are provided in Chapters 6, 7, and 8.

BOX 3.6:   THE MODULARITY SCORE OF A SINGLE HEDGE FUND NETWORK.

```
#Run cluster algorithms and compute modularity

clp<-cluster_label_prop(as.undirected(netz_pcor_shf))
cfg<-cluster_fast_greedy(as.undirected(netz_pcor_shf))
clei<-cluster_leading_eigen(as.undirected(netz_pcor_shf))
cim<-cluster_infomap(as.undirected(netz_pcor_shf))
csg<-cluster_spinglass(netz_pcor_shf)
cwt<-cluster_walktrap(netz_pcor_shf)
clo<-cluster_louvain(as.undirected(netz_pcor_shf))
modularity(clp)
modularity(cfg)
modularity(clei)
modularity(cim)
modularity(csg)
modularity(cwt)
modularity(clo)
#select the clo with the highest modularity score
V(netz_pcor_shf)$community<-clo$membership
```

Once the algorithm with the highest modularity score is selected, it is essential to compute the length, which provides the number of communities. Enumerating the sizes is reasonable to see the number of nodes assigned to each community. When plotting the network, it is reasonable to adjust the color group according to the number of communities.

Box 3.7 provides the code to compute the minimum spanning tree (MST) of the single hedge fund network according to the number of communities detected once the algorithm with the highest modularity score is selected.

BOX 3.7: A MINIMUM SPANNING TREE FOR THE SINGLE HEDGE FUND NETWORK WITH COMMUNITIES.

```
sizes(clo)
length(clo) #gives the number of communities
colrs <- adjustcolor(c("black","gray20", "gray30","gray40", "gray50", "gray70","gray90",
"white"), alpha=.6)
#use MST algorithm to plot a graph optimizing the structure
plot(mst(netz_pcor_shf), vertex.color=colrs[V(netz_pcor_shf)$community],
layout=layout_with_gem, vertex.label.cex=0.5, vertex.size=5,edge.color="grey85")
#Show the components of the SHF
components(netz_pcor_shf)$csize


#Plot SHF network with components
plot(netz_pcor_shf, vertex.color=coreness(netz_pcor_shf), layout=layout_with_gem,
vertex.label.cex=0.5, vertex.size=5)

#Plot SHF network with components in a MST with GEM-Algorithm
plot(mst(netz_pcor_shf), vertex.color=coreness(netz_pcor_shf), layout=layout_with_gem,
vertex.label.cex=0.5, vertex.size=5,edge.color="grey85")

#Run cluster algorithms and compute modularity

clp<-cluster_label_prop(as.undirected(netz_pcor_shf))
cfg<-cluster_fast_greedy(as.undirected(netz_pcor_shf))
clei<-cluster_leading_eigen(as.undirected(netz_pcor_shf))
cim<-cluster_infomap(as.undirected(netz_pcor_shf))
csg<-cluster_spinglass(netz_pcor_shf)
cwt<-cluster_walktrap(netz_pcor_shf)
clo<-cluster_louvain(as.undirected(netz_pcor_shf))


modularity(clp)
modularity(cfg)
modularity(clei)
modularity(cim)
modularity(csg)
modularity(cwt)
modularity(clo)
```

(Continued)

(*Continued*)

```
#select the highest modularity score and adjust the color group according to the number of
communities
V(netz_pcor_shf)$communities<-clo$membership
colrs <- adjustcolor(c("black","gray20", "gray30","gray40", "gray50", "gray70","gray90",
"white"), alpha=.6)
plot(mst(netz_pcor_shf), vertex.color=colrs[V(netz_pcor_shf)$communities],
layout=layout_with_gem, vertex.label.cex=0.5, vertex.size=5,edge.color="grey85")
```

BOX 3.8:   CODE FOR ESTIMATING THE COMPACTNESS OF A GRAPH.

```
comp.graph <- function(g) {
  net.geodesic <- distances(g) # computes geodesics
  net.rdist <- 1/net.geodesic  # get reciprocal value of geodesics according to the
nominator
  diag(net.rdist) <- NA   # assign NA to the main diagonal of the matrix
  net.rdist[net.rdist == Inf] <- 0 # replace infinity with 0
  #compactness is the mean of reciprocal distances - see the denominator
  comp.graph <- mean(net.rdist, na.rm=TRUE)
  return(comp.graph)
}
```

Compactness and Breadth

Borgatti et al. (2022) argued that compactness is a highly informative metric using distances in a network. The measure of compactness involves taking the reciprocal distances in a graph. The main intuition behind this metric, which is informative for association networks widely used in finance, is that the inverse of higher reciprocal distances indicates shorter paths between nodes. Thus, more compact networks tend to have shorter paths.

$$Compactness = \frac{\sum_{i \neq j}\left(1/d_{ij}\right)}{n(n-1)} \tag{3.11}$$

where d_{ij} is the geodesic distance between node i and j.

The code for estimating the compactness of a graph is shown in Box 3.8.

Bridge Ties

An important property of networks is the existence of nodes referred to as "bridge ties". These nodes are essential because they might link two distinct components or clusters of a network. Technically, a bridge tie is a node that, after its removal, causes the network to be separated into two subgraphs. In other words, bridge ties effectively partition a graph into subgraphs.

The most convenient way to identify bridge ties is by using a large network, as smaller networks may exhibit different separations. For example, when analyzing directed networks of 322 bond and equity funds, Konstantinov and Rusev (2020) identified several bridge ties critical in transferring risk.[10] Economically, the absence of an edge between two subgraphs implies that the risk transfer between the nodes of the two networks does not occur.

Bridge ties can indeed have different degree scores, but it's the ones with high-degree centrality that concern risk managers the most. To illustrate their importance, let's consider an example of a bond and equity funds network. In such a network, bridge ties act as crucial connectors between different communities of funds. These segments may represent distinct funds – bonds or equities. When bridge ties have high-degree centrality, it means they are heavily connected to many other nodes in the network. This implies that they play a significant role in facilitating the flow of risk or information between different network parts.

For example, imagine a bridge tie between the network's clusters of bond funds and equity funds. If this bridge tie node has high-degree centrality, it suggests that it is involved in numerous transactions or relationships with other funds in both clusters. As a result, any disruptions or shocks affecting this bridge tie node could potentially propagate quickly throughout the network, affecting a wide range of funds. Therefore, risk managers closely monitor bridge ties with high-degree centrality because their importance lies in their ability to transmit risk across different parts of the network, making them potential focal points for systemic risk. Figure 3.9 illustrates the bridge ties for that fund network. A direct application of funds that are bridge ties in investment management is to avoid allocating to such funds.

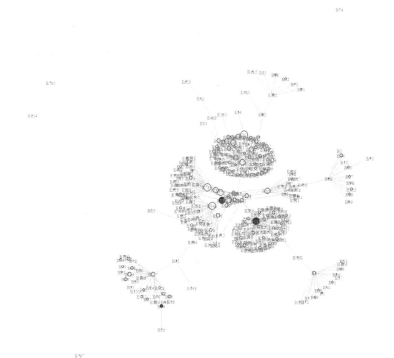

FIGURE 3.9 Bridge Ties of a Bond and Equity Fund Network.

---

[10]The network is sparse with a density of 0.04 and reciprocity of 0.35. For more details see the study of Konstantinov and Rusev (2020).

```
mai2006<-as.matrix(mai2006[,2:323])
mai2006<-graph_from_adjacency_matrix(mai2006)
E(mai2006)$arrow.size<-0 # sets the arrow size to zero
degmai2006<-degree(mai2006) # compute the degree centrality
articulation_points(mai2006) # shows the bridge ties: B16 B14 B21 E838 E581
#highlight the bridge ties
V(mai2006)$label.color="grey55"
V(mai2006)$color[V(mai2006)$name==articulation_points(mai2006)$name[1]]<-"black"
V(mai2006)$color[V(mai2006)$name==articulation_points(mai2006)$name[2]]<-"black"
V(mai2006)$color[V(mai2006)$name==articulation_points(mai2006)$name[3]]<-"black"
V(mai2006)$color[V(mai2006)$name==articulation_points(mai2006)$name[4]]<-"black"

V(mai2006)$color[V(mai2006)$name==articulation_points(mai2006)$name[5]]<-"black"
plot(mst(mai2006),vertex.size=sqrt(degmai2006/10),layout=layout_with_kk, edge.
color="grey85", vertex.label.cex=.4)
```

According to the study performed by Konstantinov and Rusev (2020), the code found in Box 3.9 is used to identify the bridge ties for a bond and equity fund network. The data shows five bridge ties weighted by corresponding degree centrality scores.

In Figure 3.9, there are five bridge ties, two of which possess a high- degree of centrality. This indicates that the two nodes with large degree scores (E 838 and E 581, in this case) are highly connected and play a crucial role in risk transmission within the bond-equity network. From a risk management perspective, retaining such bridge ties in a portfolio poses risk.[11] Granovetter (1973) argued that bridge ties are the most relevant links, both economically and topologically. The existence of bridge ties in large funds or graphs comprising financial securities means that very few nodes connect clusters that might be large market segments of funds or instruments.

KEY TAKEAWAYS

- Common properties of a network include connectivity, geodesic distance, size, degree, density, reciprocity, diameter, assortativity, clustering coefficients, and community structure.
- The mathematical formulation of connectedness refers to the Intermediate Value Theorem, path-connectedness, and simple connectedness.
- Like descriptive statistics used to represent financial time series, networks are characterized by specific metrics.

---

[11]Note that network analysis applies to all asset classes and is highly relevant to apply to funds, as fund-of-fund portfolio managers might want to investigate the connectedness of funds to other funds. Similar investigations have been made in financial research on other asset classes, such as private equity – Mezzeti, Marechal, David, Maillart, and Mermoud (2024), and real estate – Krautz and Fuerst (2016).

■ Common properties of a network include size, connectivity, degree, density, reciprocity, diameter, assortativity, and clustering coefficients, among others.

■ Network metrics vary, depending on the type of network and its characteristics.

■ A deep understanding of these metrics is essential for comprehending network dynamics and interconnectedness.

■ Metrics like network size, diameter, and distance are general descriptors, while average degree, density, and compactness measure interconnectedness.

■ Reciprocity and transitivity assess the balance in the network, while centrality scores and centralization measure the dominance of specific nodes.

Network Centrality Metrics

Contents

The network literature offers various metrics to measure connectedness. Connectedness is typically measured at the node level, and centrality scores are the appropriate metrics for this purpose. In network analysis, centrality measures are frequently used to examine the spreading of systemic risk. Time-varying centrality scores identify highly connected nodes that concentrate risks and transmit them to others, acting as a proxy for a node's embeddedness within the network. These scores are essential metrics for understanding network interconnectedness. In this chapter, we will focus on the most widely applied centrality metrics. While degree and eigenvector centrality are the most used, other centrality measures become valuable depending on the node connectivity, network structure, and information flow dynamics.

It's important to emphasize that node centrality plays a crucial role in modeling, explaining, and simulating networks because the connectedness of nodes is essential in determining mutual relationships. Nearly all network models revolve around node activities gauged by their degrees.

Konstantinov, Aldridge, and Kazemi (2023) demonstrated that, like mathematics providing the toolkit in physics, measuring connectedness requires different mathematical tools. Research on financial networks extensively uses various network measures to capture and explain interconnectedness. The choice of graph-theoretical tools depends on a network's classes, types, underlying properties, and processes. Financial markets represent money flow networks with dynamic properties, where nodes (i.e., financial assets) change connections over time. Centrality metrics precisely inform about current interconnectedness at the node level.

NODE CENTRALITY METRICS

Kara et al. (2015) offer a brief overview of centrality metrics commonly applied to investigate financial networks. Some of the most important centralities include eigenvector centrality, betweenness centrality, degree centrality, alpha centrality, closeness centrality, hub centrality, and authority centrality.

However, not all centrality metrics apply to the same types of graphs, as the underlying network structure determines which centrality metric is most suitable.[1] For instance, alpha centrality applies to networks where a node might be disjoint, while eigenvector centrality applies to most undirected networks. Betweenness centrality seeks the shortest path but requires following a path rather than a walk. Closeness centrality requires the definition of geodesic distance between nodes. Hubs and authorities are meaningful for directed networks.

One significant difference exists between alpha and eigenvector centralities, primarily in dealing with asymmetric networks and self-edges between nodes. Centrality measures reflect the number of connections of a specific node and its importance in information flow. Economically, an importance score, as measured by centrality, increases if a node connects to other nodes that are strongly connected and important.

Degree Centrality

Degree centrality measures the average connectedness of each individual node in the network, irrespective of their connections to other nodes. In essence, it quantifies the number of edges connected to a node. The degree centrality of a network is simply the average of the degree centralities of all its nodes. Mathematically, it is calculated as the sum of the edges connected to each node in the network.

Wasserman and Faust (1994) first introduced the concept of degree centrality, which they defined as the row or column sums of the adjacency matrix, which captures the connections between nodes in the network.

$$\hat{k}_i^{in} = \sum_{j \in n} a_{ij} = \hat{k}_j^{out} = \sum_{j \in n} a_{ji} \tag{4.1}$$

where a_{ij} are the entries in the adjacency matrix A and the k_i^{in} is the in-degree centrality of a node i measured as column sums of the adjacency matrix.

The *out-degree centrality* is calculated as the row-sums of the adjacency matrix and is equivalent to the in-degree centrality in undirected networks. However, in directed networks, the in-degree and out-degree may differ.

It's important to understand the properties of degree centrality in the context of portfolio and risk networks. One key advantage of degree centrality is that it measures the immediate impact of risk on a node level. It quantifies the exposure of a node within the network, indicating the flow of risk through that node. In contrast, *eigenvector centrality* measures both the direct and indirect long-term impact on a node.

According to Borgatti et al. (2022), degree centrality is particularly informative in networks where information flow follows a random walk process. However, it may be less informative in networks where flows are based on specific paths or trails. Figure 4.1 illustrates the degree centrality for all assets and factors in a network. Node degree is a fundamental property of any network, and distribution can vary based on the type of graph and construction method. Box 4.1 contains the code used to plot the degree centralities of the asset and factor networks.

BOX 4.1:   PLOTTING DEGREE CENTRALITIES OF THE ASSET AND FACTOR NETWORKS.

```
#Plotting all Centralities with Names


allem<-list(netz_dir_gct,netz_pcor,netz_undir,netz_corf, netz_dir,netz_dir_mcn, netz_cor,
netz_dir_cvd, netz_dir_conf, netz_undir_lasso, netz_dir_dist, netz_dir_p)
```

---

[1]See Bonacich and Lloyd (2001) and Borgatti (2005).

```
all.netz<-c("netz_dir_gct","netz_pcor","netz_undir","netz_corf", "netz_dir","netz_dir_
mcn", "netz_cor", "netz_dir_cvd","netz_dir_conf", "netz_undir_lasso", "netz_dir_dist",
"netz_dir_p")
par(mfrow=c(4,3))

foreach (i=all.netz, j=allem) %do% {
  barplot(sort(degre(j), decreasing=TRUE), lwd=0.5, cex.names=0.7,cex.axis=0.7,las=2,
main=bquote(paste('Eigen Centrality ',.(i))))

}
```

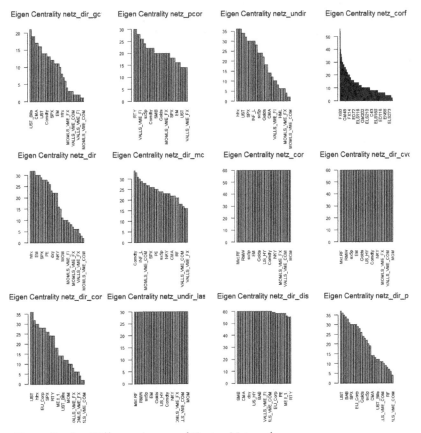

FIGURE 4.1 Degree Centrality for Different Asset and Factor Networks.
Note: The R code for all these asset and factor networks is provided in Chapter 2 and on https://finance-resolution.com/. The network of "netz_cor" is an undirected correlation (complete) network, "netz_pcor" is an undirected partial correlation network, "netz_corf" is an undirected correlation test network, "netz_dir" is a directed network, "netz_dir_gct" is a directed Granger-causality network, "netz_undir" is a undirected network with Fischer transformation, "netz_dir_conf" is a directed network estimated with confounders, "netz_dir_cvd" is a directed network estimated using the Cholesky variance decomposition technique, "netz_undir_lasso" is a Gaussian network estimated using least absolute shrinkage and selection operator (LASSO), "netz_dir_mcn" is a directed Markov chain network, "netz_dir_dist is Markov Manhattan distance probability network, and "netz_dir_p" is a directed multigraph network.

Visualizing networks in different layouts based on node properties and weighting the edges according to specific parameters can provide valuable insights into network structure. In Figure 4.2, the asset and factor network is represented using degree centralities, node types (asset or factor), bridge ties, and edge widths corresponding to link strength. Additionally, nodes with degrees exceeding a certain threshold, such as the mean degree of all nodes, are highlighted. This visualization enables researchers to identify nodes with high immediate connectedness within the network, providing a clearer understanding of important network properties. Figure 4.2 provides a visual impression of assets and factors with high degrees of connectivity. Specifically, Figure 4.2a shows the bridge ties for a directed network and Figure 4.2b shows the bridge ties for an undirected network.

The code provided in Box 4.2 can be used to plot the networks, highlighting the bridge ties and the nodes with an average degree larger than the mean degree of the corresponding network. It's worth noting that in both cases, there are two articulation points (i.e., bridge ties), so the code remains similar for both networks. Whereas the bridge ties for the directed Granger-causality network (netz_dir_gtc) are the momentum (MOM) and the profitability factor (conservative minus aggressive, denoted as CMA), the bridge ties for the undirected asset and factor network are the US Treasury bills (US_Treasury_bills), and the Commodity Value factor network (VALLS_VME_COM). Note that the code in Box 4.2 run for each of the networks provides the bridge ties.

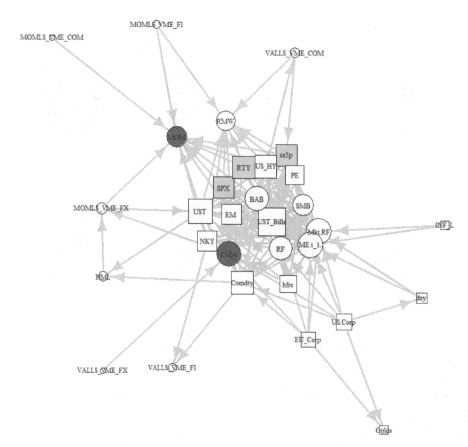

FIGURE 4.2A Bridge Ties for Degree Centrality-Weighted Directed Granger Causality.

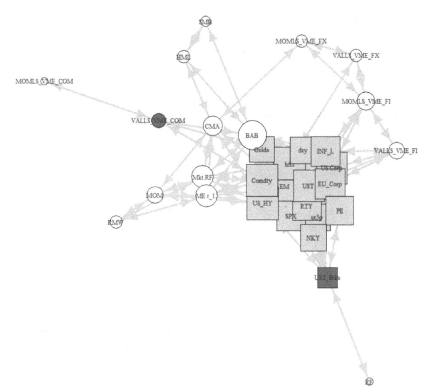

FIGURE 4.2B An Undirected Asset and Factor Network.
Note: We plot the degree centralities and the bridge ties of the netz_dir_gtc and the netz_undir networks and highlight the nodes that exceed the average value of the node degree in the correspondent network. For netz_dir_gct network, the mean degree is 9.8, and the average degree for netz_undir is 19.8.

BOX 4.2: BRIDGE TIES FOR A DEGREE CENTRALITY-WEIGHTED DIRECTED ASSET AND FACTOR NETWORK.

```
articulation_points(netz_dir_gct) #provides the bridge ties, which are two
V(netz_dir_gct)$color[V(netz_dir_gct)$name==articulation_points(netz_dir_gct)$name[1]]<-
"red"
V(netz_dir_gct)$color[V(netz_dir_gct)$name==articulation_points(netz_dir_gct)$name[2]]<-
"red"
V(netz_dir_gct)[V(netz_dir_gct)>mean(degree(netz_dir_gct))]$color<-"purple"
plot(netz_dir_gct,vertex.size=sqrt(degree(netz_dir_gct))*3,edge.color="grey85", vertex.
label.cex=.5, edge.width=E(netz_dir_gct)$weight*2)
```

The degree centrality is crucial for assessing and simulating networks, including those with disconnected nodes. However, it may be less informative for representing the connectedness of nodes relative to the entire network. However, the degree centrality provides an average measure of the most central assets within a network. In this context, the average connectedness of an asset becomes less significant if its connectedness increases substantially more than the average number would imply.

For example, consider an equity market index such as the S&P 500, with an average connectedness of 20 and a US Treasury bond index with a connectedness of 50. Simply knowing the average connectedness does not adequately convey the risk, especially if the 20 assets to which an equity index is connected are more crucial due to their connections with other highly connected assets. Therefore, the average number of connected nodes may not be as crucial as the potential for a node to be connected to other highly connected nodes. This perspective is vital from both portfolio and risk management standpoints.

Another significant aspect of degree centrality is the degree distribution, which represents the weighted sum of individual node degrees, considering the probability that a node is randomly connected to another node.

Eigenvector Centrality

Eigenvector centrality is widely used in network analysis, assigning higher scores to nodes connected to other central nodes. This relationship is captured mathematically as follows:

$$x_i = \frac{1}{\lambda} \sum_{j \in n} A_{ij} x_j \tag{4.2}$$

where x is the eigenvector, A is the adjacency matrix, and λ is constant representing the eigenvalue. Importantly, the nodes must be in a connected network.

The matrix notation of the eigenvector centrality is widely used in network analysis.

$$Ax = \lambda x \tag{4.3}$$

Kolaczyk and Csardi (2020) argue that eigenvector centrality applies to undirected but connected networks. In this case, the largest eigenvalue of matrix A exists, and its eigenvector will have nonzero entries in the range [0,1] due to the orthonormality of eigenvectors.

However, a major challenge arises when applying eigenvector centrality to directed networks. It struggles to properly assign scores to disconnected nodes in a network. For example, consider the risk-free asset, which might be disconnected following the economic reasoning of the Separation Theorem (Tobin, 1958). The assumption holds that the risk-free asset is unrelated or disconnected (e.g., non-existing path, walk, or trail) to all other risky assets. Eigenvector centrality cannot accurately assign a score to that asset, despite network models in portfolio management showing that the risk-free rate is well-connected to other assets. Figure 4.3 illustrates the eigenvector centrality for asset and factor networks.

Box 4.3 provides the code for the computation of the eigenvector centrality scores for all asset and factor networks.

BOX 4.3: EIGENVECTOR CENTRALITY METRICS FOR THE ASSET AND FACTOR NETWORKS.

```
##Plotting all Eigen Centrality Metrics for the Asset and Factor Networks with Names

allem<-list(netz_dir_gct,netz_pcor,netz_undir,netz_corf, netz_dir,netz_dir_mcn, netz_cor,
netz_dir_cvd, netz_dir_conf, netz_undir_lasso, netz_dir_dist, netz_dir_p)
all.netz<-c("netz_dir_gct","netz_pcor","netz_undir","netz_corf", "netz_dir","netz_dir_
mcn", "netz_cor", "netz_dir_cvd","netz_dir_conf", "netz_undir_lasso", "netz_dir_dist",
"netz_dir_p")
```

```
par(mfrow=c(3,4))

foreach (i=all.netz, j=allem) %do% {
    barplot(sort(eigen_centrality(j)$vector, decreasing=TRUE), lwd=0.5, cex.names=0.7,cex.
axis=0.7,las=2, main=bquote(paste('Eigen Centrality ',.(i))))

}
```

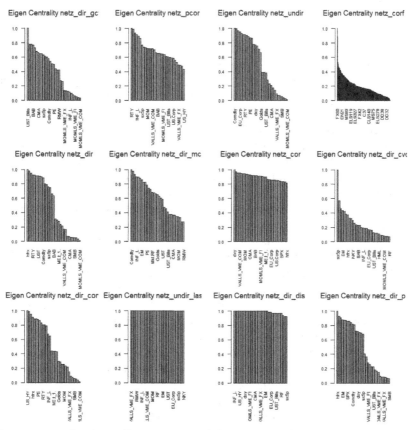

FIGURE 4.3 Eigenvector Centrality for Different Asset and Factor Networks.
Note: The "R" code for all these asset and factor networks is provided in Chapter 2 and on https://finance-resolution.com/. The network of "netz_cor" is undirected correlation (complete) network, "netz_pcor" is an undirected partial correlation network, "netz_corf" is an undirected correlation test network, "netz_dir" is a directed network, "netz_dir_gct" is a directed Granger-causality network, "netz_undir" is a undirected network with Fischer transformation, "netz_dir_conf" is a directed network estimated with confounders, "netz_dir_cvd" is a directed network estimated using the Cholesky variance decomposition technique, "netz_undir_lasso" is a Gaussian network estimated using LASSO, "netz_dir_mcn" is a directed Markov chain network, "netz_dir_dist is Markov Manhattan distance probability network, and "netz_dir_p" is a directed multigraph network.

Alpha and Bonacich Centrality

Alpha and power centralities scores are particular solutions of eigenvector centrality, enhanced to reflect the demands of networks with unconnected nodes.

Alpha centrality was initially developed by Katz (1953), and later extended by Bonacich (1987) and Bonacich and Lloyd (2001). It assigns a score to every node that is proportional to the sum of the scores of its neighboring nodes.

$$x = \alpha Ax + e1 \tag{4.4}$$

where a is a constant, I is the identity matrix, A is the adjacency matrix, and e is a vector of exogenous variables usually set to ones.

Recasting in matrix notation, we have:

$$x = (I - \alpha A)^{-1} e1 \tag{4.5}$$

Note that a is a constant inversely related to the largest eigenvalues of A, or $a = 1/\lambda_1$.

The existence of a maximum eigenvalue is a necessary condition. According to Bonacich (1972) and Bonacich and Lloyd (2001), λ_1 is assumed to be larger than all other eigenvalues to apply eigenvector centrality. When e is a vector of ones, the centrality measure is defined as the Katz centrality (Katz, 1953). The development of graph theoretical models has shown that we can assume e to take on any values associated with external effects on the network. The reason is that e might take values different from zero because, as shown by Newman (2010) for social networks, individuals might have attributes independent of their network affiliation, such as age, wealth, club memberships, publications, and education, among others. This attribute is essential in portfolio management because e might incorporate exogenous attributes to the nodes, which are assets or factors. For example, consider the possibility of attaching specific risk or return scores to the assets in the network. Using e, as demonstrated by Konstantinov and Rebmann (2019), one can build currency factor portfolios, which is the topic of Chapter 11.

Following Bonacich and Lloyd (2001) and Newman (2010), the major differences in the application of alpha centrality compared to eigenvector centrality are built on two essential properties. First, alpha centrality enables the analysis of importance scores of nodes or assets disconnected from the entire network. Meaning that even if a node is not directly connected to other nodes, its importance can still be assessed based on its indirect connections. Second, the underlying adjacency matrix can contain self-edges. In other words, the main diagonal of the adjacency matrix does not contain only zeros, indicating that nodes can connect with themselves. This property is essential because it enables a more nuanced understanding of node importance, particularly in cases where nodes may have significant self-influence. Economically, a node's importance might increase as a result of increased leverage and complex capital structure that represents a self-edge, systemic relevance, and importance in financial markets.

These two properties make alpha centrality particularly useful in scenarios where the network structure includes disconnected nodes or self-connections such as in multigraphs with weights and self-edges. In such cases, alpha centrality provides a more accurate metric for measuring the importance of nodes in a portfolio than eigenvector centrality.[2] Figure 4.4 captures the power centralities for all asset and factor networks.

A notable extension of alpha centrality is Bonacich centrality, introduced by Bonacich (1987) and known as power centrality. Borgatti and Everett (2006) highlight the efficacy of this centrality metric,

---

[2]This point has been raised by Konstantinov, Chorus, and Rebmann (2020), in case of portfolio allocation to factors and assets.

emphasizing its ability to model directed networks and flows and incorporate exogenous factors. Bech and Atalay (2011) have successfully applied this method to analyze government money market funds, demonstrating their utility in financial market contexts. Another advantageous property of Bonacich centrality is its compatibility with weighted graphs. Formally, the Bonacich centrality is defined as follows:

$$b(\alpha, \beta, A) = \alpha (I - \beta A)^{-1} A 1 \tag{4.6}$$

where α is a scaling parameter that determines the length (i.e., size of the network), A is the weighted adjacency matrix, β is a decay factor that is inversely proportional to the absolute values of eigenvalue of the adjacency matrix A, and 1 is a vector of ones.

One of the most powerful properties of the Bonacich centrality metric is its ability to model the current node's activities as well as the activities of its successors. This functionality is governed by the beta parameter given by equation (4.6). When β is set to 0, the Bonacich centrality score of a vertex becomes independent of the scores of other vertices. However, when β is greater than 0, vertices with higher importance scores

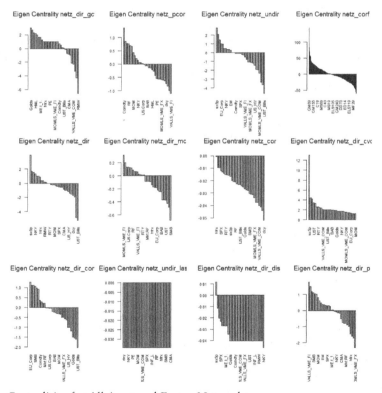

FIGURE 4.4 Bonacich Centralities for All Asset and Factor Networks.
Note: The "R" code for all these asset and factor networks is provided in Chapter 2 and on https://finance-resolution.com/. The network of "netz_cor" is an undirected correlation (complete) network, "netz_pcor" is an undirected partial correlation network, "netz_corf" is an undirected correlation test network, "netz_dir" is a directed network, "netz_dir_gct" is a directed Granger-causality network, "netz_undir" is a undirected network with Fischer transformation, "netz_dir_conf" is a directed network estimated with confounders, "netz_dir_cvd" is a directed network estimated using the Cholesky variance decomposition technique, "netz_undir_lasso" is a Gaussian network estimated using LASSO, "netz_dir_mcn" is a directed Markov chain network, "netz_dir_dist is Markov Manhattan distance probability network, and "netz_dir_p" is a directed multigraph network.

exert a greater influence on the centrality scores of their neighbors. Essentially, this means that the more connected a node is, the larger its impact on the connectedness of neighboring nodes.

An intriguing observation suggested by Bech and Atalay (2011) is that both the regular matrix A and the transpose of A can be utilized. It's important to note that in directed graphs, A is not equal to its transpose, denoted as A^T, or $A \neq A^T$. This implies that the information flow is reversed, which can be beneficial for investigating reverse causality or information flows between nodes. By using the transpose of the adjacency matrix, the links are reversed, offering insights into the reverse properties of causality or information flows within the network. For example, the regular matrix might capture how interest rate connectedness affects currencies, while the transposed adjacency matrix gauges the reverse effect—how currency flows impact interest rates.

Hub and Authority Centrality

Directionality in finance is paramount due to the causal relationships and the flow of economic information. Directed networks offer a key advantage over undirected networks by enabling us to discern which nodes point to other highly connected nodes, as measured by centrality scores. Hubs and authorities are properties unique to directed networks because undirected networks cannot differentiate information flow. As a result, the concepts of hubs and authorities effectively segregate information related to centrality within the network (see Benzi, Estrada, and Klymko, 2013).

Authorities represent nodes possessing valuable information in a network, while *hubs* indicate nodes that provide information on where to locate authoritative nodes. For instance, in risk analysis within directed networks, hubs aid in identifying reliable sources of risk information (i.e., authorities). The role of hubs is to guide users to authoritative sources of information.

The relationship between authority and hub centrality is based on the idea that nodes with high hub centrality scores connect to other nodes with high authority centrality scores. This relationship is quantified by the leading eigenvalue of the adjacency matrices, with AA^T governing authority centrality and A^TA governing hub centrality. The matrix equations for authority and hub centralities are as follows:

$$AA^Tx = \lambda x \quad A^TAy = \lambda y \tag{4.7}$$

where λ is the leading eigenvalue of A^TA and AA^T, A is the adjacency matrix, x is the centrality vector or the authority score, and y is the centrality vector for the hub score.

Figure 4.5 plots the hub and authority centrality for a directed network.

A major advantage of hub and authority centralities is their ability to address a limitation of eigenvector centrality, particularly in networks with disconnected nodes. In eigenvector centrality, nodes that are disconnected from the rest of the network are assigned centrality scores of zero, which can obscure their potential importance or influence. However, hub and authority centrality metrics offer a solution to this problem. Even in networks with disconnected nodes, hub, and authority centralities can still assign meaningful scores to these nodes based on their connections to other nodes within the network. This capability enables for a more comprehensive analysis of node importance and influence within the network, even when specific nodes are not directly connected to others. Thus, hub and authority centralities provide a more nuanced and informative perspective on network structure and node importance than eigenvector centrality alone.

Closeness Centrality

Closeness centrality is a metric that assesses the importance of nodes within a network by considering their proximity to other nodes. The underlying concept is that nodes with shorter distances to many other vertices are more critical. This metric is based on the work of Sabidussi (1966) and Freeman (1979), who observed that node importance is inversely related to its geodesic distance to other nodes.

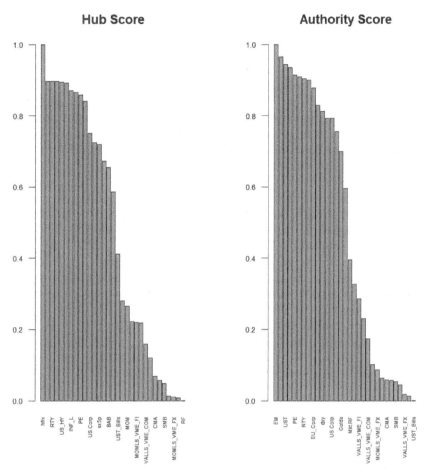

FIGURE 4.5 Hub and Authority Centrality of a Directed Asset and Factor Network.
Note: We use the "netz_dir" for this example.

It is important to note, however, that distance itself is not a centrality metric; rather, it serves as a basis for calculating closeness centrality. In network analysis, centrality metrics are typically higher for more central nodes. Therefore, to ensure consistency with other centrality metrics and facilitate comparison, the reciprocal of the geodesic distance is often used as the closeness centrality metric. This reciprocal value reflects that nodes with shorter distances are considered more central.

The mean geodesic distance is a measure that averages the reciprocal distances of a node to all other nodes in the network. It provides insight into the network's overall connectedness and accessibility, with lower values indicating greater closeness centrality and tighter integration among nodes.

$$l = \frac{1}{n-1}\sum_{i=j} d_{ij} \qquad (4.8)$$

where d_{ij} is the geodesic distance between node i and j.[3]

---

[3]To normalize the matrix to receive values in the interval [0,1], the score is divided by *n–1*.

The closeness centrality using the inverse of the distance metric is then:

$$C_i^{Closeness} = \frac{1}{l} = \frac{1}{\sum_{i \in n} d_{ij}} \tag{4.9}$$

Closeness centrality, as described by Borgatti (2005), identifies nodes with short distances to other nodes, implying that information reaches them sooner than nodes with longer distances. In financial networks, assets or institutions with low closeness centrality scores are assumed to respond more rapidly to information or risk compared to those with higher scores. This metric is economically relevant as it helps identify assets or institutions that may be significantly impacted by events, potentially posing risks to the entire financial system.

Distance, represented by the shortest path between nodes, is crucial in closeness centrality. Nodes with shorter distances are considered more central regarding information flow or risk transmission. However, for closeness centrality to be applicable, the graph must be connected, meaning a path must exist between any pair of nodes. For instance, if the risk-free rate is disconnected from other nodes at a specific time, closeness centrality cannot be computed for it because no path exists to reach other nodes in the network. Path connectedness is necessary for the application of closeness centrality.

Moreover, closeness centrality assumes that information flows randomly along paths without duplication, meaning each node is visited only once. This makes the metric suitable for analyzing systems where information spreads through connected pathways. However, computing closeness centrality can be challenging for large and dense networks, as highlighted by Knickerbocker (2023). In Figure 4.6, closeness centrality plots for all asset and factor networks are displayed, providing insights into the nodes' centrality.

Betweenness Centrality

Developed by Freeman (1978, 1979), betweenness centrality quantifies the significance of a node in terms of its position along the shortest paths between pairs of other network nodes. Essentially, it measures how much a node acts as a bridge or lies on the geodesic path connecting other nodes. The betweenness importance score assigned to a vertex depends on its position within the network. Nodes on many shortest paths between pairs of nodes receive higher betweenness centrality scores.

Mathematically, betweenness centrality is calculated as the number of shortest paths that pass through a node, normalized by the total number of shortest paths between all pairs of nodes in the network. This metric provides insights into the nodes that are crucial in facilitating communication or information flow between different parts of the network.

In summary, betweenness centrality is a valuable metric for identifying nodes that serve as critical intermediaries or connectors within a network, facilitating efficient communication and information exchange between disparate nodes.

$$C_s^{Betweenness} = \sum_{i \in n} \frac{g_{isj}}{g_{ij}}, i \neq j \neq s \tag{4.10}$$

where node s (whose centrality is being measured), in order for node i to reach a node j via the shortest path g_{ij}, is the total number of shortest paths between nodes i and j, and g_{isj} is the number of shortest paths between nodes i and j that pass through s.

The application of betweenness centrality to financial networks hinges on the underlying flow process within the network. Unlike metrics such as closeness centrality that assume random path selection, betweenness centrality is well-suited for networks where the flow of resources or information follows specific, predetermined paths. In financial networks, where transactions involve directed flows such as funds transferring from buyers to sellers, betweenness centrality becomes particularly relevant.

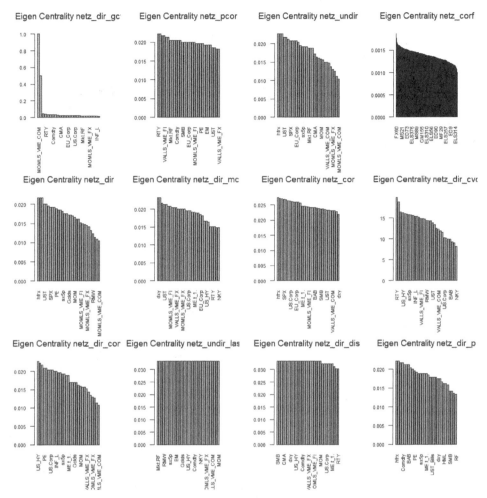

FIGURE 4.6 Closeness Centrality for the Asset and Factor Networks.

Note: The "R" code for all these asset and factor networks is provided in Chapter 2 and on https://finance-resolution. com/. The network of "netz_cor" is undirected correlation (complete) network, "netz_pcor" is a undirected partial correlation network, "netz_corf" is an undirected correlation test network, "netz_dir" is a directed network, "netz_dir_gct" is a directed Granger-causality network, "netz_undir" is an undirected network with Fischer transformation, "netz_dir_conf" is a directed network estimated with confounders, "netz_dir_cvd" is a directed network estimated using the Cholesky variance decomposition technique, "netz_undir_lasso" is a Gaussian network estimated using LASSO, "netz_dir_mcn" is a directed Markov chain network, "netz_dir_dist is Markov Manhattan distance probability network, and "netz_dir_p" is a directed multigraph network.

By quantifying the number of shortest paths that pass through a node in relation to the total number of shortest paths in the network, betweenness centrality identifies nodes that serve as critical intermediaries or bridges in facilitating the flow of resources or information. These nodes play a crucial role in connecting different parts of the network and are essential for efficient transactional processes.

Figure 4.7 displays the betweenness centrality scores for both the asset and factor graphs, providing insights into the nodes that act as key intermediaries in facilitating transactions or information exchange within the network.

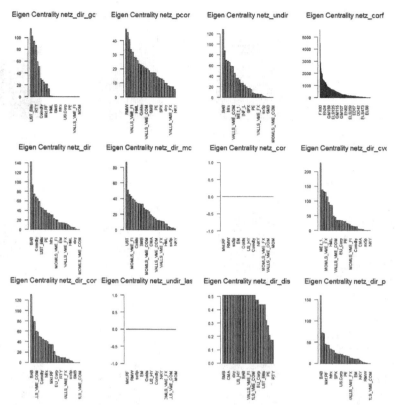

FIGURE 4.7 Betweenness Centrality for the Asset and Factor Networks.

Note: The "R" code for all these asset and factor networks is provided in Chapter 2 and on https://finance-resolution. com/. The network of "netz_cor" is undirected correlation (complete) network, "netz_pcor" is an undirected partial correlation network, "netz_corf" is an undirected correlation test network, "netz_dir" is a directed network, "netz_dir_gct" is a directed Granger-causality network, "netz_undir" is an undirected network with Fischer transformation, "netz_dir_conf" is a directed network estimated with confounders, "netz_dir_cvd" is a directed network estimated using the Cholesky variance decomposition technique, "netz_undir_lasso" is a Gaussian network estimated using LASSO, "netz_dir_mcn" is a directed Markov chain network, "netz_dir_dist is Markov Manhattan distance probability network, and "netz_dir_p" is a directed multigraph network.

DESCRIPTIVE STATISTICS AND NETWORK SUMMARY

A direct comparison between centrality measures offers a more comprehensive understanding of the network structure, highlighting both central and peripheral nodes. To demonstrate this, we present a simple example using one of the asset and factor networks comprising only 31 nodes. For larger networks (size >500 nodes), utilizing distribution statistics to summarize properties and visualizations that effectively convey the key insights in graphical form is advisable.

Table 4.1 shows the scores of the nodes for a directed network estimated using the Markov Chain algorithm, which is introduced in Chapter 8. We compute that network's eigenvector, closeness, betweenness, power, alpha, and degree scores. Visual inspection reveals that the importance of assets or factors varies, depending on the centrality metric used. For example, the commodity possesses the highest importance score according to the eigenvector centrality (1.00) and degree scores (34). However, its node connectivity, as measured by alpha centrality, is among the lowest, with a score of –0.43,

The code in Box 4.4 provides the centrality scores for an example network (netz_dir_mcn).

The code in Box 4.4 calculates and displays all centrality metrics for the directed Markov chain network (netz_dir_mcn), as detailed in Chapter 8.

TABLE 4.1 Centrality Metrics for a Directed Markov-Chain Network.

Name	Node	Eigenvector	Closeness	Betweenness	Power	Alpha	Degree
Market Excess	Mkt.RF	0.68	0.60	0.03	0.03	0.08	24
Size	SMB	0.35	0.58	0.04	0.03	−0.69	17
Value	HML	0.34	0.57	0.01	0.02	−0.18	18
Profitability	RMV	0.27	0.57	0.02	0.02	−0.49	16
Investments	CMA	0.37	0.61	0.02	0.03	−0.37	22
Risk Free	RF	0.38	0.60	0.01	0.04	0.09	21
EuroStoxx50	Sx5p	0.74	0.45	0	0.03	0.02	24
S&P500	SPX	0.82	0.45	0	0.03	0.01	26
Russel 2000	RTY	0.82	0.45	0	0.03	0.01	26
MSCI EM	EM	0.86	0.49	0.01	0.04	0.13	27
Hedge Funds	HF	0.98	0.50	0.04	0.03	−0.14	33
US Dollar	DXY	0.38	0.70	0.01	0.04	−0.09	22
Gold	Golds	0.65	0.59	0.04	0.03	0.07	24
US Treasuries	UST	0.58	0.64	0.1	0.03	−0.38	27
US Corporates	US.Corp	0.90	0.59	0.06	0.03	0.13	29
US High Yield	US_HY	0.88	0.50	0.01	0.03	0.02	28
Inflation-Linked	INF_L	0.9	0.59	0.05	0.03	−0.24	30
EU Corporates	EU_Corp	0.93	0.56	0.04	0.03	−0.18	31
Commodity	Comdty	1.00	0.55	0.04	0.03	−0.43	34
Private Equity	PE	0.79	0.45	0.01	0.03	−0.09	25
US Treasury Bills	USTBills	0.41	0.61	0.03	0.04	0.12	23
Nikkei 225	NKY	0.73	0.45	0.00	0.03	0.07	23
Betting-Against-Beta	BAB	0.68	0.62	0.05	0.03	−0.25	26
FX Value	VALLS_VME_FX	0.28	0.61	0.01	0.03	−0.38	16
FX Momentum	MOMLS_VME_FX	0.45	0.60	0.01	0.02	0.13	23
FI Value	VALLS_VME_FI	0.45	0.70	0.03	0.06	0.06	22
FI Momentum	MOMLS_VME_FI	0.60	0.62	0.05	0.03	0.32	25
Commodity Value	VALLS_VME_COM	0.37	0.65	0.02	0.02	−0.17	18
Commodity Momentum	MOMLS_VME_COM	0.63	0.64	0.03	0.03	0.20	28
Liquidity	ME.t_1	0.66	0.58	0.02	0.03	−0.08	23
Momentum	MOM	0.35	0.60	0.04	0.03	−0.22	21

Note: The nodes for the asset and factor network have been defined in Chapter 1. The centralities are computed given specific *p*-value threshold (0.05) for all graphs.

BOX 4.4:   COMPUTATION OF ALL CENTRALITY METRICS FOR AN ASSET AND FACTOR NETWORK.

```
tab.central<-cbind(
  ec=eigen_centrality(netz_dir_mcn)$vector,
  cc=closeness(netz_dir_mcn, normalized=TRUE),
  bc=betweenness(netz_dir_mcn, normalized=TRUE),
  pc=power_centrality(netz_dir_mcn, rescale = TRUE),
```

(Continued)

(Continued)

```
  ac=alpha_centrality(netz_dir_mcn),
  dc=degree(netz_dir_mcn))
colnames(tab.central)<-c("Eigenvector", "Closeness", "Betweenness", "Power", "Alpha",
"Degree")
tab.central<-round(tab.central,digits=2)
print(tab.central)
```

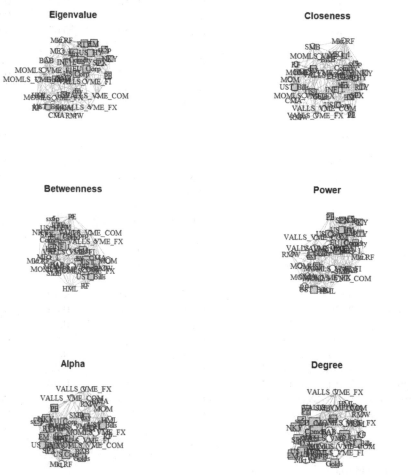

FIGURE 4.8   Comparison of Centrality Metrics in Network Analysis – A Directed Markov Chain Network.

Keep in mind that the scores are subject to the network inference algorithm applied to estimate a portfolio network. When visualizing the importance scores of the nodes in a graph, one should choose larger nodes corresponding to higher centrality scores. Displaying node properties, such as asset or factor categories, and weighting nodes by their centrality scores enhances network visualization. Such visualization provides valuable information about the least and most connected nodes in a network. Figure 4.8 provides an overview of this book's most applied centrality metrics for the factor networks. The code for plotting all centrality metrics for a directed Markov Chain network is provided in Box 4.5. The code for the computation of all centrality metrics for an asset and factor network in case of a Markov chain network is provided in Box 4.6

BOX 4.5: PLOTTING ALL CENTRALITY METRICS FOR A DIRECTED MARKOV CHAIN ASSET AND FACTOR NETWORK.

```
clp<-cluster_label_prop(as.undirected(netz_dir_mcn))
cfg<-cluster_fast_greedy(as.undirected(netz_dir_mcn))
clei<-cluster_leading_eigen(as.undirected(netz_dir_mcn))
cim<-cluster_infomap(as.undirected(netz_dir_mcn))
csg<-cluster_spinglass(netz_dir_mcn)
cwt<-cluster_walktrap(netz_dir_mcn)
clo<-cluster_louvain(as.undirected(netz_dir_mcn))

modularity(clp)
modularity(cfg)
modularity(clei)
modularity(cim)
modularity(csg)
modularity(cwt)
modularity(clo)
##select the community algorithm with the highest modularity score, which is "cwt"
V(netz_dir_mcn)$com<-cwt$membership

E(netz_dir_mcn)$arrow.size<-0
plot(netz_dir_mcn, layout=layout_with_lgl, edge.color="grey80", vertex.color=V(netz_dir_
mcn)$com,vertex.size=sqrt(eigen_centrality(netz_dir_mcn)$vector)*20, main="Eigenvalue")
plot(netz_dir_mcn, layout=layout_with_lgl, edge.color="grey80",vertex.color=V(netz_dir_
mcn)$com,vertex.size=sqrt(closeness(netz_dir_mcn, normalized=TRUE))*20, main="Closeness")
plot(netz_dir_mcn, layout=layout_with_lgl,edge.color="grey80", vertex.color=V(netz_dir_
mcn)$com,vertex.size=sqrt(betweenness(netz_dir_mcn, normalized=TRUE))*100,
main="Betweenness")
plot(netz_dir_mcn, layout=layout_with_lgl,edge.color="grey80", vertex.color=V(netz_dir_
mcn)$com,vertex.size=sqrt(power_centrality(netz_dir_mcn, rescale = TRUE))*100,
main="Power")
plot(netz_dir_mcn, layout=layout_with_lgl,edge.color="grey80", vertex.color=V(netz_dir_
mcn)$com,vertex.size=sqrt(1+(alpha_centrality(netz_dir_mcn)))*20, main="Alpha")
plot(netz_dir_mcn, layout=layout_with_lgl, edge.color="grey80",vertex.color=V(netz_dir_
mcn)$com,vertex.size=degree(netz_dir_mcn),main="Degree")
```

BOX 4.6: COMPUTATION OF ALL CENTRALITY METRICS FOR AN ASSET AND FACTOR NETWORK.

```
#made for the undirected MCN network
netz_dir_mcn<-set.vertex.attribute(netz_dir_mcn, "category", value=c("F", "F", "F", "F",
"F", "F", "A", "A", "A", "A", "A", "A", "A", "A", "A", "A", "A", "A", "A", "A", "A", "A",
"F", "F", "F", "F", "F", "F", "F", "F", "F"))
#Assign different shapes and color according to the asset or factor clusters
par(mfrow=c(3,2))
V(netz_dir_mcn)$shape <- V(netz_dir_mcn)$category
V(netz_dir_mcn)$shape <- gsub("F","circle",V(netz_dir_mcn)$shape)
V(netz_dir_mcn)$shape <- gsub("A","square",V(netz_dir_mcn)$shape)
```

(Continued)

(*Continued*)

```
V(netz_dir_mcn)$color <- V(netz_dir_mcn)$category
V(netz_dir_mcn)$color <- gsub("F","grey90",V(netz_dir_mcn)$color)
V(netz_dir_mcn)$color <- gsub("A","white",V(netz_dir_mcn)$color)

#compute network partition algorithms
clp<-cluster_label_prop(as.undirected(netz_dir_mcn))
cfg<-cluster_fast_greedy(as.undirected(netz_dir_mcn))
clei<-cluster_leading_eigen(as.undirected(netz_dir_mcn))
cim<-cluster_infomap(as.undirected(netz_dir_mcn))
csg<-cluster_spinglass(netz_dir_mcn)
cwt<-cluster_walktrap(netz_dir_mcn)
clo<-cluster_louvain(as.undirected(netz_dir_mcn))

#Compute modularity and select the algorithm with the highest modularity score
modularity(clp)
modularity(cfg)
modularity(clei)
modularity(cim)
modularity(csg)
modularity(cwt)
modularity(clo)

#Selects cwt based on the highest modularity
V(netz_dir_mcn)$com<-cwt$membership

E(netz_dir_mcn)$arrow.size<-0
plot(netz_dir_mcn, layout=layout_with_lgl, edge.color="grey80", vertex.color=V(netz_dir_
mcn)$com,vertex.size=sqrt(eigen_centrality(netz_dir_mcn)$vector)*20, main="Eigenvalue")
plot(netz_dir_mcn, layout=layout_with_lgl, edge.color="grey80",vertex.color=V(netz_dir_
mcn)$com,vertex.size=sqrt(closeness(netz_dir_mcn, normalized=TRUE))*20, main="Closeness")
plot(netz_dir_mcn, layout=layout_with_lgl,edge.color="grey80", vertex.color=V(netz_dir_
mcn)$com,vertex.size=sqrt(betweenness(netz_dir_mcn, normalized=TRUE))*100,
main="Betweenness")
plot(netz_dir_mcn, layout=layout_with_lgl,edge.color="grey80", vertex.color=V(netz_dir_
mcn)$com,vertex.size=sqrt(power_centrality(netz_dir_mcn, rescale = TRUE))*100,
main="Power")
plot(netz_dir_mcn, layout=layout_with_lgl,edge.color="grey80", vertex.color=V(netz_dir_
mcn)$com,vertex.size=sqrt(1+(alpha_centrality(netz_dir_mcn)))*20, main="Alpha")
plot(netz_dir_mcn, layout=layout_with_lgl, edge.color="grey80",vertex.color=V(netz_dir_
mcn)$com,vertex.size=degree(netz_dir_mcn),main="Degree")
```

As explained in Chapter 2, visualization is among the most powerful properties of graph theory. Therefore, with the different designs and algorithms, it is possible to attach and arrange more information and properties to the nodes and edges to better understand the relationships. Hence, adding additional node properties when visualizing networks is more informative. This helps to understand the node structure and the possible cluster affiliation resulting afterward. The node properties are external data, such as country or geographical region, sector or industry group, asset or subasset class classification. The cluster or community classification uses the network data and the adjacency matrix. Therefore, the community algorithm and the modularity score can be used to determine the optimal community algorithm, which can properly show the interconnectedness structure according to communities.

Not only do different networks have different layouts and structures, but the centrality scores also differ substantially. Network data might challenge the underlying principles of assets by showing their affiliation to different clusters, groups, and even importance scores than initially thought. Assets and factors might belong to the same underlying community, which is evident when inspecting Figure 4.9. For example, the asset class US Treasuries (UST) possesses high-degree and betweenness centrality scores but much lower scores for eigenvector and alpha centrality. The nodes in Figure 4.9 are assigned to communities, whereas in Figure 4.8 the nodes are differentiated according to their categorization – assets and factors.

Summarizing network properties and key network metrics is often more informative than providing lengthy descriptions. Descriptive statistical tables should include essential metrics such as nodes, correlation coefficients, reciprocity (for directed graphs), diameter, distances, components, and mean connectivity, as determined by clustering algorithms. Table 4.2 illustrates these descriptive statistics for all asset and factor networks discussed in this book. The underlying codes and algorithms are detailed in Chapters 6, 7, and 8. Besides basic statistical properties like node and edge counts and density, other metrics, such as mean degree, diameter, clustering coefficient, and transitivity, are crucial for understanding networks. Centralization metrics offer additional insights into node connectivity, while community structure scores, derived from community detection algorithms, reveal the degree of community separation within the graphs.

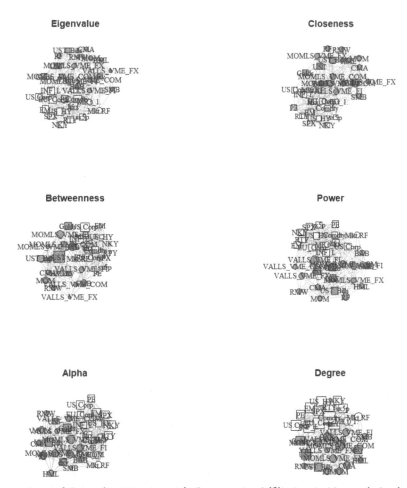

FIGURE 4.9 A Comparison of Centrality Metrics with Community Affiliation in Network Analysis – A Directed Markov Chain Network with Community-Affiliation.
Note: The cluster affiliation is estimated using the largest modularity score of 0.295, which is the cluster walktrap algorithm for network partitioning as shown.

TABLE 4.2 Descriptive Statistics for Asset and Factor Networks.

Network Statistics	Directed Network (nerz_dir_p)	Undirected Network (netz_undir_dist)	Undirected Network (netz_undir_lasso)	Directed Network (netz_dir_conf)	Directed Network (netz_dir_cvd)
Algorithm	Regression	Dsitance Metric	LASSO	Regression Confounder	VAR/Variance Decomposition
Links	324	916	465	284	930
Nodes	31	31	31	31	31
Density	0.35	0.98	1	0.31	1
Average Degree	20.9	59.1	30	18.3	60
Compactness	0.67	0.99	1	0.61	2631.8
Reciprocity	0.89	1	1	1	1
Transitivity	0.62	0.99	1	0.61	1
Clustering	0.30	−0.08	NaN	0.19	NaN
Diameter	4	2	1	5	0.01
Degree Centralization	0.28	0.02	0	0.3	0
Eigen Centralization	0.52	0.01	0	0.53	0
Distance	1.85	1.02	1	1.96	0
Components	1	1	1	1	1
Mod. Cluster Infomap	0.00	0	0	0	0
Mod. Cluster Louvain	0.23	0	0	0.23	0.18
Mod. Cluster Walktrap	0.19	0	0	0.14	0.17
Mod. Cluster Leading Eigen	0.23	0	0	0.18	0.18
Mod. Cluster Fast Greedy	0.23	0	0	0.22	0.19

KEY TAKEAWAYS

- The choice of graph-theoretical tools depends on a network's classes, types, underlying properties, and processes.
- Financial markets represent money flow networks with dynamic properties, where nodes (i.e., financial assets) frequently alter connections.
- Centrality metrics provide precise information about the current interconnectedness of nodes.
- Centrality scores are fundamental metrics for understanding node interconnectedness.
- Centrality measures reflect both the number of connections of a specific node and its importance in terms of information flow.

Undirected Network (netz_cor)	Directed Network (netz_dir_mcn)	Directed Network (netz_dir)	Undirected Network (netz_corf)	Undirected Network (netz_undir)	Undirected Network (netz_pcor)	Directed Network (netz_dir_gct)
Correlation Coefficients	Markov Chain	Regression	Correlation/Fisher Transformation	Correlation Test	Partial Correlation	Granger Test
930	376	282	234	308	320	152
31	31	31	31	31	31	31
1	0.40	0.30	0.25	0.33	0.34	0.16
60	24.26	18.2	15.1	19.9	20.6	9.8
0.77	0.75	0.63	0.61	0.62	0.67	0.62
1	0.78	0.90	1	1	1	0.11
1	0.64	0.66	0.26	0.69	0.3	0.48
NaN	−0.04	0.39	−0.32	0.26	−0.09	0.03
1.87	4	5	3	5	3	8
0	0.17	0.24	0.26	0.28	0.16	0.19
0	0.41	0.53	0.5	0.50	0.34	0.61
1.35	1.78	2.05	1.86	1.94	1.67	2.45
1	1	1	1	1	1	1
0	0	0.14	0	0	0	0
0	0.29	0.22	0.25	0.18	0.17	0.14
0	0.3	0.16	0.23	0.15	0.12	0.05
0	0.3	0.22	0.23	0.18	0.16	0.11
0	0.29	0.21	0.21	0.18	0.17	0.14

Note: The corresponding algorithms for the network estimation are provided in Chapters 6, 7, and 8. The current representations aim to provide descriptive statistics as a broad overview of the different asset and factor networks. We compute an undirected asset and factor network using the Wasserstein distance in Chapter 6 and a Bayesian network in Chapter 7. We omitted these two networks here purposely.

- The most widely used centrality scores are degree, eigenvector, alpha, betweenness, closeness, and power centrality.
- Among centrality metrics, degree and eigenvector centralities are the most widely used.
- Degree centrality measures each node's average connectedness independently within the network.
- Eigenvector centrality assigns a higher score to a node whose neighbor nodes are more central themselves. It is suitable for all connected networks, including those with asymmetric relationships. For networks with unconnected nodes, alpha centrality provides higher precision.

Network Modeling

Contents

In this chapter, we will cover the development of asset networks for use in portfolio management. The scarcity or difficulty in observing empirical real asset networks in portfolio management necessitates that researchers and portfolio managers create these networks using available data to infer potential connections between assets. Traditionally, time series data has been the primary source of information for this purpose in portfolio management.

Traditional models employed to analyze asset relationships in portfolio management predominantly use time series data. Key models include the minimum-variance portfolio developed by Markowitz (1952) and the Black–Litterman approach developed by Black and Litterman (1992) to portfolio allocation, which both use the variance-covariance matrix of assets. In this chapter, we focus on networks built using time series data, which can be utilized as both traditional and alternative allocation tools. However, time series data used in network modeling are susceptible to estimation risks. The recent surge in financial data science has brought about innovative trends and tools for handling data in portfolio management. Models that prevent overfitting and address multiple testing are important enhancements that should be considered in portfolio allocation models that utilize networks.

The primary chapter theme is the network simulation used in portfolio allocation models. Understandably, the chapter's focal point is network construction in portfolio management using mathematical models. The key idea is representing the assets or individual securities within a portfolio as a network. This is an essential task that should yield portfolio allocation networks, comprising different asset classes. It can also be applied to portfolio selection using individual securities, such as bonds, stocks, and derivatives. The nodes of the network and their connections must be modeled using mathematical, statistical, probabilistic, or other econometric models. In this chapter, we focus on the mathematical models. Modeling the connections between assets in a portfolio represents a fundamental yet complex task, given that the nodes are preestablished. We explore association and causal models for building asset networks. We offer solutions on how to utilize these networks in portfolio management. In the final section, we demonstrate how researchers can select networks and address issues like overfitting and network prediction using models from financial data science.

NETWORK MODELS

The goal of networks is to gauge the relationships between assets. When we model networks, the objective is to estimate proper graphical representations effectively characterized by nodes and their mutual links. In Chapter 3, essential network properties and metrics were provided. Here, we investigate the four critical phases of a random network and their implications for its structure, which depend on the nodes, links, and the probabilities of node connections.

The fundamental question is: when does a network become critical on the node level? In Chapter 3, we explained the construction of networks and how links, nodes, and other metrics are interrelated. The answer to this question is determining the probability that a network behaves in either a weak or highly connected regime. A highly connected regime is associated with strong relationships between the nodes, as measured by degree centrality. Models presented in previous chapters and financial literature indicate that financial networks tend to be dense rather than sparse, compared to biological, Internet, and other real networks (Newman, 2010). We apply the mathematical framework developed for network science to model financial networks. The role of simulations is critical in this endeavor.

GENERAL FRAMEWORK

Suppose a portfolio is a network in which the assets are the nodes and links exist between them. Network simulation can be employed in portfolio and risk management to model the inclusion of a new asset (i.e., node) to a portfolio. Alternatively, simulations can provide information about the portfolio's network behavior once a security is bought or sold. Portfolio and risk managers can utilize network simulations to gather valuable insights into the connectedness of assets and their potential behavior when a link(s) are removed or added. Network simulation is arguably the most important aspect when using networks in portfolio and risk management.

There are many reasons for this, but one of them lies in the conceptual difference between the definition of a static or random network and a dynamic or growing network, whose nodes and links might change over time. Another reason can be attributed to the necessity of evaluating simulated and real networks. In this section, we focus on the major differences between simulated and real networks, which can be broken down into two key properties:

- *Node growth*: the constantly increasing number of nodes n in a network
- *Preferential attachment of links*: the probability p of nodes n being connected by a link

To better understand these properties, recall that a network is represented by nodes (n) and links (m) between them. Formalistically, $G = (n,m)$ is the number of *nodes*, or *vertices* n (assets) and *links*, or *edges* (connections) m, where $n \in \mathbb{R}^n$ and $m \in \mathbb{R}^{n \times n}$ ($m_{i,j} \neq m_{j,i}$) for directed networks and ($m_{i,j} = m_{j,i}$) for undirected networks.

There are two possible approaches to building a network:

1. Modeling the data on the edge level while keeping the nodes fixed
2. Modeling a network on the node level, given the edges between them

To illustrate the advantages of graph theory (as already evident in the previous simple example), it is easier to define nodes in a network and model the links. Financial research has identified two types of networks commonly applied to hedge funds and asset portfolios: correlation networks and directed networks.

Different types of networks exist depending on the flow process between nodes, as discussed by Borgatti (2005). Kara, Tian, and Yellen (2015) provide various measures of financial interconnectedness. A simple example using social networks illustrates the difference. Consider the social network Facebook. Once two people are connected, the link is symmetrical in any direction. This argument supports the consideration of Pearson correlation as a measure of connectedness (e.g., Facebook is undirected and, thus, a symmetric network). Because correlation coefficients are widely used in finance, undirected networks are a practical and convenient way to map relationships. Alternatively, consider social networks like X (formerly Twitter) or Instagram. An individual might be linked to or following another but that does not imply reciprocity. This concept can be applied to hedge funds or any type of asset or factor. To illustrate, consider hedge funds and factor exposure. A hedge fund manager might have sources of information regarding factor exposure independent of those of other fund managers, such as data science, market analysis, or machine-learning approaches. The intuition behind a directed hedge fund network is that a hedge fund might be linked to another fund based on different criteria, such as risk and return exposure, but that does not imply a reciprocal link. To model such networks, the links are assigned specific probabilities p. The network is then defined as $G(n, p)$ as defined by Gilbert (1959).

Importantly, we either model the links while holding the nodes constant, or we hold the links constant and model the emergence of nodes into the network. Notably, Barabási (2016) demonstrated that real networks exhibit both properties – a growing number of nodes and an increasing number of links between them. For instance, consider social networks where the number of nodes (i.e., individuals) constantly increases along with the links between them. This dynamic interaction is a fundamental property of real networks, and Barabási and Albert (1999) developed a model to capture these interactions dynamically.

However, in finance, nodes are often considered finite, at least in the short term. Nodes can be defined as assets, factors, countries, sectors, or indices. While new factors may be constantly discovered by researchers, new equity and bond indices may be developed, and new sectors in the economy and financial assets may emerge (e.g., cryptocurrencies), the increase in nodes can be seen as finite in the short term. Similarly, a portfolio or benchmark representing the investment universe has a finite number of assets. The number of assets may increase or decrease over time, but as the portfolio is estimated or derived by an asset allocation model, it comprises a finite number of nodes.[1]

Let's consider another example of funds available in the market. Funds are constantly emerging, but their inclusion in an analytical process typically requires a proven track record of success and establishment, often spanning two to three years. Therefore, the number of nodes in finance can be deemed relatively constant. This essential property of a relatively constant number of nodes reflects the notion of a network analyzed by mathematicians Paul Erdös, Alfréd Rényi,[2] Duncan J. Watts, and Steven Strogatz.[3] The main property of their models is their static nature – the number of nodes is fixed, and the focus is on the time-dependent development of the links between the nodes governed by probabilistic models. These models are known as *random networks*. Because financial networks can be deemed static in the short run, we can easily model the links using probabilities.

By fixing the number of nodes in a financial network, such as the number of assets, factors, indices, or other variables considered in a portfolio, we can define a random network model that governs the probability of assets, factors, or other portfolio and risk variables connecting. The biggest challenge lies in connecting disparate entities, such as a bond index to an equity index or an equity momentum factor to a currency momentum factor. In this model, the probability p of two connected nodes is fixed. This is a fundamental aspect of random financial or portfolio networks. Thus, the available number of nodes determines the likelihood that a random network comprises a fixed number of assets.

---

[1] In Chapter 10, we show alternative models to portfolio allocation using networks whose number of nodes is finite.
[2] Together, Erdös and Rényi made significant contributions to the field of random graphs (discussed later). The Erdös-Rényi model (discussed later) for analyzing random graphs has been influential in the development of network theory.
[3] Watts and Strogatz advanced network theory through their analysis of small-world network modeling (Watts-Strogatz model).

$$p = \frac{1}{n-1} \approx \frac{1}{n} \tag{5.1}$$

Within this framework, the maximum number of links in a network, given the fixed number of nodes n, would be:

$$m_{max} = \frac{n(n-1)}{2} \tag{5.2}$$

where m^{max} is the maximum number of links in a network, and the other variables have been defined previously.

In a random network, some nodes may connect to other connected nodes via links, while others may remain unconnected. The probability of this occurrence is given by the degree distribution, which represents the probability that a random node has a certain degree. Barabási (2016) demonstrated that the degree distribution of a random network follows a binomial distribution rather than a Poisson distribution. Empirical results indicate that the degree of large networks exceeds the predictions of the Poisson distribution, and the standard deviation is larger than predicted. Therefore, by applying the binomial distribution and considering that the average degree of an undirected network is $2m/n$, where m is the number of links and n is the number of nodes, the average degree of a random network would be determined:

$$k_i = \frac{2m}{n} = p(n-1) \tag{5.3}$$

where the average degree k is the product of the probability p and two nodes are connected and the number of nodes is n.

Now that we have identified the basic properties of random networks – (i.e., degree, links, and the fixed number of nodes), let's explore how a portfolio network simulation can be programmed.[4]

RANDOM PORTFOLIO NETWORK SIMULATION AND NETWORK REGIME

Random graph models developed by Erdos and Renyi (1959, 1960) and Gilbert (1959) assume a fixed number of nodes, with the edges assigned equal probability. Consequently, the degree distribution follows a Poisson distribution, as each node's degree is distributed as a binomial random variable with $n-1$ nodes and edge probability p. One of the most distinctive properties of random graph models is the fixed a priori node degree sequence. However, numerous extensions have been developed to enable more network constraints. The random network model is considered a benchmark network model because it identifies critical connectedness regimes.

General Framework for Random Network Models

The foundational work on random graph models goes back to the studies by Rapoport (1957, 1968), Gilbert (1959), and Erdös and Renyi (1959, 1960, 1961). In this section, we demonstrate how portfolio networks form and how nodes become connected using a sample of asset and factor returns representing a broad asset allocation. Networks consisting of assets may alter their connectedness over time, necessitating simulation from a risk management perspective to understand how network connectivity evolves. Specifically, a giant

---

[4]This topic is highly complex. Detail coverage is beyond the scope of this book. Our focus here is on the implications of these tools for financial markets, rather than conducting a mathematical analysis of them. The reader seeking further information should refer to Barabási (2016) and Newman (2010).

component emerges as risk increases, where nodes become heavily interconnected. Recall that the average number of links in a network is *n(n–1)/2*. The probability of a node connecting to another node is given by:

$$p = \frac{1}{n} \tag{5.4}$$

where *n* is the number of nodes and *p* is the probability of any two nodes to be connected.

Let's investigate a portfolio comprising 31 assets. In this case, the simple probability is 1/31 = 3.2%. This simple probability can be considered as a baseline scenario where the average degree *k* of a node is equal to one. At this stage, the asset network is in a critical regime, meaning that some nodes are connected while others are not. In a portfolio with 31 assets, the maximum number of links is 31× (31 – 1)/2= 465. Following a binomial distribution, Barabási (2016) demonstrated that when the average degree exceeds 1, we are adding nodes to the network with an expected probability of two nodes being connected by a link.

$$p^m = \frac{pn(n-1)}{2} = pm^{max} \tag{5.5}$$

This is why in a graph *G(n,p)*, we try to model the probability of two assets to get connected. The average degree *k* of a random directed network is

$$k = \frac{m}{n} = p(n-1) \tag{5.6}$$

The average degree for an asset allocation network with 31 assets (nodes) is then $k = p \times (31 - 1)$. The average degree is the product of the probability of two nodes getting linked and the maximum number of links a node might have in a network. Accordingly, we can derive the probability of connectedness given the expected average degree *k* in the equation. From an asset management perspective, the network comprises several clusters or communities. Once the probability of node connectedness increases more than 1/*n*, the network becomes supercritical. In our example, with a network comprising 31 nodes, the critical point would be reached if the probability exceeds 3.2%. Again, as a result, the possible links are 31(31 – 1)/2 = 465 links.

To determine the threshold level for a connected regime of a network, recall that the average degree at which this occurs depends on the number of nodes *n* in the network. Barabási (2016) showed that the critical point is when the average degree exceeds the logarithm of the node size, or:

$$p = \frac{\ln(n)}{n} \tag{5.7}$$

This corresponds to a probability of two nodes being connected of ln (*n*)/*n* = ln(31)/31 = 11.07%.

In simpler terms, if the probability of two assets being connected exceeds 11.07%, then the network enters a connected phase. At this point, nodes tend to attract each other, forming a large uniform cluster known as a giant component. This giant component absorbs many nodes, indicating that the assets are highly interconnected. In such a scenario, financial turmoil could easily impact all connected nodes, increasing fragility. For the network comprising 31 nodes, the average degree threshold is 3.43. As mentioned previously, the node degree sequence is fixed and is a function of the number of nodes in the network. The following expression then gives the average degree:

$$k = \ln(n) \tag{5.8}$$

Once the average degree of the network surpasses the threshold level of 3.43, the network becomes connected. A reasonable question is how to relate this threshold number to the general network metrics. In a directed network, the average node degree *k* would be 465/31 = 15, and the critical level for the average degree would be ln (31) = 3.43. For degrees larger than 3.43, the network becomes highly connected, and the formation of a giant cluster that absorbs the nodes is evident. Following Das (2016), if a network's connections, or links, are concentrated in a few nodes (i.e., the degree of the nodes), the risk is transmitted widely and immediately into the network. Obviously, the node degree and number of links are essential in this case. In other words, the more concentrated a network is, or the higher the number of links and the fewer the nodes, the higher the fragility. Figure 5.1 illustrates this with a network simulation comprising 31 assets using the Erdös–Renyi random model.

Using the code in Box 5.1, an asset and factor network with 31 nodes in the four regimes can be simulated. Note that the number of nodes is fixed, and we vary the probability of an edge between any pair of vertices. The edge probability in the first random graph is 1.6%, the edge probability in the second random graph is 3.2%, and the edge probability of the third random graph equals 11.02%, which is the probability for the critical connected regime. The fourth edge probability is a randomly selected probability that should generate a highly connected random graph.

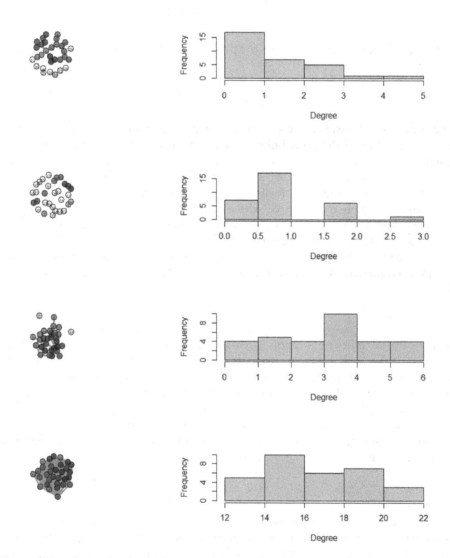

FIGURE 5.1   Network Simulation for the 31 Assets and Factors Used for Asset Allocation.

BOX 5.1: CODE FOR ESTIMATING THE DIFFERENT GRAPHS.

```
#simulates Random: Sub, Critical, and Connected Regimes for Erdös-Renyi Model
set.seed(123456)
#Simulate Sub Regime
ste<-seq(from=1, to=1, by=31)
x=0
outg<-foreach(x=ste,.combine=rbind) %do% {
  test=erdos.renyi.game(31,1/15,directed=FALSE)
  degs=mean(degree(test))
  degs=as.matrix(degs)
}
csg=cluster_louvain(test)
modularity(csg)
plot(csg,test, vertex.size=5)
print(outg)
hist(degree (test))

ste<-seq(from=1, to=1, by=31)
x=0
outg<-foreach(x=ste,.combine=rbind) %do% {
  test=erdos.renyi.game(31,1/31,directed=FALSE)
  degs=mean(degree(test))
  degs=as.matrix(degs)
}
csg=cluster_louvain(test)
modularity(csg)
plot(csg,test, vertex.size=5)
print(outg)
hist(degree (test))

ste<-seq(from=1, to=1, by=31)
x=0
outg<-foreach(x=ste,.combine=rbind) %do% {
  test=erdos.renyi.game(31,log(31)/31,directed=FALSE)
  degs=mean(degree(test))
  degs=as.matrix(degs)
}
csg=cluster_louvain(test)
modularity(csg)
plot(csg,test, vertex.size=5)
print(outg)
hist(degree (test))

#Connected Graph with Gianat Component
x=0
outg<-foreach(x=ste,.combine=rbind) %do% {
  test=erdos.renyi.game(31,5*log(31)/31,directed=FALSE)
  degs=mean(degree(test))
  degs=as.matrix(degs)
}
csg=cluster_louvain(test)
modularity(csg)
plot(csg,test, vertex.size=5)
print(outg)
hist(degree (test))
```

Simulating Random Networks

To understand network modeling, it is reasonable to delve into the simulations and the results. The first network has an average degree of 0.77, which indicates $k < 1$. The network is in a subcritical regime where some assets are building connections while others remain disconnected, resulting in numerous clusters. The second network has an average degree of 1.5, corresponding to $k = 1$, placing it at a critical point. Here, the emergence of clusters and connected groups begins to appear.

Finally, the third network is in a critical regime, associated with an average degree $k > 1$. This suggests a higher level of connectivity compared to the previous networks. Once the average degree exceeds 1, the network enters a supercritical regime. The average node degree for the second network is 1.2 (slightly above 1), indicating that the regime is supercritical. In the fourth network, the average degree for the highly connected network, which forms a giant component, is 16. It is evident that, for random matrix simulations intended to model asset behavior in a specific regime, it is necessary to keep the average degree constant. Recall that the average degree is the relationship between the links m and the nodes n. Given a fixed number of nodes, the links are simulated. Because we make assumptions about the connection probability between two nodes, the network simulation depends on that probability. The larger the probability, the more connected the nodes in the network. We plot the simulation for the node degrees in Figure 5.2. Box 5.2 summarizes the code for the simulation.

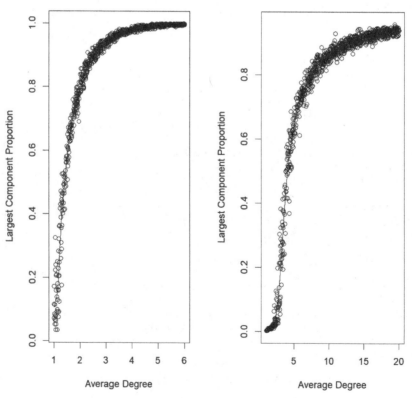

FIGURE 5.2   An Average Degree of Simulated Networks.

BOX 5.2:   CODE FOR SIMULATION OF RANDOM GRAPHS WITH FIXED DEGREE AND COMPONENT SIZE.

```
#Average Degree of Random Network with node probability of 1/p
crnd<-runif(1000,1,6)
cmp_prp<-sapply(crnd,function (x) max(clusters(erdos.renyi.game(1000,x/1000))$csize/1000))
plot(crnd,cmp_prp, xlab="Average Degree", ylab="Largest Component Proportion")
sm_spl<-smooth.spline(crnd, cmp_prp)
lines(sm_spl)

#Average Degree of Random Network with ln(p)/n
crnd<-runif(1000,1,20)
cmp_prp<-sapply(crnd,function (x) max(clusters(erdos.renyi.game(1000,log(x)/999))
$csize/1000))
plot(crnd,cmp_prp, xlab="Average Degree", ylab="Largest Component Proportion")
sm_spl<-smooth.spline(crnd, cmp_prp)
lines(sm_spl)
```

Such simulations are crucial for asset allocation models, which aim to estimate a portfolio's connected regime of assets. It's important to note that mainstream financial theory targets low-risk portfolios. From a graph-theoretical perspective, this implies an asset network with low connectedness. However, estimated financial networks often exhibit high levels of average degrees, and forming a giant component in such networks suggests elevated risk for a portfolio. Financial market volatility exhibits clustering and transitions from periods of low to periods of heightened volatility and vice versa. Low volatility states have a low entropy, but the portfolio entropy, which measures the evolution in a system, is not stable because of constant endogenous and exogenous interactions and information flow. As a result, low-volatility portfolios are not persistent and cannot be aligned with static networks, because dynamic systems are characterized by phase transitions in which interaction takes place. Given a path connectedness, the distance between the nodes is changing. In other words, phase transitions correspond to emerging properties coined by persistent or transitory interactions (see Prigogine, 1997).

According to Barabási (2016), the formation of a giant component for networks at the critical point or in subcritical regimes is not large enough. However, for networks with numerous average degrees, the giant component attracts every node, resulting in a completed graph when the average degree approaches 30 in our example.

DYNAMIC NETWORK MODELS

We have already explored how random networks are modeled. However, in portfolio management networks the constraint of a constant number of nodes exists, and the possibility that nodes may be added or excluded is a fundamental property. For instance, consider how the number of assets changes over time due to globalization and increased information exchange velocity in financial markets. Portfolios evolve as the number of bonds, for example, changes based on portfolio allocation and optimization processes.[5]

---

[5] See, for example, Konstantinov, Fabozzi, and Simonian (2023) for detailed explanation of the portfolio allocation and optimization process for global bond portfolios. Portfolio allocation is the process of deriving an optimal risk-return mix of the assets in the portfolio, and mathematical tools are employed to find the solution.

Similarly, benchmark indices representing the investable universe of assets change as new constituents are added and others are removed. Take, for instance, the J.P. Morgan World Sovereign Bond Index, where index constituents may change monthly as new bonds are included or others mature or are removed. Another example is hedge funds included in representative indices like the HFRX Global Hedge Fund Index, where the number of index constituents (i.e., hedge funds) may change as new funds are added or others are removed due to closures.

Therefore, the primary task is to model the growth of assets in a portfolio or benchmark and their connections to other nodes as a network. This is because not only do the nodes (i.e., assets, funds, and financial instruments) change, but their connections change over time as well. For example, an asset or financial instrument may be strongly connected to other securities during heightened financial market stress but become disconnected during normal times. Proper network models can capture the changing nature of financial market interactions. Such models are dynamic because they enable the modeling of the number of links or edges between nodes. Prigogine (1997) argued that solving dynamical systems requires the specification of probabilities that gauge the changing structure of interactions between nodes. To model these interactions probabilistically, we look at the degree distribution.

Degree Distribution

The small-world phenomenon is the most important property of real networks, not adequately reflected by random and static networks. According to this concept, some nodes have a substantial number of links or are connected to many nodes, while most are weakly connected to others. Barabási and Albert (1999), Albert and Barabási (2002), Broder et al. (2000), Strogatz (2001), Dorogovtsev and Mendes (2002), and Lilijeros et al. (2001) found such scale-free properties in real networks, and Tse, Liu, and Lau (2010) found evidence of scale-free properties in financial markets.

Statistically, these networks exhibit a fat-tail degree distribution and follow a power-law. The following mathematical expression gives the power-law distribution for the degree distribution:

$$p_k = Ck^{-\gamma} \tag{5.9}$$

where γ is a constant that usually ranges $2 < \gamma < 3$ observed in real networks, k is the node degree, and C is a fixed constant for normalization.

Figure 5.3 illustrates the fat-tail properties of an undirected partial correlation network comprising 239 hedge funds in the market, as reported in the study by Konstantinov and Simonian (2020). Upon visual examination of the figure, it becomes apparent that there are a small number of hedge funds with high degree scores and a larger number of funds with small degree scores, as depicted on the left-hand side. The right-hand part of the figure provides a visualization of the log-log scale.

Another example is an undirected network comprising 380 global equity funds, where the power-law degree distribution is evident (see Figure 5.4). In this visualization, it is observed that only a small number of funds exist with high degree scores, compared to a larger number of funds exhibiting low node degree or connectedness to other funds.

In real-world scenarios, nodes are typically connected to other nodes sequentially or gradually, unlike the simultaneous connections assumed by the random model. For instance, an individual joining a social network is more likely to establish connections with existing members over time. Similarly, in financial markets, a newly introduced asset is probabilistically linked to other assets already present in the market. For instance, when a corporate bond is added to a benchmark index, it is likely to be connected to other bonds with similar characteristics already part of the index. Consider cryptocurrencies as an asset. Despite that they are considered uncorrelated assets, they resemble the asset properties of currencies serving for payments buying goods and services. The blockchain technology underlying behind, associates them with

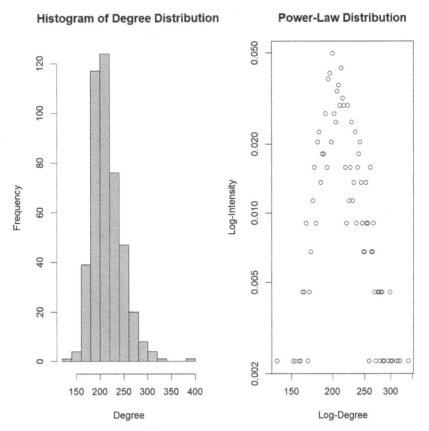

FIGURE 5.3 An Undirected Network Using the Fisher Transformation of the Partial Correlations Between 239 Single Hedge Funds: Fat-Tail Degree Distribution.
Note: Based on the study of Konstantinov and Simonian (2020), in which the connectedness of single hedge funds is investigated. The single hedge funds are from the MercerInsight categorization and include these categories: global macro, credit long-short, distressed debt, equity long-short, equity market neutral, multi strategies, alternative risk premia, foreign exchange, tail hedge, commodities, liquid alternatives, and event-driven.

other digital assets. This sequential linking of nodes necessitates a model that considers the probability of a node being connected to existing nodes in the network.[6]

Advancements in graph theory have been made to apply this concept to bond networks within a benchmark or portfolio. These advancements enable the modeling of probabilities regarding which nodes are likely to be connected. Such dynamic models are highly valuable in portfolio management and trading because they enable the continuous and adaptive modeling of changing network structures. Trading platforms, for instance, could leverage these models by simulating networks and comparing them to real networks that emerge when securities are exchanged.

---

[6]There are several parameters usually used to proxy for the tradability of a bond to other similar bonds – maturity bucket, option-adjusted spread, coupon, yield-to-maturity, rating, issuer-specific information, sector, industry, to name a few.

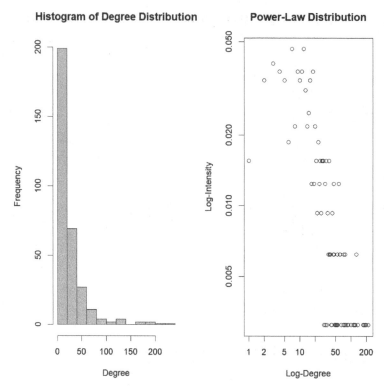

FIGURE 5.4　An Undirected Network Using the Fisher Transformation of the Partial Correlations of 380 Global Equity Funds.
Note: Based on the study of Konstantinov and Rusev (2020), the connectedness of global bond and equity funds is investigated. The global bond and equity mutual funds are from the MercerInight database.

The Preferential Attachment Model

One of the most prominent approaches in network science is the model proposed by Barabási and Albert (1999) and Albert and Barabási (2000, 2002), which facilitates the growth of both vertices (i.e., nodes) and their links. Unlike static models like random networks, the Barabási-Albert model enables the modeling of dynamic networks, which can provide more insightful information in portfolio management. For instance, it can account for the continuously expanding or contracting investment universe where new financial instruments (i.e., nodes), such as bonds, equities, commodities, or currencies, are regularly introduced and others exit the market.

The Barabási–Albert model facilitates the monitoring of network development, including the addition and removal of nodes. It operates as a probabilistic model that assigns a link to a new node's link to an existing one, based on the latter's node degree. This model falls into the category of scale-free models, indicating that the degree distribution follows a power-law distribution (Barabási, 2016). Notably, Nobel Prize-winning economist Herbert Simon (1955) observed the presence of power-laws in various economic data and wealth distribution. Sociologist Robert K. Merton (1968) introduced the concept of the "Matthew effect," which describes the accumulation of advantage and can be seen in the "rich get richer" phenomenon. These concepts help explain the dynamics behind growing networks.

The Barabási–Albert model's strength lies in its ability to accommodate both node growth and preferential attachment. At each step, a new node is attached with m links to an already existing node in the network, and the probability of the new node being connected to any existing node depends on the node's degree.[7] Formally, the probability that a node is chosen follows the power-law distribution, augmented by an additional autonomous constant that accounts for nodes without any adjacent connections:

$$p_i = k_i^{\gamma} + a \tag{5.10}$$

where k is the degree of a node, γ is a power constant that usually ranges $2 < \gamma < 3$ as observed in real networks, and a is a constant that gives the attractiveness of nodes without adjacent links. Usually, the model uses a constant $a = 1$. In case the power coefficient is equal to 1, the preferential attachment is a linear model.

Applying the Barabási–Albert model is highly informative in finance. The application might be to model a benchmark network, of say, 500 (e.g., the S&P 500 Index) or 2,000 (e.g., Russel 2000 Index), or even more than 20,000 nodes (e.g., the Bloomberg Barclay Global Aggregate Bond Market Index). Its major advantage and usefulness is to model a network with a changing number of nodes (or growth) and changing edges (or preferential attachment). A more appropriate example of such networks is the trading networks that capture the exchange of different, individual securities.

Figure 5.5A and Figure 5.5B show two simple examples of the Barabási–Albert Model for an undirected network with 500 nodes that match the S&P 500 Index, in which the nodes with an average mean

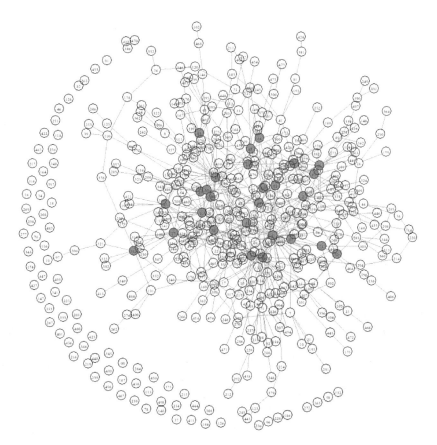

FIGURE 5.5A The Barabási–Albert Preferential Attachment Network.

---

[7]Barabási (2016) and Newman (2010) provide for a detailed and formalistic explanation of the Barabási–Albert model.

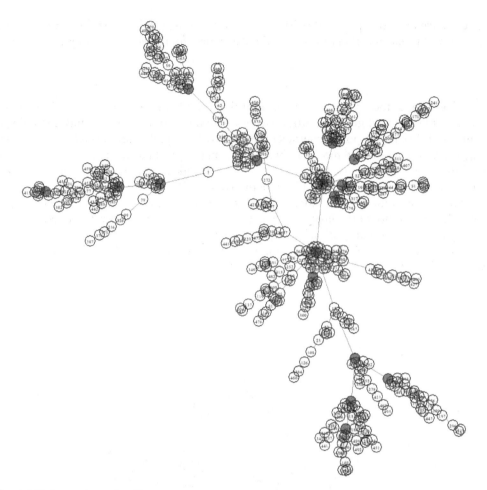

FIGURE 5.5B A Minimum Spanning Tree.

degree above the threshold level of 6.21 (6.21 = ln (500)) are highlighted. The network is an undirected network whose preferential attachment is modeled and whose preferential attachment is modeled using randomly selected probabilities. Specifically, the first probability (10%) is that no edges are added, the second probability (25%) indicates that one edge is added, and so on.

The code for the simple Barabási–Albert Model of the S&P 500 Index is shown in Box 5.3.

The advantage of this model is that researchers can attach a new node to exactly one existing node or even model the links probabilistically. In Figure 5.6, we plot an equity fund network using the model Barabási and Albert (1999) suggested, with preferential node attachment of the nodes to nodes with large-node degree scores. It is worth investigating such a network and comparing it to a "real" network in finance. For this example, we use a single hedge fund network with 239 nodes, based on the study of Konstantinov and Simonian (2020). We plot the simulated and partial correlation single hedge fund networks in Figure 5.6A and 5.6B.

The codes in Boxes 5.4 and 5.5 show the computation of partial-correlation and correlation test networks for single hedge funds, which are central for Figure 5.6A and 5.6B.

BOX 5.3:   CODE FOR THE BARABÁSI–ALBERT MODEL WITH PREFERENTIAL ATTACHMENT.

```
#Simple Barabási Preferential Attachment Model for the S&P 500 Index
ba.model<-barabasi.game(500, directed=FALSE,zero.appeal=1)
E(ba.model)$arrow.size<-0.1
V(ba.model)$size<-5
V(ba.model)[degree(ba.model)>log(500)]$color="grey60"
plot(ba.model, vertex.label.cex=.3)


# Barabási Preferential Attachment Model with attachment probabilities
ba.model<-barabasi.game(500,out.dist=c(0.1,0.25,0.25), directed=FALSE,zero.appeal=1)
E(ba.model)$arrow.size<-0.1
V(ba.model)$size<-5
V(ba.model)[degree(ba.model)>log(500)]$color="grey60"
plot(ba.model, vertex.label.cex=.3)
```

Barabasi-Albert Simulated Hedge Fund Network

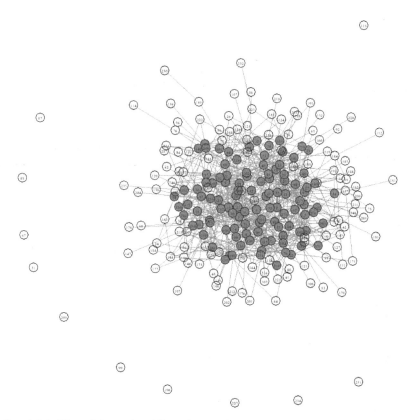

FIGURE 5.6A   The Barabási–Albert Network with Preferential Attachment for Single Hedge Funds.

Partial Correlation Hedge Fund Network

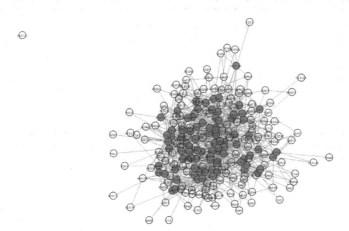

FIGURE 5.6B The Partial Correlation Single Hedge Fund Network.
Note: We highlight the nodes with a degree higher than a threshold level of mean node degree for the corresponding network. The code is found in Box 5.5.

BOX 5.4:   CODE FOR THE PARTIAL CORRELATION SINGLE HEDGE FUND NETWORK.

```
set.seed(122)
returns<-shf
mtx_pcor_shf<-data.frame()
mtx_pcor_shf<-matrix(nrow=ncol(shf),ncol=ncol(shf))
mtx_pcor_shf<-as.matrix(mtx_pcor_shf)
mat_pcor_shf=0.5*log((1+pcor(returns)$estimate)/(1-pcor(returns)$estimate))
mat_pcor_shf=abs(mat_pcor_shf)
p.threshold=0.05/6
mat_pcor_shf<-ifelse(mat_pcor_shf[,]<p.threshold,1,0)
diag(mat_pcor_shf)<-0
colnames(mat_pcor_shf)<-colnames(shf)
print(mat_pcor_shf)
netz_pcor_shf<-as.matrix(mat_pcor_shf)
netz_pcor_shf<-graph_from_adjacency_matrix(netz_pcor_shf)
hist(degree_distribution(netz_pcor_shf))
E(netz_corf_shf)$arrow.size<-0
V(netz_corf_shf)$size<-5
V(netz_corf_shf)[degree(netz_corf_shf)>mean(degree(netz_corf_shf))]$color="grey60"
plot(netz_corf_shf, vertex.label.cex=.3,main="Partial Correlation Hedge Fund Network")
```

BOX 5.5:   CODE FOR THE CORRELATION TEST SINGLE HEDGE FUND NETWORK.

```
set.seed(3211)
returns<-shf
mtx_corf_shf<-data.frame()
mtx_corf_shf<-matrix(nrow=ncol(shf),ncol=ncol(shf))
mtx_corf_shf<-as.matrix(mtx_corf_shf)
mat_corf_shf=0.5*log((1+cor(returns))/(1-cor(returns)))
mat_corf_shf=abs(mat_corf_shf)
p.tres<-0.05/6
mat_corf_shf<-ifelse(mat_corf_shf[,]<p.tres,1,0)
diag(mat_corf_shf)<-0
colnames(mat_corf_shf)<-colnames(shf)
print(mat_corf_shf)
netz_corf_shf<-as.matrix(mat_corf_shf)
netz_corf_shf<-graph_from_adjacency_matrix(netz_corf_shf, weighted=TRUE)
hist(degree_distribution(netz_corf_shf))
E(netz_corf_shf)$arrow.size<-1
```

The essential property of such networks is that, as new nodes are added to a network, they are more likely to be linked to other highly connected nodes. Consider, for example, a network that comprises hedge funds. As a new hedge fund is added to a single hedge fund network (e.g., due to index inclusion or a newly launched strategy), it is more likely to be connected to other highly connected hedge funds.[8]

The goodness-of-fit in such models is carried out by comparing the descriptive statistics of the simulated model with the "real" model. Here, we use the partial correlation network for single hedge funds. The descriptive statistics for the estimated graph using the partial correlation coefficients and the simulated Barabási–Albert model are provided in Table 5.1. Descriptive network statistics are essential for evaluating networks and comparing simulated to observed networks. In Chapter 9, we discuss algorithms that effectively estimate the goodness-of-fit for simulated networks.

Box 5.6 represents the code for the simulation, representation, and calculation of the statistical properties of the simulated preferential attachment network according to the Barabási–Albert model. Note that the code comprises three procedures. The first code computes the Barabási–Albert Model with 239 nodes. The probability's specification of node attachment is modeled in this step with the out.dist variable. The probabilities for the single hedge fund preferential connectedness are chosen so that the probability of no edges being added is 25%. The probability that one edge is added is 65%. The probability that two edges are added is 25% and so on. Note that the probabilities sum up to 1, but the normalization occurs automatically.

Note that economic reasoning might be applied to the preferential attachment models. The probability of node addition might be the result of an economic model. Modeling the probabilities in the models represents the most challenging and compelling part of the financial analysis process. The economic intuition

---

[8]The reason for this has been highlighted by Konstantinov and Simonian (2020) and can be traced back to the style similarity of hedge fund strategies, which often experience similar style – e.g., Fung and Hsieh (1997, 2002, 2003), Khandani and Lo (2011), Billio et al. (2012), among others.

TABLE. 5.1   Descriptive Statistics for the Estimated and Simulated Single Hedge Fund Networks.

Descriptive Satistic	Barabasi–Abbert Model	Partial Correlation Network
Links	673.00	1500.00
Nodes	239.00	239.00
Density	0.02	0.03
Average Degree	5.63	12.55
Compactness	0.31	0.35
Reciprocity	1.00	1.00
Transitivity	0.08	0.02
Assortativity	–0.01	–0.33
Diameter	6.00	6.00
Degree Centralization	0.13	0.09
Egen Centralization	0.86	0.81
Distance	3.14	3.10
Components	17.00	3.00
Mod. Cluster Infomap	0.34	0.38
Mod. Cluster Louvain	0.36	0.36
Mod. Cluster Walktrap	0.23	0.32
Mod. Cluster Leading Egen	0.33	0.31
Mod. Cluster Fast Greedy	0.36	0.38

Note: the code for the statistical properties is shown in Box 5.5.

BOX 5.6:   CODE FOR THE BARABÁSI–ALBERT PREFERENTIAL ATTACHMENT SINGLE HEDGE FUND NETWORK.

```
# Barabási Preferential Attachment Model
ba.model<-barabasi.game(239,power=1, out.dist=c(0.25,0.65,0.25,0.25,0.25, 0.25,0.45),
directed=FALSE,zero.appeal=1)
E(ba.model)$arrow.size<-0
V(ba.model)$size<-5
V(ba.model)[degree(ba.model)>mean(degree(ba.model))]$color="grey60"
plot(ba.model, vertex.label.cex=.3,layout=layout_with_kk, main="Barabasi-Albert Simulated
Hedge Fund Network")
```

of this preferential attachment is arbitrarily chosen, but the intuition is that many hedge funds generate alpha returns, and thus, their strategies might be unrelated to other funds (the probability that no edge is added is 25%). However, strong academic evidence of common factor exposure may suggest that the probability of one edge being added is 65%.[9] Box 5.7 provides the entire code for all the steps conducted in this section, including the computation of network descriptive statistics in Table 5.1

---

[9]Several studies suggest that the hedge funds have common factor exposure. Some of the prominent studies are Fung and Hsieh (1997, 2002) and Konstantinov and Rebman (2020).

BOX 5.7: CODE FOR THE SIMULATION OF THE BARABÁSI–ALBERT PREFERENTIAL MODEL FOR SINGLE HEDGE FUNDS.

```
#Barabási Preferential Attachment Model
ba.model<-barabasi.game(239,power=1, out.dist=c(0.25,0.65,0.25,0.25,0.25, 0.25,0.45),
directed=FALSE,zero.appeal=1)
E(ba.model)$arrow.size<-0
V(ba.model)$size<-5
V(ba.model)[degree(ba.model)>mean(degree(ba.model))]$color="grey60"
plot(ba.model, vertex.label.cex=.3,layout=layout_with_kk, main="Barabasi-Albert Simulated
Hedge Fund Network")

#Unirected Partial-Cor Network for SHF
set.seed(122)
returns<-shf
mtx_pcor_shf<-data.frame()
mtx_pcor_shf<-matrix(nrow=ncol(shf),ncol=ncol(shf))
mtx_pcor_shf<-as.matrix(mtx_pcor_shf)
mat_pcor_shf=0.5*log((1+pcor(returns)$estimate)/(1-pcor(returns)$estimate))
mat_pcor_shf=abs(mat_pcor_shf)
p.threshold=0.05/6
mat_pcor_shf<-ifelse(mat_pcor_shf[,]<p.threshold,1,0)
diag(mat_pcor_shf)<-0
colnames(mat_pcor_shf)<-colnames(shf)
print(mat_pcor_shf)
netz_pcor_shf<-as.matrix(mat_pcor_shf)
netz_pcor_shf<-graph_from_adjacency_matrix(netz_pcor_shf)
hist(degree_distribution(netz_pcor_shf))
E(netz_corf_shf)$arrow.size<-0
V(netz_corf_shf)$size<-5
V(netz_corf_shf)[degree(netz_corf_shf)>mean(degree(netz_corf_shf))]$color="grey60"
plot(netz_corf_shf, vertex.label.cex=.3,main="Partial Correlation Hedge Fund Network")

set.seed(99)
list.nets<-list(netz_corf_shf,ba.model)
#statisti=data.frame()
statisti<-for (i in list.nets){
    list.stat<-c(ecount(i),
              vcount(i),
              edge_density(i),
              mean(degree(i)),
              compactness(i),
              reciprocity(i),
              transitivity(i),
              assortativity_degree(i),
              diameter(i),
              centr_degree(i)$centralization,
              centr_eigen(i)$centralization,
              average.path.length(i),
              components(i)$no,
              modularity(cluster_infomap(as.undirected(i))),
              modularity(cluster_louvain(as.undirected(i))),
              modularity(cluster_walktrap(as.undirected(i))),
```

(Continued)

(Continued)

```
                modularity(cluster_leading_eigen(as.undirected(i))),
                modularity(cluster_fast_greedy(as.undirected(i))))
  desc.stat<-cbind(list.stat, desc.stat)
}
desc.stat<-as.matrix(desc.stat)
rownames(desc.stat)<-c("Links","Nodes", "Density","Average Degree","Compactness",
  "Reciprocity", "Transitivity", "Clustering", "Diameter", "Degree Centralization", "Eigen
  Centralization", "Distance", "Components", "Mod. Cluster Infomap","Mod. Cluster
  Louvain","Mod. Cluster Walktrap","Mod. Cluster Leading Eigen","Mod. Cluster Fast Greedy")
desc.stat<-round(as.matrix(desc.stat), digits=2)[,1:2]
desc.stat
```

The major difference between the two networks is the number of links, resulting in a large deviation of the average degree. The estimated model has an average degree of 12.55, while the simulation has an average of 5.63. Another notable difference is observed in the clustering coefficient (i.e., assortative degree), indicating a much higher disassortative mixing for the partial correlation network where similar funds tend to be linked to dissimilar funds.

The Small-World Effect

In the Barabási–Albert simulation, a high number of components are detected. Overall, this model is more realistic than the random graph model. However, other models exist that may generate reasonable networks, such as the small-world model of Watts (1999a, 1999b) and Watts and Strogatz (1998). The Barabási–Abert model generates networks between regular (which lack small-world phenomenon but are highly clustered) and random (lacking clustering but showing evidence of small-world properties) connected regimes.

The most distinctive property of small worlds is their significant clustering alongside minimal distances between nodes. Once simulated, the Barabási–Albert model becomes particularly interesting for investigating the small-world property across many actual networks. As a result, to ascertain whether a network exhibits the small-world property, one examines its clustering coefficient and average path length, also known as the mean distance. The Monte Carlo simulation technique is valuable for understanding the evolution of clustering coefficients, mean distance, and community structure within a network over time. Network partitioning algorithms, as discussed in Chapter 2, can be employed to identify and simulate the community structure. Specifically, we can apply some powerful algorithms. In the current example, we used the cluster walktrap algorithm, which is preferred for large networks. However, the choice is not limited to this algorithm alone; other options for partition algorithms exist, such as cluster fast greedy or cluster leading eigen, and algorithm selection is based on achieving the highest modularity score.

While Table 5.2 presents the simulation statistics, Figure 5.7 plots the results of the Monte Carlo simulation with 10,000 iterations, and Box 5.8 provides the code for the small-world experiment for single

TABLE 5.2 Statistics for the Monte Carlo Simulation of Small Hedge Fund World.

	Min	1st. Qu	Median	Mean	3rd. Qu	Max
Clustering Coefficient	0.044	0.047	0.047	0.047	0.048	0.051
Mean Distance	2.50	2.515	2.517	2.517	2.519	2.534

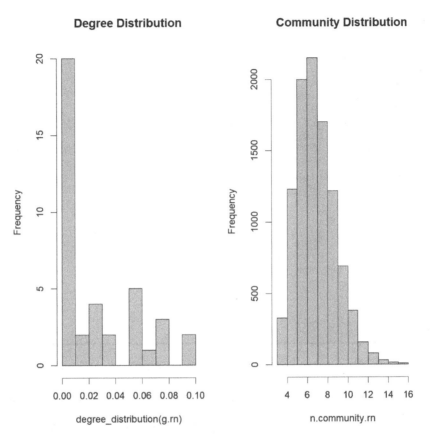

FIGURE 5.7 The Degree Distribution and Community Distribution of a Small Hedge Fund World.

hedge funds, computing the mean distance, clustering coefficient, community structure, and degree distribution. The clustering coefficient of the partial correlation single hedge fund network (netz_pcor_shf) is 0.048, and the mean distance is 2.512.

Box 5.8 summarizes the code for the small-world simulation with 10,000 iterations. The code computes the mean distance, degree distribution, and clustering coefficients. The simulation starts with the node and edge count of the partial correlation network of single hedge funds.

BOX 5.8:   CODE FOR THE SMALL-WORLD SIMULATION WITH CLUSTERING COEFFICIENT AND DEGREE DISTRIBUTION.

```
#Code for Clustering Coefficient, Mean Distance, and Community Structure
par(mfrow=c(1,2))
iteration=10000
n=vcount(netz_pcor_shf)
m=ecount(netz_pcor_shf)
cluster.rn=numeric(iteration)
mdistance.rn=numeric(iteration)
```

(Continued)

(*Continued*)

```
n.community.rn=numeric(iteration)
degree.rn=numeric(iteration)
for (i in (1:iteration)){
    g.rn<-sample_gnm(n,m,directed=TRUE)
    cluster.rn[i]<-clustering_coefficient(g.rn)
    degree.rn[i]<-degree(g.rn)
    mdistance.rn[i]<-mean_distance(g.rn)
    cwt.rn<-cluster_walktrap(g.rn)
    n.community.rn[i]=length(cwt.rn)
    as.rn[i]=assortativity.degree(g.rn)
}

hist(degree_distribution(g.rn), main="Degree Distribution")
summary(cluster.rn)
summary(mdistance.rn)
hist(n.community.rn, main="Community Distribution")
clustering_coefficient(netz_pcor_shf)
```

KEY TAKEAWAYS

- Network modeling is an essential task that should yield portfolio allocation networks comprising different asset classes.
- Random network models, or models with preferential attachment, can also be applied to portfolio selection using individual securities, such as bonds, stocks, and derivatives.
- The network's nodes and connections must be modeled using statistical, probabilistic, or other econometric models.
- The Barabási–Albert model is one of the most effective models for simulating node growth and preferential attachment.
- The Barabási–Albert model offers the capability to construct probabilistically complex and realistic models, making it highly suitable for modeling portfolio and benchmark structures, especially when simulating trading networks. Moreover, it enables comparisons with other estimated networks and facilitates the monitoring of structural changes over time.
- The most important property of real networks, not adequately reflected by random and static networks, is the small-world phenomenon.
- According to the research of real networks, the degree distribution does not follow normal distribution. Instead, some nodes have a substantial number of links or are connected to many nodes, while most nodes are weakly connected to other nodes.

## CHAPTER 6

Foundations for Building Portfolio Networks – Link Prediction and Association Models

Contents

The topic of this chapter, and the two to follow, is the development of asset networks for use in portfolio management. Nodes or vertices in networks are often known and finite. However, edges are often not directly observable in financial markets. This is because empirical real-asset networks are scarce or the ties between financial variables are challenging to observe in portfolio management. Therefore, researchers and portfolio managers must construct networks based on observable data and predict potential links between assets. Graph theoretical research proposed various models for link prediction that apply mathematical and statistical tools to enable edge prediction and simulation. In finance, statistical and econometric models commonly use time series data, traditionally the most widely used type of data in portfolio management.

Applying graph theoretical models to finance, especially in portfolio management, introduces three primary types of models for the estimation of a portfolio graph, which we cover in this book. We dedicated Chapter 5 to the mathematical structure of network models. Based on the network literature that deals with network construction models, we propose three groups of models:[1] link prediction models, association models, and statistical models. The intuition behind these three models is to estimate edges based on the available vertex information. In finance, this information might include statistical data, return time series, or other specific data referring to trading, portfolio holdings, economic publications, or any type of information that indicates or helps model-node relationships.

In this chapter and the two following chapters, we demonstrate other techniques for network construction. Whereas the network models introduced as link prediction models deal with similarity metrics, the association models comprise correlation-based and regression-based models. In the case of link prediction models, the observed and non-available edges between the nodes are modeled based on known information or node attributes. The prediction can be based on individual properties or collective data information, such as community detection or other attributes that classify the nodes. In the case of association models, the edges between the nodes are governed by specific information about the association of the node properties. The primary task in association models is to use rule-based models to estimate the edges between nodes using these attributes. Ordinary least squares regression plays a crucial role in this process.

When discussing statistical models, we primarily focus on the probabilistic models that help build directed networks. The major idea behind probabilistic models, which can be traced back to the field of statistical mechanics, is the use of various statistical and/or mathematical models to estimate the probabilities of nodes being connected based on information from neighboring nodes. A major advantage of statistical models, particularly probabilistic models, is their ability to incorporate both endogenous and exogenous properties when modeling networks, which we analyze in Chapter 9.

Figure 6.1 provides an overview of the models used for interference and inference and an estimation of graphs covered in this book. Our objective is to present some of the most useful and powerful concepts that find application in portfolio management.

Each type provides unique insights and methodologies for analyzing financial networks and portfolios. We refer to these processes as estimation, computation, and graph construction because they involve building graphs from time series data. In this chapter, we describe link prediction models and highlight the intuition behind correlation-based models, which are one type of association model. Because regression models (part of association models) are most widely used in financial economics and to model relationships in data, we dedicate Chapter 7 to them. The statistical models covered in Chapter 8 focus on probabilistic models. Association models are split into two chapters: correlation-based models are discussed in this chapter, and regression-based models are discussed in Chapter 7.

It is noteworthy that all these three types of models share a commonality: they utilize observed or historical data and attempt to establish relationships based on underlying mathematical procedures.

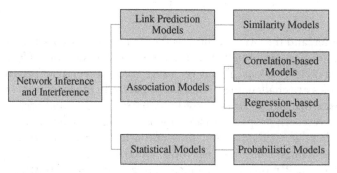

FIGURE 6.1   Models for Building Portfolio Networks.

---

[1]See Kolaczyk and Csardi (2020), Borgatti et al. (2022), and Luke (2016).

The primary difference between the models applied to edge connectivity lies in how links are estimated. Estimating probabilistic models for network structure requires statistical models or tests; similarly, correlation-based models rely on statistical tools. In essence, statistical approaches are an integral part of network theory. Econometric models are often used to derive causal relationships. The major focus is on how to use networks in asset management.

The central idea of portfolio networks is that edges connect the nodes in a network. This means that the components of a portfolio, or a benchmark, are not isolated variables but are interconnected actors, or nodes, in the language of networks and graphs, respectively. The concept of connectedness contrasts with idea of orthogonality, or absence of connections, often emphasized in the financial literature. When constructing portfolio networks, the primary task is to model the edges because the nodes are known, but the edges might be unobservable. Models that analyze asset relationships in portfolio management rely on time series data. Examples include the minimum-variance and mean-variance portfolio frameworks developed by Markowitz (1952), and the Black and Litterman (1992) approach to portfolio allocation – both which use the variance-covariance matrix of assets to represent portfolio risk.

We focus on networks built using time series data. However, the time series data used in network modeling and the resulted networks are susceptible to estimation risks. The rise and recent developments in financial data science have introduced new trends and models for handling data in portfolio management. Many of the developed techniques center on the most severe problems like overfitting, false discovery rates, and extracting causal relationships and information.[2] These questions pertain to portfolio network inference and interference, which are elaborated on in our forthcoming discussion. Models that prevent overfitting and address multiple testing represent crucial improvements for portfolio management strategies that utilize networks. These enhancements are essential for refining the accuracy and reliability of such models. We explore association and link prediction models for building asset networks using the asset and factor dataset applied by Konstantinov et al. (2020). We offer solutions on how to utilize these networks in portfolio management. We demonstrate how researchers can select networks and address issues like overfitting and network prediction, employing models from financial data science using two major types of link prediction methods: similarity metrics and correlations. We begin this chapter with a definition of link prediction models and discuss how their purpose is necessary.

PORTFOLIO NETWORK TOPOLOGY INTERFERENCE AND INFERENCE

The purpose of building networks in portfolio management is to represent the relationships between assets or individual securities. Link prediction models apply to both interference and inference. It is worth discussing the notions of interference and inference before we investigate the link prediction models in detail.

Interference and Inference

The two important aspects of interference and inference are essential for estimating links between nodes or the relation between nodes. The first aspect involves the overall method for estimating these links, while the second aspect addresses the challenges associated with multiple testing when estimating edges in a network. The asset and factor network provides a good example of a manageable node-size network.

---

[2]In his seminal paper, López de Prado (2018) identified some of most severe reasons for why portfolio (i.e., hedge fund) strategies fail. Several of the most important reasons are the backtest overfitting and the identification of causal relationships when they do not exist.

General Framework   In the context of data science, *interference* focuses on the relation of effect that a variable has on other variables. In network science, interference refers to a node's impact and effect on other nodes. This is a notion of relation or interconnectedness. *Inference* refers to making references, predictions, and projections based on observable data and empirical evidence. The edge properties are unobserved and must be inferred from measurements anticipating these properties. Statistical and observable data are crucial for classifying and estimating values through the use of tests and hypotheses. In the context of data science and machine learning, inference refers to making predictions using historical sets. Link prediction models serve both topics. We begin with interference, however, because it is essential when building portfolio networks.

The prevailing theory assumes noninterference between financial assets and factors, underlying the basic assumption of orthogonality or the absence of market relationships. However, the contrarian view driving networks suggests that interference (i.e., relations) does exist, forming the underlying intuition behind graph theory. In this theory, the central assumption is that relationships exist, and the primary aim of graph-theoretical approaches is to model this interference. This is the book's main theme; it proposes models and solutions in portfolio and risk management that model and investigate these relationships. In a graph-theoretical context, the nodes already exist, and the links must be modeled when not observed. Link prediction models help to predict the edges between the nodes. As a result, link prediction involves both inference and interference.

A simple example illustrates how interference can be modeled in finance using multivariate financial data as a set of point clouds.[3] The mathematical procedure of finding structures in objects is called *persistent homology*. The goal of persistent homology is to identify the emergence and the disappearance of (topological) structures in data. It converts unstructured data into a simplicial complex in an n-dimensional space R, from which the data are sampled. To be precise, a simplicial complex is an object in space formed by connecting other objects in space based on a specific threshold. The simplicial complexes define the structures. The financial market application of this concept is illustrated in detail by Baitinger and Flegel (2021).

Suppose that the returns, represented as clouds of two randomly chosen factors of market returns (Mkt.RF) and the value factor (HML) with specific attributes in the Fama–French three-factor model, are plotted against each other (see Figure 6.2). Using a distance measure such as the Euclidean distance (which we explain in the next section) and a threshold level, say ω, we connect the pairwise data points x and y as soon as the distance between the two points is less than the threshold level, or $dist(x,y) < \omega$.[4] Figure 6.2 visualizes the procedure, with the circles indicating a radius that is necessary to connect the points, which are set by a distance measure's threshold.

Applying a proper distance measure, the data points are connected to each other as soon as the distance metric does not exceed the threshold. Applying a graph algorithm, we can draw a network between the individual data points that represent the nodes in this network. The edges are determined using the Wasserstein distance (explained in the next section), plotted in Figure 6.3. The code for the time series network is provided in Box 6.1.

---

[3]The persistent homology goes back to the pioneer works of Edelsbrunner et al. (1983), Edelsbrunner and Mücke (1994), Edelsbrunner et al. (2002), and Edelsbrunner and Morozovy (2014). Also see Do Carmo (2016).
[4]This is the underlying mechanism behind the mathematical framework in the Renaissance hedge fund founded by Jim Simons. See Zuckerman (2023).

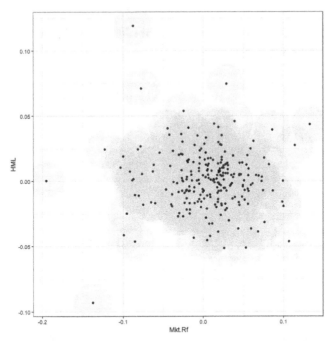

FIGURE 6.2   Returns Clouds for the Market Returns (Mkt.RF) and Value Factor (HML).
Note: Monthly returns for the period from January 2001 to December 2022 were obtained, by the authors, from Kenneth French's library. The return cloud comprises 242 observations.

FIGURE 6.3   Connecting the Unstructured Data Points with a Distance Metric.
Note: We use the pointwise Wasserstein distance and the average Wasserstein distance between Mkt.Rf and HML factors as a threshold for the network, which is 0.0388.

BOX 6.1: THE CONNECTEDNESS FOR TWO RANDOM RETURN TIME SERIES WITH A MINIMUM SPANNING TREE (MST) AS A WEIGHTED NETWORK.

```
set.seed(96)
r_2<-data.frame(structure(list(Mkt.Rf=returns[,1],HML=returns[,3])))
mtx_r2<-matrix(nrow=nrow(r_2),ncol=nrow(r_2))
for(i in 1:nrow(r_2)) {
    for(j in 1:nrow(r_2)) {
        mtx_r2[i,j]=wasserstein1d(r_2[i,1],r_2[j,2], p=1)
    }
}
w_th=mean(mtx_r2)
print(w_th)
netz_r2=as.matrix(ifelse(mtx_r2[,]<w_th,mtx_r2,0))
diag(netz_r2)<-0
netz_wd<-graph_from_adjacency_matrix(netz_r2, weighted=TRUE)
E(netz_wd)$arrow.size<-0
plot(mst(netz_wd), vertex.size=3,layout=layout_with_fr,edge.color="grey85",
vertex.label.cex=0.01,vertex.color="black")
```

Building Networks with Multiple Testing   When dealing with interference and inference in portfolio networks, the issue of multiple testing becomes apparent. In other words, when constructing networks, numerous methods are simultaneously employed. Two crucial concepts help mitigate this issue. The family-wise error rate (FWER) considers all the tests performed and provides the probability of one or more false discoveries. In statistics, this refers to the rejection of a true null hypothesis, known as a false positive or Type I error. The FWER adjusts the p-values to prevent any false positive discoveries. The false discovery rate (FDR) is the expected proportion of Type I errors among all rejected hypotheses. When some false positives are allowed, the FDR applies.

The FDR and the effect of multiple testing present significant challenges in financial analysis. Harvey and Liu (2014), Bailey and Lopez de Prado (2014), Fabozzi and Lopez de Prado (2018) have demonstrated the need to adjust p-values in multiple testing scenarios. Correlation models are particularly vulnerable to multiple testing issues due to the inherent challenges in establishing causality and inference when it barely exists. To address the multiple testing problem within the context of the FWER, methods such as Bonferroni correction and Holm adjustment can be applied. The Bonferroni method is particularly suitable for addressing a smaller number of multiple tests.

On the other hand, when multiple testing is extensive, say 1,000 networks estimated, and some false positives are acceptable, the Benjamini–Hochberg procedure is more appropriate.[5] Generally, FWER effectively mitigates inference issues in statistical analysis. Because errors in financial models can have a severe impact on portfolios, a robust correction method might be preferred. We recommend using the Bonferroni correction for its stringent control of errors. The FDR is more suitable in the early stages of the research

---

[5]The Benjamini–Hochberg procedure is easily done in five steps. The p-values are sorted in an ascending order and the assigned correspondent ranks with the smallest p-value receiving rank 1. Then the individual critical value is obtained given the specified researcher's own threshold level (e.g., 25%). The threshold level is multiplied by the total number of tests and the p-values' rank. Comparing the critical Benjamini–Hochberg to the original p-values gives an overview of the significant p-values, which are smaller than the critical values.

process, where the number of tests can grow substantially, enabling for a more balanced approach to managing Type I errors.

Portfolio and Benchmarks as Networks

The important rule when constructing networks is to determine the nodes and links based on historical data and observations. This presents an essential challenge depending on the type of network we want to derive – whether for allocation or selection purposes. The task in portfolio management – allocation or portfolio selection – impacts the assumptions regarding how to deal with the number of nodes and links. In tactical asset allocation, which typically has a short horizon (i.e., monthly or weekly), the number of assets is usually fixed or finite. New asset classes are not often added to a tactical allocation but might be included in a strategic asset allocation, which is updated on a yearly basis.[6] In the case of tactical asset allocation, the main task is to model the links between a fixed number of nodes representing asset classes such as sectors (financial, consumer, energy, information technology [IT], etc.), currencies (major currencies including emerging markets), countries (developed or emerging markets), or industry groups.

The nodes in portfolios and benchmarks are interconnected, and there are two important variables to determine: the number of nodes and the number of links. Modeling the connections between assets in a portfolio is the primary but challenging task. Nodes in a portfolio network are predetermined, or they are finite at least in the short term, say the stocks included in an equity market index (e.g., 500 for the S&P500 index). Similarly, the assets and factors used in a portfolio allocation are, in the short run, also finite, say 30. Determining the number of nodes in a portfolio or benchmark network might be directly identified by the number of entities or single securities a portfolio or benchmark comprises. However, researchers might see that the nodes in an equity index are the stocks. In a bond index, an issuer might be a node, but there might be several instruments included by the same issuer. Therefore, it is often convenient for both benchmarks and portfolios to use single instruments as nodes, not issuers.

The primary theme in this chapter is network construction used in portfolio allocation models. Understandably, this section's focal point is the various methods and models for using financial data or any type of data that helps infer node relationships for network construction. These models are statistical, and their economic relevance origin stems from data analytics. Essentially, the key idea is to represent the assets or individual securities that a portfolio may consist of as a network. In this context, we deal focus on node-level information to help estimate the edges between the nodes. This task is essential for yielding financial networks. Data used can be time series, financial and monetary flow data, transactions, or balance and portfolio holdings ledgers.

Network models can be applied to portfolio selection using individual securities, such as bonds, stocks, and derivatives. The edges of the network might be modeled using link prediction methods that incorporate similarity metrics. The similarity metrics use observable data for the portfolio constituents.

In a portfolio comprising a specific number of single securities, such as equities or bonds, neither the number of nodes (single securities) nor the links can be fixed. This is because the portfolio may include, for example, 1,000 single securities one month and 1,100 the next. However, varying both the number of nodes and links is challenging, and over short periods of time for asset networks, it is rather unrealistic, as the number of nodes in asset networks is finite in the short run.

---

[6]The asset class classification is subject to the investment process. The most common top-down asset classes are bonds, equities, commodities, and foreign exchange. However, a more granular view might break the large asset classes to more subgroups, depending on geographic clustering (US, Europe, Asia, or even more country-specific), sectoral (government, corporate, financial), rating (IG vs. HY, or granular decomposition into the rating classes), to name a few.

An important question to address is related to the size of the portfolio network, which is associated with the top-down or bottom-up portfolio management approaches. It is worth elaborating on this question. While top-down portfolio management prioritizes asset allocation, the networks considered within this framework are relatively small, typically consisting of a finite number of nodes – perhaps 10, 20, or 30 – depending on how asset classes or factors are defined in a network. For instance, portfolio managers and researchers might consider factors, and the network might include over 300 factors, as identified by Harvey and Liu (2014). However, factor investing in the literature typically employs a finite number of factors ranging between 5 and 30.[7]

The bottom-up portfolio process involves considering many individual securities, from which the asset allocation is derived, once the selection process is conducted and the most attractive securities are chosen. This approach necessitates large networks – single security networks derived from the benchmark universe. While benchmark networks, or networks comprising the securities of a benchmark index, are large, portfolio networks are comparatively smaller.

Therefore, a preselection model should be applied in portfolio management to fix the number of nodes. An example of such a model might be a return estimator or a scoring system that selects the number of individual securities to be considered in a portfolio. In this case, the portfolio manager might fix the number of nodes to, for example, 60 bonds in the case of bond portfolios.

Building a network for the benchmark is another vital source of information and a challenging task. Consider the S&P 500 index, which comprises 500 single securities. We can construct the network using these 500 instruments. However, a bond index comprises many more securities. For instance, the Bloomberg Barclays Global Aggregate Bond Index (LEGATRUU Index) includes over 20,000 bonds. Building a network with, say 1,000 bonds that meet specific predefined filter criteria might be more relevant than simply estimating a large network with over 20,000 nodes, which would be considered a large network.[8] Regardless of the question of whether a portfolio or benchmark network is desired, the models that play an effective role are similarity metrics and correlation-based models.

LINK PREDICTION MODELS

The primary objective of link prediction models is to utilize existing data and observations to generate scores that indicate the likelihood of links between vertices which are not directly observable. However, observable market data can be used to model these relationships. In the literature, numerous models have been identified for estimating scores between variables of interest, where higher scores correspond to greater link probabilities between these variables. Among the most important and commonly used models are similarity metrics.

Similarity Models

In this section, we focus on simple models for link prediction and modeling edges, primarily utilizing similarity metrics to identify associations.

The concept of similarity is crucial, yet complex in network science. Newman (2010) and Borgatti et al. (2022) have argued that understanding the distinction between structural and regular equivalence is

---

[7]No unified factor set exists. The Fama and French (1992, 1993, 2005) five factors and the Carhart (1997) equity momentum factor are the benchmark factors used in factor research. For example, Bender, Sun, and Thomas (2019) use 14 factors,

[8]According to Yang et al. (2016), a network that comprises more than 500 nodes is considered large network.

pivotal in determining similarity. However, the most prevalent and commonly applied techniques revolve around structural similarity, typically measured using common metrics, such as correlations and distance metrics.

Provost and Fawcett (2013) offer an overview of various methods for estimating similarity between variables, including cosine similarity, Manhattan distance, Jaccard distance, and the Euclidean distance metric. Another distance metric, drawn from statistical geometry, is the Mahalanobis distance, which Kritzman and Li (2010) have applied to financial time series data. However, some distance metrics necessitate observable inputs to generate scores that measure distances. Here, we highlight some significant distance metrics commonly used in data science for link prediction.

The rationale behind distance metrics is intuitive: the shorter the distance between two vertices, the shorter the path through which information travels between them. Borgatti, Everett, Johnson, and Agneessens (2022) demonstrated that shorter distances between nodes correspond to higher transmission levels through the network. Therefore, understanding the definition of a distance metric is crucial. We will highlight some of the most important and widely used distance metrics in graph theory applicable to portfolio management later.

It is also necessary to explain the concept of structural equivalence, which is vital when applying similarity metrics like correlations and distance metrics. Lorrain and White (1971) defined structural equivalence as the mathematical property of nodes in a network having identical links to and from all other nodes in the network.[9] An essential property of structural equivalence is that nodes in a graph, or actors in a network, have identical links to and from identical nodes. Consequently, nodes that are structurally equivalent can be substituted without any information loss because their links are equivalent. However, equivalence does not immediately imply that the networks are complete. It indicates that the rows and columns in the adjacency matrix for structurally equivalent nodes are identical. It is noteworthy that structural equivalence is easy to detect for dichotomous relations but almost impossible to measure for weighted graphs.

Structural equivalence applies to both directed and undirected graphs. The inclusion of self-edges depends on the definition. Specifically, the definition of self-edges relies on the meaningfulness of self-connections within the context of interconnectedness. In the context of financial markets, self-edges for correlations might be meaningless. However, a financial institution that has issued several instruments leveraging its own capital structure might be deemed meaningful. One example is Lehman Brothers preceding the 2007 to 2008 Global Financial Crisis in 2008.

Applying models of structural equivalence to financial networks requires the following steps, as identified by Wasserman and Faust (1994):

Definition of equivalence for the node properties: which properties must be measured

1. *Definition of proper metric that captures equivalence:* Euclidean, Manhattan distance, or other proper distance metrics
2. *Representation of the equivalence, based on economic reasoning:* assets, factors, industry groups, and sectors, to name a few
3. *Adequacy measurement of the applied metrics:* goodness-of-fit and simulation for robustness

Note that these steps are necessary when applying structural equivalence models but are not limited to them. We refer to these steps in several later chapters in this book. In general, applying models that help to construct portfolio graphs requires these steps.

---

[9] See Wasserman and Faust (1994) for detailed explanation.

Euclidean Distance   The use of Euclidean distance in social networks can be traced back to the work of Burt (1980, 1988). According to Wasserman and Faust (1994), using the Euclidean distance is intuitive and captures structural equivalence between pairwise nodes. The equivalence is zero if the nodes are structurally equivalent and higher if the two nodes are not structurally equivalent. Formally, in a network context, the distance is calculated as the square root of the squared differences between the node attributes, as shown here:

$$d_{ij}^{Euclidean} = \sqrt{\left(i_{1i} - j_{1j}\right)^2 + \left(i_{2i} - j_{2j}\right)^2 + \cdots + \left(i_{qi} - j_{qj}\right)^2} \tag{6.1}$$

The attributes of every asset are vectors with particular realizations (i.e., coordinates) in the form $(y_1,\ldots,y_q)^T$. Note that the attributes can be estimated for any form of assets – sectors, countries, indices, and individual securities.

In a financial context, a crucial question revolves around identifying scoring models that effectively provide node attributes. These attributes can comprise raw data, but more informative solutions are often derived using observed data or analytically with the aid of financial models. Fortunately, financial research has developed numerous such models. For instance, when evaluating equities, Altman's Z-score model, introduced by Altman (1968), is widely used to assess a company's credit risk within a sector. Altman's Z-Score utilizes corporate data, such as liquidity, profitability, leverage, solvency, and activity of a firm as input variables in a regression model, to evaluate the risk of default of a company and to compare the metric to other companies in the same cluster, such as financials or industrials.[10]

The literature provides numerous examples of how distance metrics can be applied using common properties of financial instruments, institutions, and other variables. A notable example is the utilization of distance metrics in the fixed-income space. Heckel et al. (2020) conducted a study measuring the distances between individual bonds within an investment universe. Two risk metrics commonly applied to bonds are the option-adjusted spread (OAS) and the duration-times-spread (DTS). Both metrics are derived using observed market data. By utilizing OAS and DTS, bond managers can assess a bond's riskiness within a particular bond rating or sector bucket.[11]

Another important aspect to consider in distance computations is the integration of all node properties of securities. These properties may include liquidity metrics, such as notional amount outstanding, traded prices and size, rating scores, duration, yields, expected returns, currency notions, and factor premiums. Integrating these variables into distance calculations provides a more comprehensive understanding of the relationships between securities within a network.[12] Analysts can utilize such metrics to assess similarity in risk and apply these metrics to the data to quantify distances between securities.

---

[10]The exact input parameters to the five-factor model suggested by Altman (1968) are: working capital/total assets, retained earnings/total assets, earnings before interest and taxes/total assets, book value/total assets, and the sales/total assets. Altman developed threshold levels for the Z-scores to interpret and compare the scores between firms. See Kazemi, Black, and Chambers (2016).

[11]The OAS is the spread of a bond that is added to the underlying spot curve to estimate the observable bond price. When a bond's spread duration is multiplied by the spread change, the result is the DTS metric. The DTS metric is a good indicator for positive and negative spread effects. Positive DTS values are associated with favorable bond price effects of decreasing spreads, while negative values for the DTS means spread widening, which has a negative price impact. A detailed explanation of OAS and DTS and its role in bond management is provided by Konstantinov, Fabozzi, and Simonian (2023) and de Jong (2022).

[12]See Konstantinov, Fabozzi and Simonian (2023) for a detailed explanation of possible factors and drivers of returns for international bonds.

Consider, for example, three bonds in the same currency (say, the Australian dollar) with the following three attributes: OAS, DTS, and the roll-down returns as a metric for expected return of a bond.[13] Table 6.1 summarizes the data.

We can now compute the pairwise Euclidean distances and construct a matrix containing these distances. The pairwise Euclidean distances represent the differences between the respective dimensions, which can have arbitrarily many features (three in this simple example).

$$d_{AB}^{Euclidean} \sqrt{(-0.44 + 0.04)^2 + (-0.11 + 0.01)^2 + (-0.34 + 0.69)^2} = 0.29 \tag{6.2}$$

$$d_{AC}^{Euclidean} \sqrt{(-0.44 + 0.17)^2 + (-0.11 + 0.03)^2 + (-0.34 - 0.21)^2} = 0.38 \tag{6.3}$$

$$d_{BC}^{Euclidean} \sqrt{(-0.04 + 0.17)^2 + (-0.01 + 0.03)^2 + (-0.69 - 0.21)^2} = 0.82 \tag{6.4}$$

As a result, we measure the structural equivalence as the distance between the ties to and from the nodes. We can utilize the distance coefficients d_{ij} between all pairs of bonds to construct a distance matrix that represents an undirected three-node network. Table 6.2 is the distance matrix that represents the observed distances for these three bonds. Note that the distance matrix is symmetric and represents adjacency matrices for undirected networks, regardless of the nodes (i.e., assets in the network). This approach can be successfully implemented for bonds or other types of asset indices with many individual securities.

Pearson Product-Moment Similarity   The Pearson product-moment correlation coefficient is similar to the Euclidean distance but uses the time series returns and mean returns of the assets that should comprise the network. It has a broad use in social networks, as shown by Wasserman and Faust (1994). It is computed on the rows and columns of the matrix between nodes, which has been introduced by Bonanno et al. (2004) to equity markets and applied to asset networks by Papenbrock and Schwendner (2015).

TABLE 6.1   Simple Return (%) Statistics for Three Bonds.

	Bond A	Bond B	Bond C
DTS	−0.44	−0.04	−0.17
OAS	−0.11	−0.01	−0.03
Roll Down	−0.34	−0.69	0.21

TABLE 6.2   A Distance Matrix for the Three Bonds.

	Bond A	Bond B	Bond C
Bond A	0	0.29	0.38
Bond B	0.29	0	0.82
Bond C	0.38	0.82	0

---

[13]The roll-down return is the expected return of a bond, derived from the underlying yield curve, under the expectation that the yield curve remains relatively constant for a short time period. The roll-down returns are widely used in portfolio management and estimated for individual securities as well as for countries and indices. See more in Konstantinov (2022) and Konstantinov, Fabozzi, and Simonian (2023).

The Pearson product-moment correlation coefficient is measured using the time series of asset returns over a specific time period and is a measure of linear dependence.

$$\rho_{ij} = \frac{\sum r_i r_j - \sum r_i \sum r_j}{\sqrt{\sum r_i^2 - (\sum r_i)^2}\sqrt{\sum r_j^2 - (\sum r_j)^2}} \tag{6.5}$$

where r_i and r_j are the returns of the individual nodes (i.e., assets) i and j, respectively.

Jaccard Distance Following Provost and Fawcett (2013), the Jaccard distance is of particular use in network science because it deals with sets of characteristics in which the existence of a common characteristic is relevant. In this case, the common absence of a characteristic is less important. This distance metrics deal with the union of the attributes i and j $|i \cup j|$ of two objects relative to the intersection of the characteristics of two objects (e.g., assets) $|i \cap j|$. In other words, the Jaccard distance is the ratio of the attributes that each of the nodes share by the two objects. That is,

$$d_{ij}^{Jaccard} = 1 - \frac{|y_i \cap y_j|}{|y_i \cup y_j|} \tag{6.6}$$

The Jaccard distance is also used to compare networks because investigating common links might be more emphasized when investigating the properties of two networks.

Manhattan Distance Manhattan distances is of particular interest in network analysis because it relates to the earth mover's distance – a measure to identify similarities between vectors, sets, and distributions. It identifies the shortest paths in a network using the L1-norm. Specifically, named after the grid layout of Manhattan, it measures the distance between two points in a grid as the absolute value of the differences of their coordinates or returns, as shown here:

$$d_{ij}^{Manhattan} = |r_i - r_j| \tag{6.7}$$

where the variables have been declared previously.

Mahalanobis Distance Another interesting distance metric is the Mahalanobis distance, introduced in Mahalanobis (1936) and used by Kritzman and Li (2010) to identify financial turbulence in risk management.[14] Unlike the previous distance metrics within Euclidean geometry, this is a statistical geometry distance metric. When applied to networks, the Mahalanobis metric measures the distance between any two nodes using their inverse covariance matrix. The lower the distance, the higher the similarity between the nodes.

Mathematically, it considers the inverse of the covariance between the points and is measured as:

$$d_{ij}^{Mahalanobis} \sqrt{(r_i - r_j)' \Sigma^{-1}(r_i - r_j)} \tag{6.8}$$

where Σ^{-1} is the inverse covariance matrix of historical returns between r_i and r_j.

---

[14]Chow et al. (1999) introduced the Mahalanobis distance to measure turbulence of returns. That is, asset returns exhibit uncharacteristic patterns in times of heightened financial risk and deviate significantly from their long-term historical patterns. The larger the deviation, the larger is the Mahalanobis distance between asset points.

Wasserstein Distance   In the previous section, we discussed the simplicial complex, which determines a structure in a point cloud such as asset returns. It is time to consider the mechanism that sets points to be connected or the appropriate metric. The Wasserstein distance is one of the most compelling distance metrics because it differs substantially from the other distance metrics. It finds its application in transport systems, where the optimal traveling routes must be estimated between two objects. The Wasserstein distance measures the "mass distance" between two objects and is often used to compute the probability distributions of two variables.[15]

Notably, the Wasserstein distance is suitable for comparing the distribution of positive definite matrices, making it ideal for comparing networks, as we shall see in Chapter 9. The larger the Wasserstein distance, the more dissimilar the networks might be. In this context, we focus on the Wasserstein distance and its application in network construction.

For univariate time series data with normal distributions, the first moment of the statistical distribution can be used as a mass point. Using the Euclidean space as a distance function, the 2-Wasserstein metric W_2 can be computed using the squared distance of means of the two variables as follows:

$$W_2(\mu_i, \mu_j)^2 = \left\| \mu_i - \mu_j \right\|_2^2 \tag{6.9}$$

where μ_i and μ_j are the expected values (i.e., means) of node i and node j. The application of the L1-norm to the Wasserstein distance is commonly referred to as the "earth mover's distance."

The code for computing the Wasserstein distance for the asset and factor network is provided in Box 6.1. The generated network is a weighted network, with edge distances used as weights. To avoid self-edges, the main diagonal is set to zero. The width of the edges corresponds to the edge weight; the shorter the distances between the nodes, the larger the weights. Categorization in the network is based on the asset and factor affiliation of the variables. The network is an undirected network because the pairwise distances between node i and node j are equal. Both degree and eigencentrality metrics are computed. The node size in the plot represents the degree centrality score: the larger the score, the larger the node size. Interestingly, the momentum (MOM) factor serves as a bridge, connecting two major components in the network with its weighted edges.

The asset and factor network using the code in Box 6.2 is plotted in Figure 6.4.

BOX 6.2:   THE WASSERSTEIN NORM DISTANCE ASSET AND FACTOR NETWORK.

```
returns<-AssetsFactors
mtx_undir_wd<-matrix(nrow=ncol(AssetsFactors),ncol=ncol(AssetsFactors))
for(i in 1:ncol(returns)) {
    for(j in 1:ncol(returns)) {
        mtx_undir_wd[i,j]=wasserstein1d(returns[,i], returns[,j], p=2)

    }
}
```

(Continued)

---

[15] See Rachev (1991), Rachev and Rüschendorf (1998), and Bhatia et al. (2019) for more details on the Wasserstein distance. We discuss the p-th Wasserstein distance in Chapter 12. Nevertheless, we use in this section, the second order of the Wasserstein distance denoted as 2-Wasserstein distance order. See Aktas et al. (2019).

(*Continued*)

```
netz_undir_wd=as.matrix(abs(mtx_undir_wd))
netz_undir_wd=ifelse(netz_undir_wd[,]<mean(mtx_undir_wd),netz_undir_wd,0)
diag(netz_undir_wd)<-0
colnames(netz_undir_wd)<-colnames(AssetsFactors)
print(netz_undir_wd)
netz_undir_wd<-graph_from_adjacency_matrix(netz_undir_wd, weighted=TRUE)

hist(degree_distribution(netz_undir_wd))
E(netz_undir_wd)$arrow.size<-1

#DegreeCentrality
barplot(sort(degree(netz_undir_wd), decreasing=TRUE), lwd=0.5,
cex.names=0.7,cex.axis=0.7,las=2)

#Centrality
barplot(sort(eigen_centrality(netz_undir_wd)$vector, decreasing=TRUE), lwd=0.5,
cex.names=0.7,cex.axis=0.7,las=2)
ecs<-as.matrix(eigen_centrality(netz_undir_wd)$vector)


netz_undir_wd<-set.vertex.attribute(netz_undir_wd, "category", value=c("F", "F", "F", "F",
"F", "F", "A", "A", "A", "A", "A", "A", "A", "A", "A", "A", "A", "A", "A", "A", "A", "A",
"F", "F", "F", "F", "F", "F", "F", "F", "F"))

V(netz_undir_wd)$color <- V(netz_undir_wd)$category
V(netz_undir_wd)$color <- gsub("F","white",V(netz_undir_wd)$color)
V(netz_undir_wd)$color <- gsub("A","grey85",V(netz_undir_wd)$color)

V(netz_undir_wd)$shape <- V(netz_undir_wd)$category
V(netz_undir_wd)$shape <- gsub("F","circle",V(netz_undir_wd)$shape)
V(netz_undir_wd)$shape <- gsub("A","square",V(netz_undir_wd)$shape)
E(netz_undir_wd)$arrow.size<-0
plot(netz_undir_wd, vertex.size=sqrt(degree(netz_undir_wd))*3, vertex.label.cex=0.4,
layout=layout_with_fr, edge.width=E(netz_undir_wd)$weight*100)
```

ASSOCIATION MODELS

There are two types of association models for building portfolio networks that fall within the group of association models. These are correlation-based and regression-based models.

Correlation-Based Models

Perhaps the most widely used networks in finance are correlation networks, which represent a complete graph. A suitable method for association is necessary to construct a network based on observational data. Note that association networks are not affiliation networks because the nodes are not necessarily affiliated. That is, the edges between the nodes do not follow a strict contractual or causal relationship.

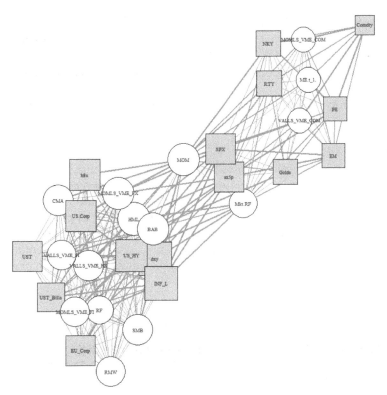

FIGURE 6.4 A Wasserstein Distance L2-Norm Asset and Factor-Weighted Network.

Pairwise correlation coefficients represent associations between the nodes. Under correlation-based association criteria, the interaction between nodes is modeled using different types of statistical tests. Many tests can be applied to measure association, such tests form the backbone of financial models.

Correlation coefficients are fundamental in financial modeling and portfolio theory. They are intuitive and informative, serving as indicators for association. Because correlations are nondirectional metrics of pairwise association, many financial networks are built using correlation coefficients. Next, we discuss three examples of correlation-based networks that represent undirected networks.

Correlation (Complete) Networks   In correlation networks used in portfolio management, the similarity or association between nodes is determined by the Pearson correlations represented in the entries of the covariance matrix $\Sigma = \{\sigma_{ij}\}$, which are based on the time series returns of the assets in a portfolio. The correlation coefficient is defined as the relationship between the pairwise variances of the asset returns:

$$\rho_{ij} = \frac{\sigma_{ij}}{\sqrt{\sigma_{ii}\sigma_{jj}}} \tag{6.10}$$

where σ_{ij} is the covariance between the returns of node i and node j, σ_{ii} is the variance of node i, and σ_{jj} is the variance of node j.

The statistical test for association between the assets (i.e., nodes) in a network based on the correlation coefficient implies that we test the H_0: $\rho_{ij} = 0$ against the H_A: $\rho_{ij} \neq 0$. A natural consequence of using the correlation coefficient to measure association is that it is nonzero. We evaluate this statistical association using an appropriate test statistic. Box 6.3 provides the code for the correlation (completed) asset and factor network.

The classical correlation network using the Prim's distance metric applied by Onnela et al. (2003) is drawn in Figure 6.5.

Correlation Distance Metrics Financial literature employs metrics to directly estimate associations based on correlation coefficients. A critical notion stressed by López de Prado (2023) and others is that correlation does not imply causation. To construct correlation networks, correlation coefficients must be transformed into distance metrics. Various distance types can convert correlations into network distances.

The process of selecting an appropriate method is often described as choosing a kernel. Phoa (2013) and Kolaczyk and Csardi (2020) emphasize that a kernel is a function necessary for generating similarity matrices. These matrices are symmetric and contain the similarity metrics between nodes, essentially modeling the edges of a graph. In the following sections, we demonstrate how to build practical networks using time series data and models that serve as kernels.

BOX 6.3:   A CORRELATION (COMPLETED) ASSET AND FACTOR NETWORK.

```
#Undirected Completed Network with Volatility as Compromise
set.seed(321)
returns<-AssetsFactors
mtx_cor<-data.frame()
mtx_cor<-matrix(nrow=ncol(AssetsFactors),ncol=ncol(AssetsFactors))
mtx_cor<-as.matrix(mtx_cor)
matrize_cor=sqrt(2*(1-cor(returns)))
matrize_cor=abs(matrize_cor)
diag(matrize_cor)<-0
colnames(matrize_cor)<-colnames(AssetsFactors)
print(matrize_cor)
netz_cor<-as.matrix(matrize_cor)
netz_cor<-graph_from_adjacency_matrix(netz_cor, weighted=TRUE)
hist(degree_distribution(netz_cor))
E(netz_cor)$arrow.size<-0


netz_cor<-set.vertex.attribute(netz_cor, "category", value=c("F", "F", "F", "F", "F", "F",
"A", "A", "A", "A", "A", "A", "A", "A", "A", "A", "A", "A", "A", "A", "A", "F", "F",
"F", "F", "F", "F", "F", "F", "F"))

V(netz_cor)$color <- V(netz_cor)$category
V(netz_cor)$color <- gsub("F","white",V(netz_cor)$color)
V(netz_cor)$color <- gsub("A","grey85",V(netz_cor)$color)

V(netz_cor)$shape <- V(netz_cor)$category
V(netz_cor)$shape <- gsub("F","circle",V(netz_cor)$shape)
V(netz_cor)$shape <- gsub("A","square",V(netz_cor)$shape)
plot(netz_cor, layout=layout_with_kk, vertex.size=15, edge.arrow.size=.1,
edge.color="grey85",vertex.label.cex=.6)
```

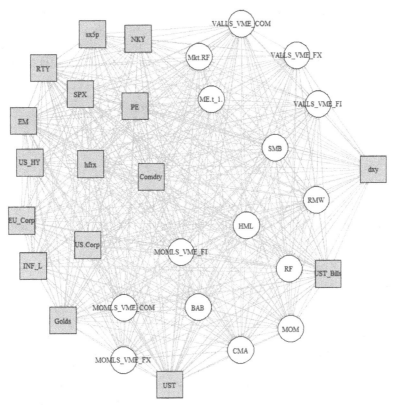

FIGURE 6.5 A Completed Asset and Factor Network.

Transforming correlations into distance metrics, as discussed by Prim (1957) and applied by Mantegna (1999) and Onnela et al. (2003), is essential for converting simple correlations into a graph represented by an adjacency matrix. Perhaps the most widely used is the Mantegna distance metric (Mantegna, 1999):

$$d_{ij}^{Mantegna} = \sqrt{2(1 - \rho_{ij})}, \; with \; i \neq j \qquad (6.11)$$

where the distance metrics d_{ij} enable for adjusting the pairwise correlation coefficients ρ_{ij}.

Applying equation (6.10) to a financial network results in a complete graph, with zeros along the main diagonal. Off-diagonal elements represent the pairwise correlation coefficients. Another correlation distance metric used in financial research on portfolio management is the correlation kernel, utilized by Phoa (2013) for equities and by Konstantinov (2022a) for emerging market bond portfolios. This kernel ensures that all distances are nonnegative:

$$k_{ij} = 1 + \rho_{ij} \qquad (6.12)$$

Another alternative for a correlation kernel that might be used is the goodness-of-fit metric, denoted by R^2, of a linear least-squares regression between the returns of asset i and j. The square root of this measure is the correlation coefficient:

$$\rho_{ij} = \sqrt{R^2} \qquad (6.13)$$

A significant limitation of using correlation coefficients is their tendency to produce complete networks with an edge density close to 1. Researchers need to recognize that actual networks typically exhibit much lower-edge densities. Once the distance metric and kernel function are defined and applied to the time series data, the resulting values populate the $n \times n$ distance matrix $D(n,n)$, which is straightforward to interpret. That is,

$$D_{ij}^{l} = \begin{pmatrix} d_{11}^{g} & d_{12}^{g} & \cdots & d_{1j}^{g} \\ d_{21}^{g} & d_{22}^{g} & \cdots & d_{2j}^{g} \\ \vdots & \vdots & \ddots & \vdots \\ d_{i1}^{g} & d_{i2}^{g} & \cdots & d_{ij}^{g} \end{pmatrix} \tag{6.14}$$

where D_{ij}^{g} is the distance matrix computed using a predefined kernel function for a geodesic distance d_{ij}^{g} defined earlier (e.g., Mahalanobis, Manhattan, Jacquard, or Euclidean). Note that the distance matrix $D(n, n)$ is a square, symmetric matrix that gauges the node distances and is directly related to the size of the network.[16]

Correlation Test Networks   Correlation networks represent undirected graphs. However, using direct correlation coefficients and estimating the adjacency matrix for a complete graph can be misleading for several reasons.

First, the constructed network is complete, which may not be realistic, as it implies that all nodes are highly connected. Second, the pairwise correlation coefficients may be biased by the influence or association of a third node. Third, an adjacency matrix comprising only 1s and 0s would be more informative than one where the main diagonal is zero, but all other elements are nonzero. To construct an indirect correlation network, we might use the p-values of the pairwise correlations, assigning 1 if the p-value is significant and 0 if the correlation is not significant. This approach reduces the possibility of false discovery rates associated with multiple testing. Finally, correlation networks are vulnerable to multiple testing and false discovery rates, necessitating adjustment of the p-values.[17]

Relying solely on the correlation coefficient to assign edges in a financial network can lead to significant overfitting issues. This occurs because real networks typically have far fewer edges than what is suggested by simple correlation analysis. Newman (2010) and Barabási (2016) have demonstrated that real networks are typically sparse. To mitigate this problem, it's crucial to apply the FDR, which corrects for the multiple testing problem arising from the large number of potential edges, quantified as $n(n-1)/2$, in a network.

One advantage of correlation test networks is that adjusting for p-values enables for a sparser adjacency matrix, resulting in more realistic networks. Box 6.4 provides the code used to create a correlation test network that includes both assets and factors, while Figure 6.6 illustrates the resulting network. A powerful, but less applied metric in finance, is the Fisher transformation, which provides a variance-stabilizing transformation of the correlation coefficients (see Kolaczyk and Csardi [2020]) as given by:

$$z_{ij} = \frac{1}{2} log \left[\frac{1 + \rho_{ij}}{1 - \rho_{ij}} \right] \tag{6.15}$$

---

[16]A graph is defined as $G(n,m)$ or $G(V,E)$, where n (V) is the number of nodes and m (E) is the number of edges.
[17]See Harvey and Liu (2014).

where ρ_{ij} is the pairwise correlation coefficient between asset i and j. Applying p-value adjustment to the correlation coefficients for multiple testing might reduce the adjacency matrix, and thus, the network from a complete one to a less sparse network. To show the differences between correlation tests and correlation-based networks with the Fisher transformation, we compute two undirected networks.

Box 6.5 includes the code for constructing an undirected correlation-test network, and the resulting network is displayed in Figure 6.7.

BOX 6.4: AN UNDIRECTED CORRELATION-BASED FISHER TRANSFORMATION ASSET AND FACTOR NETWORK.

```
#Undirected Correlation Network with Fischer Transformation
set.seed(3211)
returns<-AssetsFactors
mtx_corf<-data.frame()
mtx_corf<-matrix(nrow=ncol(AssetsFactors),ncol=ncol(AssetsFactors))
mtx_corf<-as.matrix(mtx_corf)
mat_corf=0.5*log((1+cor(returns))/(1-cor(returns)))
mat_corf=abs(mat_corf)
p.adjusted=0.05
mat_corf<-ifelse(mat_corf[,]<p.adjusted,1,0)
diag(mat_corf)<-0
colnames(mat_corf)<-colnames(AssetsFactors)
print(mat_corf)
netz_corf<-as.matrix(mat_corf)
netz_corf<-graph_from_adjacency_matrix(netz_corf, weighted=TRUE)
hist(degree_distribution(netz_corf))
E(netz_corf)$arrow.size<-1

#Degree
barplot(sort(degree(netz_corf), decreasing=TRUE), lwd=0.5,
cex.names=0.7,cex.axis=0.7,las=2)

#Centrality
barplot(sort(eigen_centrality(netz_corf)$vector, decreasing=TRUE), lwd=0.5,
cex.names=0.7,cex.axis=0.7,las=2)
ecs_corf<-as.matrix(eigen_centrality(netz_corf)$vector)

netz_corf<-set.vertex.attribute(netz_corf, "category", value=c("F", "F", "F", "F", "F",
"F", "A", "A", "A", "A", "A", "A", "A", "A", "A", "A", "A", "A", "A", "A", "A", "A", "F",
"F", "F", "F", "F", "F", "F", "F", "F"))

V(netz_corf)$color <- V(netz_corf)$category
V(netz_corf)$color <- gsub("F","orange",V(netz_corf)$color)
V(netz_corf)$color <- gsub("A","lightblue",V(netz_corf)$color)

V(netz_corf)$shape <- V(netz_corf)$category
V(netz_corf)$shape <- gsub("F","circle",V(netz_corf)$shape)
V(netz_corf)$shape <- gsub("A","square",V(netz_corf)$shape)

plot(netz_corf, layout=layout_with_kk, vertex.size=15, edge.arrow.size=.1,
edge.color="grey85",vertex.label.cex=.6)
```

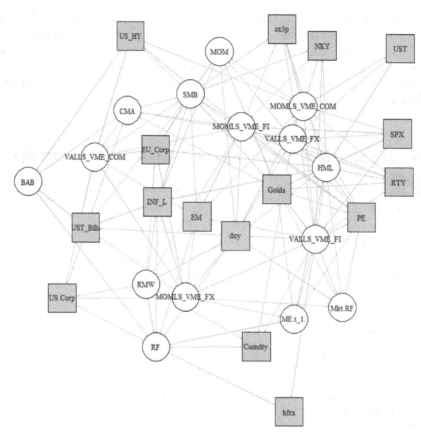

FIGURE 6.6   An Undirected Correlation-Based Fischer Transformation Asset and Factor Network.

BOX 6.5:   AN UNDIRECTED CORRELATION TEST ASSET AND FACTOR NETWORK.

```
#Undirected Cor-Test Network with Volatility as Compromise and Bonferroni-Adjustment

returns<-AssetsFactors
mtx_undir<-data.frame()
mtx_undir<-matrix(nrow=ncol(AssetsFactors),ncol=ncol(AssetsFactors))
for(i in 1:ncol(returns)) {
    for(j in 1:ncol(returns)) {
        mtx_undir[i,j]=cor.test(returns[,i],returns[,j])$p.value
        matrize<-as.matrix(mtx_undir)
        p.t.adj=0.05/6
        matrize<-ifelse(matrize[,]<p.t.adj,1,0)
        diag(matrize)<-0
    }
}
colnames(matrize)<-colnames(AssetsFactors)
print(matrize)
netz_undir<-as.matrix(matrize)
```

```
netz_undir<-graph_from_adjacency_matrix(netz_undir, weighted=TRUE)
E(netz_undir)$arrow.size<-1

hist(degree_distribution(netz_undir))


#DegreeCentrality
barplot(sort(degree(netz_undir), decreasing=TRUE), lwd=0.5,
cex.names=0.7,cex.axis=0.7,las=2)

#Centrality
barplot(sort(eigen_centrality(netz_undir)$vector, decreasing=TRUE), lwd=0.5,
cex.names=0.7,cex.axis=0.7,las=2)
ecs_undir<-as.matrix(eigen_centrality(netz_undir)$vector)

netz_undir<-set.vertex.attribute(netz_undir, "category", value=c("F", "F", "F", "F", "F",
"F", "A", "A", "A", "A", "A", "A", "A", "A", "A", "A", "A", "A", "A", "A", "A", "A", "F",
"F", "F", "F", "F", "F", "F", "F", "F"))

V(netz_undir)$color <- V(netz_undir)$category
V(netz_undir)$color <- gsub("F","white",V(netz_undir)$color)
V(netz_undir)$color <- gsub("A","grey85",V(netz_undir)$color)

V(netz_undir)$shape <- V(netz_undir)$category
V(netz_undir)$shape <- gsub("F","circle",V(netz_undir)$shape)
V(netz_undir)$shape <- gsub("A","square",V(netz_undir)$shape)
plot(netz_undir, layout=layout_with_kk, vertex.size=15, edge.arrow.size=.1,
edge.color="grey85",vertex.label.cex=.6)
```

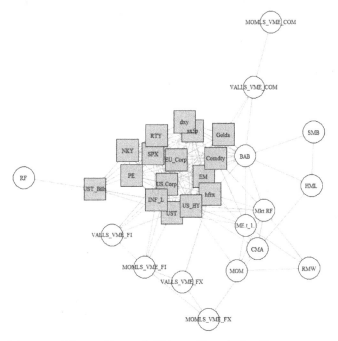

FIGURE 6.7   An Undirected Asset and Factor Network Using a Correlation Test.

Partial Correlation Networks To mitigate the strong associations implied by correlation coefficients, partial correlations may offer a more meaningful approach. This is because pairwise correlations could be high due to one-off events or the influence of a third variable or asset.[18] In other words, correlation coefficients can be biased or influenced by the indirect impact of associations with other assets. Partial correlations, on the other hand, measure the immediate impact of node associations more directly. They account for the pairwise correlations between any two assets while adjusting for the effects of other assets. This adjustment is measured as follows:

$$\rho_{ij|s} = \frac{\rho_{ij} - \rho_{is}\rho_{is}}{\sqrt{\left(1 - \rho_{is}^2\right)\left(1 - \rho_{js}^2\right)}} \tag{6.16}$$

where ρ_{ij} is the correlation coefficient between the returns of node i and node j, ρ_{is} is the correlation coefficient of node i to a third node s, and ρ_{js} is the correlation coefficient of node j to a third node s.

The statistical test for association between all assets (i.e., nodes) in a network, which is based on the partial correlation coefficient, implies that we test the $H_0: \rho_{ij|s} = 0$ against the $H_A: \rho_{ij|s} \neq 0$. Again, we test the statistical association using appropriate test statistic given by:

$$z_{ij|s} = \frac{1}{2}log\left[\frac{1 + \rho_{ij|s}}{1 - \rho_{ij|s}}\right] \tag{6.17}$$

We provide the code for a partial-correlation network in Box 6.6 and the network in Figure 6.8.

BOX 6.6:   A PARTIAL-CORRELATION ASSET AND FACTOR NETWORK.

```
set.seed(3211)
returns<-AssetsFactors
mtx_pcor<-data.frame()
mtx_pcor<-matrix(nrow=ncol(AssetsFactors),ncol=ncol(AssetsFactors))
mtx_pcor<-as.matrix(mtx_pcor)
mat_pcor=0.5*log((1+pcor(returns)$estimate)/(1-pcor(returns)$estimate))
mat_pcor=abs(mat_pcor)
p.t.adj=0.05
mat_pcor<-ifelse(mat_pcor[,]<p.t.adj,1,0)
diag(mat_pcor)<-0
colnames(mat_pcor)<-colnames(AssetsFactors)
print(mat_pcor)
netz_pcor<-as.matrix(mat_pcor)
netz_pcor<-graph_from_adjacency_matrix(netz_pcor, weighted=TRUE)
hist(degree_distribution(netz_pcor))
E(netz_pcor)$arrow.size<-1
#Centrality
```

---

[18]We discuss this issue in detail in the next section when we analyze regression-based models.

```
barplot(sort(degree(netz_pcor), decreasing=TRUE), lwd=0.5,
cex.names=0.7,cex.axis=0.7,las=2)
#Centrality
barplot(sort(eigen_centrality(netz_pcor)$vector, decreasing=TRUE), lwd=0.5,
cex.names=0.7,cex.axis=0.7,las=2)
ecs_pcor<-as.matrix(eigen_centrality(netz_pcor)$vector)
netz_pcor<-set.vertex.attribute(netz_pcor, "category", value=c("F", "F", "F", "F", "F",
"F", "A", "A", "A", "A", "A", "A", "A", "A", "A", "A", "A", "A", "A", "A", "A", "A", "F",
"F", "F", "F", "F", "F", "F", "F", "F"))
V(netz_pcor)$color <- V(netz_pcor)$category
V(netz_pcor)$color <- gsub("F","orange",V(netz_pcor)$color)
V(netz_pcor)$color <- gsub("A","lightblue",V(netz_pcor)$color)

V(netz_pcor)$shape <- V(netz_pcor)$category
V(netz_pcor)$shape <- gsub("F","circle",V(netz_pcor)$shape)
V(netz_pcor)$shape <- gsub("A","square",V(netz_pcor)$shape)
plot(netz_pcor, layout=layout_with_fr, vertex.size=15, edge.arrow.size=.1,
edge.color="grey85",vertex.label.cex=.6)
```

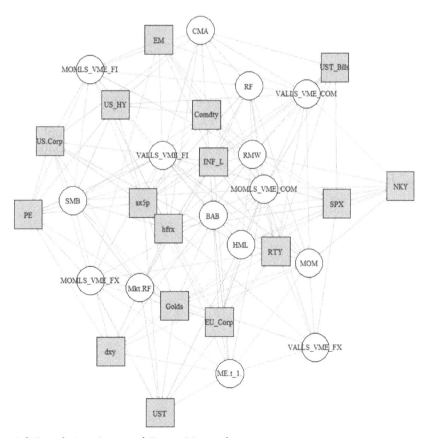

FIGURE 6.8 A Partial Correlation Asset and Factor Network.

KEY TAKEAWAYS

- Both portfolio and benchmark networks can be conceptualized as graphs, where the components are interconnected actors or nodes, rather than isolated variables.
- Interconnectedness, fundamental to network theory, contrasts with the notion of orthogonality or the lack of connections often emphasized in the financial literature.
- A key challenge in constructing portfolio networks is modeling the edges, which connect the known nodes but might themselves be unobservable.
- In network science, the term "interference" refers to the influence and effect that one node exerts on others, highlighting the notion of relationships or interconnectedness within the network.
- Inference involves drawing conclusions, making predictions, and forming projections based on observable data and empirical evidence.
- Statistical and observable data help classify and estimate values using tests and hypotheses.
- Distance measures are applied to model edges in a network. Depending on the economic and statistical procedure, several distance metrics might be applied, with the Wasserstein distance and the correlation metric suggested by Prim among the most powerful.
- In the context of data science and machine learning, inference refers to the process of making predictions based on historical data sets. Link prediction models and similar techniques are commonly used in both disciplines. The central challenge in network modeling involves using link prediction models, such as correlation tests or similarity and distance metrics, to effectively model the connections between nodes.
- Link prediction models are susceptible to false discovery rates and require specialized handling.
- Despite the thematic categorizations applied to link-prediction models, most tests and models share more similarities than differences.
- The models for analyzing interference and inference in asset and factor networks can be grouped into link prediction, association, and statistical models.
- Although link prediction and association models leverage the extensive application of association models in finance, which offer an intuitive method for modeling edges, association models, which are more sophisticated, require a solid economic foundation to justify their use.
- Statistical models are the most sophisticated, emphasizing probabilistic modeling of relationships.

## CHAPTER 7

Foundations for Building Portfolio Networks – Statistical and Econometric Models

Contents

In this chapter, we describe the application of statistical and econometric models in analyzing asset networks. While nodes or vertices in networks are typically known and finite, edges are often not directly observable in financial markets. Statistical and econometric models play a crucial role in modeling these edges. In finance, these models utilize time series data, with regression models – both linear and nonlinear – being among the most widely applied. These models may consist of multifactor or single-factor structures, incorporating one or multiple explanatory variables, and possibly interaction terms governing cross-relationships between these variables. They involve both independent and dependent variables where they seek to clarify the dependent variable with the aid of other variables known as regressors. These models are inherently statistical, as statistical reasoning is essential for exploring data structures. Moreover, they are economic, as they are rooted in relationships among variables – both dependent and independent. Essentially, these models operate on the premise that the interplay observed in graph theory exists within markets and can be captured using statistical and econometric methodologies. Consequently, they facilitate the construction of networks.

Our focus in this chapter is on networks built using time series data. However, time series data used in statistical and econometric network modeling and the resulting networks are susceptible to estimation risks, such as overfitting, underfitting, heteroscedasticity, and multicollinearity, to name a few. Recent developments in the field of financial data science have introduced new trends and tools for handling data in portfolio management. Many of the techniques developed focus on addressing critical issues, such as overfitting, multicollinearity of the explanatory variables, heteroscedasticity of the variance of the error terms, outliers in data, and serial correlation of residuals.[1]

---

[1] For the most severe problems of regression and statistical models, see James et al. (2013).

The chapter's primary themes are network construction used in portfolio allocation models, based on different types of regression models that we describe as statistical and econometric models. Many of these models are used in the modern world of statistical thinking or machine learning (James et al., 2013). Understandably, the chapter's central focus is the description of various methods and models for utilizing financial data in statistical and economic frameworks for network construction. These models are inherently statistical, with their economic significance stemming from econometrics. In contrast to the previous chapter that delved into link prediction models, the data utilized in statistical and econometric models primarily consist of time series data. The statistical and econometric network models can be applied to portfolio selection using individual securities, such as bonds, stocks, and derivatives. We explore association and causal models for building asset networks using the asset and factor dataset applied by Konstantinov et al. (2020).

PORTFOLIO NETWORK TOPOLOGY INTERFERENCE AND INFERENCE WITH STATISTICAL AND ECONOMETRIC MODELS

As in the previous chapter where we discussed portfolio network interference and inference, it is necessary to discuss these topics in the context of statistical and econometric models. The prevailing intuition behind statistical and econometric models assumes noninterference between dependent and independent variables, or financial assets and factors in our case. This underscores the basic assumption of orthogonality or the absence of relationships in markets. In contrast, graph theory posits that relationships do exist, and the primary objective of statistical and econometric approaches is to model this interplay. The process of defining an appropriate method for modeling interference is referred to as employing a regression model. Specifically, interference is modeled as a function between one or more independent variables and a dependent variable, assessing the statistical significance of the estimated regression coefficients. These coefficients are then utilized to populate the entries of the adjacency matrix, representing relationships. A regression equation's explanatory variables (i.e., independent variables) may include lagged variables or independent regressors, each with an economic function. In essence, this process involves modeling the links in a graph. In the following sections, we demonstrate how to build practical networks using time series data and different regression models, and statistical tests that use regression models as interference.

The regression-based models applied in graph theory and financial networks aim to bridge the gap between statistically rigorous theory and economic reasoning. In this context, regression models used in financial economics serve as a valuable tool for assessing the relationships between economic variables. In networks, their role is to offer structure to the data and relationships, with economic rationale regarding explanatory variables in regression models taking center stage while statistical modeling provides support. However, applying regression models may have some caveats. On the one hand, they serve an associational role, while on the other hand, when using regression models in finance, the objective is often to represent possible causal relationships. Overfitting and economic reasoning are always challenges. For this reason, several models are introduced to help model interference. The aim of regression models is to provide the entries for the adjacency matrix.

In a network context, the dependent and independent variables function as nodes within the network. Regression models establish at least an association between two variables – whether assets, factors, or other financial instruments – acting as nodes in a graph, as evidenced in the works of Barigozzi and Brownlees (2018). Essentially, using regression models to estimate the relationship between nodes involves assuming that the dependent variable in the model represents a set (such as the US High Yield Index), while the independent variable represents another node or financial asset (such as the S&P 500 Index). Similarly, individual stocks, like the time series of Coca-Cola (node i) and the time series of 3M (node j), can also be used. Therefore, the results of the regression models are used to populate the elements of the adjacency matrix, mapping the pairwise links between the nodes.

The use of linear models in finance in a network context can be traced back to the work of Stevens (1998), who demonstrated that the inverse of the covariance matrix can be used to derive hedging risk information. The network information is directly related to the inverse of the covariance matrix. Regression models serve as tools for illustrating the relationship between independent and dependent variables. These variables encompass economic and financial time series or quantitative variables. They may also include qualitative variables, such as products, scores, or any categorical or binary variables, that take values of 1 or 0. In this sense, regression models are association models. While statistical inference focuses on explaining the relationship between the dependent and independent variables, prediction aims to find a model that efficiently predicts the dependent variable. The prediction feature of regression models can be further applied to networks when predicting possible associations between nodes. Regression models in networks satisfy the idea of both statistical inference and interference, with prediction being of less concern.

Finally, regression models and hypothesis testing for the regression model's estimated coefficients are prone to false discovery rates. That is, based on multiple testing, the selection of adequate p-values is highly relevant in determining the entries for the adjacency matrix. The Bonferroni p-value adjustment and/or the Benjamini–Hochberg adjustment are essential for mitigating overfitting in regression models and effectively building sparse networks.[2]

REGRESSION-BASED MODELS

Various types of regression functions are utilized in statistical and economic models to construct networks. These can range from simple models employing one explanatory and one dependent variable, to more complex ones where multiple independent variables explain the dependent variable. Additionally, some models utilize lagged time series of the same regressors to capture relationships. A straightforward analogy for such models is factor investing. The modern development of statistical thinking and the rise of factor investing can be interpreted as explaining the variance of returns of a variable, say an asset using other independent factors. The intuition behind using regression models is simple and intuitive. The models might be linear or nonlinear and the aim is to explain the relationship.

Here we explain some of the most-used regression models for network interference, which include linear models incorporating additional regressors or explanatory variables, among others. Subsequently, we introduce several intuitive and widely employed regression models. Towards the end of this section, we delve into more intricate statistical and econometric models tailored for network construction.

Linear Models with Confounders

A linear model captures the relationship between the independent variables and dependent variable linearly. Essentially, it assumes a linear relationship between the dependent and independent variables. Applying linear models to network construction provides a straightforward approach to modeling the links between nodes, extending the use of linear models originally proposed for measuring social interaction by Wasserman and Faust (1994), which was further developed by Bramoulle et al. (2009), as well as Lee, Lin, and Lin (2010).

Crucially, nodes can symbolize various financial assets within financial networks – a topic extensively explored in network literature. The fundamental idea driving the use of regression models for interactions is to capitalize on the significance of the regression coefficients (i.e., independent variables) as indicators of

---

[2] See Harvey and Liu (2014, 2015) and Kolaczyk and Csardi (2020) for more information on p-value hacking and the p-value correction for false discovery rates using the Bonferroni and the Benjamini–Hochberg adjustments.

the association with the dependent variable.[3] Essentially, the goal is to analyze which variables are linked to the dependent variable and the nature of their relationship. The significance of the regression parameters plays a crucial role in determining the entries of the adjacency matrix. It's essential to grasp this intuition thoroughly to effectively interpret the regression analysis results in the context of network construction. We will discuss the regression models in detail in the forthcoming sections.

Suppose we run two regression models for two assets, i and j, against each other. A simple linear model that governs the relationship between two assets (nodes) has the following form:

$$R_i = \alpha_{ij} + \beta_{ij} R_j + \varepsilon_i \qquad (7.1)$$

$$R_j = \alpha_{ji} + \beta_{ji} R_i + \varepsilon_i \qquad (7.2)$$

where R_i is the return of asset i regressed against the returns of asset j $\left(R_j\right)$, α is the intercept of the regression, β_{ij} is the slope coefficient that gauges the association, and ε is a random error term. Similarly, the R_j is the return of asset j regressed against the returns of the asset i $\left(R_i\right)$, and the β_{ji} is the slope coefficient that measures the change of the returns of asset of asset j by a unit change in the returns of asset i.

In the studies that use regression models for statistical graph inference, the use of the intercept is not documented. It needs explanation.

The intuition of the regression model as an inference technique in graph theory can be found in the work of Wasserman and Faust (1994). Whereas β coefficients explain the response of the dependent variable for a change in the independent variable, they represent the tendency of node i to receive ties at node j. The term for this phenomenon is referred to as *popularity*. In other words, this is a node-level dependence. The intercept represents the tendency of node i to send links to node j, which is referred to as *expansiveness*. Clearly, the extent of node i's influence is captured by α_{ij}, while its popularity is indicated by β_{ij}. Likewise, the extent of node j's influence is represented by α_{ji}, and its popularity by β_{ji}. Hence, the relationship between assets can be estimated by assessing the statistical significance of these variables. If the main objective is solely to measure the response, the preferable method is to utilize the beta coefficients of the regression. As the explanatory variables vary, the significance of the coefficients will also differ, resulting in various entries in the adjacency matrix. The result will be a directed network given by

$$a_{ij} = \begin{cases} 1, & \text{if } |t_\beta| > t_{t-(k+1);1-\frac{\alpha}{2}} \\ 0, & \text{otherwise} \end{cases} \qquad (7.3)$$

---

[3] Several important studies have explored broad international asset markets, contributing significantly to our understanding of global financial dynamics. They include: König (2014) who analyzed equity fund managers invested in the DAX index, providing insights into strategies and performance metrics specific to this market segment; Barigozzi and Brownlees (2018) who focused on broader equity markets, employing advanced statistical techniques to analyze market volatility and co-movements; Konstantinov and Rebmann (2019) who provided a detailed study on currency managers, highlighting their risk management strategies and performance in volatile markets, Konstantinov et al. (2020) who discussed the application of linear models across multiple asset classes, examining their effectiveness in asset allocation and risk assessment; Konstantinov and Rusev (2020) who conducted a comprehensive analysis of global bond and equity funds, focusing on their correlations and the impact of global economic events on their performance; Konstantinov and Simonian (2020) who provided an in-depth look at single hedge funds, exploring their investment strategies and market behavior; and Konstantinov (2022) who analyzed hedge fund indices, assessing their predictive power and the implications for portfolio diversification.

where a_{ij} represent the components of the adjacency matrix, assuming a binary value only if asset i is linked to asset j.

The significance of β coefficients is relevant for determining the entries in the adjacency matrix. The rationale for utilizing significant β coefficients, which exhibit a strong positive correlation with centrality scores in the network, has been illustrated by Peralta and Zareei (2016). In essence, it indicates a noteworthy relationship between elevated systematic risk and importance score within the network, as demonstrated by Konstantinov (2022b) in developing a risk hedge fund index. If β measures the systematic risk of an asset and a higher β is associated with greater risk, then a β-weighted network would reflect the risk at a node level. Therefore, we can leverage the magnitude of the β coefficients to construct a weighted adjacency matrix. Once the appropriate model is specified, the statistical significance of the β coefficients is crucial for computing elements in the adjacency matrix. The slope from a regression model indicates systematic risk, reflecting the sensitivity of the dependent variable to a unit change in the independent asset.

Nonlinear Relationships with Linear Models

Using linear models is intuitive, and the results are easy to interpret. However, often the relationship, association, and causation between the dependent and independent variables are nonlinear in nature. For instance, Baitinger and Papenbrock (2017) demonstrated that mutual-based information is nonlinear. They argue that quadratic terms, among other terms, capture this connectedness and suggest that linear models should not be used when the underlying connectedness is nonlinear. Therefore, regression models that include squared terms of the explanatory variables and confounders (i.e., variables that are related to both the independent and dependent variables, as explained later) may be favored when employed for classification and association tasks.

The most-used nonlinear models are polynomial models, which use polynomial functions of the independent variables within the model. The easiest to interpret is a quadratic model, which takes the following form:

$$R_i = \alpha + \beta R_j + \gamma R_j^2 + \varepsilon \tag{7.4}$$

where R_i is the return of asset i regressed against the returns of the asset $j\left(R_j\right)$ and against the squared returns $\left(R_j^2\right)$ of asset j, α is the regression intercept, β is the slope coefficient, and ε is a random error term.

Of course, we can add a confounder variable Z_j into the model, which in certain cases could represent the return of the S&P500 index, the value of the US dollar, or other relevant factors. That is,

$$R_i = \alpha + \beta R_j + \gamma R_j^2 + \varphi R_C + \varepsilon \tag{7.5}$$

where all other variables have been defined earlier.

The code for a directed network using regression models is shown in Box 7.1, and the network is shown in Figure 7.1. In this network, we incorporate squared terms of the independent variables to account for nonlinearity in the regression model using equation (7.4).

BOX 7.1: A REGRESSION-BASED DIRECTED ASSET AND FACTOR NETWORK.

```
returns<-AssetsFactors
mtx_dir<-matrix(nrow=ncol(AssetsFactors),ncol=ncol(AssetsFactors))
for(i in 1:ncol(returns)) {
  for(j in 1:ncol(returns)) {

mtx_dir[i,j]=coef(summary(lm(formula=returns[,i]~returns[,j]+I(returns[,j]^2))))[11]
      netz_dir=as.matrix(abs(mtx_dir))
      #boni<-p.adjust(netz_dir, method="bonferroni")
      #boni.p<-matrix(boni,31,31)
      p.t=0.05/6
      netz_dir=ifelse(netz_dir[,]<p.t,1,0)
      diag(netz_dir)<-0
  }
}
colnames(netz_dir)<-colnames(AssetsFactors)
print(netz_dir)
netz_dir<-as.matrix(netz_dir)
netz_dir<-graph_from_adjacency_matrix(netz_dir, weighted=TRUE)
hist(degree_distribution(netz_dir))
E(netz_dir)$arrow.size<-1

#DegreeCentrality
barplot(sort(degree(netz_dir), decreasing=TRUE), lwd=0.5, cex.names=0.7,
cex.axis=0.7,las=2)

#Centrality
barplot(sort(eigen_centrality(netz_dir)$vector, decreasing=TRUE), lwd=0.5,
cex.names=0.7,cex.axis=0.7,las=2)
ecs<-as.matrix(eigen_centrality(netz_dir)$vector)

#set vertex color and shapes according to the category - asset or factor
netz_dir<-set.vertex.attribute(netz_dir, "category", value=c("F", "F", "F", "F", "F", "F",
"A", "A", "A", "A", "A", "A", "A", "A", "A", "A", "A", "A", "A", "A", "A", "A", "F", "F",
"F", "F", "F", "F", "F", "F", "F"))

V(netz_dir)$color <- V(netz_dir)$category
V(netz_dir)$color <- gsub("F","orange",V(netz_dir)$color)
V(netz_dir)$color <- gsub("A","lightblue",V(netz_dir)$color)

V(netz_dir)$shape <- V(netz_dir)$category
V(netz_dir)$shape <- gsub("F","circle",V(netz_dir)$shape)
V(netz_dir)$shape <- gsub("A","square",V(netz_dir)$shape)
plot(netz_dir, layout=layout_with_kk, vertex.size=15, edge.arrow.size=.3,
edge.color="grey85",vertex.label.cex=.6)
```

Note that the risk of false discovery rate (FDR) increases substantially when conducting multiple tests. Hence, p-value adjustment becomes imperative. While the Bonferroni method is commonly favored, it entails a significant reduction in p-values.[4]

---

[4]See Harvey and Liu (2014) for the application of the Bonferroni and Holms methods when adjusting the p-values for multiple testing.

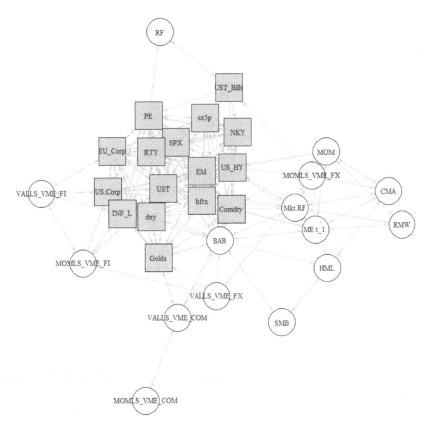

FIGURE 7.1   A Directed Asset and Factor Network.

When using regression models, it is necessary to focus on model specification and accuracy, as they are prone to errors related to both the dependent and independent variables. López de Prado (2018, 2023) has questioned the economic interpretation of these models, highlighting the lack of significant relationships often postulated in regression models.

Frequently, relationships inferred from regression models can be misleading due to the lack of underlying economic relationships, which can result in statistical effects identifying apparent relationships that do not exist. To address the issues of overfitting and false associations between economic and statistical relationships, López de Prado (2023) and Simonian (2023) propose the use of factors known as confounders. Confounders affect the statistical results of a regression model aimed at explaining relationships and causality between variables. Remember, causality forms the backbone of directed networks. Confounders must be correlated with the independent variable and may have a causal relationship with it, but this is unnecessary. They must be causally related to the dependent variable, however.

Formally, the simple regression model is extended by the inclusion of a confounder variable as follows:

$$R_i = \alpha + \beta R_j + \varphi R_C + \varepsilon \qquad (7.6)$$

where R_i is the return of asset i regressed against the returns of the asset j (R_j), R_C is the return of the confounder variable related to the dependent variable, α is the intercept of the regression, β is the slope coefficient, and ε is a random error term.

The selection of a confounder depends on quantitative economic analysis. Supporting this economic choice is the assertion by Leibowitz (2011) that equity exposure exists in every asset. Economic research has revealed that equity exposure is apparent in various other asset classes. For instance, it has been observed in government and corporate bonds (Houveling and van Zundert, 2017), high-yield bonds, and hedge funds (Asness et al., 2001; Asness et al., 2015), among others. Therefore, equity market returns might economically fulfill the role of a confounder. That is,

$$R_i = \alpha + \beta R_j + \varphi R_C + \varepsilon \tag{7.7}$$

where R_i is the return of asset i regressed against the returns of the asset $j\left(R_j\right)$; and R_C is the return of the confounder variable, which is, in this case, the returns of the S&P500 index related to the dependent variable. For the sake of brevity, we only show the general model.

The role of confounders is not limited to equities. Konstantinov and Fabozzi (2021), for example, analyzed global and US bond indices and found that US dollar risk is a major determinant of bond benchmark performance. This intuition holds, as the US dollar predominantly influences global markets, and its volatility, appreciation, or depreciation significantly affects asset portfolios. Hence, the US dollar could serve as a suitable confounder, enabling the construction of a directed network.

The code for generating the directed network using a regression model with the US dollar as a confounder is presented in Box 7.2, and the resulting network is depicted in Figure 7.2.

BOX 7.2: A DIRECTED ASSET AND FACTOR NETWORK USING A REGRESSION MODEL AND THE US DOLLAR AS A CONFOUNDER.

```
#Directed Network with Confounders
returns<-AssetsFactors
mtx_dir_conf<-matrix(nrow=ncol(AssetsFactors),ncol=ncol(AssetsFactors))
for(i in 1:ncol(returns)) {
  for(j in 1:ncol(returns)) {

mtx_dir_conf[i,j]=coef(summary(lm(formula=returns[,i]~returns[,j]+usd[,1])))[11]
netz_dir_conf=as.matrix(abs(mtx_dir_conf))
p.t=0.05/6
netz_dir_conf=ifelse(netz_dir_conf[,]<p.t,1,0)
diag(netz_dir_conf)<-0
  }
}
colnames(netz_dir_conf)<-colnames(AssetsFactors)
print(netz_dir_conf)
netz_dir_conf<-as.matrix(netz_dir_conf)
netz_dir_conf<-graph_from_adjacency_matrix(netz_dir_conf, weighted=TRUE)


netz_dir_conf<-set.vertex.attribute(netz_dir_conf, "category", value=c("F", "F", "F", "F",
"F", "F", "A", "A", "A", "A", "A", "A", "A", "A", "A", "A", "A", "A", "A", "A", "A", "A",
"F", "F", "F", "F", "F", "F", "F", "F", "F"))

V(netz_dir_conf)$color <- V(netz_dir_conf)$category
V(netz_dir_conf)$color <- gsub("F","orange",V(netz_dir_conf)$color)
V(netz_dir_conf)$color <- gsub("A","lightblue",V(netz_dir_conf)$color)
```

```
V(netz_dir_conf)$shape <- V(netz_dir_conf)$category
V(netz_dir_conf)$shape <- gsub("F","circle",V(netz_dir_conf)$shape)
V(netz_dir_conf)$shape <- gsub("A","square",V(netz_dir_conf)$shape) plot(netz_dir_conf,
layout=layout_with_kk, vertex.size=15, edge.arrow.size=.3, edge.color="grey85",vertex.
label.cex=.6)
```

Applying a regression model to asset returns requires several tests and data analyses of the factors and return time series used. Some issues are highly relevant when applying linear models. However, before and after the model is estimated, the following necessary diagnostic tests must be run:[5]

- Nonlinearity in the data
- Correlation of the residual terms
- Heteroscedastic variance of error terms
- Identification of outliers associated with the dependent variable
- High-leverage points associated with unusual values for the independent variables
- Multicollinearity between the independent variable and a confounder

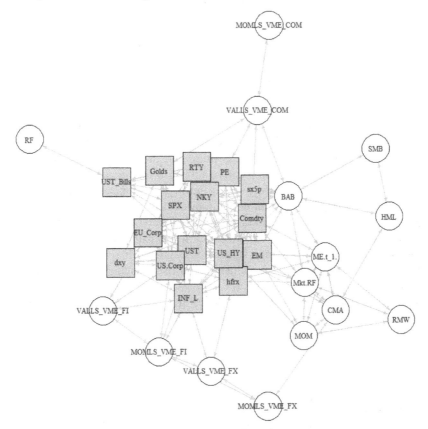

FIGURE 7.2   A Directed Asset and Factor Network with a Confounder.

---

[5]Detailed explanation is provided in James et al. (2013) and Fabozzi and Konstantinov (2022).

Dichotomous Node Relations with Regression Models

We now turn our attention to the regression models but focus on both the regression's intercept and slope coefficients. Using regression models, we can estimate directed multigraphs using an adopted version of the Wasserman and Faust (1994) dichotomous relations model. This model revolves around regression models that employ distinct parameters to distinguish between the effects of receiver and sender relations. Regression models that model social interactions within network structures have been studied by Bramoulle et al. (2009), Lee et al. (2010), König (2014), and Konstantinov and Simonian (2020). These models incorporate a significant advancement in the form of the α_{ji} and β_{ji} parameters. Specifically, α_{ji} quantifies the propensity of a node to *send* information, whereas β_{ji} is used to measure the tendency of a node to *receive* information. The regression models described in equation (7.1), which are applied in various studies, primarily assess the tendency of nodes to receive information. However, in the enhanced model that considers dichotomous relationships, both sender and receiver dynamics are analyzed. This model utilizes operators for both sending and receiving, incorporating coefficients that are statistically and economically significant within a regression framework. Consequently, these enhanced regression models are instrumental in estimating direct networks and delineating explicit relationships between nodes.[6]

As a result, we can use the β_{ij} significant parameter of the regression model to populate the off-diagonal entries in the adjacency matrix, and the intercept α for the diagonal entries of the adjacency matrix. That is,

$$a_{ij} = \begin{cases} 1, & \text{if } |t_{\beta}| > t_{t-(k+1);1-\frac{q}{2}} \\ 0 & Otherwise \\ diag(1) & \text{if } |t_{\alpha}| > t_{t-(k+1);1-\frac{q}{2}} \end{cases} \qquad (7.8)$$

Because beta can be a negative or positive number, the question arises of how to deal with negative weights in an adjacency matrix. Typically, weights in a network are positive numbers (such as money transfers, notional amounts, or the number of individuals). However, according to Newman (2010), negative weights can also make sense. Borgatti et al. (2022) presented the Positive-Negative Index (PN) centrality measure, which deals with both negative and positive entries in the adjacency matrix.

Based on the social concept of friendship versus enmity, or homophile versus homophobe, negative weights in financial networks might represent economic relations, such as net money inflows or outflows, negative risk exposure, or short exposure to assets, among others. In this case, they can manifest as negative or positive beta coefficients. To represent such relationships, Harary (1953) proposed that the network structure be clustered or grouped into structural balance, in which we can represent a network containing the positive weights and a separate cluster built using the negative weights (converted to positive numbers).

Box 7.3 displays the code for generating the dichotomous network with information receivers and senders, and Figure 7.3 visualizes the resulting network.

---

[6]See the studies by Konstantinov and Rebman (2019), Konstantinov and Rusev (2020), Konstantinov and Simonian (2020), Konstantinov et al. (2020), and Konstantinov (2022). To properly estimate such networks, confounders and additional regressors might be used.

BOX 7.3: A DIRECTED ASSET AND FACTOR NETWORK WITH SENDERS AND RECEIVERS OF REGRESSION MODELS.

```
returns<-AssetsFactors
mtx_dir_p<-matrix(nrow=ncol(AssetsFactors),ncol=ncol(AssetsFactors))
mtx_p<-matrix(nrow=ncol(AssetsFactors),ncol=ncol(AssetsFactors))
for(i in 1:ncol(returns)) {
  for(j in 1:ncol(returns)) {

mtx_dir_p[i,j]=coef(summary(lm(formula=returns[,i]~returns[,j]+I(returns[,j]^2))))[8]
    mtx_p[i,j]=coef(summary(lm(formula=returns[,i]~returns[,j]+I(returns[,j]^2))))[7]
    netz_dir_p=as.matrix(abs(mtx_dir_p))
    netz_p=as.matrix(abs(mtx_p))
    p.t=abs(qt(0.05/6,nrow(AssetsFactors)))

    diag(netz_dir_p)=diag(netz_p)
    netz_dir_p=ifelse(netz_dir_p[,]>p.t,1,0)
  }
}
colnames(netz_dir_p)<-colnames(AssetsFactors)
print(netz_dir_p)
netz_dir_p<-as.matrix(netz_dir_p)
netz_dir_p<-graph_from_adjacency_matrix(netz_dir_p, weighted=TRUE)
hist(degree_distribution(netz_dir_p))
E(netz_dir_p)$arrow.size<-1

#DegreeCentrality
barplot(sort(degree(netz_dir_p), decreasing=TRUE), lwd=0.5, cex.names=0.7,
cex.axis=0.7,las=2)

#Centrality
barplot(sort(eigen_centrality(netz_dir_p)$vector, decreasing=TRUE), lwd=0.5,
cex.names=0.7,cex.axis=0.7,las=2)
ecs_p<-as.matrix(eigen_centrality(netz_dir_p)$vector)

netz_dir_p<-set.vertex.attribute(netz_dir_p, "category", value=c("F", "F", "F", "F", "F",
"F", "A", "A", "A", "A", "A", "A", "A", "A", "A", "A", "A", "A", "A", "A", "A", "A", "F",
"F", "F", "F", "F", "F", "F", "F", "F"))

V(netz_dir_p)$color <- V(netz_dir_p)$category
V(netz_dir_p)$color <- gsub("F","orange",V(netz_dir_p)$color)
V(netz_dir_p)$color <- gsub("A","lightblue",V(netz_dir_p)$color)

V(netz_dir_p)$shape <- V(netz_dir_p)$category
V(netz_dir_p)$shape <- gsub("F","circle",V(netz_dir_p)$shape)
V(netz_dir_p)$shape <- gsub("A","square",V(netz_dir_p)$shape)
plot(netz_dir_p, layout=layout_with_fr, vertex.size=15, edge.arrow.size=.1,
edge.color="grey85",vertex.label.cex=.6)
```

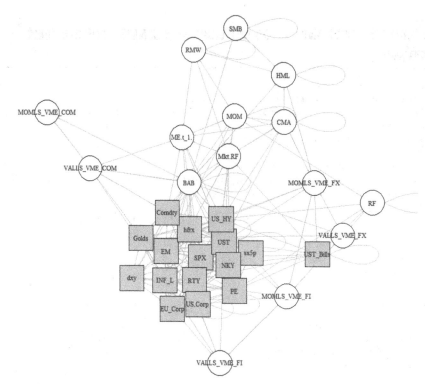

FIGURE 7.3   A Directed Asset and Factor Network with Receiver/Sender Operators.

Gaussian Graph Models

A more efficient approach to association network construction is using the least absolute shrinkage and selection operator (LASSO) model. This model has been applied to equity market networks by Barigozzi and Brownlees (2018). It is valuable for inference for modeling networks as demonstrated by Kolaczyk and Csardi (2014). It has absolute terms for the β_i coefficients, meaning they have a value of zero if their impact is significantly small. The aim is to find the best model by minimizing the squared errors between the node returns R_i and a model $\widehat{R}_i$ fitted to explain node returns using other asset returns and confounders.

The LASSO model has the following form as suggested by Tibshirani (1996):

$$\underset{\beta \in R^p}{\text{argmin}}\left[\sum_{i=1}^{K}\left(R_i - \widehat{R}_i\right)^2\right] = \sum_{i=1}^{K}\left(R_i - \alpha - \sum_{j=1}^{P}\beta_j F_{ij}\right)^2 + \lambda \sum_{j=0}^{P}|\beta_j| \tag{7.9}$$

where R_i is the asset's return, α_i is the intercept, $F_{j,t}$ are style factors, and β_i is a coefficient of factor loading that measures the sensitivity of the nodes' return to the factor.[7]

It is worth discussing LASSO model in more detail. The summation of the β_i coefficients in equation (7.9) could encompass any of the factors commonly employed by portfolio managers. The novel part of the equation is the last term on the right-hand side. This term defines the values that calibrate the β_i coefficients, which are in absolute terms $|\beta_j|$. This process is called *factor shrinkage*. Note that the shrinkage effect

---

[7]James et al. (2013) provide a detailed overview of the model specification.

depends on the penalty parameter λ in equation (7.9). A λ of zero will produce the same model as the ordinary least squares model. However, a sufficiently large λ value would force some of the coefficients β_j to become zero. Thus, different estimated values for λ determine the outcome of a model and the variability of coefficients. Therefore, λ is a tuning parameter.

One major advantage of the LASSO model is its ability to select relevant factors. This feature is crucial, because it makes the coefficients easier to interpret compared to regression models such as the ridge regression model. The reason behind this lies in the assumption of the LASSO model that some of the true coefficients in the model are indeed zero. Specifically, LASSO shrinks the least squares coefficients toward zero by the same magnitude.

The code for generating this network is outlined in Box 7.4, and Figure 7.4 illustrates the resulting network. The LASSO network is estimated using the "huge" package and requires the covariance matrix of the asset and factor returns.

BOX 7.4:   THE LASSO MODEL FOR ASSET AND FACTOR NETWORK.

```
test.mat<-cov(AssetsFactors)
m.inv.cor<-solve(test.mat) %*% test.mat
huge.out<-huge(m.inv.cor,method = "glasso" )
huge.opt<-huge.select(huge.out,criterion = "ric")
plot(huge.opt)
g.huge<-graph_from_adjacency_matrix(huge.opt$refit, "undirected")
netz_undir_lasso<-g.huge
V(netz_undir_lasso)$name<-colnames(AssetsFactors)
netz_undir_lasso<-set.vertex.attribute(netz_undir_lasso, "category", value=c("F", "F",
"F", "F", "F", "F", "A", "A", "A", "A", "A", "A", "A", "A", "A", "A", "A", "A", "A",
"A", "A", "F", "F", "F", "F", "F", "F", "F", "F", "F"))

V(netz_undir_lasso)$color <- V(netz_undir_lasso)$category
V(netz_undir_lasso)$color <- gsub("F","orange",V(netz_undir_lasso)$color)
V(netz_undir_lasso)$color <- gsub("A","lightblue",V(netz_undir_lasso)$color)
V(netz_undir_lasso)$shape <- V(netz_undir_lasso)$category
V(netz_undir_lasso)$shape <- gsub("F","circle",V(netz_undir_lasso)$shape)
V(netz_undir_lasso)$shape <- gsub("A","square",V(netz_undir_lasso)$shape)
plot(netz_undir_lasso, vertex.size=eigen_centrality(netz_undir_lasso)$vector*20,
layout=layout_with_gem)
```

Regression Models with Interaction Terms

Incorporating interaction terms is another method to properly estimate the association between nodes when constructing asset networks using regression models. The primary reason for including interaction terms is to address the additive assumption issue in multifactor models.

Recall that in a linear model using, for example, a dependent variable, an independent variable, and a confounder variable, if the effect of the increase of the returns R_j by one unit, then returns R_i will rise by an average of β_i units. In this case, the inclusion of a confounder does not impact the result. That is, regardless of the cofounder's value, a one-unit increase in R_j will lead to a β_j-unit increase of R_i. Following the hierarchical principle that econometric models should include the main effects of the variables R_j and a

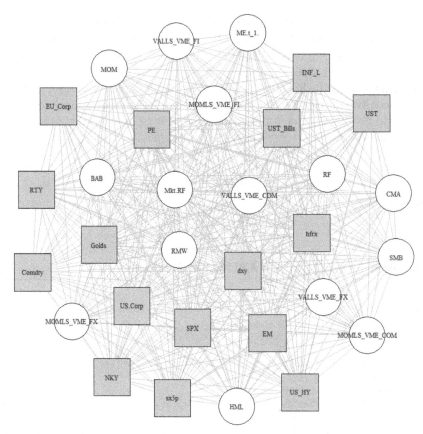

FIGURE 7.4   A LASSO Asset and Factor Network.

confounder, the model can be extended to use the interaction term between the confounder and the independent variable as follows:

$$R_i = \alpha + \beta R_j + \gamma R_C + \phi R_j R_C + \varepsilon \tag{7.10}$$

where R_i is the return of asset i regressed against the returns of the asset j $\left(R_j\right)$, and R_C is the return of the confounder variable related to the dependent variable, and the product (i.e., interaction) between the returns of the confounder and the independent variable, α is the intercept of the regression, β is the slope coefficient, and ε is a random error term. The inclusion of interaction terms in regression models results in variations in parameter estimates for the slope of the regression line, thereby influencing the calculated values for the association variable. Consequently, the significance of the beta coefficients can be interpreted as elements of the adjacency matrix, enabling for a better understanding of the relationships within the network.

$$a_{ij} = \begin{cases} 1, & \text{if } |t_\beta| > t_{t-(k+1);1-\frac{a}{2}} \\ 0, & \text{otherwise} \end{cases} \tag{7.11}$$

where a_{ij} represents the components of the adjacency matrix, assuming a binary value only if node i is linked to node j.

The resulting network is a graph without loops, as the main diagonal entries are zeros. When considering only the β parameter, the researcher focuses solely on the popularity or direct impact of other nodes on the current node, neglecting the effects of sending ties or expansiveness.

Granger Causality Tests

Perhaps the most well-known study on interconnectedness between financial institutions using the Granger causality tests suggested by Granger (1969) is the work by Billio et al. (2012). The authors employed pairwise statistical Granger causality tests, using lagged asset returns to estimate the forecasting power of pairwise variables.[8] The node i is said to *Granger cause* node j if past values of i help to predict j, beyond the information contained in the past values of the time series of j. The statistical test for causality between assets (i.e., nodes) in a network, based on the Granger causality test, involves testing the null hypothesis (H_0) that node i does not cause time series j to Granger-cause itself against the alternative hypothesis (H_A) that time series i cause time series j to Granger-cause itself. The mathematical notion is based on the following pairwise regression models:

$$R^i_{t+1} = a_i R_{i,t} + b_j R_{j,t} + e_{i,t} \tag{7.12}$$

$$R^j_{t+1} = a_j R_{j,t} + b_i R_{i,t} + e_{j,t} \tag{7.13}$$

where $e_{j,t}$ and $e_{i,t}$ are the uncorrelated residuals, and a_i, a_j, b_i, b_j are the coefficients of a linear model. Importantly, node i is said to be a Granger cause node j, if b_i is different from zero.

To account the influence of confounders, following the approach of Lopez de Prado (2023) and to align the methodology of Billio et al. (2012), we extend the equations by incorporating additional predictors and different lag levels. The identification of these predictors is subject to model order-selection procedure as follows:

$$R_{i,t+1} = \sum_{i=1}^{\infty} a_i R_{i,t-i} + \sum_{j=1}^{\infty} b_j R_{j,t-j} + \varphi_i R_{C,t} + e_{i,t+1} \tag{7.14}$$

$$R_{j,t+1} = \sum_{j=1}^{\infty} a_j R_{j,t-j} + \sum_{i=1}^{\infty} b_i R_{i,t-i} + \varphi_j R_{C,t} + e_{j,t+1} \tag{7.15}$$

where $R_{C,t}$ are the returns of a confounder variable but might be the returns of an equity market index, and all other variables are the lagged specification of the variables that have been declared previously.[9]

It's important to emphasize that model evaluation, parameter checks, and proper model specification are essential for accurately estimating the network. The specification of lag and significance tests must be carried out with careful consideration to ensure robustness and reliability of the results. We reject the null hypothesis and infer that the time series of node i Granger causes time series associated with asset j, if the p-value is less than a specified threshold significance level (e.g., 5%). Because the test generates an F-statistic with a p-value, we can use the p-values to populate the elements of the adjacency matrix with 1 if the test

---

[8]Note that this method does not provide a true causality estimation, as Bayesian networks do, but rather conducts a statistical test for causality.

[9]Instead of the S&P500 index returns, Billio et al. (2012) use a vector that comprises multiple explanatory factors like the Fama and French (1992, 1993, and 2005) factors combined with macroeconomic variables. This is a reasonable choice when estimating a network of individual securities (equities or bonds), but less appropriate for asset and factor networks that comprise the same regressors.

is significant, and 0 if the *p*-value is not significant. The results of the tests are used to build adjacency matrices that represent directed networks. The entries in the adjacency matrix are:

$$a_{ij} = \begin{cases} 1, & \text{if node } i \text{ and } j \text{ are connected, or } \{i,j\} \in m \\ 0 & \text{Otherwise} \end{cases} \tag{7.16}$$

The code for generating the Granger Causality test-based directed network is presented in Box 7.5, and the resulting network is visualized in Figure 7.5.

BOX 7.5: A GRANGER-CAUSALITY-BASED DIRECTED ASSET AND FACTOR NETWORK.

```
#Directed GCT-Test Network
#library (lmtest)
returns<-AssetsFactorsp.t=0.05/6
mtx_dir_gct<-matrix(nrow=ncol(AssetsFactors),ncol=ncol(AssetsFactors))
for(i in 1:ncol(returns)) {
  for(j in 1:ncol(returns)) {
      x=ts(returns[,i])
      y=ts(returns[,j])
      mtx_dir_gct[i,j]=ifelse(x != y,(grangertest(x,y,3))[-1,4],0)[1]
      mat_gct<-as.matrix(mtx_dir_gct)

      mat_gct<-ifelse(mat_gct[,]<p.t,1,0)
      diag(mat_gct)<-0
  }
}
colnames(mat_gct)<-colnames(AssetsFactors)
print(mat_gct)
netz_dir_gct<-as.matrix(mat_gct)
netz_dir_gct<-graph_from_adjacency_matrix(netz_dir_gct, weighted=TRUE)
E(netz_dir_gct)$arrow.size<-1
hist(degree_distribution(netz_dir_gct))
#DegreeCentrality
barplot(sort(degree(netz_dir_gct), decreasing=TRUE), lwd=0.5, cex.names=0.7,
cex.axis=0.7,las=2)
#Centrality
barplot(sort(eigen_centrality(netz_dir_gct)$vector, decreasing=TRUE), lwd=0.5,
cex.names=0.7,cex.axis=0.7,las=2)
ecs_netz_dir_gct<-as.matrix(eigen_centrality(netz_dir_gct)$vector)

netz_dir_gct<-set.vertex.attribute(netz_dir_gct, "category", value=c("F", "F", "F", "F",
"F", "F", "A", "A", "A", "A", "A", "A", "A", "A", "A", "A", "A", "A", "A", "A",
"F", "F", "F", "F", "F", "F", "F", "F", "F"))

V(netz_dir_gct)$color <- V(netz_dir_gct)$category
V(netz_dir_gct)$color <- gsub("F","orange",V(netz_dir_gct)$color)
V(netz_dir_gct)$color <- gsub("A","lightblue",V(netz_dir_gct)$color)

V(netz_dir_gct)$shape <- V(netz_dir_gct)$category
V(netz_dir_gct)$shape <- gsub("F","circle",V(netz_dir_gct)$shape)
V(netz_dir_gct)$shape <- gsub("A","square",V(netz_dir_gct)$shape)
plot(netz_dir_gct, layout=layout_with_lgl, vertex.size=15, edge.arrow.size=.3,
edge.color="grey85",vertex.label.cex=.6)
```

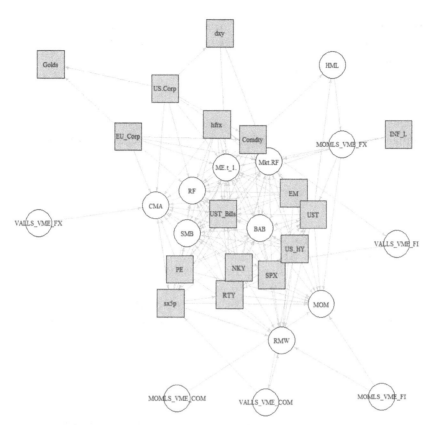

FIGURE 7.5   A Granger Causality Test Asset and Factor Network.

Vector Autoregression and Variance Decomposition Models

The econometric time-series models of vector autoregression (VAR), along with the technique of variance decomposition, are fundamental components of the directed network approach proposed by Diebold and Yilmaz (2009, 2012, 2014, 2015). While the networks presented in previous chapters are more return-based, focusing on modeling the connectedness at the node level, variance decomposition networks are volatility-based. They aim to model the connectedness at the edge level, specifically focusing on the relationships between the nodes gauged by their mutual links.

Variance decomposition networks offer two important differences compared to other networks. First, the adjacency matrix represents a complete directed graph, wherein all nodes are connected by links. Second, the shocks in variance decomposition networks are not orthogonal. Meaning that the shocks occur simultaneously to all nodes in the graph, rather than in a sequential ordering.

By applying variance decomposition to each variable (i.e., node) in the network, we can estimate the response of each node to such shocks. In this respect, all nodes (i.e., assets and factors) are treated equally. The variance decomposition network aims to estimate the cascade effects that transmit shocks over the links.

The model starts with a multivariate vector autoregression model for the asset returns, which computes the variance dynamically following the notation of Diebold and Yilmaz (2014):

$$Y_t = \sum_{i=1}^{p} \phi_i Y_{t-i} + \epsilon_t \tag{7.17}$$

where Y_t is the vector of lagged asset returns, ϕ_i is the $n \times n$ coefficient matrix, and ϵ_t is the normally distributed error vector. In addition, the moving-average model is essential to understand the dynamic nature of the model and is represented by the following equation:

$$Y_t = \sum_{i=1}^{\infty} \theta_i \epsilon_{t-i} \tag{7.18}$$

where θ are the moving average coefficients for all assets in the analysis and that represent the nodes in the network. The h-step ahead error is the squared difference of the realized asset values and the expected or forecasted ones. The equation has the following form:

$$\xi(H) = Y_{t+H} - E\left(Y_{t+H} | Y_t, X_{t-1}, Y_{t-2, \ldots}\right) = \sum_{i=1}^{H-1} \theta_i \epsilon_{t+H-i} \tag{7.19}$$

Note that model calibration and detailed model investigation are required for every model, and VAR models are no exception. Due to the complex characteristics of the variables and tests, it is reasonable to follow the established procedures for VAR implementation.

Variance decompositions enable the decomposing forecast error variances of each variable into components attributable to different system shocks. To model interconnectedness represented by the nodes in the adjacency matrix, Diebold and Yilmaz (2011) define an $n \times n$ "connectedness table," with entries being the h-step-ahead forecast error variance decomposition coefficients, following Pesaran and Shin (1998). That is,

$$\zeta_{ij}^g(H) = \frac{\sigma_{jj}^{-1} \sum_{h=0}^{H-1} \left(e_i' \theta_h \Sigma e_j\right)^2}{\sum_{h=0}^{H-1} \left(e_i' \theta_h \Sigma \theta_h' e_i\right)} \tag{7.20}$$

where e_j is a zero vector with unity on the j-th position, θ_h is the coefficient matrix multiplying the h-lagged shock vector in the moving-average representation of the nonorthogonalized vector autoregression, Σ is the covariance matrix of the nonorthogonalized vector autoregression, and σ_{jj}^{-1} is the j element of the covariance matrix Σ. Then the connectedness table with entries $\left[\zeta_{ij}\right]$ has the following form:

$$\begin{pmatrix} \zeta_{11}^{gH} & \zeta_{12}^{gH} & \cdots & \zeta_{1j}^{gH} \\ \zeta_{21}^{gH} & \zeta_{22}^{gH} & \cdots & \zeta_{2j}^{gH} \\ \vdots & \vdots & \ddots & \vdots \\ \zeta_{i1}^{gH} & \zeta_{i2}^{gH} & \cdots & \zeta_{ij}^{gH} \end{pmatrix}$$

Note that the main diagonal of the connectedness matrix defined, as by Diebold and Yilmaz (2009, 2014), contains nonzero elements, indicating self-edges or self-connectedness. Again, asking about the meaningfulness of self-edges is essential. Whereas self-edges in a network of financial institutions might be highly reasonable, in portfolio networks, a self-connectedness might require economic reasoning. Whereas such rationale is easy to find for financial institutions, countries, or other business units, stronger arguments might be necessary for asset markets.

One of the most important advantages of modeling interconnectedness at the edge level is that it helps when investigating risk propagation between the nodes. The row sums represent the connectedness "From Others," and the column sums express the connectedness "To Others." As a result, the volatility-based networks suggested by Diebold and Yilmaz aim to evaluate the spread and transmission of systemic risk. This property makes these networks useful from a risk-management point of view, and we discuss their risk management application properties in Chapters 11 and 12.

When implementing variance decomposition networks, the first step is to run the VAR model using the multivariate time series. The intuition behind the approach is that the model assumes covariance stationarity of a VAR process. The stationarity process selects the optimal lag structure using information criteria that estimates the difference between the observations and model. Such information criteria are the Bayesian information criteria and Schwarz criterion. Once the model is estimated, a set of diagnostic tests should be conducted. Examples are the test for stability of the coefficients and residuals and normality of the VAR residuals, and tests for the serial correlation, heteroscedasticity, or non-normality (i.e., Portmanteau test) of the residuals.[10] The *p*-values are used to interpret these statistical tests for the VAR model. When the *p*-value is greater than a specific threshold value, the null hypothesis is rejected.

Once the VAR model is estimated, the results are used to estimate the forecast error variance decompositions. According to Lütkepohl (2005), the variance decomposition aims to show the information that each variable contributes to each variable in the VAR model. In other words, it measures the effect of each forecast error variance. The error variance is the one that produces an exogenous shock of one variable to the other variables. The Cholesky variance distribution is a widely applied technique to measure such shocks by decomposing the positive-definite covariance matrix. The code for generating and running diagnostic tests for the VAR and Cholesky variance-decomposition network is provided in Box 7.6, and the resulting network is illustrated in Figure 7.6. The code requires the package "vars" in the software R.

BOX 7.6: A VECTOR-AUTOREGRESSION AND CHOLESKY VARIANCE DECOMPOSITION DIRECTED ASSET AND FACTOR NETWORK.

```
#Select the lag structure and the type of VAR model
VARselect(returns,lag.max=12, type="const")$criteria
VARselect(returns,lag.max=12, type="none")$criteria
VARselect(returns,lag.max=12, type="trend")$criteria

info.var<-VARselect(returns,lag.max=12, type="trend")
info.var$selection
#estimate the VAR model
var.est<-VAR(returns, p=2,type="const", season=NULL,exog=NULL)
#summary of the VAR estimation and parameters
#summary(var.est)

#VAR Diagnostics
#verify the variance stationarity of the VAR process
v.stability<-stability(var.est, type="OLS-CUSUM")
#plot(v.stability)
#Normality test for the residuals
v.normality<-normality.test(var.est)
v.normality
#Portmanteau serial correlation test for the absence of autocorrelation in the errors
v.serial<-serial.test(var.est,lags.pt=12, type="PT.asymptotic")
v.serial
#ARCH test for the heteroscedasticity
#arch.test(var.est)
```

(Continued)

---

[10] See Pfaff (2008) for a detailed explanation of the VAR package in R. Practical examples can be found in Nagarajan et al. (2013).

(*Continued*)

```
#Cholesky Variance Decomposition
v.vardec<-fevd(var.est,n.ahead = 10)
v.vardec<-do.call("rbind", lapply(bv.vardec, "[", 3,))
var.dec<-as.matrix(v.vardec)
diag(var.dec)<-0
netz_dir_cvd<-graph_from_adjacency_matrix(var.dec, weighted=TRUE)


netz_dir_cvd<-set.vertex.attribute(netz_dir_cvd, "category", value=c("F", "F", "F", "F",
"F", "F", "A", "A", "A", "A", "A", "A", "A", "A", "A", "A", "A", "A", "A", "A", "A", "A",
"F", "F", "F", "F", "F", "F", "F", "F", "F"))

V(netz_dir_cvd)$color <- V(netz_dir_cvd)$category
V(netz_dir_cvd)$color <- gsub("F","white",V(netz_dir_cvd)$color)
V(netz_dir_cvd)$color <- gsub("A","grey85",V(netz_dir_cvd)$color)

V(netz_dir_cvd)$shape <- V(netz_dir_cvd)$category
V(netz_dir_cvd)$shape <- gsub("F","circle",V(netz_dir_cvd)$shape)
V(netz_dir_cvd)$shape <- gsub("A","square",V(netz_dir_cvd)$shape)


E(netz_dir_cvd)$arrow.size<-0.2
plot(netz_dir_cvd, vertex.size=sqrt(eigen_centrality(netz_dir_cvd)$vector)*50,
edge.width=sqrt(E(netz_dir_cvd)$weight)*5)
```

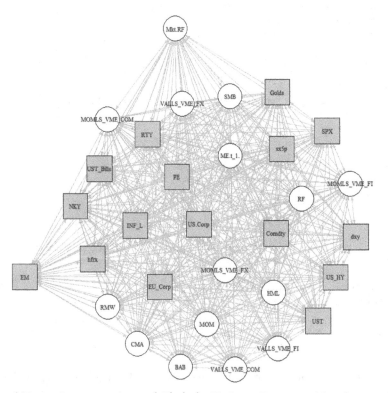

FIGURE 7.6   A Directed Vector-Autoregression and Cholesky Variance Decomposition Asset and Factor Network.

KEY TAKEAWAYS

- The primary task when constructing portfolio networks using statistical and econometric models is to model the edges using regression models and other statistical processes using ordinary least squares models because the nodes are known, but the edges might be unobservable.
- The major challenge lies in modeling the links using link prediction tools, such as linear models, linear models with confounders, linear models with interaction terms, LASSO and VAR models, and the Granger causality test.
- Statistical models rely on tests and statistical hypothesis testing regarding the significance of the regression coefficients. These models might be prone to false discovery rates and need special treatment. Notably, most of the tests and presented models here have much more in common than the thematic clustering that we assigned to them.
- Regression-based approaches are generally more sophisticated and often require a solid economic foundation compared to link prediction models. These regression-based models are among the most employed in both directed and undirected network models within finance.
- The interference for regression-based approaches is modeled as a function between an independent variables, or variables and dependent variable, and the statistically significance of the estimated regression coefficient. The explanatory variables in a regression equation might be lagged variables, or independent regressors, which have an economic background.
- The coefficients in a regression-based model are used to populate the entries of the adjacency matrix that represent relationship.

## CHAPTER 8

Building Portfolio Networks – Probabilistic Models

Contents

The topic of this chapter is the development of portfolio networks using statistical tools and probability theory. Again, the starting point is that nodes or vertices in networks are often known and finite, but that the edges must be modeled using time series or other types of underlying data, from which relationships can be extracted or extrapolated. The chapter's essential idea is to present portfolio and possible benchmark networks as graphs using statistical models.

The probabilistic theory offers a direct way to implement a mathematical and statistical toolkit to enable edge prediction and simulation. Probabilistic models fall within the larger group of statistical models extensively discussed by Kolaczyk and Csardi (2020) and Luke (2015), forming a subset of statistical models overall. We define the models as probabilistic because their goal is to build networks probabilistically using statistical models, and not to investigate, simulate, or pattern the underlying statistical process of an already existing network. The probabilistic models discussed in this chapter are the Markov chain network models and the Bayesian networks, which generate models without a priori information about an underlying network structure.

According to Kolaczyk and Csardi (2020), statistical models comprise exponential random graph models (ERGMs), network block models, and latent network models. The authors also highlight models effective in predicting statistical processes in graphs, such as nearest neighbor models, Markov random fields, and statistical kernel models. Chapter 9 delves into investigating statistical processes in networks, employing statistical models and utilizing node and edge attributes as graph determinants. That chapter provides detailed explanations of the ERGM and latent network models. A common characteristic of these statistical models is the presence of structural equivalence, which refers to the similarity of the links between the nodes.[1]

---

[1] See Chapter 6 for an explanation of the structural equivalence.

As with the previous chapters, the networks derived from statistical and probabilistic models extend beyond asset and factor network models. They can also be applied to portfolio selection involving individual financial instruments (e.g., bonds, stocks, and derivatives). To maintain consistency with discussions in the previous chapters and the models highlighted there, we use the asset and factor data set used by Konstantinov et al. (2020).

PORTFOLIO NETWORK TOPOLOGY INTERFERENCE AND INFERENCE WITH PROBABILISTIC MODELS

Constructing statistical and, specifically, probabilistic networks in portfolio management represents the relationships (i.e., edges) between assets or individual securities as probabilities. The objective is to model the probability of pairwise connectedness between nodes (i.e., pairs) and populate the adjacency matrix with these probabilities.

An important rule to follow when constructing probabilistic networks is to determine the nodes and links based on historical data and observations. Doing so presents a major challenge, depending on the type of network from which we want to derive – whether for allocation or selection purposes. The task in portfolio management – allocation or portfolio selection – impacts the assumptions regarding how to deal with the number of nodes and links. Probabilistic networks are flexible and can accommodate both a large and small number of vertices.

Consider the previous example of a portfolio that comprises a specific number of single securities, such as equities or bonds. The number of nodes (i.e., single securities) and links cannot be fixed because the portfolio may include, for example, 1,000 single securities one month and 1,100 the next. Managing both the number and the links over short periods is challenging and somewhat unrealistic for asset networks, as the number of nodes is generally finite in the short term. This variability is where probabilistic models excel due to their ability to handle time-specific structures. In other words, the only relevant information is the present one.

A key attribute of probabilistic models is that they are deterministic in their estimation approach: the current network structure of a portfolio is determined independently of its previous structure and interconnections, implying that there is no memory of edge connectivity. A probabilistic edge might exist now but can disappear in the next period. The resulting graph is not necessarily a completed graph. If the pairwise probability is zero, there is no edge between the two nodes.

Moreover, applying the false discovery rate (FDR) and family-wise error rate (FWER) is also relevant to those networks. Setting an appropriate probability threshold can lead to a sparser network than originally estimated. However, to maintain the integrity of the network's probabilistic mode when applying a threshold, it is critical to ensure that the probabilities remain positive and sum up to one.

To construct a probabilistic network such as the Markov chain model from observational data, a suitable method for establishing connectedness is crucial, and link prediction techniques and association tools can be applied, with correlation kernels being a particularly effective way to estimate distances and relationships. The selection of a suitable kernel, the initial step, is fundamental. As highlighted by Phoa (2013) and Kolaczyk and Csardi (2020), a kernel is a function essential for generating similarity matrices, effectively modeling the edges within a graph.

Here we present the Bayesian net model that facilitates the construction of networks based on causality. This model uses regression models to define edge relationships. In the following sections, we will demonstrate how to build practical networks using time series data and present tests and models that serve as kernels.

PROBABILISTIC MODELS

Compared to link prediction and association models, probabilistic network models might seem less economically intuitive. However, these probabilistic models offer a better way to model relationships using mathematics and statistical properties, relying less on subjective interpretation and analysis regarding possible explanatory factors and variables of interest. They offer a robust foundation for determining causality more rigorously and effectively. Nevertheless, these models are structural and enable financial markets to be modeled in a structured and intuitive way.

Two major probabilistic models highlighted in this section are the Markov chain model and the Bayesian net model. These models share the common property of modeling the links between nodes as probabilities using the statistical toolkit. Probabilistic models are essential in graph theory because they enable the probabilistic estimation of connectedness and edge probabilities, especially in fields where node relationships are not observable or are difficult to detect.

Financial markets often fall into this category, where some observations are hard to detect. Transaction data or direct relationships may be challenging to observe, or they may be proprietary to investment banks and data providers, remaining in private hands. Additionally, probabilistic models play a central role in portfolio management because they enable the modeling of unobservable outcomes and future scenarios.

Diffusion Maps and Markov Chain Networks

The origin of Markov graphs can be attributed to the work of Frank and Strauss (1986), who introduced the concept of relationships between nodes conditioned on the overall edge connectedness. This dependence on probabilistic structures in a network context is termed Markov graphs.

Computation   One major advantage of Markov chain networks is their ability to compute links within a network probabilistically. This approach enables the modeling of transition probabilities at any given point in time. Essentially, this approach functions as a diffusion map, assigning coordinates in Euclidean space and measuring the distance (i.e., similarity) between points. To apply graph theory, these spatial points must be converted to geodesic distances. Phoa (2013) outlined a method to calculate such probabilities for a diffusion map.

To compute these probabilities, which we define as links in a network, each row of the correlation kernel matrix is divided by the row sums to obtain the probability transition coefficients. For instance, each entry in the resulting matrix can be interpreted as the probability of risk transferring from one country index to in the case of country portfolio allocation or from one industry sector to another in the case of industry portfolios.

In essence, this approach estimates the probability of transitioning between assets in the network, with a higher likelihood of switching between two assets if they are more similar, based on similarity. Each entry in the probabilistic adjacency matrix represents the probability of switching from one asset to another in a single time step. The transition rates can be computed using a kernel function, with commonly used distance kernels suggested by Prim (1957), Mantegna (1999), Phoa (2013), and Konstantinov (2022b).

$$d_{ij}^{Mantegna} = \sqrt{2\left(1 - \rho_{ij}\right)} \tag{8.1}$$

$$d_{ij}^{Phoa} = 1 + \rho_{ij} \tag{8.2}$$

$$d_{ij}^{K} = 1 + |\rho_{ij}| \tag{8.3}$$

The distances are the entries in a distance matrix. Using the distance metrics in a distance matrix $D(n, n)$, we can compute the transition rates. The transition probabilities are calculated by dividing each of $D(n, n)$ by the row sums. The use of a stochastic matrix of transition probabilities $\eta_i(n)$ describes a Markov chain transition rates from node i to node j $(i \rightarrow j)$. The result is the transition probability matrix $P(n, n)$.

Mathematically, the main diagonal contains nonzero entities. In this case, the diagonal entry represents the probability of no switch from one node to another. Next, the eigenvalues and eigenvectors of the assets from the probability matrix can be estimated. We can use the eigenvectors and eigenvalues to estimate the diffusion map $(n \times 1)$ vector given by

$$\Psi(n) = \begin{pmatrix} \lambda_1 \psi_1(n) \\ \lambda_2 \psi_2(n) \\ \vdots \\ \lambda_{N-1} \psi_{N-1}(n) \end{pmatrix} \tag{8.4}$$

where ψ_i is eigenvectors, and λ_i are the eigenvalues.

The inverse of the covariance matrix here is a measure of the concentration of nodes and can be expressed as a square root of the inverse of the trace of the covariance matrix $\left(\frac{1}{\sqrt{tr\Sigma}} \right)$.

The following example uses the asset correlation matrix to highlight the intuition. In our case, the probability of switching from the market risk premium (MktRF in the Fama–French model) to the size factor (Small minus Big [SMB] in the Fama–French model) is 3.3% (3.3 = 1.08/33.2). In comparison, the probability of switching from SMB to MktRF is 3.4% (3.4 = 1.09/32.3). Notice that the magnitude of the correlation distances (i.e., kernels) determines the row-sums, and thus, the probability of a switch. The probabilistic matrix's design depends on the kernel function's selected. Different kernel estimations generate different probability matrices. We show the eigenvectors of the Markov chain probability matrix in Figure 8.1.

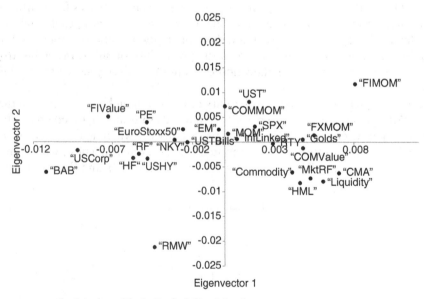

FIGURE 8.1 Eigenvectors of a Markov Chain Probability Matrix.

Practical Implementation   Practical applications of directed Markov chain networks can be found for the estimation of the country allocation of emerging market bond portfolios and hedge funds, but the use in portfolio management is enormous.[2] The probabilistic adjacency matrix represents a weighted directed network, with the probabilities serving as the node weights. The application of Markov chain networks in portfolio management has been recognized for its efficacy, particularly highlighted by Konstantinov, Aldridge, and Kazemi (2023), who demonstrated its power in assigning probabilities at every portfolio construction stage.

Markov chain networks find utility beyond portfolio management, extending into risk management where specific models leveraging connectedness are used to estimate node and edge robustness and fragility. These applications are extensively discussed in sections dedicated to risk management.

However, a notable drawback is associated with Markov chain networks. The inherent assumption of randomness in each period means that the current interconnectedness of assets in the portfolio is independent of the interconnectedness in preceding periods. This assumption diverges from reality, as many financial time series exhibit memory, often detected as an autoregressive process with specific lag structures.[3] Indeed, considering the time-dependent structures of financial data is crucial for accurately modeling interconnectedness and risk propagation in financial networks. While Markov chain and probabilistic models are well-suited for risk and portfolio allocation models involving a significant number of assets, they may not be as appropriate for modeling networks of single securities.

In networks with many individual securities, the small probabilities inherent in Markov processes can be averaged out, potentially diminishing the centrality scores of individual assets. As a result, these models may not effectively capture the nuanced relationships and importance of individual securities within the network. Therefore, alternative approaches may be more suitable for modeling networks at the level of single securities, such as regression-based models or correlation networks. These methods may offer more granularity and sensitivity to the unique characteristics of individual assets.[4] Consider, for example, an equity market index, such as the Russell 2000 index, which comprises 2,000 stocks. The Markov decision probability matrix estimated using the correlation coefficients would comprise many small probabilities.

To mitigate this issue, clustering and community structures of the benchmark or portfolio network might be applied. Hierarchical clustering is one possible solution, which we investigate in Chapter 10. Nevertheless, computing transition probability matrices is necessary for asset allocation purposes and portfolio optimization, particularly for networks with few vertices. Given the reduced granularity in the asset allocation process, where the assets, factors, industry, and sector groups are broadly defined, a portfolio allocation network with up to 30 nodes might be a reasonable threshold level. It enables effective modeling and optimization while maintaining manageable complexity.

To overcome these issues, we present an algorithm that penalizes some of the probabilities when estimating the adjacency matrix using the connected regime probability of $p = 1/n$, as discussed in the previous section. The reason for this filtering is that, according to the random network model suggested by Erdős and Rényi (1959, 1960), the probability that a network enters a critical regime is given by $1/n$, where n is the number of nodes, and the degree of the network is $k = 1$. Thus, as a probability filtration, the probability that two nodes are connected must exceed $1/n$, which, for a network of 31 nodes, is 3.2%. Removing self-edges is not essential because self-edges or self-loops in large probabilistic networks, computed using the correlation coefficients, account for a smaller amount in the overall connectedness (see Barabási, 2016).

---

[2] See Konstantinov (2022a, 2022b).

[3] The detection of an autoregressive process in time-series data is an indication of the memory effect. The underlying theory is that the current data contains past information.

[4] The R codes are available at https://finance-resolution.com/.

The code for the Markov chain network is provided in Box 8.1. Note that this code includes the computation of the eigenvectors. The specific network code is independent of this computation, which provides an overview of the eigenvector geometry. Also, note that considering the economic relevance of self-edges is essential when deciding whether to remove them. The directed Markov chain-based asset and factor network is drawn in Figure 8.2.

BOX 8.1:   A MARKOV CHAIN-DIRECTED ASSET AND FACTOR NETWORK.

```
#Compute Markov Chain Network
set.seed(67)
returns<-AssetsFactors
trans.mat<-as.matrix(1+cor(returns))
mtx_markov<-matrix(nrow=ncol(AssetsFactors),ncol=ncol(AssetsFactors))
mtx_markov<-t(apply(trans.mat,1,function(x) x/sum(x)))
trans.mat<-as.matrix(mtx_markov)
#Compute the eigenvectors of the assets
eigen(trans.mat)$vector
eig.vec1<-eigen(trans.mat)$vector[,1]
eig.vec2<-eigen(trans.mat)$vector[,2]

asset.vec1<-foreach(x=1:ncol(trans.mat), .combine=cbind) %do% {
   einzel=trans.mat[,x]
   res.vec1=einzel%*%eig.vec1
}
asset.vec2<-foreach(x=1:ncol(trans.mat), .combine=cbind) %do% {
  einzel=trans.mat[,x]
  res.vec1=einzel%*%eig.vec2
}
#Plots the Diffusion Map based on the Eigenvalues 1 & 2
plot(asset.vec1, asset.vec2)
text(asset.vec1,asset.vec2, labels = rownames(trans.mat),cex = 0.6, pos = 4, col = "red")

#Make a network from the probability Matrix
trans.prob.matrix<-as.matrix(trans.mat)
diag(trans.prob.matrix)<-0
p.t<-1/31
trans.prob.matrix<-ifelse(trans.prob.matrix[,]>p.t,1,0)
Tr.pr.net<-graph_from_adjacency_matrix(trans.prob.matrix, weighted=TRUE)

#DegreeCentrality
barplot(sort(degree(Tr.pr.net), decreasing=TRUE), lwd=0.5,
cex.names=0.7,cex.axis=0.7,las=2)
#Centrality
barplot(sort(eigen_centrality(Tr.pr.net)$vector, decreasing=TRUE), lwd=0.5,
cex.names=0.7,cex.axis=0.7,las=2)
E(Tr.pr.net)$arrow.size<-0
plot(Tr.pr.net, layout=layout_with_fr)
netz_dir_mcn<-Tr.pr.net
hist(degree_distribution(netz_dir_mcn))

#DegreeCentrality
barplot(sort(degree(netz_dir_mcn), decreasing=TRUE), lwd=0.5,
cex.names=0.7,cex.axis=0.7,las=2)
```

```
#Centrality
barplot(sort(eigen_centrality(netz_dir_mcn)$vector, decreasing=TRUE), lwd=0.5,
cex.names=0.7,cex.axis=0.7,las=2)
ecs_dir_mcn<-as.matrix(eigen_centrality(netz_dir_mcn)$vector)
netz_dir_mcn<-set.vertex.attribute(netz_dir_mcn, "category", value=c("F", "F", "F", "F",
"F", "F", "A", "A", "A", "A", "A", "A", "A", "A", "A", "A", "A", "A", "A", "A", "A", "A",
"F", "F", "F", "F", "F", "F", "F", "F", "F"))


V(netz_dir_mcn)$color <- V(netz_dir_mcn)$category
V(netz_dir_mcn)$color <- gsub("F","orange",V(netz_dir_mcn)$color)
V(netz_dir_mcn)$color <- gsub("A","lightblue",V(netz_dir_mcn)$color)


V(netz_dir_mcn)$shape <- V(netz_dir_mcn)$category
V(netz_dir_mcn)$shape <- gsub("F","circle",V(netz_dir_mcn)$shape)
V(netz_dir_mcn)$shape <- gsub("A","square",V(netz_dir_mcn)$shape)
#some varaints for plotting this network are
plot(netz_dir_mcn, layout=layout_with_kk, edge.width=E(netz_dir_mcn)$weight*2)
plot(netz_dir_mcn, layout=layout_with_lgl,
edge.width=(E(netz_dir_mcn)$weight^0.5)*2, edge.color="grey85")
#we show the network with this line of code
plot(netz_dir_mcn, layout=layout_with_kk, vertex.size=15, edge.arrow.size=.3,
edge.color="grey85",vertex.label.cex=.6)
```

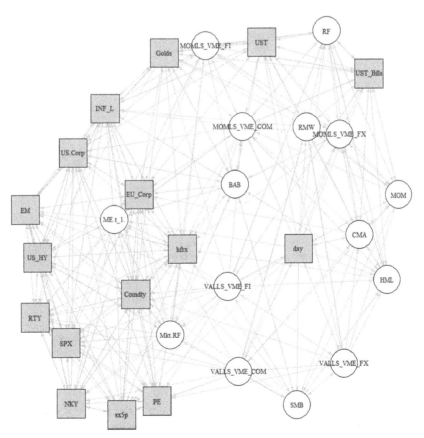

FIGURE 8.2 A Markov Chain-Directed Asset and Factor Network.

In Chapter 6, we defined the link prediction models and described similarity metrics that aim at capturing relationships. The various distance metrics gauge the edge connection differently. For example, between the Euclidean distance and the Manhattan distance, there exists a substantial difference. Extending this intuition to the networks, we can compute a Markov chain probability matrix using the Manhattan distance of the node structure. The advantage of the Manhattan distance is that it is a proxy used in the market curvature estimation, which is discussed in detail in Chapters 11 and 12. The code is provided in Box 8.2, and the graph is shown in Figure 8.3.

Bayesian Networks

Bayesian networks in finance, used to gauge causality, are introduced by Jensen (2001), Pearl (2000, 2009) and extensively discussed by Nagarajan et al. (2013), and Rebonato and Denev (2013).[5] Specifically, the nodes (i.e., assets) are connected by edges, whose nature and estimation follow a probabilistic model. A table with conditional probabilities in line with the Bayesian framework is needed to build such a network. Because the real probability distribution in financial markets is not observable, financial research

---

BOX 8.2: A MARKOV CHAIN MANHATTAN DISTANCE-BASED DIRECTED ASSET AND FACTOR NETWORK.

```
set.seed(67)
returns<-AssetsFactors
tra.mat<-as.matrix(dist(cor(returns), method="manhattan"))
mtx_markov_m<-matrix(nrow=ncol(AssetsFactors),ncol=ncol(AssetsFactors))
mtx_markov_m<-t(apply(tra.mat,1,function(x) x/sum(x)))

tra.mat<-as.matrix(mtx_markov_m)

#Make a network from the probability Matrix
trans.prob.matrix.m<-as.matrix(tra.mat)
diag(trans.prob.matrix.m)<-0
p.t<-0.05/6
trans.prob.matrix.m<-ifelse(trans.prob.matrix.m[,]>p.t,1,0)
netz_dir_dist<-graph_from_adjacency_matrix(trans.prob.matrix.m, weighted=TRUE)

netz_dir_dist<-set.vertex.attribute(netz_dir_dist, "category", value=c("F", "F", "F", "F",
"F", "F", "A", "A", "A", "A", "A", "A", "A", "A", "A", "A", "A", "A", "A", "A", "A",
"F", "F", "F", "F", "F", "F", "F", "F", "F"))

V(netz_dir_dist)$color <- V(netz_dir_dist)$category
V(netz_dir_dist)$color <- gsub("F","orange",V(netz_dir_dist)$color)
V(netz_dir_dist)$color <- gsub("A","lightblue",V(netz_dir_dist)$color)

V(netz_dir_dist)$shape <- V(netz_dir_dist)$category
V(netz_dir_dist)$shape <- gsub("F","circle",V(netz_dir_dist)$shape)
V(netz_dir_dist)$shape <- gsub("A","square",V(netz_dir_dist)$shape)

plot(netz_dir_dist, layout=layout_with_kk, vertex.size=15, edge.arrow.size=.3,
edge.color="grey85",vertex.label.cex=.6)
```

---

[5]The literature on Bayesian networks has grown substantially. The aim of this section is to provide an overview of the Bayesian causal networks. The readers can approach the dedicated literature on these types of networks, which exceeds the purpose of this book.

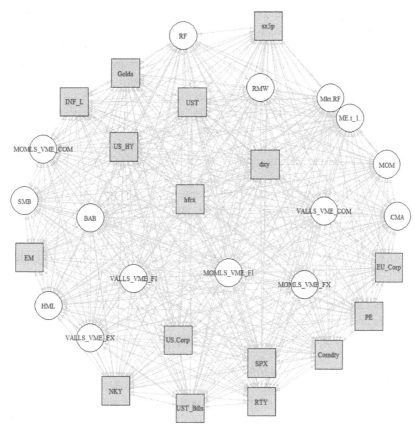

FIGURE 8.3   A Markov Chain Manhattan Distance-based Directed Asset and Factor Network.

often uses bootstrapping methods. Within the framework suggested by Pearl (2000), the edges of graphical causal nets are arrows pointing to the probabilistic connectedness and causation between the nodes. In that respect, probabilistic models can be classified as structural statistical models.

Theoretical Framework and Connectedness   The intuition of the Bayesian approach to network modeling follows paths. Therefore, Bayesian nets underlie the mechanism of paths (contrary to walks and trails). Path simulation is essential when it comes to the identification of causality. Consequently, the intuition of Bayesian networks enables them to be modeled as path structures, in which information travels only once through a node and aims to affect other nodes, rather than randomly traveling across the network. In other words, in Bayesian networks, a node is visited only once – e.g., information, infections, or disease networks.

Formally, the structure of a Bayesian network is represented by the probabilistic dependencies between the nodes in a directed acyclic graph, denoted by $G(n,m)$, where n is the number of nodes and m is the number of edges. Because we model the edges probabilistically, the directed acyclic graph might be denoted as $G(n,p)$, where n is the number of nodes and p is the probability of an edge. Every node in the Bayesian network corresponds to one random variable. Estimating the real networks underlying the Bayesian network structure poses challenges for several reasons. Nagarajan et al. (2013) highlight the following three crucial assumptions for causal networks:

- The nodes in the network represent an independence map, meaning that nodes are independent of their direct and indirect effects. This independence map is governed probabilistically based on a

Markov probability chain, where there is a one-to-one correspondence between the random variables and the nodes of $G(n,m)$. The dependency map works the other way around; it exists when there is a one-to-one correspondence between the nodes in G and the random variables.

- The relationship between the conditional independence structure modeled probabilistically and the directed acyclic graph should be isomorphic. Wassermann and Faust (1994) define two graphs as isomorphic if there is a one-to-one mapping of the nodes in the graph $G(n,m)$ and the probabilistic graph $G^p(n^p, m^p)$.[6] Isomorphism implies the coexistence of both independence and dependency maps.

- There must be no unobservable variables influencing the nodes in the network. These variables are referred to as latent variables, which act as confounders and introduce bias into the causal relationships within Bayesian network structures. Unfortunately, such latent variables often exist but are difficult to detect. In financial networks, even minor variations in the directionality of these latent variables, reflected in the direction of the edges, can result in significantly different network structure. In Chapter 9, we discuss the opposite case, in which latent variables exist and extensively influence the network structure. In that chapter, we provide information on how to estimate and evaluate such portfolio network structures. Consequently, there is no universal causal network; it is contingent on how variables and network models are defined. In general, the network's structure is highly data dependent.

- The major distinction between the regression models presented in the previous sections is their inclusion of all vertices in the modeling and their significance estimation. This approach differentiates the directional links between nodes. Bayesian structure might also identify indirect causal relationships. Bayesian networks are a compact tool used to represent conditional independencies. Sometimes conditional independencies can be given causal meaning, but not always. Their advantage can be summarized in the d-separation of causal events between the nodes in a network. D-separation helps to clarify the relationships by specifying the distance or direction of connectedness, typically revealed in three specific configurations, as outlined by Rebonato and Denev (2013):

  1. **Serial Connection:** Also known as a "chain," serial connection represents a linear sequence of cause and effect. For instance, node i is connected to node j, which in turn is connected to node u. Here, node j acts as a blocker, interrupting the direct connection between nodes i and u.

  2. **Diverging Connection:** Also known as a "form," the diverging connection is characterized by a single node influencing multiple other nodes. For example, node i might impact nodes j, u, and k. Importantly, nodes j, u, and k are unrelated. Suppose that, in practical terms, this might be seen in an economic scenario where an interest rate increase (node i) influences bond losses (node j). The rise in interest rates then impacts equities and commodities (nodes u and k). However, the causal link between equities and commodities is unclear, and these two assets might not directly relate to each other. Another example captured in Figure 8.4, illustrates the point with three assets. In this example, the rise of interest rates (node n_1) might cause bond losses (node n_3) and currency appreciation (node n_2).

  3. **Converging Connection:** This configuration, also referred to as a "collider," occurs when multiple causes lead to the same effect. For example, a combination of an interest rate increase, a credit rating upgrade, and the inclusion of a country in a global index might all contribute to the appreciation of that country's currency.

It is worth discussing these three types of connectedness. Bayesian connections, such as divergent, convergent, and serial connections can be visualized and formally expressed as probabilities. Figure 8.4 illustrates the connectedness in Bayesian networks, using three nodes and two directional edges between them. The code for this illustrative example is shown in Box 8.3. Again, the node relationships in the Bayesian networks are driven by the differences between serial, convergent, and divergent connectedness.

---

[6]Two isomorphic graphs have identical number of nodes, edges, and other statistical properties like diameter and density.

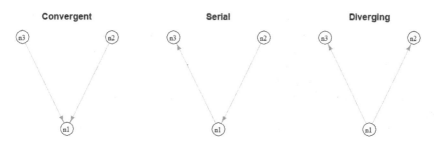

FIGURE 8.4   Connectedness in Bayesian Networks.

BOX 8.3:   A BAYESIAN NETWORK WEIGHTED DIRECTED ASSET AND FACTOR NETWORK.

```
par(mfrow=c(1,3))
#serial connectedness
A <- matrix(c(0,0,0,
       1,0,0,
       1,0,0), ncol = 3, byrow = TRUE)
a<-graph_from_adjacency_matrix(A)
E(a)$arrow.size<-0.5
plot(a, vertex.size=30,vertex.color="white", main="Convergent", vertex.label.cex=2,
layout=layout.mds, vertex.label=c("n1", "n2", "n3"))


#serial connectedness
A <- matrix(c(0,0,1,
       1,0,0,
       0,0,0), ncol = 3, byrow = TRUE)
a<-graph_from_adjacency_matrix(A)
E(a)$arrow.size<-0.5
plot(a, vertex.size=30,vertex.color="white", main="Serial", vertex.label.cex=2,
layout=layout.mds, vertex.label=c("n1", "n2", "n3"))

#diverging connectedness
A <- matrix(c(0,1,1,
       0,0,0,
       0,0,0), ncol = 3, byrow = TRUE)
a<-graph_from_adjacency_matrix(A)
E(a)$arrow.size<-0.5
plot(a, vertex.size=30,vertex.color="white", main="Diverging", vertex.label.cex=2,
layout=layout.mds, vertex.label=c("n1", "n2", "n3"))
```

In the convergent connectedness between three nodes, node n_1 becomes directional edges (as paths in Bayesian network context) from two other nodes – n_2 and n_3. Consequently, node n_1 does not d-separate nodes n_2 and n_3 they are not independent given node n_1. In other words, node n_1 depends on the joint probabilities of nodes n_2 and n_3. Following Nagarajan et al. (2013), node n_1 depends on the joint distributions of nodes n_2 and n_3. Given the Markov properties, the probability of nodes n_1, n_2, and n_3 are:

$$P(n_1,n_2,n_3) = P(n_1|n_2,n_3)P(n_2)P(n_3) \tag{8.5}$$

Convergent connections in financial markets can occur when different causes lead to the same effects. For example, during periods of financial market fragility, simultaneous central bank purchases of financial instruments, when implementing monetary policy and investor demand for those same instruments, can create such connections. Notable instances include the European Central Bank's (ECB) purchases of government and corporate bonds, and the Federal Reserve's (Fed) activities in the US Treasury market, particularly during their respective interventions and tapering programs. These events have often coincided, especially during times of economic uncertainty, illustrating how multiple factors can converge to influence market outcomes.

Considering the serial connectedness between the three nodes reveals a different picture. The nodes n_2 and n_3 are independent given node n_1. The probabilities for the three nodes given serial connectedness are:

$$P(n_1,n_2,n_3) = P(n_1|n_2)P(n_3|n_1)P(n_2) \tag{8.6}$$

The serial effects are not easy to detect in financial markets. A scenario commonly considered by portfolio managers illustrates serial connectedness: for instance, an increase in interest rates can trigger capital flows into a country, subsequently elevating the exchange rate due to heightened demand. This surge in demand for the currency then boosts demand for bonds, leading to higher returns in the bond market.

The formula for the divergent connected probabilities nodes n_2 and n_3 that depend on the n_1 is

$$P(n_1,n_2,n_3) = P(n_3|n_1)P(n_2|n_1)P(n_1) \tag{8.7}$$

Suppose, for example, a country's central bank increases interest rates. An example for divergent connections in financial markets would be the causal relationship of interest rates on both bonds and currencies.

Practical Implementation   A successful model for Bayesian causal graphs was proposed by Carvalho et al. (2021) and Hahn, Murray, and Carvalho (2020), in which the bootstrapping method generates data and identifies the structure or relations between the nodes. The resulting structure follows the intuition of structural equation modeling, according to which the links are modeled using causal equational models. These models are usually linear. In other words, estimating causal relationships, which are the core of Bayesian networks, relies on the statistically significant coefficients of linear equations.[7] Once the coefficients indicate relationships, this relationship is directional, and the edges are represented as arrows pointing toward causality. Bayesian networks incorporate regression-based models and probabilistic thinking. A linear equation represents the directional relation or structure of each node.

For example, consider a network comprising five nodes. The directional structure of the five nodes can be expressed by linear models gauging the edge between the node and other nodes:[8]

$$n_1 = f_1(n_4,n_5)$$

$$n_2 = f_2(n_1,n_2,n_3)$$

$$n_3 = f_3(n_1) \tag{8.8}$$

$$n_4 = f_4(n_1,n_3,n_5)$$

$$n_5 = f_5(n_3)$$

---

[7] In the continuous case.
[8] See Kanas (2025).

where f_i are linear models gauging the directional relations for the respective nodes n_1, n_2, n_3, n_4, n_5. As suggested by Lefcheck (2015), the causal relationship is given by the significant coefficient multiplied by the standard deviation of the independent variable and divided by the standard deviation of the dependent variable. That is,

$$m_i = \beta_{ij} \frac{\sigma_j}{\sigma_i} \tag{8.9}$$

where m_i is the link or edge of node i that depends on the coefficient β_{ij}, σ_j is the standard deviation of the independent variable j, and σ_i is the standard deviation of the dependent variable i.

Note that the term "causality" should be relaxed. Under causation in Bayesian nets, causality means that there might exist other effects that cause something to happen, which might remain unknown. In Box 8.4, we show the code for a simple asset and factor Bayesian network, and Figure 8.5 shows the network using the package *bnlearn* in R developed by Scutari (2010, 2017). Visual inspection confirms the findings by Kanas (2025) that the market factor (Mkt.RF) is the most connected and takes central stage in causal relationships.

BOX 8.4:   A BAYESIAN NETWORK WEIGHTED DIRECTED ASSET AND FACTOR NETWORK.

```
#Define a clustering algorithms with bootstrapping method
cl <- bnpa::create.cluster()
data.bn.boot.strap <- bnlearn::boot.strength(
  data = AssetsFactors,
  R = 1000, #set the iteration to 1000
  algorithm = "hc",
  cluster = cl,
  cpdag = FALSE
)
bn.nodes<-as.matrix(colnames(AssetsFactors)) #define the nodes
bn.edges<-data.bn.boot.strap #use the Bayesian algorithm results for edges


edge.w<-data.bn.boot.strap$strength
edge.d<-data.bn.boot.strap$direction
#run the algorithm using a data frame comprising "From" and "To" node information
netz_dir_bay<-graph_from_data_frame(d=bn.edges, vertices=bn.nodes, directed=T)

#identify the node categories
netz_dir_bay<-set.vertex.attribute(netz_dir_bay, "category", value=c("F", "F", "F", "F",
"F", "F", "A", "A", "A", "A", "A", "A", "A", "A", "A", "A", "A", "A", "A", "A", "A",
"F", "F", "F", "F", "F", "F", "F", "F", "F"))

V(netz_dir_bay)$color <- V(netz_dir_bay)$category
V(netz_dir_bay)$color <- gsub("F","white",V(netz_dir_bay)$color)
V(netz_dir_bay)$color <- gsub("A","grey85",V(netz_dir_bay)$color)

V(netz_dir_bay)$shape <- V(netz_dir_bay)$category
V(netz_dir_bay)$shape <- gsub("F","circle",V(netz_dir_bay)$shape)
V(netz_dir_bay)$shape <- gsub("A","square",V(netz_dir_bay)$shape)
#plot the network
plot(netz_dir_bay, layout=layout_with_lgl, vertex.size=15, edge.arrow.size=.3,
edge.width=edge.w*5, edge.color="grey85",vertex.label.cex=.6)
```

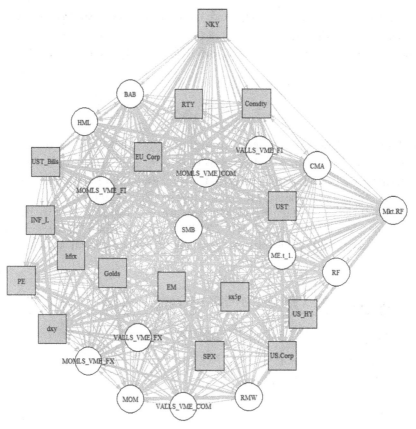

FIGURE 8.5   A Bayesian Asset and Factor Network.

In Chapter 9, we discuss and model causal network interference, which is centered around probabilistic thinking and the manipulation of networks according to some prespecified node structure. In Box 8.5, we provide a code that sets the edge colors according to the strength. The network is then plotted in Figure 8.6.

BOX 8.5:   SETTING THE EDGE WIDTH IN A BAYESIAN NETWORK: A WEIGHTED DIRECTED ASSET AND FACTOR NETWORK.

```
#Set Edge Color and plot the network
palf<-grep("grey5", colors(), value=T)
E(netz_dir_bay)$color <- palf[E(netz_dir_bay)]
edge.start <-ends(netz_dir_bay, es=E(netz_dir_bay), names=F)[,1]
edge.col <-E(netz_dir_bay)$color[edge.start]
plot(netz_dir_bay, layout=layout_with_lgl,
vertex.size=15,edge.arrow.size=.3,vertex.label.cex=.6, edge.color=edge.col,
edge.width=edge.w*5)
```

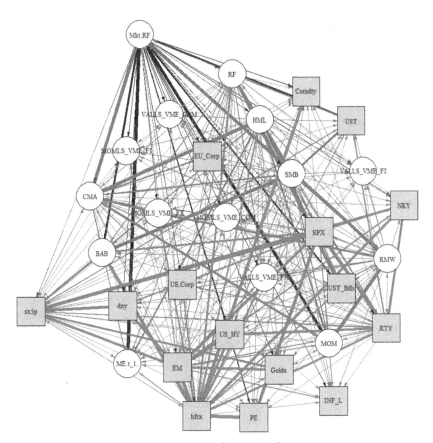

FIGURE 8.6   A Bayesian Asset and Factor Network with Edge Strength.

AN OVERVIEW OF THE NETWORKS

In this chapter, we explained methods to estimate various financial networks through probabilistic models, which are integral to constructing network frameworks using statistical techniques. The fundamental idea of these models is to represent network connectedness through probabilistic reasoning, specifically by modeling the likelihood of connections between two nodes based on the overall network structure and a defined distance metric. An alternative we discussed is using Bayesian nets, whose intuition is to model the interactions between the nodes using a causality structure. Essentially, Bayesian networks are probabilistic in nature and offer a structured approach to understanding complex network dynamics. Estimating these networks is straightforward, and their analysis extends to advanced features such as prediction, simulation, and learning algorithms, making them a robust tool for financial network analysis.

Several studies performed on network experiments in asset management show that the factors driving connectedness are not consistent and persistent. Umar et al. (2024) detected strong interaction effects between the country and industry returns by applying correlation networks. They found that on an industry-portfolio level, momentum, and value are leading factors in interconnectedness. Implementing variance decomposition networks, Diebold and Yilmaz (2015) showed that the equity markets possess the strongest connectedness, followed by bond and foreign-exchange markets. Applying the same method for network construction for a dataset of asset and factors, Konstantinov and Fabozzi (2022) show that the equity markets and currencies play a vital role to risk transfer. Applying regression-based networks, Konstantinov et al. (2020) found that US Treasuries are central within interconnected markets. Generally, the characteristics of the network – such as the type of network, the absence of latent variables, and the choice of an estimation algorithm based on similarities, statistical methods, or association models – not only influence the structure of the edges but also affect node connectivity. These factors collectively contribute to the distinct properties of the network.

The major task in network modeling is to predict links or apply various mathematical and statistical models to determine the often-unobservable edges between nodes, which can represent assets, factors, or other economic variables. Our aim is to provide a comprehensive overview of some of the models widely applied in asset management beyond the commonly used simple correlation networks in finance. Several purposes guided us in this chapter. First, providing examples of directed and undirected asset and factor networks is essential. Second, the networks have different properties and edge structures underlying information flow. Third, we focused on asset and factor networks because asset allocation is the most important step in portfolio construction and takes central stage in asset management industry. Fourth, our aim is to provide a brief overview of some tools and ways to estimate and generate portfolio graphs, which are the building blocks for both portfolio and risk management. The presented networks and the models applied to generate them are indicative with the aim at highlighting the methods of building portfolio networks.

The algorithm for building portfolio networks might be generalized into the following three steps:

1. Definition of proper metric that captures inference and interference – a distance or other proper metric, statistical model or test, or mathematical equation
2. Representation of both the inference and interference, based on economic reasoning modeling unobservable edges and possible interconnectedness
3. Adequacy measurement of the applied interference model – goodness-of-fit and simulation for robustness

We focused on the 12 asset and factor networks for brevity to provide a broad picture of the different algorithms. Bayesian networks were purposely not investigated or used in this book, because a substantial amount of research literature is already dedicated to this specific type of network. The asset and factor networks comprising 31 nodes and various edges presented in this chapter are summarized in Table 8.1, and the code to plot all networks simultaneously is shown in Box 8.6. The design algorithm used is the Kamada–Kawai, and the node size corresponds to the node degree of the specific network. The names of the networks that we use in the book are provided in Table 8.1. Note that we use only one node attribute for the network representations, but the use of other attributes simultaneously is possible and may enhance the network's information. For example, we can add liquidity in addition to the node property of asset and factor category. Alternatively, we can split the nodes into other explanatory types or categories like capital appreciation or capital accumulation or similar node attributes that might be specific to the underlying investment process. Figure 8.7 captures the node degree centrality in the 12 networks.

Note that networks are computed using the same dataset and categorization provided in Chapters 6 and 7. Network centrality is extensively discussed in Chapter 4.

TABLE 8.1 An Overview of the Asset and Factor Networks.

Name and Description	Type	Short Name	Algorithm
Correlation network (completed network)	undirected	netz_cor	Correlation coefficients
Undirected network	undirected	netz_undir	Correlation test
Partial -correlation network	undirected	netz_pcor	Partial correlations
Correlation test network	undirected	netz_corf	Correlation by Fischer transformation
Directed network	directed	netz_dir	Regression with squared term
Directed network with confounder	directed	netz_dir_conf	Regression with US dollar
Probabilistic Markov chain network	directed	netz_dir_mcn	Markov chain by correlations
Probabilistic network with Manhattan distance	directed	netz_dir_dist	Markov chain by Manhattan distance
Cholesky variance decomposition network	directed	netz_dir_cvd	Vector autoregression (VAR) and Cholesky decomposition
Granger causality network	directed	netz_dir_gct	Granger causality test
Gaussian network (least absolute shrinkage and selection operator [LASSO])	undirected	netz_undir_lasso	LASSO
Dichotomous regression model network	directed	netz_dir_p	Regression with dual operators
Bayesian network*	directed	netz_dir_bay	Bayesian probabilistic model
Wasserstein distance network*	undirected	nertz_dir_wd	Wasserstein distance L2-norm

Note: Throughout this book, we use all the networks except netz_dir_bay and netz_dir_wd.

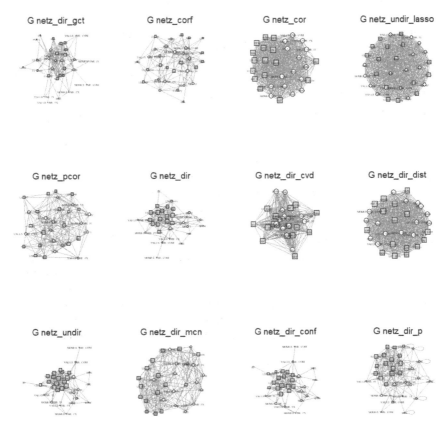

FIGURE 8.7 All Asset and Factor Networks with Node Degree Centrality.

BOX 8.6:   PLOTTING AN ALL ASSET AND FACTOR NETWORK.

```
#Plots all Networks with Degree Centralities
allem<-list(netz_dir_gct,netz_pcor,netz_undir,netz_corf, netz_dir,netz_dir_mcn,
netz_cor, netz_dir_cvd, netz_dir_conf, netz_undir_lasso, netz_dir_dist, netz_dir_p)
all.netz<-c("netz_dir_gct","netz_pcor","netz_undir","netz_corf",
"netz_dir","netz_dir_mcn", "netz_cor", "netz_dir_cvd","netz_dir_conf",
"netz_undir_lasso", "netz_dir_dist","netz_dir_p")
par(mfcol=c(3,4))
foreach (i=all.netz, j=allem) %do% {
   E(j)$arrow.size<-0
   plot(j, vertex.label.cex=0.4, layout=layout_with_kk,
vertex.size=sqrt(degree(j))*2,main=
bquote(paste('G ',.(i))))
}
```

KEY TAKEAWAYS

- To effectively model edges in networks where nodes are known and finite in the short-term but the edges may be unobservable, Markov chains and Bayesian networks can be used. These approaches provide robust frameworks for understanding and predicting the dynamics of network connections.
- The Markov chain network approach estimates the probability of transitioning between assets in the network, assigning a higher probability to switches between more similar assets based on similarity. The probabilistic adjacency matrix then details these probabilities, with each entry indicating the chance of transitioning from one asset to another within a single time step.
- The major advantage of Markov chain networks is their ability to probabilistically compute links within a network. This approach enables the modeling of transition probabilities at any given point in time. Essentially, this approach functions as a diffusion map, assigning coordinates in Euclidean space and measuring the distance (i.e., similarity) between points.
- The Bayesian approach to network modeling is fundamentally based on the concept of paths, distinguishing it from other forms such as walks and trails.
- Bayesian networks are specifically designed to simulate paths where information travels through each node only once, facilitating the identification of causality. This structure enables for a directed flow of influence across the network, ensuring that each node's impact on others is deliberate, rather than random.
- In Bayesian networks, each node is visited only once, whether for the flow of information, infections, or other process classifications. The resulting graph structure aligns with the principles of structural equation modeling, where the connections between nodes are defined using causal equations. This approach emphasizes the causal relationships inherent in the network's design.
- The estimation of causal relationships, the core of Bayesian networks, involves estimating cause relationships, which depend on the statistically significant coefficients of linear equations. When these coefficients indicate relationships, these relationships are directional, and the edges are represented as arrows pointing in the direction of causality, illustrating the influence of one node on another.

## CHAPTER 9

Network Processes in Asset Management

Contents

This chapter has two primary objectives. The first objective is to introduce several methods for evaluating network models and types. Given the variety of approaches to constructing networks, a key challenge in portfolio management is selecting the most suitable network model to meet specific investment criteria. The network models discussed in this chapter enable portfolio managers to simulate graphs based on predetermined inputs, thereby enhancing the investment process with deeper insights into the risks and potential outcomes associated with market factors represented in these graphs.

The second objective is to describe the pivotal role of network choice in portfolio management, especially from a graph-theoretical perspective. This choice critically influences portfolio allocation and the overall success of a portfolio strategy. Markowitz's foundational work (1952) established the importance of optimizing portfolios for risk and return. Selecting the right network model is a modern extension of this theory.

Choosing the best network model, however, involves complex decision-making. While traditional backtesting methods like calculating the Probabilistic Sharpe Ratio (PSR) and adjusting p-values for multiple testing are essential for validating portfolio strategies, the selection and examination of network models should occur earlier in the process. This is because these networks form the basis of subsequent portfolio strategies. The appropriate network selection is contingent upon the specific data and algorithms used. It requires a thorough model evaluation, a process supported by advancements in data science that offers the necessary algorithms for this task. Proper evaluation helps ensure that the network model chosen aligns well with the strategic objectives and data characteristics of the portfolio management endeavor.

The aim of the statistical models discussed in this chapter is to use different types of unobservable and empirical attributes and adjacency matrices of already constructed or observed networks to generate new graphs and model edges. In network literature, these models are defined as statistical models for network processes, because the underlying mechanisms are intrinsic or unobserved properties of networks. Such models include the Exponential Random Graph Model (ERGM), Latent Network Model (LNM), and Laplacian Graph Kernel and Spectral Partitioning Model (LKSP).

As an example, we discuss the ERGM, a leading approach in statistical network modeling, by Harris (2013), which has become a benchmark for its robust capabilities in modeling network data. The underlying principle of ERGM is that the edges of a network are a function of the properties of an existing network. These characteristics often include the idea of structural equivalence, where nodes are connected based on similar roles or positions within the network, expressed through real values. Alternatively, connections might be explained by homophily – the tendency of nodes to connect with others that are similar to them – measured using specific distance metrics.[1]

Often, the model integrates both these concepts to more accurately depict the network's structure. ERGM stands out by pinpointing the statistically significant attributes that influence the formation of connections within the network. It employs sophisticated statistical inference techniques to align the model closely with the observed data, ensuring that the model captures the essential dynamics of the network. This approach enables researchers and analysts to understand and predict network behaviors based on underlying structural properties.

A powerful model that relies on simulated data and underlying networks is the LNM. The LNM assumes that the observed network is influenced by unobserved (i.e., latent) variables, which determine the edges in the network. LMN's major advantage is that it models and uses latent structures to correct the observed network, which might be prone to noise or errors such as misspecification of edges. As mentioned in previous chapters, portfolio networks are vulnerable to estimation errors, and the LNM model serves as a corrective measure for these inaccuracies. The LNM approach involves estimating probabilistic models for latent variables, which helps refine the network analysis's accuracy. It does so by accounting for unobserved factors that influence network dynamics. By doing so, the model increases the reliability of the network's representation of interconnections and dependencies within a portfolio, offering a more robust framework for managing and understanding portfolio risks.

The LKSP model uses kernels to produce a similarity matrix representing graphs. This model integrates the adjacency matrix and the degree matrices of predefined graphs, extracting the information in the form of eigenvalues and eigenvectors from the Laplacian matrix. Eigenvalues describe the variance within the dataset, with larger eigenvalues explaining a greater portion of the variance. The eigenvalues and the corresponding eigenvectors describe a dataset. The information contained within the eigenvectors is used to

---

[1]Homophily, in a network context, refers to the social phenomenon according to which similar individuals attract and connect to other individuals with similar characteristics.

represent the community structure of a network. The methods used in the LKSP approach primarily involve sophisticated algebraic operations and matrix manipulations, enabling for a deeper understanding and visualization of the network's underlying structure.

The shared property of the statistical models for network processes discussed in this chapter is that network modeling requires a predefined or existing network in which the node and edge properties are used as covariates, or input variables (referred to as attributes), to model and simulate a network. The network models presented in this chapter require an observed or at least a predefined network, such as a partial-correlation network. The advantage of the three models – ERGM, LKSP, and LNM – is that they provide visualization and graph simulation using node attributes or intrinsic information.

These three models offer different perspectives and serve different purposes when analyzing portfolio networks. LNM is primarily concerned with identifying the underlying structure, which is often hidden, that generates the observed network. By doing so, it provides insight into the unobserved dynamics impacting the network's behavior. ERGM directly models the probability of observing specific network structures, modeling the network formation based on network statistics. LKSP produces clusters and edge patterns in the networks using intrinsic information encoded in the eigenvalues and eigenvectors.

In the last section of this chapter, we investigate one of the most interesting applications of graph theory that intersects with causality: casual network inference under interference. This section provides a comprehensive overview of casual network inference and interference, using examples from asset and factor networks to examine causal relationships and the effects of node manipulation in various forms. Potential sources of this manipulation could be analyst predictions, direct actions by financial market regulatory authorities, policy interventions by central banks, or other market interventions. This section aims to elucidate how different influences within a network can affect its overall dynamics and the implications of these changes on network behavior and performance. Causal network inference investigates the potential outcomes under network interference, examining how the influence on any specific nodes might affect the entire network.[2]

Network models used to shape the statistical process of a graph, which are not covered in this book, include the network block model and the nearest neighbor model. The major reason for this exclusion is that financial and specifically portfolio networks usually do not exist a priori but are modeled. The simulation and network experiments for already-defined graphs are the main purposes of this chapter.

NETWORK EVALUATION

Various methods are available to evaluate the accuracy of a network model in aligning with real-world data. Due to the unobservability of the true network in finance, we rely on assumptions. Therefore, simulations serve as powerful instruments when the actual interactions between financial instruments are hidden or difficult to detect. Among these tools, the Monte Carlo simulation is widely used in finance. It is particularly useful for modeling scenarios where direct observation may be impractical. These simulations help in approximating the behavior and dynamics of financial networks under various hypothetical scenarios.[3]

---

[2]In Chapter 12, we describe risk management approaches that investigate the node and link behavior from a risk management perspective. That is, Chapter 12's objective is to describe risk management techniques that examine node behavior during periods of elevated risk and the potential impact of spillover effects. While Part 3 continues to concentrate on portfolio management, the introduction of causality network inference serves as a pivotal link to the risk management aspects of the book. We believe this approach will improve your understanding of how interconnectedness within networks can influence overall risk management strategies.

[3]To evaluate the significance of a strategy, we apply the technique developed by Bailey and Lopez de Prado (2014) and Harvey and Liu (2014). The Probabilistic Sharpe Ratio (PSR) is required to evaluate strategies and expresses the

It is important to understand that the focus of the simulation procedure here is not to construct a new network. Rather, its primary purpose is to evaluate existing or predefined networks to select the most appropriate choice for use in portfolio and risk management. The network selection process can be divided into two main components: the estimation of goodness-of-fit, which relies on simulation techniques; and the network intersection method. The latter is more intuitive and heuristic, making use of the descriptive statistics of graphs outlined in Chapter 2. This structured approach ensures that the chosen network effectively aligns with the specific requirements of risk and portfolio management strategies.

Goodness-of-Fit

The most fundamental characteristics of networks, such as density, degree centrality, diameter, and reciprocity, along with their distributions, are typically used to measure the goodness-of-fit of a network. The purpose of assessing goodness-of-fit is to determine whether the model's characteristics adequately match the values observed in the simulated graph. A significant difference between the model and the simulated graph is an indication of a lack of goodness-of-fit.

While useful, the concept of goodness-of-fit, can be somewhat misleading. Its primary goal is to assess how well the underlying model aligns with the original model it is meant to represent. As discussed later in this chapter, the ERGM deals with the original and simulated versions of the model to assess the alignment, applying the original principles of the goodness-of-fit concept. The key objective of the goodness-of-fit concept is to select the best model by generating numerous random networks from the fitted model, and then comparing these graphs with the initially estimated network.

To evaluate the goodness-of-fit concept across different network models, we employ stochastic models based on Hoff's eigenmodel.[4] The intuition behind this approach is to identify the model with the highest area under the curve (AUC) among all the models for networks constructed from financial data, a metric for evaluating the predictive acurrary of network models.

Cross-validation is widely applied in data science and helps evaluate the networks' accuracy for portfolio construction. This is an essential undertaking, as an overfitted or too sparse asset network might greatly impact the portfolio strategy. Cross-validation provides information on the ability to predict the behavior of the network given an underlying structure and a specific subset. The results of the predictions generated using each underlying network used in portfolio management can be assessed by examining the receiver operating characteristic (ROC) curves. The ROC curve is a graphical representation used to evaluate the performance of a binary classifier system. By plotting the true positive rate on the vertical axis and the false positive rate on the vertical axis, the ROC summarizes the proportion of actual positive models, which are correctly identified relative to the actual negative models that are incorrectly identified as

---

deflated Sharpe ratio (DSR) as a probability. Where s is the skewness, k is the kurtosis, γ is the Euler–Mascheroni constant 0.5772, N is the number of strategies, T is the length of the time-series, [SR*] is the threshold Sharpe ratio, $\widehat{SR}$ is the annualized Sharpe ratio using monthly data $(\sqrt{12})$, and Z is the cumulative distribution function of the standard normal distribution.

$$\widehat{PSR}[SR^*] = Z\left[\frac{(\widehat{SR} - SR^*)\sqrt{T-1}}{\sqrt{1 - \hat{s}\widehat{SR} + \frac{\hat{k}-1}{4}\widehat{SR}^2}}\right], \quad SR^* = \sqrt{Var\left[\{\widehat{SR}_n\}\right]}\left[(1-\gamma)Z^{-1}\left[1 - \frac{1}{N}\right] + \gamma Z^{-1}\left[1 - \frac{1}{N}e^{-1}\right]\right]$$

[4] See Hoff et al. (2002) for the description of latent network effects, and Hoff (2007) and the description of the "Package 'eigenmodel'" at https://cran.r-project.org/web/packages/eigenmodel/eigenmodel.pdf

positives at various threshold levels. Specifically, in a classification algorithm, the threshold is the point at which a decision is made about whether a given network model belongs to a specific class.[5]

The AUC value is a measure of the effectiveness of the classification algorithm. The higher the AUC value, the better the classifier is. A larger AUC indicates that the characteristics of the simulated model closely match those of the network model used as a benchmark model. To compare networks for the respective data (e.g., assets and factors, bond and equity funds, and single hedge funds), it is reasonable to run the eigenmodel simulation without specific covariates.

Figure 9.1 illustrates the AUC curves for various asset and factor networks. The AUC values are as follows: 0.83 for the overall network, 0.44 for netz_pcor, and 0.85 for netz_dir_gct. The AUC for netz_undir is slightly higher at 0.86, while netz_dir_conf also has an AUC of 0.83, and netz_dir_m stands at 0.80. The AUC value for netz_corf is relatively lower at 0.63, but it increases to 0.88 for netz_dir_mcn. It is evident that netz_pcor and netz_corf have significantly lower AUC values, suggesting that these networks exhibit poorer characteristics compared to others. The methodology used for these estimations is detailed in Box 9.1.

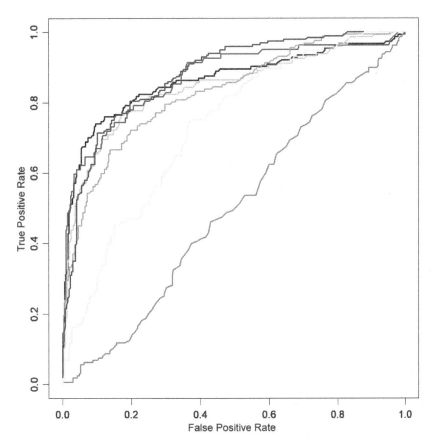

FIGURE 9.1 ROC Curves Comparing the Goodness-of-Fit for the Different Eigenmodels for Asset and Factor Networks.

---

[5]See Provost and Fawcett (2013).

BOX 9.1: AN UNDIRECTED CORRELATION-BASED FISCHER TRANSFORMATION ASSET AND FACTOR NETWORK.

```
# Generate a sample index for cross-validation
p.index <- sample(1:465) # Total number of links is 930 for a 31-node network

# Define the number of folds
nfolds <- 5
nmiss <- 465 / nfolds

# Get the adjacency matrix of the underlying network
A <- as_adjacency_matrix(netz_dir, sparse = FALSE)
vect <- A[lower.tri(A)]
vect <- as.numeric(vect)
vect.pred <- numeric(length(vect))

# Perform cross-validation
for (i in seq_len(nfolds)) {
  # Determine missing indices for the current fold
  missing.index <- seq(((i - 1) * nmiss + 1), (i * nmiss))
  A.missing.index <- p.index[missing.index]

  # Create a temporary vector with missing values
  vect.temp <- vect
  vect.temp[A.missing.index] <- NA

  # Convert the temporary vector back to a 31-nodes symmetric matrix
  a.temp <- matrix(0, 31, 31)
  a.temp[lower.tri(a.temp)] <- vect.temp
  a.temp <- a.temp + t(a.temp)

  # Fit the model
  model.fit <- eigenmodel_mcmc(Y = a.temp, R = 2, S = 1100, burn = 1000)

  # Get the predicted values
  model.pred <- model.fit$Y_postmean
  model.pred.vec <- model.pred[lower.tri(model.pred)]
  vect.pred[A.missing.index] <- model.pred.vec[A.missing.index]
}

# Plot the ROC and AUC for the simulation
predicted.g <- prediction(vect.pred, vect)
perf.g <- performance(predicted.g, "tpr", "fpr")
plot(perf.g, col = "red", lwd = 2)
perf.g.auc <- performance(predicted.g, "auc")
print(slot(perf.g.auc, "y.values"))
```

Figure 9.2 displays the ROC curves comparing the goodness-of-fit for three different networks: an equity-bond fund directed network with 322 nodes proposed by Konstantinov and Rusev (2020), equity markets network, and a correlation test network for 239 single hedge funds studied by Konstantinov and Simonian (2020). The AUC value for the Granger causality-based directed equity-bond fund network is 0.90, while the AUC value for the hedge fund network is 0.97.

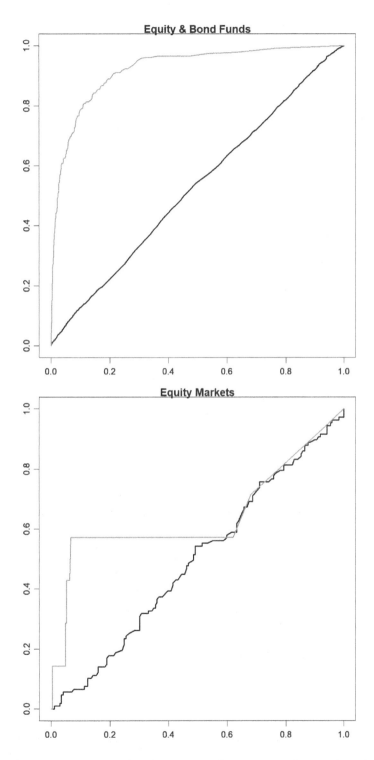

FIGURE 9.2 Examples for AUC Curves: Bond and Equity Funds, Equity Markets, and Single Hedge Funds.
Note: we use a directed Granger causality network and a partial correlation network for the equity and bond funds and the equity markets. For the single hedge funds, we used a directed network, a partial correlation network, and an undirected network.

(*Continued*)

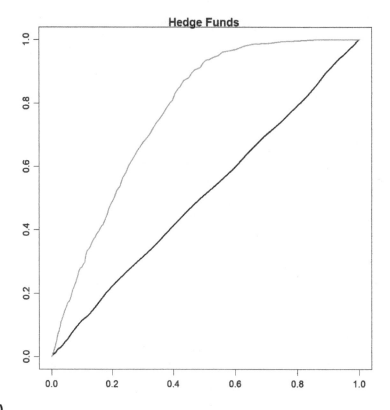

FIGURE 9.2 (CONT'D)

The Intersection Method

The network literature provides several powerful methods to measure network similarities.[6] In this section, we employ a more direct approach that is based on comparing network descriptive statistics such as degree distribution, centrality, density, reciprocity, diameter, distance, transitivity, and clustering.

Several mathematical models enable the comparison of different network types, with an extensive summary provided by Kara et al. (2015). One of the simplest and most intuitive methods applicable to portfolios is the comparison of edge distances. The main idea behind the intersection procedure is to assess the links between nodes, and then determine the differences based on the adjacency matrices. This procedure, known as the Hamming distance, is like the Manhattan distance (Hamming, 1950). The primary distinction between Manhattan distance and Hamming distance is that Hamming distance considers cases where $i \neq j$. One fundamental rule is that the networks being compared should have the same number of nodes. The main concept involves computing the distance between the two adjacency matrices and is akin to the similarity ratio developed by Baitinger and Papenbrock (2017a), which measures the intersection of edges in two adjacency matrices divided by the node count.

---

[6]Tantardini, Ieva, Tajoli, and Piccardi (2019) and Shimada, et al. (2016) provide a comprehensive study describing and comparing network comparison techniques. There are two main methods: the known-node-correspondence method, which compares networks with same node set; and the unknown-node-correspondence method, which enables the comparison of different networks with different sizes, degrees, and connections.

The distance between pairwise networks can be estimated as the difference between the adjacency matrices's edge counts. Let us define this relation as the network intersection ratio, representing the disparity between the edge counts of pairwise networks minus the intersection of mutual edges between the two networks:

$$NIR = \sum_i m_a + \sum_i m_b - 2\sum_i m_{a,b} \tag{9.1}$$

where m_a is the number of edges in the first graph, m_b is the number of edges of the second graph, and $m_{a,b}$ is the number of joint edges between the two graphs.

Because in portfolio and risk management there may be a large number of simulated matrices, the result of the comparison would be a pairwise Hamming distance matrix comprising the differences in edges. The shorter the distance (i.e., lower the number), the fewer the differences in the networks. It's important to note that the number of nodes, or network size, must be equal when comparing the networks and estimating the intersection.

A simple example illustrates the logic. Consider three different graphs computed for 31 nodes: a directed network (netz_dir), an undirected network (netz_undir), and the completed correlation-based network (netz_cor). Table 9.1 captures the details for the intersection analysis for these three examples of asset and factor networks. Figure 9.3 displays the intersection graph between the completed and the directed network in the the netz_dir vs netz_cor example. For illustrative purposes, the edges are curved and bidirectional, showing the arrows. The code is provided in Box 9.2.

The primary purpose of the graph intersection method is to extract information about the estimated graphs and to identify possible information loss related to undetected edges in the original estimations. By comparing the networks using the intersection method, one can determine how closely the different networks align and identify any discrepancies that may arise from undetected edges. This method helps to ensure that the chosen network model is robust and reliable for portfolio and risk management purposes.

Once the intersection analysis is computed, it is necessary to compute all descriptive network statistics for the networks that result from the intersection method. A simple code is provided in Box 9.3.

TABLE 9.1 Network Intersection for the Directed, Undirected, and Completed Asset and Factor Network

Links (Degree)	Directed	Undirected	Completed
Directed	0		
Undirected	271 (17.41)	0	
Completed	282 (18.19)	308 (19.87)	0

Note: We use netz_undir, netz_dir, and netz_cor networks for this example.

BOX 9.2: ESTIMATING THE EDGE DIFFERENCE BETWEEN TWO NETWORKS.

```
#Estimate the difference in the intersection that has common edges of two networks with
same size:
int<-graph.intersection(netz_dir,netz_cor)
#to compute the difference in edges between the graphs:
```

(Continued)

(Continued)

```
difference<-ecount(netz_dir)+ecount(netz_cor)-2*ecount(int)
mean(degree(int))
#consider whether a graph is simple, that is whether the network comprises multiple edges
and loops
is.simple(int)
#print the summary of the intermediate network
summary(int)
E(int)$arrow.size<-0.1
plot(int, vertex.size=5,vertex.label.cex=0.6,
layout=layout_with_kk,vertex.color="grey90",edge.curved=.2)
```

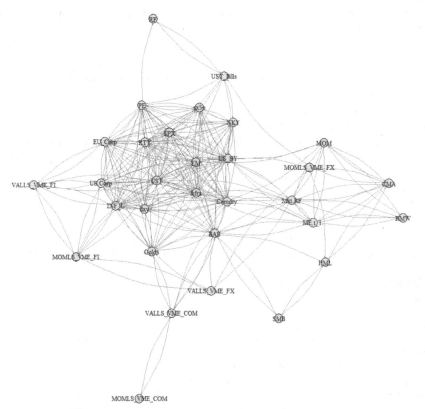

FIGURE 9.3   A Graph Intersection: A Directed vs. a Completed Graph.

BOX 9.3:   PRINTING ALL NETWORK STATISTICS AN INTERSECTED NETWORK.

```
list.stat<-c(ecount(int),
        vcount(int),
        edge_density(int),
        mean(degree(int)),
```

```
            compactness(int),

            reciprocity(int),

            transitivity(int),

            assortativity_degree(int),

            diameter(int),

            centr_degree(int)$centralization,

            centr_eigen(int)$centralization,

            average.path.length(int),

            components(int)$no,

            modularity(cluster_infomap(as.undirected(int))),

            modularity(cluster_louvain(as.undirected(int))),

            modularity(cluster_walktrap(as.undirected(int))),

            modularity(cluster_leading_eigen(as.undirected(int))),

            modularity(cluster_fast_greedy(as.undirected(int))))
desc.stat<-cbind(list.stat)
rownames(desc.stat)<-c("Links","Nodes", "Density","Average Degree","Compactness",
"Reciprocity", "Transitivity", "Clustering", "Diameter", "Degree Centralization", "Eigen
Centralization", "Distance", "Components", "Mod. Cluster Infomap","Mod. Cluster
Louvain","Mod. Cluster Walktrap","Mod. Cluster Leading Eigen","Mod. Cluster Fast Greedy")
desc.stat
#evaluate whether the intersection graph is isomporphic ot the two initial graphs
is_isomorphic_to(int,netz_dir)
is_isomorphic_to(int,netz_cor)
```

The result is a matrix displaying distances between the networks, quantified by the number of differing edges. The distance between the directed and the undirected networks is the smallest, involving only 271 edges, which raises important questions from a portfolio management perspective: Do the differences between these networks signify a loss of information, and what could be the implications if the distances are significantly large? Moreover, it raises the question as to whether there might be an informational gain in the intermediate network configurations. This inquiry can be addressed in two ways.

The first approach is to evaluate whether the intermediate network captures significant information potentially crucial for portfolio allocation. It involves assessing whether this network operates within a connected regime. By applying insights from network theory, particularly regarding the subcritical and connected regimes, researchers can determine the likelihood that the network is fully connected. This analysis aids in understanding the network's structure and its implications for information flow and decision-making in portfolio management. In other words, a network in a subcritical regime contains no useful information, while a network in a supercritical regime offers information gain.

The second step when evaluating networks is to investigate the informational gain that might result from considering the network-in-between and running the goodness-of-fit procedure, then estimating the area under the ROC curve for that network. The ROC curve for the intersection network between the undirected and the correlation network is 0.86, suggesting valuable information in this graph worth considering.

Jaccard Distance for Network Similarity   An alternative way to estimate network similarity is to implement the similarity ratio suggested by Baitinger and Papenbrock (2017a), which involves the Jaccard distance discussed in Chapter 6. In this context, the Jaccard distance is applied to the edge structure of networks of the same size. The similarity ratio measures the intersection of graph edges relative to the network size (i.e., number of vertices). It is important to note that this method is suitable for comparing networks with an equal number of nodes. Formally, the ratio is given by:

$$\text{Similarity} = \frac{|m^{G_1} \cap m^{G_2}|}{n-1}, \text{ with } G_i(n, m_i) \tag{9.2}$$

where n is the number of nodes, and m is the number of edges in the corresponding graph $G(n, m)$. This ratio provides a measure of how similar or different two networks are, based on their edge structures.

The Wasserstein Distance for Network Similarity   One of the major ideas in Chapter 6 was to provide an overview of the association models used to build networks. One of these models estimates the distance between nodes using the p-th Wasserstein distance, the p-th root of the total cost incurred to transport masses. Comparing the distance between networks using the Wasserstein distance assumes that the adjacency matrices of the networks represent the empirical distribution of the node edge relationships. In other words, the Wasserstein distance metric is used to estimate the distances between networks of same size. The larger the distance, the more dissimilar the networks are, indicating that there is information not captured by the two networks. A threshold level may also be used for estimating this distance.

STATISTICAL MODELS FOR NETWORK PROCESSES

This section enhances the previously established analytical framework by examining further aspects of network construction and manipulation within the context of portfolio management. Here, we introduce statistical models rooted in graph theory. The key distinction between the models discussed in this section and the probabilistic models discussed in Chapter 8 lies in their approach to network modeling.

The models discussed in this section are designed to work with a preexisting network architecture. They leverage endogenous node and edge characteristics, or attributes, to statistically model the process of network connectedness. In contrast, the models discussed in Chapter 8 focused on explicitly modeling networks. Now, we shift to using attributes or other functional variables to predict the behaviors of nodes and edges. The methods covered in this section are kernel methods, which focus on ERGM, LKSP, and LNM. These models include subnetwork separation, adjacency matrix enhancements, and modeling of external factors, all which are valuable enhancements in portfolio allocation.

Exponential Random Graph Model

The ERGM is perhaps the most powerful and flexible model for analyzing network structures. The major distinction between ERGM and more traditional models, such as regression models, lies in their approach to modeling relationships. While regression models directly predict the response or edges, ERGM uses a logistic function to model the probability of link formation between nodes, based on specific attributes or covariates. This enables the ERGM to incorporate and test various local node and edge characteristics, extending these to model the entire network. Within the model, these characteristics are treated as covariates.

ERGM operates on the statistical principles of the Monte Carlo Markov Chain simulation that uses maximum likelihood estimation (MLE) to analyze data. This enables the model to generate numerous potential networks that should reflect the model's estimated parameters. Although this a rigorous approach, the ERGM remains fundamentally probabilistic, estimating the likelihood of an edge forming between two nodes conditional on the presence of all other edges in the network, thereby taking into consideration complex interdependencies within the network structure.

General Overview   ERGM's purpose is to model edges. In this respect, the ERGM is like the Erdös-Renyi model discussed in Chapter 5, in which the nodes are fixed and the edge probability is modeled. Recall that edge density is the network metric used to provide information regarding the graph's completeness given the number of nodes ranging between zero and one. The ERGM uses network and observational data to statistically estimate the edge structure and simulate several graphs that might possess properties similar to the empirically observed networks. An underlying network that serves as information from which to extract edge and node structure represented by the adjacency matrix is necessary for the ERGM.

According to Borgatti et al. (2022), estimating parameters in an ERGM involves using MLE. The objective of MLE is to find the parameter values, denoted as θ_k, which maximize the likelihood of observing the actual network given the model. This is achieved by maximizing the exponent of the probability, of the observed network, relative to the sum of the exponent probabilities for all possible networks with the same number of nodes. The results of the MLE procedure is convergence towards an optimal estimation that captures network properties like triangles, degrees, density, paths, reciprocity (in the case of directed networks), and assortative mixing. Generating a distribution for node degrees, density, and triangles among others, MLE seeks to match the criteria of the observed network by maximizing the probability of finding such a network from a set of randomly generated networks.

The formalistic part of the model is worth discussing. The model estimates the probability of a link between nodes i and j in a graph $G(n, m)$, which is a random graph, and the edges m of the graph are represented by random variables q_{ij} that are the entries of the random adjacency matrix $[Q]_{ij}$. Formalistically, the ERGM suggested by Hunter et al. (2008), Morris et al. (2008) and Harris (2013), and applied by Luke (2015) and Kolaczyk and Csardi (2020), is given by:[7]

$$P\left(q_{ij} = 1 \mid n \text{ nodes}, Q_{ij}^C\right) = \frac{1}{c} e^{\sum_{k=1}^{K} \theta_k \delta_k(q)} \tag{9.3}$$

where here θ_k is the coefficient for the edges term, $\delta_k(q)$ is the change statistic for the any of the k terms included in the model, and c is a normalizing constant that ensures that the probabilities lie always between 0 and 1 over all estimated networks. The logistic function of the model is more intuitive and easier to interpret probabilistically in the range from 0 to 1.[8] In the adjacency matrix $[Q]_{ij}$, the entry q_{ij} represents dyads, taking a value of 1 if nodes i and j share a link, and zero, otherwise.

Harris (2013) and Hunter et al. (2008) aptly describe the ERGM as being like a binary logistic model, where the presence of an edge in a network is influenced by network properties and attributes that aim to predict the probability of that edge. In this model, edge predictions are calculated using the principles of logistic regression, where coefficients are multiplied by specific attribute values to express the log odds as probabilities. These network properties facilitate hypothesis testing to explore the association of these attributes with edge formation. Statistical confidence intervals are employed to assess the significance of the coefficients, enabling the ERGM to model interactions between network attributes included in the model equation while acknowledging the inherent nonindependence among nodes in a network.

Luke (2015) highlights the following ERGM's four major advantages:

1. It considers complex interaction structures.
2. It can deal with a large number of characteristics that can be used as edge predictors.

---

[7] The authors developed the *ERGM* package in the statistical software *R*, which we use in this chapter.
[8] See James et al. (2013) and Borgatti et al. (2022) For a detailed explanation, see Harris (2013). The logistic function expresses directly the probability $P(q_{ij})$.

3. It is integrated into statistical models that enable easier implementation.
4. The entire network interconnectedness and structure might be influenced by local node and edge dependencies and relationships.

The ERGM is a powerful approach wherein the simulated networks differ from the initial null model, enabling the newly generated graphs to show different properties from the graphs obtained as compared to those obtained in previous steps. This is achieved by using four characteristic groups as edge predictors: node-level, edge-level, dyad-level, and local structure predictors. These edge predictors determine the network's connectedness. In other words, the addition of any type of attributes aims to examine its influence on the formation of a links between the nodes. Statistically speaking, we test the null hypothesis that there is no association between any attribute (e.g., node, edge, local structure, or dyadic) and the formation of an edge, against the alternative hypothesis that there is an association. We use the reported statistics to evaluate the significance of the parameters in the model and to determine whether to reject or accept the null hypothesis regarding the added attributes.

According to Harris (2013), the null hypothesis is rejected in favor of the alternative hypothesis when p-values are lower than a certain threshold level, say $p < 5\%$. Stated differently, as soon as the p-value is less than the threshold level, there is a significant association between the probability of an edge and the specific attribute or covariate used. Because we are running multiple tests, adjusting the p-values for FWER and FDR is highly necessary. Starting from a null model, in which the edges are determined using observed data, new edge connectedness and network are simulated using vertex attributes and data obtained from exogenous or endogenous properties. For example, local parameters such as diameter, degree, or density as well as individual node properties and attributes, can be generalized across the entire network. Consequently, the ERGM enables the creation of customized networks, which are customized for a portfolio manager's needs by incorporating a mix of qualitative and quantitative attributes for nodes and edges. This tailored approach enables a nuanced analysis of the network structures, enhancing the relevance and applicability of the model in strategic portfolio management.

The determination of which model to select is based on the use of the Akaike Information Criterion (AIC) and the Schwarz Criterion (SC), also known as the Bayesian Information Criterion (BIC). The formula for the AIC and SC are:[9]

$$AIC = 2k - ln\left(\frac{RSS}{n}\right) \tag{9.4}$$

$$SC = n\,ln\left(\frac{RSS}{n}\right) + k\,ln(n) \tag{9.5}$$

where n is the number of data points in the time-series, RSS is the residual sum of squares, and k is the number of factors in a model.

The intuition behind model selection and the AIC and BIC is that when researchers identify a model, a certain amount of information is always lost. That is, an ERGM applied cannot be better than the true model that describes the network. Therefore, portfolio managers should select the model with the smallest information loss, which is what AIC or BIC seek to do.

The starting point in ERGMs is the building of the null model, which provides a basic network structure determined by the edges. Therefore, we discuss the null model first and provide an example. Before we

---

[9] James, Witten, Hastie, and Tibshirani (2013) show how machine- and statistical-learning algorithms can be used in model selection. See Akaike (1973) and Schwartz (1978).

start with the null model, it is necessary to define the algorithm for ERGM. It can be split into the following steps:

1. Select observed or estimated network and extract the adjacency matrix of that network.
2. Run the null model and estimate the base edge density.
3. Define and run models with node-level, edge-level, dyadic-level, and local-structure attributes and run the corresponding models.
4. Drop all nonsignificant coefficients in every step and consider the model selection criterions AIC or BIC.
5. Estimate the goodness-of-fit model.
6. Run simulations and visualize the original and simulated networks.

The Null Model   The null model represents the basic network model without any predictors. That is, the only property used in the mathematical expression of the logistic function is that of the intercept. The intercept of the null model represents the edges of the network like that of the underlying network. Note that the coefficient of the intercept is multiplied by 1, which is the variable representing the change statistic of the network, which in our case is the edges themselves. This is because the model estimates the probability of one edge or link between the nodes. In other words, we estimate the coefficient of producing one link between the nodes.

For example, if we use an observed or estimated asset and factor network comprising 31 nodes with, say, 50 edges between them, then the null model assumes the same number of edges. Taking the logistic transformation of the edges parameter from the model gives the edge density, or the probability of edges between nodes i and j in the network. The edge probabilities between nodes i and j are estimated using the edge term parameter obtained from an observable network in the null model.

$$p_{ij} = \frac{1}{\left(1 + e^{-(\theta\delta)}\right)} \tag{9.6}$$

where θ is the coefficient for the edges term, and δ is the change statistic for the edges term.

To demonstrate the ERGM, we apply the ERGM procedure to one of the networks previously constructed in Chapter 6. It's important to note that the selected network for this analysis must not be a complete graph. Meaning that it should not have an edge density of 1. In other words, it is useless to use completed (correlation-based) networks with a density of 1 in the ERGM model. The summary output from the null model analysis of this network is presented in Table 9.2.

We select the undirected correlation test network (netz_corf). The null model comprises only one variable, which is the edges of the observed graph. The edges parameter is typically negative and statistically significant for real networks. Using the code in Box 9.4, the probability of the edges in the ERGM network is roughly 25%.

TABLE 9.2   The Null Model Output.

```
Call:
ergm(formula = g ~ edges, control = control.ergm(seed = 31))

Maximum Likelihood Results:

        Estimate Std. Error MCMC % z value Pr(>|z|)
edges  -1.09003    0.07557      0   -14.43  <1e-04  ***
---
Signif. codes:   0 '***' 0.001 '**' 0.01 '*' 0.05 '.' 0.1 ' ' 1
     Null Deviance: 1289  on 930  degrees of freedom
 Residual Deviance: 1049  on 929  degrees of freedom

AIC: 1051 BIC: 1056 (Smaller is better. MC Std. Err. = 0)
```

BOX 9.4:   AN ERGM NULL MODEL FOR AN UNDERLYING UNDIRECTED CORRELATION TEST ASSET AND FACTOR NETWORK.

```
#Set the original (observed) network in the igraph package
        A.sm<-as.matrix(as_adjacency_matrix(netz_corf))
library(ergm)
        g<-network(A.sm) #set a network in ergm & network package using the adjacency
matrix of an observed network.

#Building the Null Model with the only term available as intercept which is edges
        model0<-ergm(g~edges, control=control.ergm(seed=31))
        summary(model0)
        1/(1+exp(coef(model0)[1])) #compute the edge density of the null model
        plogis(coef(model0)[1])#compute the edge probability using the logistic model
#edges
0.2516
```

TABLE 9.3 An ERGM Including Node-Level Attributes.

```
Call:
ergm(formula = g ~ edges + nodefactor("liquidity") + nodefactor("category") +
    nodecov("volatility") + nodecov("exp.returns"))

Maximum Likelihood Results:
```

	Estimate	Std. Error	MCMC %	z value	Pr(>|z|)
edges	-1.44671	0.29383	0	-4.924	<1e-04***
nodefactor.liquidity.L	0.06408	0.12908	0	0.496	0.620
nodefactor.category.F	0.56934	0.11836	0	4.810	<1e-04***
nodecov.volatility	-1.93738	3.00417	0	-0.645	0.519
nodecov.exp.returns	-33.05746	20.58799	0	-1.606	0.108

```
---
Signif. codes:   0  '***'  0.001  '**'   0.01   '*' 0.05  '.'   0.1    ' '    1

     Null Deviance: 1289  on 930  degrees of freedom
 Residual Deviance: 1013  on 925  degrees of freedom

AIC: 1023   BIC: 1048   (Smaller is better. MC Std. Err. = 0)
```

Node-Level Attributes   Once the null model is generated, node attributes are typically the first added. Generally, node-level covariates are properties of the nodes that can shape and determine the network structure. These attributes can be qualitative or quantitative expressions. Qualitative attributes often include node categories such as sectors, industry groups, ratings, currencies, or other local properties in asset management. Quantitative node properties may include specific returns, risk metrics, or other factors derived using econometric models or other analytical functions.

We add node factor attributes based on the liquidity and category of the factors and assets as well as node covariates based on expected returns and volatility. The ERGM run that incorporates node-level attributes is presented in Table 9.3. Box 9.5 provides a summary of the code that utilizes node-level attributes.

BOX 9.5: ADDING NODE-LEVEL ATTRIBUTES AND RUNNING THE ERGM MODEL WITH NODE COVARIATES.

```
#Set Node qualitative and quantitative Covariates
      #set categorial attributes
      g %v% "liquidity"<-c("L", "L", "L", "L", "L", "L", "L", "L", "L", "L", "I", "I",
"L", "L", "L", "L", "I", "I", "I", "L", "I", "L", "L", "L", "L", "L", "I", "I", "I", "I",
"L") #Liquidity as node categorial attribute
      g %v% "category"<-c("F", "F", "F", "F", "F", "F", "A", "A", "A", "A", "A", "A",
"A", "A", "A", "A", "A", "A", "A", "A", "A", "A", "F", "F", "F", "F", "F", "F", "F", "F",
"F") #Category as node categorial attribute
      #run model 1 with qualitative attributes
      model1<-ergm(g~edges+nodefactor("liquidity")+nodefactor("category"))
      summary(model1)
      #set quantitative attributes
      volatility<-(apply(returns,2, function(x) sd(x))) #compute volatility
      g %v% "volatility"<-volatility #set volatility as node attribute
      expected.returns<-(apply(returns,2, function(x) mean(x))) #compute mean returns
      g %v% "exp.returns"<-expected.returns #set expected returns as node attribute
      #run model 2 with both qualitative and quantitative attributes
      model2<-ergm(g~edges+nodefactor("liquidity")+nodefactor("category")+nodecov
("volatility")+nodecov("exp.returns"))
      summary(model2)
plogis(coef(model2)[1]+coef(model2)[3])#estimate the edge probability given singificant
coefficients
#edges
0.2937
```

The attributes found to be statistically significant are included in the next step when dyad-level attributes are added to the ERGM. In our illustration, the coefficients for the edges and the node-factor attributes based on the category show statistically significant coefficients, while not statistically significant variables are dropped from the model. After incorporating node covariates, the edge probability in the ERGM is approximately 29%. Note that the ERGM with node covariates exhibits a significant improvement, according to both the AIC and BIC.

Dyad-Level Attributes   Dyad-level attributes capture a key aspect of networks known as homophily, which describes the tendency of similar nodes to connect with one another or, conversely, to dissimilar nodes. Originating from the social sciences, this concept explains how individuals with similar characteristics are more likely to form connections based on specific criteria. In financial networks, a common hypothesis to test might be whether assets with similar liquidity levels tend to connect more frequently than with assets of differing liquidity levels. While it is possible to include specifications of other qualitative and quantitative attributes, integration of both node-level attributes and relational or interaction terms is contingent upon the available degrees of freedom and predefined criteria.[10]

Harris (2013) and Luke (2015) suggest that the most effective method to analyze the dyadic structure is through a mixing matrix. This matrix displays the raw frequencies between different node types based on classifications such as category or other node attributes. The matrix's elements describe the dyadic structure as a flow in columns and rows. For example, Table 9.4 provides examples from the asset and factor

---

[10]See Harris (2013). Note that, in our case, we defined both liquidity and category as binary criteria. More heterogenous definitions and attribute definition is generally preferredl.

networks under two classifications – category and liquidity – offering insights into the correlation test for an undirected network asset and factor network (netz_corf). It is important to note that the sums of rows and columns for each category should ideally be equal, as large discrepancies in these sums are undesirable. The model's results are displayed in Table 9.5, where both liquidity-related attributes and categories show statistical significance. The code incorporating dyad-level attributes is outlined in Box 9.6.

TABLE 9.4 Mixing Matrices for the Asset and Factor Undirected Correlation Test Network.

From/To	Assets	Factors	Sum
Assets	10	85	95
Factors	85	54	139
Sum	95	139	234
Illiquidity	12	61	73
Liquidity	61	100	161
Sum	73	161	234

TABLE 9.5 The Model Output for Dyad-Level Attributes.

```
Call:
ergm(formula = g ~ edges + nodefactor("category") + nodematch("liquidity") +
nodematch("category") + absdiff("volatility") + absdiff("exp.returns"))


Maximum Likelihood Results:

                     Estimate    Std. Error    MCMC%    z value    Pr(>|z|)
Edges                 -1.6232       0.2699          0     -6.014    <1e-04***
nodefactor.category.F  1.0925       0.1821          0      6.000    <1e-04***
nodematch.liquidity   -0.5061       0.1605          0     -3.154    0.00161**
nodematch.category    -1.5255       0.2050          0     -7.443    <1e-04***
absdiff.volatility     4.7534       4.8720          0      0.976    0.32924
absdiff.exp.returns   25.3642      29.6242          0      0.856    0.39189
---
Signif.  codes:  0  `***'  0.001  `**'  0.01  `*'  0.05  `.'  0.1  ` '  1


    Null Deviance: 1289.3  on  930  degrees of freedom
 Residual Deviance:  935.1  on  924  degrees of freedom

AIC:  947.1   BIC:  976.1   (Smaller is better. MC Std. Err. = 0)
```

BOX 9.6:   ADDING DYAD-LEVEL COVARIATES AND RUNNING THE ERGM MODEL WITH DYADIC COVARIATES.

```
#Set Dyadic Covariates
    #estimate the mixingmatrix that show the raw frequences between the different types
of nodes
    mixingmatrix(g, 'liquidity')
```

```
        mixingmatrix(g, 'category')
        #select the more appropriate as a covariate
        #run model with qualitative, quantitative and homophily attributes
        model3<-ergm(g~edges+nodefactor("category")+nodematch("liquidity")+nodematch
    ("category")+absdiff("volatility")+absdiff("exp.returns"))
        summary(model3)
```

TABLE 9.6   An ERGM Output with Edge-Level Covariates.

```
Call:
ergm(formula = g ~ edges + nodefactor("category") + nodematch("liquidity") +
    nodematch("category") + edgecov(dist.mat) + edgecov(sharpe))

Maximum Likelihood Results:

                          Estimate    Std. Error  MCMC%    z value    Pr(>|z|)
edges                     -1.59714     0.35754       0     -4.467     < 1e-04***
nodefactor.category.F      1.06262     0.18073       0      5.879     <1e-04***
nodematch.liquidity       -0.49112     0.15994       0     -3.071     0.00214**
nodematch.category        -1.52301     0.20463       0     -7.443     <1e-04***
edgecov.dist.mat           0.56905     0.88595       0      0.642     0.52068
edgecov.sharpe             0.04212     0.09347       0      0.451     0.65229
---
Signif. codes:   0 '***' 0.001 '**' 0.01 '*' 0.05 '.' 0.1 ' ' 1

      Null Deviance: 1289.3  on 930   degrees of freedom
  Residual Deviance:  936.4  on 924   degrees of freedom

AIC: 948.4   BIC: 977.4   (Smaller is better. MC Std. Err. = 0)
```

Edge-Level Attributes   The edge-level attributes differ from the node-level covariates in that they are relational. Specifically, the objective of the edge-level attributes is to gauge the relations between the nodes on the edge level, and then this information is used to predict the edges in the network. The relationships might be estimated and managed over distance and similarity metrics. The distance matrices are one of the most widely used choices (Luke, 2015). For example, the larger the distance between the nodes, the less likely that an edge might justify their information exchange. A closed-node distance means that the information exchange might result in a stronger edge. The edge-level covariates are usually in symmetric $n \times n$ matrix form.

We can enhance the ERGM by incorporating edge covariates such as a distance matrix and the Sharpe ratio. The Sharpe ratio, which measures returns relative to volatility, is a useful metric for comparing portfolios and investments due to its ability to quantify the differences in return per unit of risk. Therefore, we include it as an edge covariate. Specifically, the absolute difference in Sharpe ratios between two nodes might suggest the probability of one node imitating the other's investment strategy. To operationalize this, we calculate the outer product of the vectors of expected returns and volatility, enabling us to use the Sharpe ratio as an edge covariate in matrix format. The results of this model are displayed in Table 9.6, and the corresponding code is detailed in Box 9.7.

The results show that none of the edge-level covariates are statistically significant.

BOX 9.7:   ADDING EDGE-LEVEL COVARIATES AND RUNNING THE ERGM MODEL WITH EDGE COVARIATES.

```
#Set Edge Covariate
        #set edge covariatesas Euclidean Distance
        dist.mat<-as.matrix(dist(returns, method="euclidean"))

        #set edge covariates as Sharpe Ratio and Low Volatility
        sharpe<-abs(outer(g %v% "exp.returns",g %v% "volatility","/"))
        low.vol<-abs(outer(g %v% "volatility",g %v% "volatility","-"))
        #run model with both edge and node covariates
        model4<-ergm(g~edges+nodefactor("category")+nodematch("liquidity")+nodematch
("category")+edgecov(dist.mat)+edgecov(sharpe))
        summary(model4)
#Compute the edge probability using the significant coefficients
plogis(coef(model4)[1]+coef(model4)[2]+coef(model4)[3]+coef(model4)[4])#estimate the edge
probability given significant coefficients
```

TABLE 9.7   The ERGM Model with Local Structure Attributes.

```
Call:
ergm(formula = g ~ edges + nodefactor("category") + nodematch("liquidity") +
  nodematch("category") + gwesp(0.2, fixed = TRUE) + gwdsp(log(13),
  fixed = TRUE))

  Monte Carlo Maximum Likelihood Results:
```

	Estimate	Std. Error	MCMC%	z value	Pr (>|z|)
edges	−2.223903	0.419190	0	−5.305	<1e-04***
nodefactor.category.F	0.841238	0.191842	0	4.385	<1e-04***
nodematch.liquidity	−0.455980	0.151582	0	−3.008	0.00263**
nodematch.category	−1.566004	0.235190	0	−6.658	<1e-04***
gwesp.OTP.fixed.0.2	−0.001254	0.176892	0	−0.007	0.99434
gwdsp.OTP.fixed.2.56494935746154	0.082674	0.039395	0	2.099	0.03585*

```
---
Signif. codes:  0 `***' 0.001 `**' 0.01 `*' 0.05 `.' 0.1 ` ' 1

    Null Deviance: 1289.3  on 930  degrees of freedom
Residual Deviance:   933.3  on 924  degrees of freedom

AIC: 945.3  BIC: 974.3   (Smaller is better. MC Std. Err. = 0.2625)
```

Local Structure Attributes   Local structures help to model and fit the desired network using more complex dependencies for both edge and node levels. Specifically, there are three local structure predictors.

The first refers to the degree distribution and puts more weight on the nodes with high-degree scores. The second is the edgewise-shared partnerships measuring the local clustering calculated by the transitivity. Recall from Chapter 3 that transitivity measures the clusters in a network, and densely connected nodes form clusters. The third component is the dyadwise-shared partnerships. All node pairs in a network are dyads according to Harris (2013). This covariate assesses the tendency for nodes in a network with numerous pairwise connections to share many partners. The dyadwise-shared partnerships, which pertain to nodes, and the edgewise-shared partnerships are often closely linked because they are typically found within clusters. The results for the ERGM including local structure attributes are shown in Table 9.7. The code is summarized in Box 9.8.

Inspection of Table 9.7 reveals that only one parameter for the local structures covariates is statistically significant. This is the parameter that governs the clustering coefficient.

Goodness-of-Fit and Network Simulation   Model evaluation is critical for assessing the ERGM's performance. Visualization plays a key role in network science, and by plotting both the simulated and original networks, their interconnected structures can be visually compared.

The code in Box 9.9 demonstrates the model's goodness-of-fit using standard evaluation parameters and overall model statistics. It utilizes the "igraph" package to plot the simulated network, constructing it from the adjacency matrix provided by the "ergm" package. To ensure consistency in visual comparison, we apply the same properties, layout, and node sizes to both the simulated and original networks when plotting them in "igraph".

The goodness-of-fit diagnostics plot the relevant information in Figure 9.4. The statistics for all relevant variables are plotted. The grey lines indicate the 95% interval for the statistics, and the bold line indicates the fit of the model relative to the original network. As a rule of thumb, a well-fitting model should have statistics within the 95% confidence interval indicated by the grey lines. The code for the goodness-of-fit and the plot of the simulated and originally estimated graphs are shown in Box 9.9. The model parameters lie within the 95% confidence interval bands. The graphs are shown in Figure 9.5.

BOX 9.8:   ADDING LOCAL STRUCTURES AND RUNNING THE ERGM MODEL WITH LOCAL STRUCTURES.

```
#Set Local Structures or dyad dependency
        model5<-ergm(g~edges+nodefactor("category")+nodematch("liquidity")+nodematch("ca
tegory")+gwesp(0.2, fixed=TRUE)+gwdsp(log(13), fixed=TRUE))
        summary(model5)

        plogis(coef(model5)[1]+coef(model5)[2]+coef(model5)[3]+coef(model5)[4])#estimate
the edge probability given significant coefficients
```

BOX 9.9:   ESTIMATING THE GOODNESS-OF-FIT AND SIMULATION.

```
#Goodness-of-Fit
        model5.gof<-gof(model5)#evaluate the model comparing it to the original graph
        model5.gof
        plot(model5.gof)

#Simulation
        A.sim.model5<-as.matrix.network.adjacency(sim.model5)
        #detach ergm and attatch igraph
        set.seed(733)
        sim.g<-graph_from_adjacency_matrix(A.sim.model5)

        ecs_sim.g<-as.matrix(eigen_centrality(sim.g)$vector)

        sim.g<-set.vertex.attribute(sim.g, "category", value=c("F", "F", "F", "F", "F",
"F", "A", "A", "A", "A", "A", "A", "A", "A", "A", "A", "A", "A", "A", "A", "A", "A", "F",
"F", "F", "F", "F", "F", "F", "F"))
```

(Continued)

(Continued)

```
        V(sim.g)$color <- V(sim.g)$category
        V(sim.g)$color <- gsub("F","white",V(sim.g)$color)
        V(sim.g)$color <- gsub("A","grey85",V(sim.g)$color)

        V(sim.g)$shape <- V(sim.g)$category
        V(sim.g)$shape <- gsub("F","circle",V(sim.g)$shape)
        V(sim.g)$shape <- gsub("A","square",V(sim.g)$shape)

#Plot the original and simulated networks in igraph
        par(mfrow=c(1,2))
        library(igraph)
        plot(sim.g,layout=layout_with_kk,vertex.size=sqrt(ecs_sim.n)*20,vertex.label.
cex=.6, edge.arrow.size=.0, vertex.label.color="black", main="Simulated")
        plot(netz_corf,layout=layout_with_kk,vertex.size=sqrt(ecs_sim.n)*20,vertex.
label.cex=.6, edge.arrow.size=.0, vertex.label.color="black", main="Original")
```

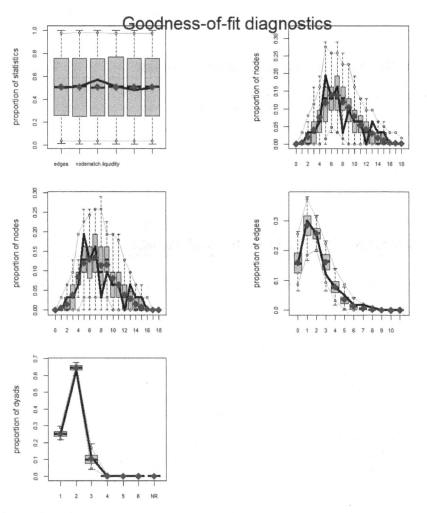

FIGURE 9.4   Goodness-of-Fit Plots.

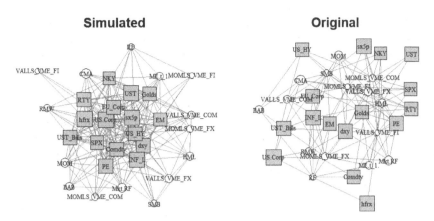

Simulated   **Original**

FIGURE 9.5   A Simulated and Original Asset and Factor Network.

Latent Network Structures

In Chapter 8, we emphasized the importance of Bayesian causal networks that lack latent variables, as such variables can act as confounders influencing edges. However, in this section, we shift our focus to latent effects that shape network structures, acknowledging that unobserved variables can significantly impact portfolio interconnectedness.

Latent network structures involve stochastic models representing unobservable node classes and properties influencing network structures. These unobserved variables, referred to as latent variables, encapsulate hidden attributes dictating the probability of edge formation. Initially explored by researchers such as Hoover (1982), Aldous (1985), Hoff (2002, 2007), Nowicki and Snijders (2001), Snijders et al. (2006) and Kolaczyk (2017), latent variables model the likelihood of nodes becoming connected. When applied to network structures, these stochastic models are known as latent network models (LNMs). While stochastic models already have found wide application in finance, incorporating statistical models into network structures introduces the concept of latent variables. For the LNM, the eigenmodel package in R is commonly utilized.

Overview   In portfolio management, the application of latent network models offers a straightforward yet powerful tool for enhancing portfolio construction and management. While briefly touched upon in the Chapter 8, in this section we provide a deeper understanding of how to leverage these models effectively. Specifically, our objective is to compute real numbers that serve as important parameters of nodes influencing each other to form links within the portfolio network.

Expected returns serve as one intuitive application of such variables in portfolio management. Additionally, other variables such as risk metrics (e.g., Altman's Z-score, liquidity scores, etc.) or any other orthogonal node properties can be incorporated. The key point is to model node effects through a function that captures the relationships and dependencies between nodes.

There are three major principles/properties for modeling node probabilities using latent effects. It is important to highlight their relevance and differences in the context of financial markets:

Latent Class Effects: This approach applied to financial networks involves categorizing nodes into latent classes based on certain characteristics or attributes. Nodes within the same class are assumed to have similar probabilities of forming links, enabling for a more nuanced understanding of the underlying network structure. For example, nodes within the same asset class might share more similar properties compared to those across differing asset classes. Similarly, nodes within the same industry group, such as capital goods, might exhibit similar properties, and therefore, have a higher probability to share a link. For instance, 3M, General Electric, and Honeywell are more likely to be interconnected due to their shared-industry characteristics.

Homophily Principle: This principle posits that nodes with similar attributes or characteristics are more likely to form connections with each other. Proper distance metrics are used to measure the degree of similarity between nodes, which is then incorporated into the modeling process to capture the homophilic tendencies within the network. In the context of financial markets, this principle can be observed in portfolio and benchmark networks comprising securities from the same industry group, where the distances between nodes are close. In a cross-asset context, the principle might apply to bonds and currencies but is less likely to be found between currencies and equities.

Eigen-Analysis: Eigen-analysis involves analyzing the eigenvalues and eigenvectors of the adjacency matrix of the network. This approach provides insights into the global structure and connectivity patterns of the network, enabling for the identification of influential nodes and potential clusters within the portfolio network. The eigen-analysis is a pure example of a quantitative management technique that does not rely on a priori classification of asset relationships. Instead, the relationships are extracted from the mutual connections determined by the adjacency matrix.

By leveraging latent network models and the approaches outlined, portfolio managers can enhance their understanding of the intricate relationships and dependencies within the portfolio network. This deeper insight enables them to make more informed decisions regarding asset allocation, risk management, and portfolio optimization. Ultimately, this leads to more effective portfolio management strategies that are better aligned with investment objectives and risk tolerance, resulting in potentially improved portfolio performance and outcomes for investors. The latent class approach posits that the adjacency matrix A_{ij} entries a_{ij} are modeled using a function comprising a constant term and independent, identically distributed unobservable variables $u = (u_1, \ldots, u_n)$. In other words, the adjacency matrix entries a_{ij} depend on the attributes, where the u_i corresponds to the attribute of node i. The nodes relationships can be modeled using vectors comprising different but symmetric node attributes. In a network context, the adjacency A_{ij} matrix of a graph $G(n, m)$ can be estimated as a function of a constant and the latent (i.e., unobservable) variables. Importantly, these variables are latent and symmetric.

Applying the notation of Nowicki and Snijders (2001) and Kolaczyk and Csardi (2020), the latent effects for the unobservable variables are specified as real values in a symmetric matrix

$$\alpha(u_i, u_j) = m_{u_i, u_j} \tag{9.7}$$

where m_{u_i, u_j} are the real-value entries of a symmetric matrix M. It's important to note that the number of classes in latent class effects models is typically unknown. In portfolio management, these classes might represent industry groups, sectors, countries, or rating classifications, among others.

The second approach is based on the principle of homophily, which originates from the social sciences and suggests that similar individuals tend to connect with each other. Extending this intuition to financial markets suggests that nodes with a shorter distance between them are more likely to connect. Defining an appropriate distance metric is crucial. Wasserstein distance, Manhattan distance, or Euclidean distance are some of the applicable distance metrics.

In this framework, the latent variables u_i take the form of transposed real-number vectors $(u_{i1}, \ldots, u_{in})$ representing important but unknown node characteristics that influence each other and establish mutual links. Once again, with roots in the social sciences and expanded into investment management, the quest for node similarity and parameters that explain node properties (e.g., assets with similar returns, risks, and other properties) is of particular interest. The higher the similarity between nodes in terms of these characteristics, the greater the probability that they will share links. It's worth noting that this concept is directly related to the distance metrics introduced in Chapter 6, where larger distances indicate greater dissimilarity between nodes. Within the homophily concept, latent distance effects are modeled, as demonstrated by Kolaczyk and Csardi (2020).

The concept of distance between asset properties can be used to measure the homophily principle underlying the LNM. These node properties are vectors that include different node-specific variables. For example, a node-specific vector of latent variables might consist of expected returns, risk scores, or any quantitative perimeters derived using quantitative financial analysis. The smaller the distance between pairwise nodes i and j in a network, the higher the probability that they share a link, which then serves as an input variable in the LNM model as follows:

$$\alpha(u_i, u_j) = -|u_i - u_j| \tag{9.8}$$

Recall that the Euclidean distance is used to measure the similarity between nodes, as demonstrated for individual bonds in Chapter 6.

The third approach, proposed by Hoff (2007), is the eigenmodel, which combines elements of the previous two models and applies an eigenvector analysis. This model is more powerful, as it leverages eigendecomposition. Within this framework, the latent variables u_i representing class effects are n-length random vectors $u_i = (u_{i,1}, \ldots, u_{i,n})$. The vectors represent each node's unobserved characteristics as a vector. The latent variables contribution to the homophily between nodes i and j depends on the sign of the eigenvalue. These vectors are expected to be orthogonal to each other. According to Hoff (2007), the elements of the adjacency matrix a_{ij} can be modeled as a linear combination of pair-specific attributes (covariates), the latent vectors u_i and the diagonal matrix that represents the relative importance of the latent vectors:[11]

$$a_{ij} = \beta' x_{ij} + u_i^T \Lambda u_j \tag{9.9}$$

where $u_1, \ldots, u_n$ are real-number node-specific variables, Λ is an $n \times n$ diagonal matrix, and β are parameters associated with effects of pair-specific covariates x_{ij}. The $\beta' x_{ij}$ term is a linear combination of covariates.

The latent effects are the product of the vectors comprising latent variables, and matrix Λ incorporates the relative importance of each latent vector. The latent eigenmodel is then the eigen decomposition of the matrix that contains all pairwise latent effects. Behind the pure quantitative nature of the eigenanalysis, its aim is the extraction of eigenvectors from the underlying diagonal matrix as follows:

$$\alpha(u_i, u_j) = u_i^T \Lambda u_j \tag{9.10}$$

where u_i and u_j are the latent variables, and Λ is a $n \times n$ diagonal matrix, which specifies the importance of each latent vector u_i.

Note the essential property of being orthogonal in expectation. Often, in asset management, the requirement of deriving orthogonal expected returns is necessary to ensure unbiased estimation and to

---

[11]In other words, the correlation between the latent effects u_j and u_i is zero.

achieve diversified portfolios that perform well out-of-sample. In other words, asset managers can apply different techniques to estimate expected returns, and the correlation between u_j and u_i would be zero.

Following Hoff (2007), because the u_j can vary in length corresponding to the number of classes U, matrix notation can be used to represent a matrix of classes $U = (u_i, \ldots, u_n)$. We can apply eigendecomposition and eigenanalysis to the $U\Lambda U^T$, where U is then an $n \times n$ matrix comprising the latent variables, and Λ is the adjacency matrix. All pairwise latent effects $\alpha(u_i, u_j)$ are then considered. The algorithm can be summarized in the following steps:

1. Extract the adjacency matrix of the underlying network.
2. Specify vectors of latent effects and construct an $n \times n$ matrix comprising the latent vectors.
3. Run the Monte Carlo Markov Chain (MCMC) model simulation with eigenmodel and use the adjacency matrix and the matrix comprising latent variables as input variables ($U\Lambda U^T$).
4. Plot the network using the eigenvectors as coordinates.

As a result, the eigenanalysis model generalizes the principles of structural equivalence and homophily, offering portfolio managers the flexibility to incorporate various latent effects. These latent effects are node-specific and might be exogenous factor models or generated in the stages of the investment process within an organization. An example of this step at the single security level might be the estimation of covariates for fixed-income investments, such as roll-down returns, duration-times-spread, trading volumes, or other bond-specific variables of individual securities, and their incorporation at the node level in the model. In equities, covariates might be dividend projections, price-earning estimations, price-to-book value predictions, cash flow projections or other quantitative price metrics that indicate equity value and/or equity price momentum.

The eigenmodes by Hoff (2007) employ the Monte Carlo Markov Chain (MCMC) technique to model pair-specific covariates using appropriate distributions. Covariates are attributes on the edge or node level used to model relationships. The major difference between the covariates used in the latent models relative to the other models is that the covariates in the latent network models are node-level covariates.

Implementation To illustrate the advantage of the eigenmodel compared to the other two latent models, we provide three examples like the models provided by Kolaczyk and Csardi (2020).[12] In the first case, we assume that covariates do not exist, meaning that no specific characteristic variables between the pairs in the network are known. This can be interpreted as the base case model, in which the network's adjacency matrix is the only input in the eigenmodel and the MCMC simulation. To better illustrate this example, we utilize the undirected asset and factor network constructed using pairwise correlations (netz_undir).[13] We compute the average historical returns as a proxy for expected returns and apply them as a covariate effect similar to the volatility. Figure 9.6 plots the ROC curves for the three different scenarios that we tested: (a) no pairwise covariates, (b) a covariate for volatility, and (c) a covariate for expected returns, respectively. We plot the network using the spatial coordinates corresponding to the first two eigenvectors. This corresponds to Panel A in Figure 9.7. Box 9.10 provides the code for the pair-specific covariates in the eigenmodel.

---

[12] Note that this is a very simplified example for the sole purpose of showing the advantage of modeling latent effects.
[13] See Chapter 6 for the algorithm and the construction of the network.

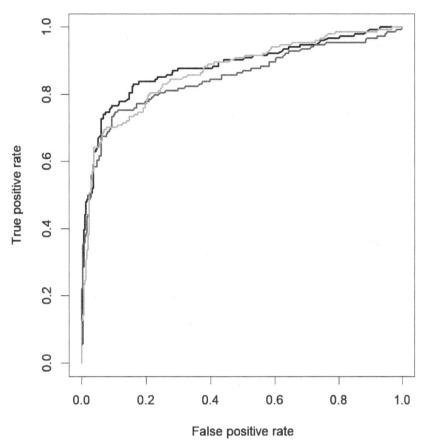

FIGURE 9.6 ROC Curves Comparing the Goodness-of-Fit to the Undirected Network with Different Eigenmodels with Specific Covariates.

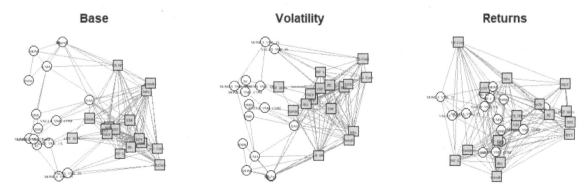

FIGURE 9.7 Network Visualizations Subject to the Different Eigenmodel Covariates.
Note: The first plot is a network with absence of pairwise covariates, the second uses the "volatility" as a covariate, and the third uses the "returns."

BOX 9.10:   EIGENMODEL WITHOUT PAIR-SPECIFIC COVARIATES (ATTRIBUTES).

```
set.seed(31)
A.undir<-as_adjacency_matrix(netz_undir,sparse=FALSE) #takes the adjacency matrix for an
undirected network netz_undir
base.fit<-eigenmodel_mcmc(A.undir, R=2, S=11000, burn=10000) #run eigenmodel simulation
with10000 iterations and 1000 iterations are used to perform posterior inference.
lat.es.base<-eigen(base.fit$ULU_postmean)$vec[,1:2] #extracts the eigenvectors for the
fitted MCMC model
plot(netz_undir,layout=lat.es.base) #plots the netz_undir network using the latent
eigenvectors as coordinates
```

BOX 9.11:   EIGENMODEL WITH VOLATILITY ESTIMATION AS PAIR-SPECIFIC COVARIATES (ATTRIBUTES).

```
#Volatility-Covariate as Latent Effect
volatility=data.frame()
volatility<-t(apply(returns,2, function(x) sd(x))) #compute the historical volatilites
as.matrix(volatility)
vol.r=as.matrix(rank(volatility))
rownames(vol.r)<-colnames(AssetsFactors)

vol.compromize.m<-vol.r%o%vol.r #make an array using the volatility data
vol.compromize<-matrix(as.numeric(vol.compromize.m%in%c(1,2,3,4,5,6,7,8,9,10)),31,31)
#select the nodes with the lowest volatility scores
vol.compromize<-array(vol.compromize,dim=c(31,31,1))
lat.fit.1<-eigenmodel_mcmc(A.undir,vol.compromize,R=2, S=1100, burn=1000) #fit the
model with the volatities as additional argument
lat.1<-eigen(lat.fit.1$ULU_postmean)$vec[,1:2] #extract the eigenvectors
plot(netz_undir, layout=lat.1)
```

In the second example, we consider the historical volatility of assets and factors as a proxy for risk, seeking to simulate latent structures using volatility scores as covariates. In this regard, as discussed in the book, we depart from the fundamental insights about unobserved variables that influence the asset and factor networks. The objective is to determine whether latent or simulated volatility metrics could influence the edges in the network. To begin, we estimate historical volatilities as a vector and construct an array that reflects the effects of a low-volatility portfolio.[14] Models that estimate expected realized volatility using econometric models might be a good enhancement. Next, we fit the eigenmodel using the low-volatility scores as arguments. In portfolio management, assets with lower volatility are often favored over those with higher volatility due to their perceived reduced risk. After fitting the model, we extract the eigenvectors used as coordinates in the network plot.

The network, with volatility as a covariate, is plotted in Panel B of Figure 9.7. The code that incorporates volatility as covariates is shown in Box 9.11.

---

[14]Note that this example is straightforward and aims to demonstrate the method. The primary criterion used here is the historical volatilities of the assets. For instance, the unobserved inputs in the eigenmodel could include the estimated expected volatility of the assets and factors.

Like the latent model implementation discussed by Kolaczyk and Csardi (2020) and depicted in Figure 9.7, we visualize the networks according to the eigenmodel and applied covariates. The graph varies based on the inputs chosen. Here, we used intrinsic values directly estimated from the graph data such as returns and standard deviations of the nodes. The rationale for using volatility as a covariate is like the approach in the ERGM from the previous section, suggesting that nodes with low volatility tend to link with other low-volatility nodes, and the same goes for high volatility. Another covariate considered is the returns of the nodes and assets, reflecting principles of momentum investing where positive returns tend to be followed by positive returns, and similarly for negative returns. This concept of linking based on returns and volatilities is consistent with the principle of homophily, where similar entities tend to connect. The ROC curves, which are tightly clustered in the upper-left part of the plot, indicate a strong model fit. The ROC curve is a visual tool used to evaluate the performance of a binary classifier system as its decision threshold changes. It displays the True Positive Rate (TPR) versus the False Positive Rate (FPR) across different threshold settings.[15]

Laplacian Graph Kernels and Spectral Partitioning

Graph kernels are powerful tools in portfolio management as they enable for the extraction of intrinsic properties from the network structure itself. By decomposing the adjacency matrix into eigenvalues and eigenvectors, these kernels can capture essential information about vertex pairs and provide real-valued outputs, enabling more nuanced analysis and decision-making in portfolio management.[16] Kernels serve this purpose in graph theory.

An Overview The concept of kernels is fundamental in data science, particularly in machine learning, as it characterizes the similarity between nodes within a network. Because a graph inherently reflects the similarities among its nodes, it's customary to derive kernels that leverage the graph's underlying data, typically assessed through the adjacency matrix, to encapsulate the network's connectivity. Graph kernels are frequently formulated based on the intrinsic data within the graph itself.

A kernel is defined as positive semidefinite if, for a set of nodes, the resulting $n \times n$ matrix – where n is the number of nodes – is symmetric and positive semidefinite. The Laplacian matrix is also an $n \times n$ matrix. In this matrix, the diagonal corresponds to the degrees of the node; that is, the entry is that the degree of node i is when i is equal to j. In the case where two nodes share a link ($\{i,j\} \in m$), then the entry is equal to -1, and zero otherwise. That is,

$$l_{ij} = \begin{cases} \deg(n_i) & \text{if } j = i \\ -1, & \text{if } j \neq i \text{ and } \{i,j\} \in m \\ 0, & \text{otherwise} \end{cases} \tag{9.11}$$

In matrix form, the graph Laplacian $[L]_{ij}$ is the difference between the $n \times n$ degree matrix $[D]_{ij}$ and the $n \times n$ adjacency matrix $[A]_{ij}$. That is,

$$L = D - A \tag{9.12}$$

---

[15] See Simonian (2024).

[16] Eigenvalues are a set of values describing a dataset. The larger the eigenvalue, the greater the portion of the variance of the dataset that it explains. Together, the eigenvalues and the corresponding eigenvectors provide a comprehensive description of the dataset.

Taking over the simple example from Chapter 2, the Laplacian matrix for an undirected graph is:[17]

$$
\begin{bmatrix} 2 & -1 & -1 & 0 \\ -1 & 3 & -1 & -1 \\ -1 & -1 & 3 & -1 \\ 0 & -1 & 0 & 1 \end{bmatrix} = \begin{bmatrix} 2 & 0 & 0 & 0 \\ 0 & 3 & 0 & 0 \\ 0 & 0 & 3 & 0 \\ 0 & 0 & 0 & 1 \end{bmatrix} - \begin{bmatrix} 0 & 1 & 1 & 0 \\ 1 & 0 & 1 & 1 \\ 1 & 1 & 0 & 1 \\ 0 & 1 & 0 & 0 \end{bmatrix} \tag{9.13}
$$

The Laplacian matrix is a symmetric matrix with real eigenvalues that are nonnegative, and at least one of which is zero.[18] Conventionally, the eigenvalues are ordered from smallest to the largest $(\lambda_1 < \lambda_2 < ... < \lambda_N)$, with $\lambda_1 = 0$. Newman (2010) demonstrated that the Laplacian matrix becomes noninvertible if a zero eigenvalue exists. Consequently, the Laplacian kernel acts as the (pseudo)inverse of the Laplacian matrix, as its eigenvalues contain more information than those of standard matrix (see Kelathaya, Bapat, and Karantha, 2023). These insights are particularly relevant in portfolio management, especially in the use of correlation matrices for network construction and the principles underlying spectral partitioning.

Traditionally, much financial research has advocated for leveraging the largest eigenvalues of the correlation matrix, often overlooking the smaller ones. Avellaneda and Lee (2010), for instance, utilized the eigenvalues of the covariance matrix to address portfolio allocation issues, a practice that can be traced back to the application of Principal Component Analysis (PCA) in portfolio optimization[19] The largest eigenvalue of the correlation matrix typically represents the global market factor, which captures the majority of observed dynamics and encompasses broad market movements. In contrast, smaller eigenvalues often reflect idiosyncratic factors.

Bouchaud and Potters (2000) and Allez and Bouchaud (2012) have noted that portfolio allocations tend to exhibit greater stability when a portion of the eigenvectors obtained from the orthogonalization of an empirical matrix of equity returns is discarded.[20] To address this issue, Bouchaud and Potters (2000) suggest using only a limited number of large eigenvalues. This strategy helps alleviate the influence of small eigenvalues, which can introduce noise into the analysis or cause structural instability in correlations.[21]

In portfolio management, portfolio weights are typically determined by the inverse of the covariance matrix. While using the largest eigenvalues might align with riskier allocations under the Markowitz (1952) framework, incorporating a smaller set of eigenvalues aligns better to diversify market risk, as per the mean-variance optimization framework that seeks to spread risk across various assets. Contrary to using the largest eigenvalues, which can lead to riskier portfolio allocations within the the Markowitz framework, incorporating a small set of eigenvalues is more consistent to diversify market risk. This is because the mean-variance framework aims to spread risk across different assets.

Aldridge (2019) demonstrated that the eigenvalues of the invertible correlation matrix are equivalent to those of its inverse matrix. Consequently, it is valuable to order the eigenvalues from smallest to largest in the inverse matrix (denoted as K). This approach is beneficial because the smallest eigenvalues, close to zero, contain significant idiosyncratic information crucial for precise portfolio management. The meaning

---

[17]Recall from Chapter 2 that for an undirected network, the in-degree is equal to the out-degree. For a directed network, it is necessary to compute the in-degree and out-degree scores, and then use one of them depending on the purpose. The result will be an in-degree, and out-degree Laplacian matrix.

[18]See Newman (2010).

[19]PCA decomposes the correlation matrix into eigenvalues and their corresponding principal components, shrinking the smaller eigenvalues to zero.

[20]This issue becomes serious when using the correlation matrix to estimate adjacency matrix, but is not exclusive to correlation networks.

[21]See Rebonato and Denev (2013).

of the inverse matrix in graph theory and portfolio management is enormous because it reflects the flow dynamics, distances and other important properties. According to Kelathaya et al. (2023), the inverse matrix highlights the properties of the flow to the nodes that are transmitted by the edges.

Using the regular matrix with only the largest eigenvalues can make the portfolio more sensitive to market factors while disregarding idiosyncratic risks associated with smaller eigenvalues. In contrast, employing the (pseudo)inverse enables for a more targeted focus on the smaller eigenvalues and the corresponding idiosyncratic risks. Therefore, the (pseudo)inverse of L, or the reduced Laplacian matrix, can be expressed as follows:

$$K = L^{-1} \tag{9.14}$$

Once the role of the inverted matrix is established, the significance of the small eigenvalues warrants discussion. A key characteristic of the graph Laplacian is that its eigenvalues $(\lambda_1, \lambda_2, \ldots, \lambda_N)$ are directly proportional to the components of the network. Empirical evidence supporting this concept traces back to the work of Fiedler (1973), who demonstrated that the second smallest eigenvalue (λ_2) is directly linked to graph partitioning and community structure. Specifically, a network exhibits distinct communities if the first eigenvalue of the graph Laplacian is zero, and the subsequent eigenvalues are greater than zero. Consequently, the community structure of a network is associated with the nonzero eigenvalues of the Laplacian L. When the second eigenvalue is close to zero but nonzero and its corresponding eigenvector indicates that the network can be effectively divided into smaller subgraphs.

Practical Implementation   It's important to note that this separation pertains to connected networks. The second eigenvalue, often termed to as the Fiedler value or algebraic connectivity, facilitates the partitioning of a connected network into distinct parts. This separation process holds significant importance in portfolio and risk management, as it isolates internal properties within vertex portfolio structures. These properties are inferred from the eigendecomposition. Figure 9.8 illustrates the eigenvalues of the graph Laplacian, arranged from smallest to largest for an undirected asset and factor network.

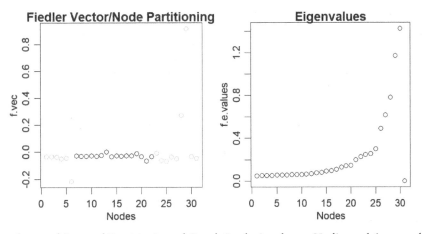

FIGURE 9.8   Eigenvalues and Spectral Partitioning of Graph Laplacian for an Undirected Asset and Factor Network.
Note: We use netz_undir for the asset and factor network and the Fiedler vector (i.e., second smallest eigenvalue) to assign properties as to "category" asset and factors.

The fundamental idea is to demonstrate that in kernel regression, the properties of node values in a graph $G(n, m)$ are forecasted through a linear combination of the eigenvectors. The approach, which leverages the (pseudo)inverse of the Laplacian matrix L, is designed to identify eigenvectors that are aligned with the weights defining the Laplacian kernel in line with the intuition suggested by Kelathaya et al. (2023).

Spectral partitioning is a procedure that connects intrinsic properties like eigenvalues and eigenvectors to the matrices associated with the network. Even a slight alteration in the eigenvectors can induce a change in the structure of the Laplacian kernel K. This precisely aligns with what spectral decomposition of the inverted Laplacian matrix achieves; it prioritizes the consideration of the smallest eigenvalues, which could exert significant influence on the asset and factor network.

From the perspective of spectral partitioning and portfolio management, the small eigenvalues of the inverse Laplacian matrix are of utmost importance. In Figure 9.8, we present the graphs illustrating this concept. Visual inspection of Figure 9.9 shows the effect of the eigenvalues on the different graphs with changing node size and connections concerning the eigenvectors. Another critical piece of information is that the local grouping of assets and factors remains preserved. The code is provided in Box 9.12.

Executing the following code generates the three graphs with different eigenvectors.

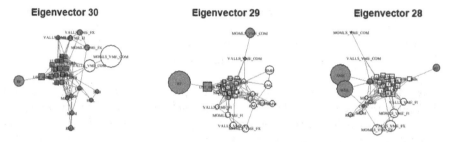

FIGURE 9.9 A Graph Laplacian with Different Eigenvectors.

BOX 9.12: LAPLACIAN GRAPH AND SPECTRAL PARTITIONING.

```
par(mfrow=c(1,2))
L<-as.matrix(laplacian_matrix(netz_undir))
eigen.L<-eigen(L)
nv<-vcount(netz_undir) ##counts the number of nodes

netz_undir<-set.vertex.attribute(netz_undir, "liquidity", value=c("L", "L", "L", "L", "L",
"L", "L", "L", "L", "L", "I", "I", "L", "L", "L", "L", "I", "I", "I", "L", "I", "L", "L",
"L", "L", "L", "I", "I", "I", "I", "L"))

f.vec<-eigen.L$vectors[,nv-1] #extract the Fiedler vector, which is the second-smallest
eigenvector
#select the feature you want to investigate "name". "category", "color", "shape"
faction<-get.vertex.attribute(netz_undir, "category")
f.colors <- ifelse(faction == "A", "grey70", "white")
plot(f.vec, col = f.colors, xlab = "Nodes", main = "Fiedler Vector and Node Partitioning")

# Compute the eigenvalues
e.values <- eigen.L$values[1:(nv - 1)]
f.e.values <- c((e.values) ^ (-1), 0)

# Plot Eigenvalues
plot(f.e.values, xlab = "Nodes", main = "Eigenvalues")
```

```
par(mfrow=c(1,3))
for (x in 1:3) {
  f.vec<-eigen.L$vectors[,node.count-x] ##extract the Fiedler vector, which is the second-
smallest eigenvector
  e.values<-eigen.L$values[1:(node.count-x)] ##computes the eigenvectors from 1:to n-1
nodes
  f.e.values<-c((e.values)^(-1),0)
  #plot(f.e.values)
  e.vector<-eigen.L$vectors[,(node.count-x)] #extract the corresponding eigenvector
  node.colors <- ifelse(e.vector < 0, "grey70", "white") #sets the color based on the
eigenvalues values
  node.size<-50*sqrt(abs(e.vector)) #the node size is proportional to its entry in the
eigenvector multiplied by a scalar
  plot(netz_undir, vertex.size = node.size, vertex.color = node.colors, vertex.label.cex =
0.5, edge.arrow.size = 0, vertex.label.color = "black", main = paste("Eigenvector", nv
- x))
}
```

CAUSAL NETWORK INTERFERENCE

In Chapter 8, we discussed the role of causal networks and introduced the Bayesian net concept that captures causal relationships within a graphical framework. This section delves into one of the most dynamic of networks in portfolio management – the application of scenario-causal interference to model and investigate the network effects of specific interventions or influences on the node level under potential outcomes. The underlying assumption is that the nodes in the network are not isolated; instead, the interactions between them define both the indirect and direct impacts of the interventions, a principle referred to as causal network interference.

In the context of financial markets, such effects could be triggered actions like central bank policies, regulatory activities affecting nodes, or "interventions" in the form of return predictions conducted within an investment process. Unlike actions that directly affect edges, these interventions impact nodes, interconnected via edges that may facilitate spillover effects to other nodes. Thus, in the causal network interference framework, each node is interconnected with the entire network structure, making the interconnectedness of nodes crucial for transmitting intervention effects throughout the network.[22] Highly connected nodes play a more important role than nodes with low-degree scores. Although widely applied in fields like economics and other disciplines (most notably in healthcare), the application of these methods in financial markets is relatively unexplored.[23]

Background and Model Fundamentals

The purpose of causal network interference is to evaluate the network impact that an intervention on some nodes and edges might have on the entire network. Originating from social sciences and healthcare, the concept of treating one individual in a network (e.g., in the case of a disease), can affect the entire network

---

[22]We use the terms intervention and treatment interchangeably. But in our view, intervention is closer to financial-markets terminology than the treatment that has more healthcare origin. Nevertheless, we use both terms.
[23]See, for example, the studies of Rosenbaum (1999), Hudgens and Halloran (2008), Aral and Walker (2011), Liu and Hudgens (2014), Leung (2016), Aronow and Samii (2017), and Fatemi and Zheleva (2023), among others

and is equally applicable to financial networks. Let us extend this framework to financial markets and interventions on asset classes or even factors rather than individual financial instruments like single bonds or equites.

Consider, for example, financial markets in which a central bank, such as the Fed, European Central Bank (ECB), or Bank of Japan, decides to influence a specific asset class, like government bonds. This type of intervention is not uncommon and has been implemented several times by these major central banks in the past. In the interconnected realms of financial markets and assets, such impacts on assets might trigger significant market events and dynamics.

Additional examples merit consideration as well. Imagine a portfolio manager who conducts extensive predictions on an asset class, such as equity market returns or government bond markets, utilizing econometric analysis, machine-learning, or other forecasting and predicting techniques. The portfolio management team would be keenly interested in understanding how these predicted returns could affect the entire network, armed with this information.

Extending causal network interference to financial markets, the focus is on investigating the impact of node influence or intervention, assessing both direct influences and potential outcomes at the node or edge level.[24] Fatemi and Zheleva (2023) argued that the problem with potential outcomes is that it is impossible to detect an impact's outcome in both the no-exposure and full-exposure (i.e., treatment) scenarios simultaneously. To overcome this, mathematical models have been developed that calculate the average outcomes between intervention and no exposure (i.e., control) by comparing the differences in means.

According to Aronow and Samii (2017), this framework consists of three major topics modeled and investigated within graph $G(n, m)$, where the nodes n interact with each other over m edges. The initial step in this process involves designing the intervention or treatment actors (i.e., nodes) and quantifying the probabilities of the interventions assigned to them. The second step entails mapping out the exposure mappings, which link the assigned interventions to the actual exposures received. In the final step, specific questions of interest are addressed through simulations employing causal estimators.

The first step is to identify the nodes that should receive intervention or treatment in the language of Aronow and Samii (2017). We separate the process not a node receives intervention with $z_i = 1$ and $z_i = 0$ when the node does not receive intervention. The condition $z_i = 1$ is called full treatment or *intervention*, and the $z_i = 0$ is defined as *full control* or *no exposure*. The vector that comprises the nodes that received an intervention is defined as the treatment assignment vector $Z = (z_1,...,z_n)$. As a result, the (n×1) treatment assignment vector comprises 1 and 0 and has number of entries equal to the size of the network. The interaction of the Z-vector with the other node features is called *intervention-induced exposures*.

The probability that a node receives treatment is generated by design and is $Pr_z = P(Z = z)$. The outcome for a node i under intervention z is denoted by $d_i(z)$. Then the idea of the model for causal interference is to investigate the causal effects of the entire network based on the interactions between the nodes.[25]

Node Representatives, Financial Market Network Exposure, and Interference

Selecting representatives or impact assets to measure causal network inference involves economic reasoning and is predicated on the recognition that interference exists in financial markets. As noted by Rosenbaum (1999), Aronow and Samii (2017), and Fatemi and Zheleva (2023), the choice of these representatives

---

[24] In the original network literature, the effect is defined as treatment. Because treatment is less suitable to financial markets, we use the term representatives or impact variables.

[25] See Rosenbaum (1999) and Aronow and Samii (2017) for a technical and mathematical detailed explanation of the framework.

should be deliberate and not arbitrary. Connections between nodes and the existence of covariates may exist even though they might be unobservable. Moreover, these nodes can have varying degrees of connectivity, influencing their exposure within the network.In a network context, the choice of treatment nodes should be subject to the node degree centrality and eventually the hub or authority score in directed network. Thee more connected and representative in clusters a node is, the higher the impact of treatment effects these nodes might have on the entire network. We discuss this topic in the next section in detail.

Node Representatives   Based on the seminal work of Asness et al. (2013), we have selected value and momentum as key factors. Their research demonstrated that the value factor defined in the Fama–French factor model[26] as high-minus-low[27] and momentum[28] exist in every asset class (e.g., commodities, fixed-income, equities, and currencies, and to name a few). Furthermore, they showed that value and momentum are economically and statistically sound factors that are fundamental to investments. Konstantinov and Fabozzi (2021), and Konstantinov (2022a) argued that the US dollar is a crucial determinant of bond markets. According to Leibowitz (2011), every asset has an equity component. Therefore, we select market excess returns, defined as the return on the market, minus the risk-free rate as a vertex in a network, which might be of particular interest in any investment process. This economic reasoning suggests that such nodes might be good candidates for treatment assignment.

Generally, the focus is on four determinants that integrate into an investment process, which asset managers might aim to predict, monitor, and analyze. These determinants have historically been directly and indirectly influenced by central bank policy or other interventions. Nevertheless, for simplicity, we limit our discussion to the basic assumption (about interference) that portfolio managers are interested in exploring the direct effects on other assets and factors when these four determinants are influenced. Equity markets and the US dollar spot index (dxy) have historically proven to be important and central in many types of investment processes. Yet, the choice of these factors is deliberate, and may also depend on their degree scores within the network.

In summary, the selected nodes to serve as representatives, which, in the spirit of Aronow and Samii (2017), are defined as treatment assignment nodes, are the market excess returns (Mkt.Rf), the value factor (HML), the US dollar spot index (dxy), and the momentum factor (MOM). The underlying rationale for choosing these representatives is their central importance in the investment process, reflecting a strategic approach to managing and understanding portfolio impacts.

Exposure Mappings   To define the effect that the selected nodes might have on the network, we need to consider how the impact on a specific node relates to the overall exposure of that node within the network. This concept, introduced in social network analysis by Rosenbaum (1999) and Aronow and Samii (2017), is referred to as *exposure mappings, which are* used to quantify the effect that an intervention or treatment on a node has on the network. Here's an approach for defining these effects:

- *Identify the key nodes*: Begin by selecting the ones of particular interest, often referred to as *treatment assignment nodes*. These nodes are chosen based on their economic and financial importance, centrality in the network, and relevance to the investment process. Examples include market excess returns, the value factor, the US dollar spot index, and the momentum factor.

---

[26]Fama and French (1992, 1993).

[27]It is measured as follows: Returns of High book-to-market stocks–Returns of Low book-to-market stocks.

[28]It is measured as follows: Returns of Winners – Returns of Losers, where Winners are the stocks that have performed the best over the chosen historical period, and Losers are the stocks that have performed the worst over the same historical period.

- *Define the adjacency matrix*: Establish the adjacency matrix that represents the connections between nodes in the network. This matrix specifies which nodes are connected and the strength of those connections.
- *Measure node centrality and degree*: Calculate each node's centrality and degree. Centrality measures a node's importance within the network, while degree measures the number of direct connections that a node has. Nodes with high centrality or degree are likely to impact the network more.
- *Define exposure mappings*: Exposure mappings quantify how much a node is influenced by other nodes. This includes assessing direct exposure, which refers to the immediate impact that connected nodes have on the node of interest, and indirect exposure, which encompasses the influence that nodes, connected indirectly through other nodes, exert on the node of interest.
- *Quantify the effects*: Using the adjacency matrix and the calculated centrality and degree, quantify the effects of the treatment or intervention on the selected nodes. Compare the mean outcomes between the scenarios where a node is treated (e.g., receives an intervention) and where it is not. Then evaluate the difference in mean outcomes to isolate the direct and indirect exposure effects.[29]
- *Adjust for interactions*: Ensure that the calculated effects account for interactions between nodes. For example, the difference in mean outcomes between $(e_{10} - e_{00})$ isolates the direct exposure from the indirect exposure, while the difference between $(e_{01} - e_{00})$ provides information on pure indirect exposure without direct interaction effects.

The main idea behind exposure mappings is to present exposure in a few intuitive situations referred to as impact or exposure conditions. These conditions can be generalized into four categories: direct and indirect impact, direct impact, indirect impact, and no impact. Following Aronow and Samii (2017), Fatemi and Zheleva (2023), and Kolaczyk and Csardi (2020), these four conditions are captured in an exposure or impact-mapping function. In this framework, node i in a network is exposed to a specific condition k. The exposure mapping function is determined by the treatment assignment vector and the elements of the adjacency matrix as defined:

$$e_k = f(z, x_i) \tag{9.15}$$

where z is the treatment assignment vector, and the x_i is a node-wise elements extracted from the adjacency matrix that provide information about the node interconnectedness to other nodes.

In other words, every node in the network is exposed to a condition e_k. Within this framework, every node belongs to only one exposure condition. The node information of every individual node as a vector is extracted from the $n \times n$ adjacency matrix A, because every node in a network stands in relation to other nodes, and the adjacency matrix gauges all relevant connectedness information. Therefore, we can use the i-th column of the adjacency matrix, instead of the vector of individual node-specific information on connectedness and relation to other nodes as follows:

$$x_i = A_{.i} \tag{9.16}$$

where the column-wise information of every individual node x_i is extracted from the adjacency matrix, which has zeros in the main diagonal. That is,

$$e_k = f(z, A_{.i}) \tag{9.17}$$

---

[29] See Kolaczyk and Csardi (2020) for a detailed description.

The choice of the underlying network and its adjacency matrix determines the impact or exposure in the four categories. That is, a sparser network will produce a completely different causal exposure than a highly denser network. The denser the network, the higher the transmission mechanisms of network flows and the interference are. However, as we shall see in Chapter 12, networks with fewer links are more fragile to node-related risk than denser networks.

Formally, for the four categories of exposure we have:

$$
f(z, A_i) = \begin{cases}
e_{11}(\text{Indirect \& Direct Impact}), \, z_i I_{\{z^T A_i > 0\}} = 1 \\
e_{01}(\text{Indirect Impact}), \, z_i I_{\{z^T A_i = 0\}} = 1 \\
e_{10}(\text{Direct Impact}), \, (1 - z_i) I_{\{z^T A_i > 0\}} = 1 \\
e_{00}(\text{No Impact}), \, (1 - z_i) I_{\{z^T A_i = 0\}} = 1
\end{cases}
\tag{9.18}
$$

where e_{11} is the condition with both direct and indirect exposure or impact, e_{01} is the condition that represents the indirect impact, e_{10} is the condition that summarizes the directed impact, and e_{00} is the condition with no impact. Again note that every node is assigned only to one specific condition; I is an inclusion indicator that assigns the node's entry in the matrix. The product $z^T A_i$ gives the number of neighbor nodes with direct exposure, which is contained in the adjacency matrix. The larger the node degree and connectedness of a node, the more neighbor nodes are involved in transmitting indirect treatment effects.

Because each node is assigned to only one category, the average causal effect measures the pure effects of intervention. That is, the adjustment of the direct effect e_{10}, reduced by the no exposure effect e_{00}, shows the pure direct effect without any interaction with the indirect effect: $(e_{10} - e_{00})$. Similarly, all other effects must be adjusted; for the combined (i.e., indirect and direct) effect we have $(e_{11} - e_{00})$, and for the indirect effect we have $(e_{01} - e_{00})$.

We calculate the four categories for each node in the network based on the exposure to a specific condition, say k. An essential aspect of this analysis is the consideration of dual exposure to k and h. The reason for the two exposures is that this framework operates under the assumption that each node is exposed to at least one condition. However, it's crucial not only to measure the exposure to that condition but also to compare it against another condition. The primary goal is to assess the fixed exposure k for node i with $p_i(e_k)$, the joint exposure probabilities of two nodes i and j to the condition k with $p_{ij}(e_k)$, and the joint exposure probabilities to both k and h with $p_{ij}(e_k, e_h)$. The average causal effect of exposure to conditions k and h is defined at the level of these exposure conditions, which are modeled probabilistically.

Recall that every node has exposure to only one of the four defined conditions: direct, indirect, combined (i.e., direct and indirect), or no exposure. In the spirit of Aronow and Samii (2017), the exposure probability is derived from the adjacency matrix of the underlying network using equations (9.15), (9.16), and (9.17). This ensures that network representations capture the notion of interconnectedness, to define proper estimations for the interconnected potential outcomes. Because we are interested in the relative results, we compute the causal effects for each node in the network under different exposure conditions. Specifically, the average causal effect is then calculated as the difference between node i's exposure to condition k versus h, as shown:

$$
\tau(e_k, e_h) = \frac{1}{N} \sum_{i=1}^{N} d_i e_k - \frac{1}{N} \sum_{i=1}^{N} d_i e_h
\tag{9.19}
$$

where N is a n-length vector that comprises ones and zeros indicating the treatment and control outcomes.

However, equation (9.19) requires the definition of contrast effects that capture the exposure to one effect versus the no-exposure effect. According to Aronow and Samii (2017) and Kolaczyk and Csardi (2020), average causal effects $\tau(e_k, e_h)$ values are set to represent specific categories of exposure – direct, indirect, combined (i.e., indirect + direct), and no exposure. The differences in the contrasts are defined as follows:

$\tau(e_{01}, e_{00})$: indirect causal effect or treated nodes versus no impact

$\tau(e_{10}, e_{00})$: direct causal effect or treated nodes versus no impact

$\tau(e_{11}, e_{00})$: total causal effect

Computing the average causal exposure under network interference that the four representatives are chosen purposely (not randomly) is essential. The aim is to investigate the interconnected (interference) effects of direct, indirect, and the total impact on the four representatives of the other neighbor nodes in the asset and factor network.

Recall that the treatment assignment is captured by the probability of treatment assignment $p_z = P(Z = z)$. As a result, the generalized probability of exposure of node i to the condition k is given by its adjacency matrix information and the exposure conditions z.

$$p_i(e_k) = \sum_z p_z I_{\{e_k = f(z, A_{\cdot i})\}} \tag{9.20}$$

where p_z is the probability of treatment assignment to z, and $e_k = f(z, A_{\cdot i})$ are the exposure to conditions, and I is an $n \times R$ matrix, where R is the number of simulation iterations for the exposure conditions and n is the number of nodes in the network. In this case, R is equal to the possible treatment assignments in the simulation, which we cannot observe empirically. Still, with the help of Monte Carlo simulation, we can approximate the observations. Then I_k is the matrix of indicators of whether nodes are in exposure conditions k over possible assignment vectors. That is,

$$I_k = \begin{bmatrix} I_{\{e_k = f(z_1, x_1)\}} & I_{\{e_k = f(z_2, x_1)\}} & \cdots & I_{\{e_k = f(z_r, x_1)\}} \\ I_{\{e_k = f(z_1, x_2)\}} & I_{\{e_k = f(z_2, x_2)\}} & \cdots & I_{\{e_k = f(z_r, x_2)\}} \\ \vdots & & \ddots & \vdots \\ I_{\{e_k = f(z_1, x_n)\}} & I_{\{e_k = f(z_2, x_n)\}} & \cdots & I_{\{e_k = f(z_r, x_n)\}} \end{bmatrix} \tag{9.21}$$

The next matrix is an $n \times n$ symmetric matrix, which comprises the individual exposure probabilities $p_i(e_k)$ and the joint exposure probabilities $p_{ij}(e_k)$ for all nodes in the network. Therefore, this is an $n \times n$ symmetric matrix:

$$I_k P I_k^T = \begin{bmatrix} p_1(e_k) & p_{12}(e_k) & \cdots & p_{1n}(e_k) \\ p_{21}(e_k) & p_2(e_k) & \cdots & p_{2n}(e_k) \\ \vdots & & \ddots & \vdots \\ p_{n1}(e_k) & p_{n2}(e_k) & \cdots & p_n(e_k) \end{bmatrix} \tag{9.22}$$

The third matrix is a nonsymmetric $n \times n$ matrix, which comprises the joint exposure probabilities p_{ij} (e_k, e_h) for all nodes i and j for all fixed exposure conditions k and h.

$$I_k P I_h^T = \begin{bmatrix} 0 & p_{12}(e_k,e_h) & \cdots & p_{1n}(e_k,e_h) \\ p_{21}(e_k,e_h) & 0 & \cdots & p_{2n}(e_k,e_h) \\ \vdots & & \ddots & \vdots \\ p_{n1}(e_k,e_h) & p_{n2}(e_k,e_h) & \cdots & 0 \end{bmatrix} \tag{9.23}$$

Note that the main diagonal of the matrix comprises zeros. This is because, as stated earlier, a node can only be assigned to one condition, not multiple conditions.

Finally, conducting a Monte Carlo simulation with many iterations ensures that the estimators remain unbiased. Visualizing the matrices for all four exposure conditions provides exposure mapping, illustrating the relationships between nodes and their interconnectedness with corresponding significant values.

Practical Implementation for an Asset and Factor Network

The algorithm to build a causal network exposure model requires defining an adjacency matrix corresponding to an existing network. Careful selection, underlined by economic rationale, is necessary when selecting the representative nodes. According to Barabási (2016), the spread of risk within a network depends on the network's density and the degree of its nodes. Nodes with high-degrees or high-centrality scores tend to have a more significant impact on the interconnected exposure model than nodes with lower degrees and centrality scores. Recall that node degree represents the immediate effect of connectedness and might be preferred over centrality metrics, which indicate the long-term connectedness score of the network. Assets with higher economic and financial importance are often most suitable for this purpose.

In any investment context (whether dealing with alternative investments, traditional investments, or other portfolio types), the equity markets play a pivotal role and could be a logical focal point. In this scenario, regulatory bodies, such as central banks or other regulatory authorities, might also focus on high-degree nodes within the financial network when selecting nodes for observation or intervention. As previously defined, the nodes designated for treatment assignment in this analysis are the market excess returns (Mkt.Rf), the value factor (HML), the US dollar spot index (dxy), and the momentum factor (MOM).

The purpose of the network experiment with average causal effects is to assess the network impact of interventions on four nonarbitrarily selected nodes. Rosenbaum (1999), Aronow and Samii (2017), and Kolaczyk and Csardi (2020) discuss how these effects, quantified as non-negative numbers, range from minimal to full receptiveness. This range is necessary to adjust the effects appropriately.

The effects are defined such that the difference in mean outcomes between $e_{10} - e_{00}$ removes the influence of direct exposure from indirect exposure. Similarly, the difference in mean outcomes for $e_{11} - e_{00}$ reveals the pure indirect exposure, excluding interaction effects of direct exposure. Additionally, the mean difference in outcomes $e_{11} - e_{00}$ underscores the interaction effects of both direct and indirect exposures.

Using the methodology proposed by Aronow and Samii (2017) and applied by Kolaczyk and Csardi (2020), the effects are scored and set as follows. We set the combined effect to $d_i(e_{11}) = 2 \times d_i(e_{00})$, the direct effect to $d_i(e_{10}) = 1.75 \times d_i(e_{00})$, the indirect effect $d_i(e_{01}) = 1.25 \times d_i(e_{00})$, and set the no-exposure effect $d_i(e_{00}) = 1$. The outcome variable can be represented by total market activity, such as the average market return.

That is, the effects should be adjusted for the interaction between the four criteria. Then we define the exposure mapping for each individual node exposed to condition k, assuring that each node takes only one specific condition. Finally, a representation of each groups shows the nodes with directed, indirect, combined, and no exposure. Table 9.8 summarizes the nodes in the four exposure categories.

Estimating the degree centrality offers initial insight into the overall connectedness of the four representatives. Generally, the connectedness of these nodes, as measured by the degree scores, should exceed the average degree score of the entire network. The average degree of the undirected network in this example is 19.87. The degree scores of the four selected nodes Mkt.RF, HML, dxy, and MOM are 17.5, 26.5, 14.0, and 22.5, respectively.

Figure 9.10 shows the initial network with the positioning of the four selected nodes highlighting the four selected nodes as exposure (i.e., treatment) assignments. The right-hand side of Figure 9.10 plots the network with the exposure conditions –directed, indirect combined, and no exposure conditions. The code for the assignment of the node representatives is shown in Box 9.13.

TABLE 9.8 Exposure in the Four Categories: – Directed, Indirect, Combined, and No Exposure.

Direct Exposure	Indirect Exposure	Combined Exposure	No Exposure
HML, dxy	SMB, RMW, CMA, SPX, RTY, EM, hfrx, Golds, UST, US.Corp, US_HY, INF_L, EU_Corp	MOM, Mkt.Rf	RF, sx5p, UST_Bills, NKY, VALLS_VME_FX VALLS_VME_FI VALLS_VME_COM MOMLS_VME_FX MOMLS_VME_FI, MOMLS_VME_COM

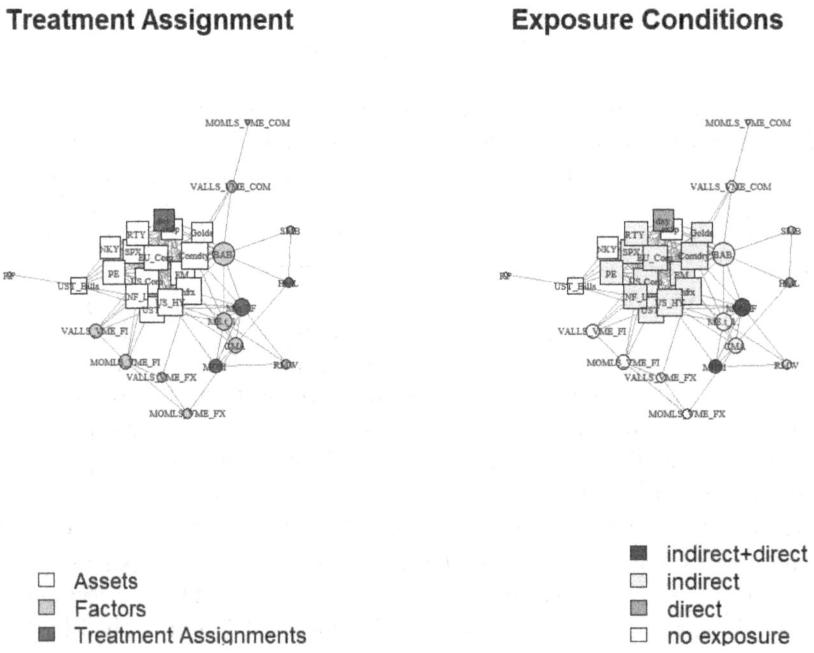

FIGURE 9.10 An Initial Undirected Network and the Network with Selected Nodes.
Note: We use the undirected correlation test asset and factor network *netz_undir* for this simulation. See Chapter 6.

BOX 9.13: NODE REPRESENTATIVE ASSIGNMENT, NETWORK PLOTS, AND EXPOSURE MAPPING.

```
#Define Assets&Factor Network first
#Use Economic Reasoning to Identify Representatives
  A<-as_adjacency_matrix(netz_undir) #extract the adjacency matrix of the underlying
network
```

```
  nodes<-vcount(netz_undir)
  z<-numeric(nodes)
  z[c(1,3,12,31)]<-1 #select the Asset and Factors with economic reasoning
#based on Asness et al. (2013) we select Value and Momentum (everywhere) - HML and MOM
#based on Konstantinov and Fabozzi (2021) we select the US dollar - DXY
#Based on Leibowitz (2011) we select Market - Mkt.Rf
  print(z)
  par(mfrow=c(1,2))
  V(netz_undir)[z==1]$names #show the names of the selected nodes
  rank(-degree(netz_undir))[z==1] #Evaluate the Rank of the Representatives using node
degree
  V(netz_undir)[z==1]$color<-"grey50" #set a color for the treatment assignment nodes
  E(netz_undir)$arrow.size<-0
#plot the netwotk with the Treatment assignment nodes
      plot(netz_undir, vertex.size=sqrt(degree(netz_undir))*3,        vertex.label.cex=0.4,
layout=layout_with_kk, main="Treatment Assignment") #plot the original network
  legend("bottomright", bty="n",legend = c("Assets", "Factors", "Treatment Assignments"),
      fill= c("white", "grey85", "grey50"))
#assign different colors to the exposure conditions
  E(netz_undir)$arrow.size<-0
  V(netz_undir)[z*I.impact.nodes==1]$color<-"grey35"
  V(netz_undir)[(1-z)*I.impact.nodes==1]$color<-"grey95"
  V(netz_undir)[z*(1-I.impact.nodes)==1]$color<-"grey75"
  V(netz_undir)[(1-z)*(1-I.impact.nodes)==1]$color<-"white"
#plot the network with the exposure conditions
  plot(netz_undir,           vertex.size=sqrt(degree(netz_undir))*3,   vertex.label.cex=0.4,
layout=layout_with_kk, main="Exposure Conditions")
  legend("bottomright", bty="n",legend = c("indirect+direct", "indirect", "direct","no
exposure"),
      fill= c("grey35", "grey95", "grey75", "white"))


  I.impact.nodes<-as.numeric(z%*%A>0) #the vector of the directly exposed neighbors of the
representative nodes selected above
  V(netz_undir)$names <- colnames(AssetsFactors)
  V(netz_undir)[z*I.impact.nodes==1]$names #Both directed and indirect exposure
  V(netz_undir)[(1-z)*I.impact.nodes==1]$names #Indirect Exposure
  V(netz_undir)[z*(1-I.impact.nodes)==1]$names #Direct Exposure
  V(netz_undir)[(1-z)*(1-I.impact.nodes)==1]$names #No Exposure
```

So far, we have seen the exposure in four categories. This is calculated using the choice of z and the number of representatives. However, network experiments require probability estimation because potential outcomes are not observable. Two important tools help to solve this issue. The first is the Monte Carlo simulation, which generates many pseudo-observations and averages out results to properly estimate the potential outcomes under causal exposure. The assumption of a proper distribution of the outcomes is vital, and the experiment requires the definition of unequal probabilities in each exposure. The distribution of the probabilities assigned to z must be adequately addressed. This is a matter of inference and is done using inverse probability weighting, according to the Horvitz and Thomson (1952) procedure.[30] The unbiased estimators for average causal effects are

$$\hat{d}(e_k) = \frac{1}{N}\sum_{z} I_{\{e_k=f(z,A_i)\}}\frac{d_i(e_k)}{p_i(e_k)} \tag{9.24}$$

---

[30] See Aronow and Samii (2017) for a detailed explanation of this and other procedures.

The result for the exposure assignments and the simulations run is presented as exposure mappings in the spirit of Aronow and Samii (2017). The results of the exposure mapping in Figure 9.11 suggest that the asset classes generally have indirect exposure. Generally, the factors do not experience exposure to the specified dilated effects. The direct exposure is relatively weak. It's important to note that results may vary in a different network context.[31] The code for the exposure mappings and the Monte Carlo simulation of treatment assignment is provided in Box 9.14.

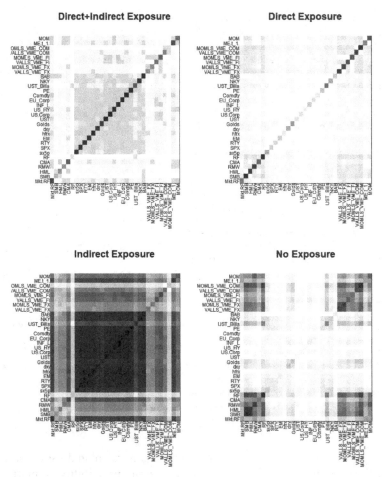

FIGURE 9.11 Exposure Mappings.

BOX 9.14:   AVERAGE CAUSAL EFFECTS MONTE CARLO SIMULATION.

```
set.seed(47)
m<-sum(z) #Number of Assets & Factors with economic Reasoning or Representatives
iterations<-10000 #number of Iterations
#Defining the Probability Matrices
```

[31] Results for different networks are provided at www.finance-resolution.com.

```
I11<-matrix(,nrow=nodes,ncol=iterations)
I10<-matrix(,nrow=nodes,ncol=iterations)
I01<-matrix(,nrow=nodes,ncol=iterations)
I00<-matrix(,nrow=nodes,ncol=iterations)

#Monte Carlo Simulation
for (i in 1:iterations){
  z<-rep(0,nodes)
  indicators<-sample((1:nodes),m,replace=FALSE)
  z[indicators]<-1
  peer.nodes<-as.numeric(z%*%A>0)
  I11[,i]<-z*peer.nodes #direct+undirect Exposure
  I10[,i]<-z*(1-peer.nodes) #direct Exposure
  I01[,i]<-(1-z)*peer.nodes #indirect Exposure
  I00[,i]<-(1-z)*(1-peer.nodes) #no Exposure
}
I11.11<-rowMeans(I11%*%t(I11))
I10.10<-I10%*%t(I10)/iterations
I01.01<-I01%*%t(I01)/iterations
I00.00<-I00%*%t(I00)/iterations


par(mfrow=c(2,2))
image(I11.11, xaxt="n",yaxt="n", main="Direct+Indirect Exposure",col=gray(100:1/100))
mtext(side=1, text=colnames(AssetsFactors), at=seq(0.0,1.0,(1/30)), las=3,cex=0.5)
mtext(side=2, text=colnames(AssetsFactors), at=seq(0.0,1.0,(1/30)), las=1,cex=0.5)
image(I10.10, xaxt="n",yaxt="n", main="Direct Exposure",col=gray(100:1/100))
mtext(side=1, text=colnames(AssetsFactors), at=seq(0.0,1.0,(1/30)), las=3,cex=0.5)
mtext(side=2, text=colnames(AssetsFactors), at=seq(0.0,1.0,(1/30)), las=1,cex=0.5)
image(I01.01, xaxt="n",yaxt="n", main="Indirect Exposure",col=gray(100:1/100))
mtext(side=1, text=colnames(AssetsFactors), at=seq(0.0,1.0,(1/30)), las=3,cex=0.5)
mtext(side=2, text=colnames(AssetsFactors), at=seq(0.0,1.0,(1/30)), las=1,cex=0.5)
image(I00.00, xaxt="n",yaxt="n",main="No Exposure",col=gray(100:1/100))
mtext(side=1, text=colnames(AssetsFactors), at=seq(0.0,1.0,(1/30)), las=3,cex=0.5)
mtext(side=2, text=colnames(AssetsFactors), at=seq(0.0,1.0,(1/30)), las=1,cex=0.5)
```

TABLE 9.9 Average Causal Effects for the Undirected Asset and Factor Network.

	Average Causal Effect	Standard Deviation	Std. Dev/Mean
$\tau(e_{11}, e_{00})$	−0.25	1.64	1.41
$\tau(e_{10}, e_{00})$	0.005	2.90	1.61
$\tau(e_{01}, e_{00})$	−0.04	2.66	1.43

Once the simulation is run, we compare the results with the initial target values for the combined, direct, indirect, and no-exposure categories. The mean statistics and the coefficients of variation for the average causal effects of the Monte Carlo simulation are shown in Table 9.9. Large deviations between the originally set values and the simulated results suggest that variance is a concern. The indirect and direct exposure values are close to the initially set values. However, the adjusted impact on the combined exposure differs substantially from the initially expected values.

The total effect $\tau(e_{11}, e_{00})$ is approximately -25%, the direct effect $\tau(e_{10}, e_{00})$ is roughly 0.05%, and the indirect effect $\tau(e_{01}, e_{00})$ is approximately -4% on the asset and factor undirected network. However, the direct effect of market intervention is slightly positive. In other words, the total effect is negative, and the network reacts negatively to the node intervention. In summary, the total and indirect effects dominate the average causal effects under interference. The ratio of standard deviation to the mean indicates that the estimators perform best for the total effects. The results can be regarded as positive for investors focusing on factor investing because any intervention on the four representatives – market excess returns, currencies, value, and momentum factor – will have low-direct exposure within the underlying network. The code for the simulation with the specification of the dilated effects is shown in Box 9.15.

BOX 9.15:   AVERAGE CAUSAL EFFECTS MONTE CARLO SIMULATION.

```
set.seed(62)
av.c11<-numeric()
av.c01<-numeric()
av.c10<-numeric()
av.c00<-numeric()

#definition of the dilated effects according to Aronow and Samii (2017)
d.c11<-2
d.c10<-1.75
d.c01<-1.25
d.c00<-1

#Monte Carlo Sampling
for (i in 1:iterations){
  z<-rep(0,nodes)
  reps.ind<-sample((1:nodes),m,replace=FALSE)
  z[reps.ind]<-1
  reps.nb<-as.numeric(z%*%A>0)

  c11<-z*reps.nb #direct & undirect
  c10<-z*(1-reps.nb) #indirect
  c01<-(1-z)*reps.nb #direct
  c00<-(1-z)*(1-reps.nb) #no exposure

  #computation of the average causal effects
  av.c11<-c(av.c11,d.c11*mean(c11/diag(I11.11)))  #the average indirect and direct effect
  av.c10<-c(av.c10,d.c10*mean(c10/diag(I10.10)))  #average direct effect
  av.c01<-c(av.c01,d.c01*mean(c01/diag(I01.01)))  #average indirect effect
  av.c00<-c(av.c00,d.c00*mean(c00/diag(I00.00)))  #no effect
}

Average_causal_effects<-list(av.c11-av.c00,av.c10-av.c00,av.c01-av.c00)

print(sapply(Average_causal_effects,mean)-c(d.c11-d.c00,d.c10-d.c00,d.c01-d.c00))
#print(sapply(Average_causal_effects,sd))
print(sapply(Average_causal_effects,sd))/c(d.c11,d.c10,d.c01)
```

KEY TAKEAWAYS

- The most fundamental characteristics of networks, such as density, degree centrality, diameter, and reciprocity, along with their distributions, are typically used to measure their goodness-of-fit.
- The purpose of assessing goodness-of-fit is to determine whether the characteristics of the model adequately match the values observed in the simulated graph. If there is a significant difference between the model and simulated graph, it indicates a lack of goodness-of-fit.
- Latent network structures involve stochastic models representing unobservable node classes and properties. Expected returns and expected volatilities are unobservable and might be used as latent node attributes. Latent variables model the probability of nodes becoming connected. In portfolio management, the application of latent network models is straightforward.
- The goal of identifying node attributes and quantitative node characteristics is to compute real numbers that serve as essential parameters influencing nodes to form links. Expected returns are an intuitive application of such variables in portfolio management, while other variables could include risk metrics like Altman's Z-score or other orthogonal properties. The key point is to model node effects through a function. Other attributes from observable networks might be used to simulate unobservable networks in the ERGMs. These attributes are building blocks of the ERGM.
- Graphs can be investigated and manipulated based on eigenvalues and input parameters such as return vectors, variances, and other exogenous factors. Graph Laplacian addresses subnetwork separation, adjacency matrix enhancements, and graph partitioning. These inputs enable portfolio managers to simulate graphs according to predefined inputs, enhancing the investment process and providing more information about risks and potential outcomes of market factors in a graph.

Portfolio Allocation With Networks

Contents

Top-down portfolio allocation involves the allocation of capital across different countries, sectors, industries, factors, commodities, currencies, funds, and other assets. This stands in contrast to bottom-up security selection, which is concerned with portfolio selection that involves the allocation of capital to individual securities within an asset class. More specifically, portfolio selection entails choosing specific securities like stocks, bonds, or other instruments, from a broader universe of candidates based on certain criteria related to asset exposures, which these selected instruments must meet to be included in the portfolio. Portfolio construction begins by choosing a set of assets, which are often based on a benchmark index of individual securities. This process continues with the development of input assumptions and the setting of constraints, and then culminates in the selection of the portfolio. This final step is typically achieved through a mathematical optimization process, or by applying a specific investment algorithm that allocates the capital to different assets. This chapter's primary task is to provide insights into the portfolio allocation framework and how networks help to overcome some of the main challenges of traditional models applied to portfolio allocation and optimization. In fact, we will show that networks successfully enhance traditional tools by capturing connectedness between assets and portfolio constituents.

GENERAL FRAMEWORK

Throughout this book, we have so far investigated how to estimate the adjacency matrices and build different types of networks that gauge node relationships (whether assets or securities). These networks serve as the building blocks for portfolio management applications. The building blocks in portfolio management can be traced back to the work of Markowitz (1952), which focused on estimating the risk relationships between assets in a portfolio. The main goal of the Markowitz mean-variance framework is to construct a portfolio with the best trade-off between risk and return. In this framework, returns are treated as the average historical returns that investors expect for each asset. Risk is measured using the variance, which gauges the uncertainty that the assets exhibit in the portfolio. The larger the variance, or variability of returns, the greater the risk. Usually, historical return data are used for both risk and return estimations. The variance-covariance matrix, which gauges asset relationships, serves as the input parameter for finding optimal portfolios that minimize risk by investing in assets with lower risk and avoiding those with higher risk.

Markowitz's framework deals with correlations, variances, and models prone to estimation errors associated with unstable correlations, fat-tailed and asymmetric return distribution, heteroscedastic variances, and the assumption that an interference does not exist between assets and factors. In finance, orthogonality is often used to describe the lack of interference between variables. This concept is typically analyzed through regression models where the dependent and independent variables are interchanged. Networks help address the challenge of unrelated assets by modeling relationships, which is the focus of this section. Portfolio allocation using network models can be applied to both portfolio optimization and the selection of individual securities.

An asset's return is its price change over a specified period. In portfolio allocation, it is common to use an asset's observed mean return over some period or apply tools to estimate asset expected returns.[1] One of the most common risk measures in investment applications is the standard deviation, which is the positive square root of the variance. It measures the deviations from the variable's expected value. In finance, standard deviation is often referred to as volatility. Investors view a larger volatility of an asset's return negatively because it signifies greater risk.

A portfolio is comprised of many assets whose return time series generally exhibit some degree of comovement, both positive and negative. As a result, the portfolio return variance is not derived solely by summing all variances or volatilities of the assets in the portfolio, but it must also consider asset covariances and correlations. This is done formally by means of what is defined as a variance-covariance matrix. As a practical matter, correlation matrices are more commonly used by portfolio managers and investors as they are invariant to scale, and thus, are generally considered more intuitive than covariance matrices. However, this approach may lead to problems. The assets in the variance-covariance matrix are not treated in their holistic connectedness. The result is often an excess amount of portfolio risk due to the inability to properly capture asset interconnectedness arising from interrelations in the portfolio (covariance), market, business cycle, macroeconomic, credit, and model risks among others.[2] The role of networks is to overcome this problem.

We can identify two major themes where networks and adjacency matrices are applied in portfolio management: optimization and nonoptimization approaches. The reason for discussing networks in both directions is straightforward. Pozzi, Di Mateo, and Aste (2013), Konstantinov and Rebmann (2019), Konstantinov and Fabozzi (2022), and later Konstantinov (2022b), Clemente et al. (2022), and Ciciretti and Pallota (2024) used centrality scores in asset allocation and argued that investors should avoid highly central nodes. By doing so, they neglected the possible positive impact of returns that such nodes might experience over time. Peralta and Zareei (2016) took a different approach and used centrality scores in optimization tools.[3] Portfolio optimization through a network approach is another way to derive portfolio

---

[1] See Ilmanen (2011) for a detailed explanation of expected returns.
[2] See Chapter 8 and Diebold and Yilmaz (2015) for a detailed explanation.
[3] The authors derived the centrality scores within the optimization.

allocation. By doing so, it is possible to utilize the advantages of optimization techniques and the network approach. Konstantinov et al. (2020), Konstantinov (2022a), Cajas (2023), and Ricca and Scozzari (2024) used networks in portfolio optimization algorithms.

Both nonoptimization and optimization approaches offer viable solutions for portfolio allocation, with empirical research demonstrating that both achieve the desired results. However, the decision to incorporate networks into the optimization process depends on the specific portfolio investment universe and objectives, necessitating further research and investigation. The easiest way to convey the intuition behind portfolio allocation is to use practical examples. Specifically, the assets and factors embody a useful example for multi-asset portfolios. A set of individual securities serves as an example for portfolio selection. Continuing with the asset and factor networks for our illustrative example comprising assets and factors, we can plot all networks (see Figure 10.1).

The code in Box 10.1 was used to plot all asset and factor networks weighting the node size by the eigen centrality score. To better visualize the graphs, we set the edge size to zero. However, setting the edge arrow size to nonzero for directed networks is more convenient.

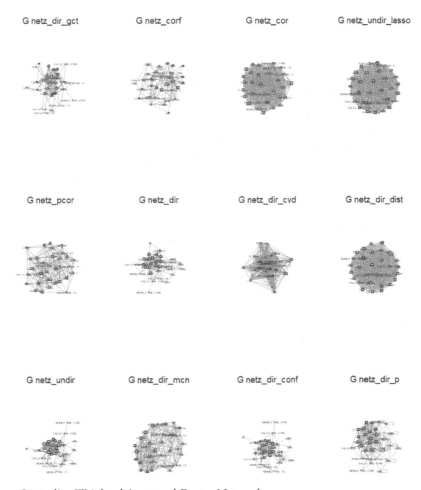

FIGURE 10.1 Eigen Centrality-Weighted Asset and Factor Networks.

BOX 10.1:   CODE FOR PLOTTING ALL ASSET AND FACTOR NETWORKS.

```
#Plots all Networks with Eigen Centralities

par(mfrow=c(1,1))
allem<-list(netz_dir_gct,netz_pcor,netz_undir,netz_corf, netz_dir,netz_dir_mcn, netz_cor,
netz_dir_cvd, netz_dir_conf, netz_undir_lasso, netz_dir_dist, netz_dir_p)
all.netz<-c("netz_dir_gct","netz_pcor","netz_undir","netz_corf", "netz_dir","netz_dir_
mcn", "netz_cor", "netz_dir_cvd","netz_dir_conf", "netz_undir_lasso",
"netz_dir_dist","netz_dir_p")
par(mfcol=c(3,4))

foreach (i=all.netz, j=allem) %do% {


  E(j)$arrow.size<-0
  plot(j, vertex.size=sqrt(eigen_centrality(j)$vector)*10, vertex.label.cex=0.4,
layout=layout_with_kk, main=bquote(paste('G ', .(i))))

}
```

RELATIONSHIP BETWEEN PORTFOLIO ALLOCATION AND NETWORKS

In this section, we will present the formal framework that establishes the connection between the Markowitz mean-variance framework and portfolio allocation using network metrics. Because networks capture relations between the nodes (i.e., assets), they find broad use in portfolio allocation models. Instead of incorporating a correlation and covariance matrix in alternative optimizations, Sandhu et al. (2016), Peralta and Zareei (2016), Výrost, Lyócsa, and Baumöhl (2019), Zareei (2019), and Konstantinov et al. (2020) used networks to derive portfolios that benefit from diversification and utilize the relationships between assets. Peralta and Zareei (2016) were among the first to show the relationship between diversification and correlation-based networks. The adjacency matrix is derived using the correlation matrix. In other words, the adjacency matrix gauges the information of connectedness regarded as association contained in the correlation matrix. Consider the Markowitz mean-variance framework, in which the portfolio weights and the variance-covariance matrix are input parameters. Portfolio allocation, in its most basic form, either minimizes risk for a given target return or maximizes return for a given target risk. Let's first consider the minimum-variance framework.

For a minimization of portfolio risk, the mathematical algorithm searches for all possible weights w that minimizes the portfolio risk captured by the portfolio variance σ_{PF}^2, which is a weighted product of the individual weights and the variance-covariance matrix $\Sigma = [\sigma_{ij}]$.[4] That is:

$$\min_{w}\ \sigma_{PF}^2 = w'\Sigma w \tag{10.1}$$

$$\text{s.t. } x \geq L$$

---

[4]See Konstantinov, Fabozzi. and Simonian (2023).

where w is a transposed n-dimensional vector of portfolio weights, and Σ is the n-dimensional variance-covariance matrix of the portfolio assets. The variable x represents the portfolio return, while L represents the minimum return value that the portfolio must satisfy. The weights that satisfy the optimizations are:

$$w_{min} = \frac{1}{1'\Sigma^{-1}1}\Sigma^{-1}1 \tag{10.2}$$

where Σ^{-1} is the inverse covariance matrix, and 1 is the vectors of ones.

Using the notion of the covariance matrix Σ that it is a product of the correlation matrix Ω and the diagonal matrix Δ whose entries are the variances with $\sigma_i = \sqrt{\sigma_{ii}}$, then the relationship is $\Sigma = \Delta\,\Omega\,\Delta$ and the weights subject to the correlation matrix are:

$$\frac{1}{1'\Sigma^{-1}1}\Sigma^{-1}1\Omega^{-1} \tag{10.3}$$

Considering the mean-variance framework, the diversification, or minimum risk given the expected level of return as measured by the portfolio variance and expected return $E(r)$, is computed as follows:

$$\min_w \sigma_{PF}^2 = w'\Sigma w \quad \text{with} \quad R_{PF} = w'E(r) \tag{10.4}$$

As a result, the weights of the mean-variance framework are a function of the expected portfolio returns and the covariance matrix of the assets, which gauges risk:

$$w_{mv} = \frac{R_{PF}}{E(r)'\Sigma^{-1}E(r)}\Sigma^{-1}E(r) \tag{10.5}$$

where Σ^{-1} is the inverse covariance matrix, and $E(r)$ are vectors of expected asset returns, and R_{PF} is the portfolio return. Similarly, using the correlation matrix, we can obtain the weights in the mean-variance framework.

Diversification in a network context is identified by the weaker relationships between the nodes in a graph. The shorter the distances between the nodes, the larger the impact of risk. This limitation, as suggested by Peralta and Zareei (2016) and Zareei (2019), has been relaxed by Konstantinov (2022a, 2022b) and used more broadly in portfolio allocation, as we will discuss later in this chapter. Essentially, the transfer of risk between the nodes is central when using networks for portfolio allocation. It's important to note that centrality scores like degree, eigenvector, or alpha centralities are essential here, because they identify how risk flows might affect the nodes. However, degree centrality is less preferred because it measures the immediate effect of connectedness compared to other node centrality metrics, which measure the interconnectedness of the node to other highly connected nodes. The asset and factor networks whose estimation and visualization we provided in the previous chapters serve as input variables in portfolio allocation, and we demonstrate how the adjacency matrices of the networks can be used in portfolio construction. There are two main lines of thought – nonoptimization and optimization approaches to portfolio allocation, and networks can be used in both techniques.

NONOPTIMIZATION APPROACHES FOR PORTFOLIO ALLOCATION

The nonoptimization approaches to portfolio allocation practically do not require optimization or the mathematical formulation of searching for a local minimum or maximum of a utility function. The intuition behind this can be traced back to the work of Simon (1962). The underlying assumption is that there is an inherent hierarchical structure in the data and economic variables, making it possible to derive structure in a portfolio without the need for optimization. Node centrality plays a crucial role in portfolio allocation with networks. It provides valuable insights into the importance of each asset within the portfolio network, enabling investors to make more informed allocation decisions.

By considering centrality metrics, such as eigenvector centrality, alpha centrality, or power centrality, investors can identify assets that are highly connected or influential within the network. This information helps in constructing portfolios that are well-diversified and resilient to systemic risks. Therefore, node centrality is a fundamental tool in network-based portfolio management, aiding investors in optimizing their investment strategies. Specifically, the approaches used for nonoptimization-based allocation include hierarchical clustering or centrality-based allocation, which identify and weight the portfolio exposure based on the underlying importance scores and clusters embedded in the network data.

Centrality-Based Portfolio Allocation

The main intuition behind centrality-based portfolio allocation is to estimate the portfolio exposure with the help of importance scores and vectors. The key advantage is that centrality vectors enable for the consideration of the interconnectedness of assets in the portfolio. To stress again, the higher the connectedness of a node to other highly connected nodes, the larger the centrality score of that node. By incorporating centrality metrics, investors can better understand the relative importance of each asset within the network and adjust their portfolio allocations accordingly. This approach provides a more holistic view of portfolio construction, considering the individual characteristics of assets and their relationships with other assets in the portfolio. In this section, we will discuss two nonoptimization approaches to portfolio construction. The first follows the algorithm suggested by Das and Sisk (2005), which builds portfolios using the assets' covariance matrix and centrality scores. The second approach, suggested by Pozzi et al. (2013) and applied to hedge fund indices by Konstantinov (2022a, 2022b) and Wang et al. (2024), utilizes centrality scores to assign weights to the assets.

The appropriate question is which centrality metric to use. The answer to this question can be easily shown by comparing different types of centrality metrics. In general, we can focus on two major centrality metrics: degree centrality and eigen centrality. Note that degree centrality identifies an important node according to its number of links. Following Konstantinov, Aldridge, and Kazemi (2023), the main advantage of degree centrality is that it measures the immediate impact of risk on a node level. In contrast, eigenvector centrality measures the immediate direct and indirect long-term impact. Therefore, we focus on eigenvector centrality. For illustrative purposes, we show the relationship between degree and eigen centrality for the partial correlation networks for assets and factors, single hedge funds, global equity markets, and equity and bond funds in Figure 10.2.

Note that the code for the partial correlation networks for single hedge funds, global equity markets, and equity and bond funds networks can be adopted from the code provided for the asset and factor partial correlation network provided in Chapter 6. The code for all four networks is provided in Box 10.2.

Eigen Centrality-Weighted Average Covariance   DeMarzo, Vayanos, and Zwiebel (2003), and Das and Sisk (2005) were among the first to notice the importance of centralities in asset management. They argued that portfolio managers might use importance scores to identify and allocate to assets (i.e., nodes) depending on their centrality. The notion of importance is essential in graph-based portfolio management. However, the decision to use centrality in portfolio allocation is not trivial. Das and Sisk (2005) proposed an approach to compute the centrality metric for all nodes in the network, and then estimate the variance-covariance

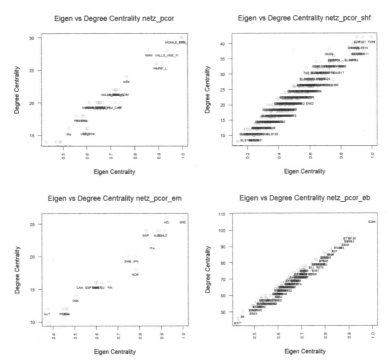

FIGURE 10.2   A Degree and Eigen Centrality Relationship.

Note: We use only one of the possible networks – a partial correlation network estimated for four different asset classes – asset and factors, hedge funds, equity markets, and equity and bond mutual funds. For this figure, we use the data used in the studies of Konstantinov et al. (2020), Konstantinov and Simonian (2020), Frazzini and Pedersen (2014), and Konstantinov and Rusev (2020).

BOX 10.2:   CODE FOR COMPARING DEGREE AND EIGEN CENTRALITY FOR DIFFERENT PARTIAL CORRELATION NETWORKS.

```
all.graphs<-list(netz_pcor,netz_pcor_shf,netz_pcor_em, netz_pcor_eb)
all.nets<-c("netz_pcor","netz_pcor_shf","netz_pcor_em", "netz_pcor_eb")
par(mfrow=c(2,2))

foreach (i=all.nets, j=all.graphs) %do% {

  ec=eigen_centrality(j)$vector
  dc=degree(j)


plot(ec,dc, lwd=0.6, cex.names=0.7,cex.axis=0.7, col="grey", bg="grey",las=2, xlab="Eigen
Centrality",ylab="Degree Centrality",main=bquote(paste('Eigen vs Degree Centrality
', .(i))))
text(ec, dc, labels = V(j)$name,cex = 0.6, pos = 1, col = "black")
}
```

matrix for the nodes. For each node, the average pairwise covariance with all other nodes is estimated. If the correlation coefficient between node centrality and return covariance is positive, nodes with high-centrality scores may be more favorable for portfolio allocation. Conversely, if the correlation between the node centrality score and return covariance is negative, these nodes should be excluded from the analysis.

Formally, we can expand the framework suggested by Das and Sisk (2005), which considers only the eigen centrality, to encompass a broader set of centrality metrics. Intuitively, the practical applications of networks for portfolio construction are closely linked to the computation of centrality scores. In the language of financial data science, centrality-based portfolio allocation reflects an unsupervised learning procedure. The reason is that when applying centrality scores, researchers do not differentiate between asset classes, industry groups, sectors, countries, geographic sectors, and other types of asset classification often used in financial analysis. When applying centrality-based allocation, it is practical to leave the hierarchical structure aside and compute the importance scores representing connected nodes. This assures that the portfolio is treated as a holistic network with all the relations represented by the links. Within this framework, the hierarchical structure of a portfolio is a function of connectedness and the importance scores.

A practical question is which centrality metric to apply. This is a reasonable question given the 100+ centrality measures that exist. In Chapter 4, we discussed the most prominent and applied importance metrics in network science, but as we stressed, the choice is driven by the network's underlying flow process and the nodes' connectedness. In this section, we will focus on two of the most prominent choices for centrality and apply them.

The purpose of proposing more centrality metrics is that the alpha and Bonacich centralities provide more robust and meaningful solutions in asymmetric networks whose nodes are unconnected. The centrality scores for all nodes in the networks are estimated using the following plan:

$$
s_i \propto x \quad
\begin{cases}
\lambda x = Ax, & \text{Eigen Centrality} \\
x = Ax + e, & \text{Alpha Centrality} \\
x = a(I - bA)^{-1} A1, & \text{Bonacich Centrality}
\end{cases}
\tag{10.6}
$$

As a result, the next step in this algorithm requires the computation of the covariance matrix of node returns. Recall from the previous section that we defined the asset variance-covariance matrix as

$$
\Sigma = \{\sigma_{ij}\}
\tag{10.7}
$$

The next step is to compute, for each node (i.e., asset), the average pairwise covariances with all other nodes in the network:

$$
\epsilon_i = \frac{1}{n-1} \sum_{i \neq j} \sigma_{ij}
\tag{10.8}
$$

In the final stage, it is necessary to compute the pairwise correlations, which we term attractiveness score g. The attractiveness score measures the correlation between the centrality scores s_i and the ϵ_i for each node in the network:

$$
g_i = \rho_{\epsilon_i, s_i}
\tag{10.9}
$$

where all ϵ_i is the average pairwise covariance for each node with all other nodes, and s_i are the eigen centrality scores for all nodes, defined previously.

Again, the higher attractiveness score g_i for a node, the more attractive the asset to be used in portfolio allocation. Conversely, negative g_i scores suggest an attractive metric for the nodes. The algorithm can be applied to all types of networks used in asset allocation and security selection. A simple example for the global equity markets is provided in Figure 10.3. The scores for France (FRA), Spain (ESP), Austria (AUT), United Kingdom (GBR), Hong Kong (HKG), and Sweden (SWE) are quite above the zero line and can be considered attractive. However, the equity market attractiveness scores for US (USA), Belgium (BEL), Canada (CAN), and Australia (AUS) are negative and considered unattractive.

The code for the centrality-weighted covariance of the global equity markets used by Frazzini and Pedersen (2014), provided by AQR Capital Management, is shown in Box 10.3. The code for computing the average pairwise covariances is shown in Box 10.4.

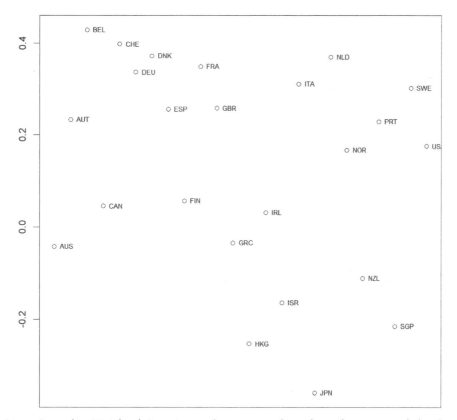

FIGURE 10.3   Eigen Centrality-Weighted Covariances for a Directed Markov Chain Network for the Global Equity Markets.
Legend: Australia (AUS), Austria (AUT), Belgium (BEL), Canada (CAN), France (FRA), Hong Kong (HKG), Japan (JAP), Spain (ESP), Sweden (SWE), United Kingdom (GBR), United States (USA), Singapore (SGP), Denmark (DNK), Switzerland (CHE), Norway (NOR), Finland (FIN), Portugal (PRT), Israel (ISR), New Zealand (NZL), Netherlands (NLD), Greece (GRC), and Germany (GER).

Note: Data for the global equity markets were obtained by the authors from AQR Capital Management, LLC. We use the algorithm for the Markov-Chain probability matrix and graph computation using the Manhattan distance of the node structure provided in Chapter 6.

BOX 10.3:   CODE FOR CENTRALITY-WEIGHTED COVARIANCE OF GLOBAL EQUITY MARKETS.

```
#Estimate a Markov Chain Network for AQR Global Equity Market Returns
returns_em<-AQR.Equity.Markets.M
trans.mat.em<-as.matrix(1+cor(returns_em))
mtx_markov.em<-matrix(nrow=ncol(AQR.Equity.Markets.M),ncol=ncol(AQR.Equity.Markets.M))
mtx_markov_em<-t(apply(trans.mat.em,1,function(x) x/sum(x)))

trans.mat.em<-as.matrix(mtx_markov_em)

#Make a network from the probability Matrix
trans.prob.matrix.em<-as.matrix(trans.mat.em)
diag(trans.prob.matrix.em)<-0
p.t<-1/24
trans.prob.matrix.em<-ifelse(trans.prob.matrix.em[,]>p.t,1,0)
netz_dir_mcn_em<-graph_from_adjacency_matrix(trans.prob.matrix.em, weighted=TRUE)
par(mfrow=c(1,1))
cor.m=data.frame()
test.c.mat=cov(AQR.Equity.Markets.M)

test.m<-upper.tri(test.c.mat, diag=FALSE)
test.s=eigen_centrality(netz_dir_mcn_em)$vector
dik<-foreach(k=1:dim(test.c.mat)[1]) %do% {
    cor.m<-(cor(test.s,test.c.mat[,k]))
}
Res.gem<-as.matrix(dik)
plot(Res.gem,xlab="",xaxt = "n",ylab="")
text(Res.gem, labels = colnames(AQR.Equity.Markets.M),cex = 0.7, pos = 4, col = "Black")
```

BOX 10.4:   CODE FOR AVERAGE PAIRWISE COVARIANCES.

```
library(extRC)
cov.matrix=cov(AssetsFactors)
cov.adj.matrix<-tril(cov.matrix)
av.p.cov=c()
for(v in 1:dim(cov.matrix)[1]) {
  av.p.cov=rbind(av.p.cov,mean(cov.matrix[1:v,1:v][lower.tri(cov.matrix[1:v,1:v])]))
}

av.p.cov #this is an n x 1 vector of pairwise average covariances.
```

Das and Sisk (2005) used the average pairwise covariances of each node to all other nodes. However, we propose a different method. For each asset and factor network, we use the covariance matrix and set the main diagonal to zero to avoid self-connectedness. In other words, we ignore the variance of each node. Because the covariance matrix corresponds to pairwise relationships, we use all columns of the matrix for each node that represent the relation of that node to all other nodes. Then we estimate the correlation between centrality scores and each node's covariances using equations (10.7), (10.8), and (10.9). Figure 10.4 illustrates the procedure along with the results for the asset and factor network using the eigen centrality and the covariance matrix of the assets and factors network. The code for this procedure is shown in Box 10.5.

Visual inspection reveals that the attractiveness scores depend on the network type and, consequently, on centrality scores. Again, the crucial first step is to estimate the covariance matrix of asset and factor returns and the eigen centrality scores of each network.

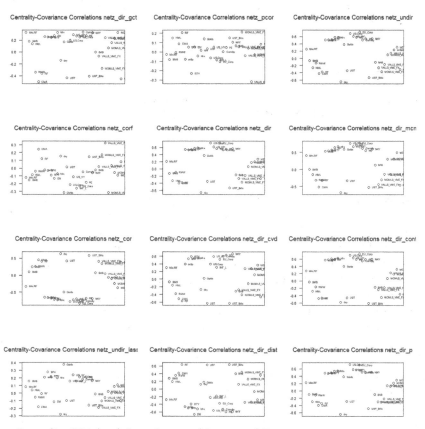

FIGURE 10.4   Eigen Centrality-Weighted Covariances of Assets and Factors.

BOX 10.5:   CODE FOR ATTRACTIVENESS SCORES WITH CENTRALITY-WEIGHTED NODES AND THE COVARIANCE MATRIX.

```
set.seed(93)
allem<-list(netz_dir_gct,netz_pcor,netz_undir,netz_corf, netz_dir,netz_dir_mcn, netz_cor,
netz_dir_cvd, netz_dir_conf, netz_undir_lasso, netz_dir_dist, netz_dir_p)
all.netz<-c("netz_dir_gct","netz_pcor","netz_undir","netz_corf", "netz_dir","netz_dir_
mcn", "netz_cor", "netz_dir_cvd","netz_dir_conf", "netz_undir_lasso", "netz_dir_dist",
"netz_dir_p")
par(mfrow=c(4,3))

foreach (i=all.netz, j=allem) %do% {

    ranking=(eigen_centrality(j)$vector)
    cov.matrix=cov(AssetsFactors) #estimate the covariance matrix
    diag(cov.matrix)<-0 #set the main diagonal to zero
```

(Continued)

(*Continued*)

```
#cov.adj.matrix<-tril(cov.matrix, k<0,diag=FALSE)
cwcm<-foreach(v=1:dim(cov.matrix)[1]) %do% {
    names(ranking)<-colnames(AssetsFactors)
    cov.cen=cor(ranking,cov.matrix[,v])


}
ergebnis<-as.matrix(cwcm)
plot(ergebnis,lwd=0.5, cex.names=0.7,cex.axis=0.7,las=2, xlab="",ylab="",xaxt =
"n",main=bquote(paste('Centrality-Covariance Correlations ', .(i))))
    text(ergebnis, labels = colnames(AssetsFactors),cex = 0.5, pos = 4, col = "red")
}
```

Centrality-Based Allocation   The centrality-based approach to portfolio construction was originally proposed by Pozzi et al. (2013) and implemented by Czasonis, Pamir, and Turkington (2019) for currencies, Konstantinov (2022a, 2022b) for hedge funds and emerging market bonds. Given that centrality scores are the main determinants of the process, it is crucial to emphasize the importance of selecting the appropriate centrality metric. Ciciretti and Pallotta (2024) showed that eigen centrality scores are inversely related to the weights in a hierarchical risk-parity portfolio. The idea can be traced back to the work of Laloux et al. (1999), who documented that the eigenvectors are directly related to systemic risk in a portfolio. That is, the higher the importance score of an asset is, the lower the portfolio allocation weight of that asset in the portfolio. This implies that the portfolio network is a completed network where no assets remain unconnected. Here comes the disadvantage of eigen centrality as an allocation tool and, to some extent, the excessive reliability on correlation-based (completed) networks.

As Bonacich and Lloyd (2001) demonstrated, eigenvector centrality for directed networks poses challenges because directed networks are asymmetric and often contain disconnected nodes. For instance, consider an asset that may be disconnected from all other assets at a specific point in time. Eigenvector centrality would not apply to such a node. In the case of directed networks, Alpha centrality serves as a better tool for capturing asymmetric relationships. The weights in a portfolio are proportional to the normalized centrality scores. However, eigenvector centrality remains applicable in cases where the directed network is asymmetric, provided that no individual node is disconnected.[5] Following Bonacich and Lloyd (2001), limiting the practical use of centrality metrics to eigenvector and alpha centrality is advisable. The Perron-Frobenius theorem is an important factor to consider in this regard.[6]

$$s \propto x \quad \begin{cases} \lambda x = Ax, & \text{Eigenvector Centrality} \\ x = Ax + e, & \text{Alpha Centrality} \end{cases} \tag{10.10}$$

where A is the adjacency matrix, λ are the eigenvalues, x is the set of eigenvectors, and s_i are the centrality scores of the assets, with each being a multiple of the leading eigenvector, the one corresponding to the largest eigenvalue.

---

[5] See Bonacich and Lloyd (2001).
[6] Which centrality applies to portfolio network depends on the flow process. See Borgatti (2005) and Wang et al. (2024).

Note again that for (completed) undirected networks, where no asset is disconnected, the eigenvector centrality applies whenever there exists a largest eigenvalue λ. However, if an asset remains disconnected from other nodes in the network, the alpha centrality applies. The intuition behind centrality-based allocation is to assign weights to assets in the portfolio inversely proportional to their centrality scores. In other words, assets with higher centrality scores are assigned a lower weight in portfolio allocation, and vice versa.

The centrality-based allocation approach assigns weights to the weakest connected assets inversely related to their normalized centrality score. That is, the allocation in the portfolio assumes the assets (i.e., nodes) with the lowest centrality or interconnectedness scores receive the highest weight in the portfolio. Specifically, the portfolio weights are inversely related to the eigen or alpha centrality scores of the nodes in a network. Once the node centrality is computed, the estimation of the weights is straightforward using

$$ w_i = \frac{s_i^{-1}}{\sum_i \left(s_i^{-1} \right)} \quad s_i \propto x \quad \begin{cases} \lambda x = Ax, & \text{Eigenvector Centrality} \\ x = Ax + e, & \text{Alpha Centrality} \end{cases} \tag{10.11} $$

where w_i is the weight associated with the centrality score of asset i.

Within this framework, the role of expected returns is neglected as only interconnectedness; thus, the risk of highly connected nodes plays a role. However, a major drawback of this method is that applying centrality scores to portfolios might alter the potential returns that nodes with high centralities might earn. Criticism arises from the possibility of a node with a large score generating both systematic and idiosyncratic returns.

Centrality-based nonoptimization allocation primarily focuses on managing risk. Such allocation is suitable for risk-averse portfolios prioritizing risk management over returns. In summary, the usefulness of centrality-based allocation lies in gaining exposure to weakly connected nodes in a portfolio, aiming to maximize diversification and minimize risk without emphasizing return perspectives.

Hierarchical Clustering for Portfolio Allocation

Hierarchical clustering is another alternative to the nonoptimization approach that utilizes graphs in portfolio management. Historically, hierarchical clustering was developed for data analytical purposes by Johnson (1967) and Lance and Williams (1967). The principal intuition behind hierarchical clustering is that it does not require specific knowledge of the data structure and separation into clusters.

Hierarchical clustering assigns the nodes into groups represented as a tree. Several criteria for grouping exist, including single linkage (i.e., nearest-neighbor method), complete linkage (i.e., diameter method), and average linkage.[7] These approaches differ significantly, and their application results in different clustering methods that consider the distances between nodes within different clusters. Complete linkage ensures that the distance between clusters is the longest distance between any node in one cluster and any node in another cluster. In contrast, the single-linkage method ensures that the distance between clusters is the shortest distance from any node in one cluster to any node in another cluster. Figure 10.5 displays dendrograms and clustering, providing more insight into the different hierarchical clusters.

Box 10.6 provides the code for the hierarchical clustering of asset and factor returns, using correlation coefficients in a Euclidean distance space.

---

[7] See Wasserman and Faust (1994) and Borgatti et al. (2022).

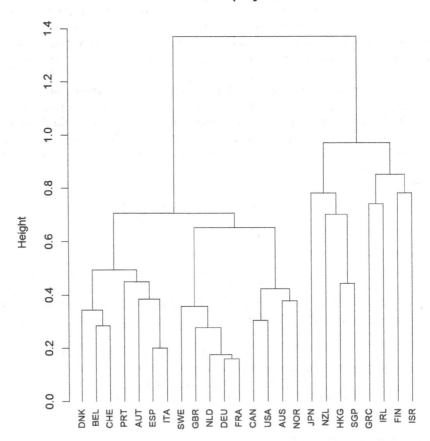

Global Equity Markets

hclust (*, "complete")

FIGURE 10.5 (CONT'D)

BOX 10.6:   CODE FOR CENTRALITY-WEIGHTED CORRELATION NODES AND COVARIANCE MATRIX.

```
hc<-hclust(dist(cor(AssetsFactors))) ##generates hierarchical cluster of the correlation
coefficients for the Assets and Factor network using the Euclidean distance
plot(hc,hang=-1, main="", xlab="", cex=0.8) #plot the dendrogramm
```

The most essential task when creating a hierarchical cluster is to have a matrix containing the structural equivalence between the nodes. Barabási (2016) refers to this step as the definition of the similarity matrix. Structural equivalence is determined by a pairwise distance metric or correlation coefficients

Assets and Factors

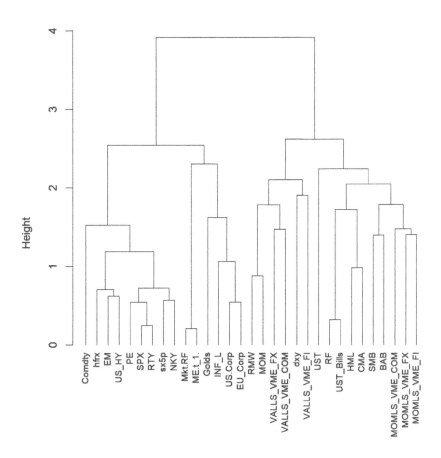

hclust (*, "complete")

FIGURE 10.5 (CONT'D)

between nodes i and j. Nodes are considered structurally equivalent if they reach a certain threshold level of similarity. When using the diameter method, all pairs are deemed similar if their similarity meets or exceeds a specified threshold value.[8] The task is to find structurally equivalent nodes at this threshold level using an appropriate measure.

Wassermann and Faust (1994) show that when using a distance metric $\left(d_{ij}\right)$, the nodes i and j are structurally equivalent when $d_{ij} \leq threshold$. If the measure of structural equivalence is the correlation

---

[8]Note that diameter is a geodesic distance following a path. Paths are essential in network science as noted by Barabási (2016).

Global Equity and Bond Funds

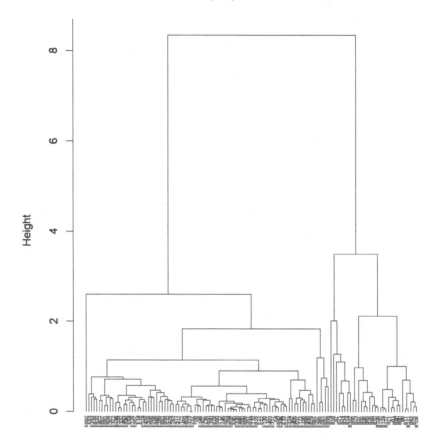

hclust (*, "complete")

FIGURE 10.5 (CONT'D)

coefficient, then the pairwise correlations should be significant above that threshold level $\rho_{ij} \geq threshold$. The algorithm is termed hierarchical because it employs less-restrictive threshold levels, and the structure is visualized in a dendrogram – a diagram showing the arrangement of a dataset's elements in a hierarchical structure. The pertinent question is how hierarchical clustering applies to financial networks, particularly to portfolio networks.

Although many financial models concentrate on hierarchical networks and their implications for investment management, two crucial questions posed by Barabási (2016) remain unanswered. First, the direct application assumes that small structures are integrated into larger communities. Second, a network could be divided into smaller, weakly connected structures, where a node may belong to multiple

Hedge Funds

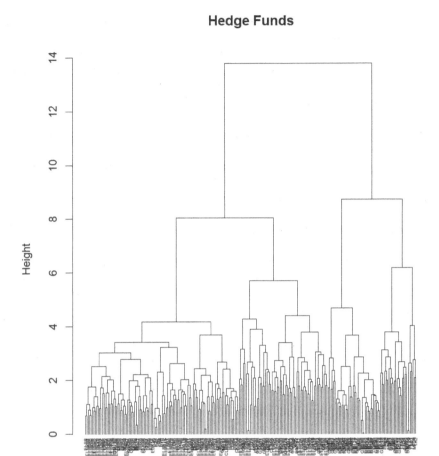

hclust (*, "complete")

FIGURE 10.5 (CONT'D)   Examples for Hierarchical Clustering in Different Markets.

Note: For the equity markets, we use AQR's monthly international equity market returns, obtained from AQR Capital Management, LLC. We use the datasets of Konstantinov et al. (2020), Konstantinov and Rusev (2020), and Konstantinov and Simonian (2020) for the asset and factor returns, equity and bond funds, and the single hedge fund returns, respectively.

communities.[9] Moreover, hubs, which are high-degree nodes, can interact with and connect several communities. The role of hubs that link a larger number of weakly connected subgraphs remains unclear. Benzi, Estrada, and Klymko (2013) investigated the ranking of hubs and authorities in networks and argued that the consistent choice of a node-ranking algorithm is central when evaluating node centrality.

---

[9]A problem referred to as overlapping communities arises when a node belongs to multiple communities. See Barabási (2016).

We address the first question through the lens of investment management. Hierarchical clustering has become a primary focus in portfolio management.[10] Often, hierarchical clustering is used with adjustments made to the covariance matrix to improve diversification by allocating to assets from different clusters, thus minimizing portfolio risk in combination with volatility targeting as a risk-budgeting approach. One major advantage is that the weights in the groups at the same level are equal, and the complete link method provides homogeneous clusters. López de Prado (2016) argued that the problem with correlation-based (complete) graphs is the lack of hierarchy and the inability to substitute highly correlated nodes to simplify the connectedness and impose a hierarchical structure. López de Prado (2018) states that weights are only rebalanced among peers at various hierarchical levels.

The potential use of hierarchical clustering for asset managers is broad because these trees can be expanded top-down from asset classes to sectors and individual securities. As noted earlier, Ciciretti and Pallotta (2024) provide algebraic proof that the weights generated by hierarchical risk parity are proportional to the inverse of the eigenvalues of the modified covariance matrix. The technique is widely used as a combination of machine learning and network analysis within a hierarchical risk parity optimization approach. Unfortunately, a dendrogram that partitions a network does not provide information about the best partitioning made by a cut. It remains an issue whether the underlying network structure is exactly as the dendrogram represents. All cuts can be equally valid. However, this makes every asset or financial network case-specific, and no underlying universal law of partitioning exists. In real networks, and even less so in financial markets, an asset strictly belongs to a predefined cluster. Similarly, a node might be a member of several clusters, which is oversimplified in simple hierarchical clustering methods. As a result, it remains unclear whether the graph comprises exactly the structure predicted by a simple dendrogram of the data. Several studies show that the structure of a network is different than the one that data dendrograms with distance metrics suggest.

Hierarchical network modeling and analysis mitigate the previously raised issues by considering the network structure based on relations between the nodes and addressing the issue with the subgraph community structure. Moreover, a critical property of nested small communities that are connected to larger communities can be addressed. The hierarchical modularity measures the relationship between the clustering coefficient and the node degree. According to Barabási (2016), there is an inverse relationship between high-degree nodes and the clustering coefficient, so that high-degree nodes tend not to connect in small communities and have a low-correlation coefficient. On the contrary, low-degree nodes are connected to small communities. The hierarchical modularity-node degree relationship is:

$$\widetilde{C}_i \sim k^{-1} \tag{10.12}$$

As discussed in Chapter 2, the clustering coefficient is defined as follows:

$$\widetilde{C}_i = \frac{2m}{k_i(k_i - 1)} \tag{10.13}$$

where k_i is the node degree, and m is the number of edges. Obviously, the larger the node degree, the lower the clustering coefficient.

---

[10]See, for example, the various application of hierarchical clustering in Bacidore, Berkow, and Polidore (2012); Papenbrock and Schwendner (2015); López de Prado (2018); Raffinot (2018); Garvey and Madhavan (2019); Molyboga (2020); Schwendner et al. (2021); Bonne et al. (2022); Ciciretti and Pallotta (2024); and Elkamhi, Lee, and Salerno (2024).

The histogram of the degree distribution provides an overview of the fat-tailed distribution of node degrees for the undirected network of assets and factors built using the partial correlation coefficients (netz_pcor). Inspecting Figure 10.6, we see that the Russell 2000 index (RTY) has the largest centrality score and the highest-node degree. In contrast, the US High Yield Market (US_HY) has the lowest eigenvector centrality score, suggesting the lowest node connectedness. Note that the lowest eigenvector centrality score is not close to zero, which indicates that the node (US_HY) is still connected to several nodes. Inspection of the degree scores provides exact information about the specific node connectedness. The lowest degree is 15, indicating that in a network size of 31, the weakly connected node is still connected to 15 other nodes.

Applying the cluster fast greedy (CFG) algorithm to the network, the modularity of 0.17 partitions the graph into four communities, comprising 12, 3, 10, and 6 nodes. The four clusters for assets and factors are summarized in Table 10.1.[11]

Figure 10.6 provides an example of portfolio analysis of an undirected network and the hierarchical structure resulting from implementing a cluster fast greedy optimization. In Figure 10.7, we show the network plots with community affiliation. To increase the information content, using the degree and eigenvector centralities to highlight the important nodes is useful. It is worth discussing the information that such representation provides.

Hierarchical clustering for portfolio allocation is usually combined with graphs that are drawn using the minimum spanning tree (MST) algorithm (see Ciciretti and Pallotta [2024]). In Chapter 6, we discussed the MST algorithm, which connected the nodes based on their eigen centrality. As such, the MST presents a network that is in a fully connected mode. In other words, the nodes in such a network are always connected because every node is itself connected to other connected nodes. The advantage of the MST algorithm is that it preserves the correlation structure by selecting the fewest possible edges between the nodes while eliminating less meaningful correlations.

Box 10.7 provides the code that reproduces Figures 10.6 and 10.7. The algorithm is run for a partial correlation asset and factor network. The code estimates the hierarchical clustering using the algorithm with the highest modularity score. In this case, we use the CFG algorithm. Finally, we plot the network with node size corresponding to the eigen and degree centralities.

TABLE 10.1   Community Affiliation for a Partial Correlation Network of Assets and Factors.

Cluster 1		Cluster 2	Cluster 3		Cluster 4	
"HML"	"RMW"	"EM"	"SMB"	"CMA"	"Mkt.RF"	"UST"
"RF"	"SPX"	"Comdty"	"sx5p"	"hfrx"	"EU_Corp"	"BAB"
"RTY"	"INF_L"	"VALLS_VME_FI"	"dxy"	"Golds"	"MOMLS_VME_FX"	
"UST_Bills"	"NKY"		"US.Corp"		"ME.t_1."	
"VALLS_VME_FX"			"US_HY"	"PE"		
"VALLS_VME_COM"			"MOMLS_VME_FI"			
"MOMLS_VME_COM"						
"MOM"						

---

[11]Note that the community structure is subject to network choice and a network community detection algorithm. The choice is made using the modularity score.

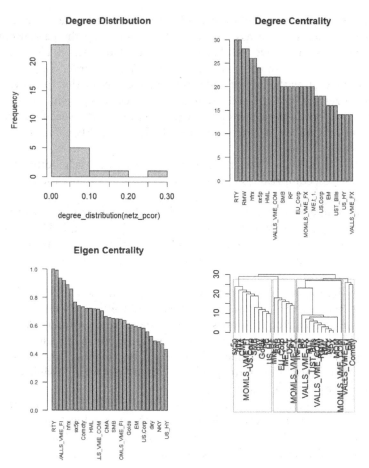

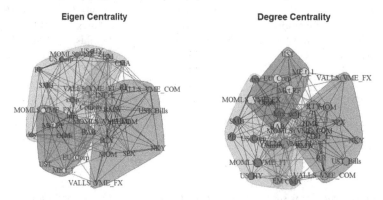

BOX 10.7: CODE FOR A PARTIAL CORRELATION ASSET AND FACTOR NETWORKS AND HIERARCHICAL CLUSTERING.

```
#Undirected Partial-Cor Network with Fischer Transformation
set.seed(3211)
returns<-AssetsFactors
mtx_pcor<-data.frame()
mtx_pcor<-matrix(nrow=ncol(AssetsFactors),ncol=ncol(AssetsFactors))
mtx_pcor<-as.matrix(mtx_pcor)
mat_pcor=0.5*log((1+pcor(returns)$estimate)/(1-pcor(returns)$estimate))
mat_pcor=abs(mat_pcor)
mat_pcor<-ifelse(mat_pcor[,]<0.05/6,1,0)
diag(mat_pcor)<-0
colnames(mat_pcor)<-colnames(AssetsFactors)
print(mat_pcor)
netz_pcor<-as.matrix(mat_pcor)
netz_pcor<-graph_from_adjacency_matrix(netz_pcor, weighted=TRUE)
hist(degree_distribution(netz_pcor))
E(netz_pcor)$arrow.size<-1 #sets the arrow size to 1
#Degree
barplot(sort(degree(netz_pcor), decreasing=TRUE), lwd=0.5, cex.names=0.7,cex.
axis=0.7,las=2)
#Centrality
barplot(sort(eigen_centrality(netz_pcor)$vector, decreasing=TRUE), lwd=0.5, cex.
names=0.7,cex.axis=0.7,las=2)
ecs_pcor<-as.matrix(eigen_centrality(netz_pcor)$vector)

#Hierarchical Clustering Plot and network plot
cfg<-cluster_fast_greedy(as.undirected(netz_pcor)) modularity(cfg) #shows the modularity
of the algorithm
sizes(cfg) #compute the size of each community.
plot_dendrogram(cfg)
E(netz_pcor)$arrow.size<-0
par(mfrow=c(1,2))
plot(cfg, netz_pcor, vertex.size=sqrt((eigen_centrality(netz_pcor)$vector)*100),
main="Eigen Centrality")
plot(cfg, netz_pcor, vertex.size=sqrt(degree(netz_pcor)*10), main="Degree Centrality")
```

PORTFOLIO OPTIMIZATION WITH NETWORKS

In this section, we will discuss optimization tools that incorporate the adjacency matrix and networks into the optimization function. Traditional approaches, such as Markowitz mean-variance optimization and the maximum Sharpe ratio optimization, can leverage instead of the covariance matrix. The main idea is to replace portfolio risk, typically measured by the variance-covariance matrix, with the adjacency matrix of interconnected assets within the underlying network.

Several key arguments exist regarding the use of different network types in portfolio optimization. One of the main considerations is preserving the connectedness between portfolio constituents, whether they are individual financial instruments or asset classes. The adjacency matrix captures this connectedness and serves as a fundamental tool in network-based portfolio optimization.

Traditionally, portfolio risk is gauged using the variance-covariance matrix in classical portfolio theory. However, networks offer a more comprehensive perspective on risk, as they capture the interconnectedness of risks between nodes. This interconnectedness is the main purpose of the adjacency matrix, making it a suitable alternative to the covariance matrix in portfolio management.

By leveraging the adjacency matrix, investors can incorporate network-based risk metrics into their optimization models, leading to more robust and insightful portfolio construction strategies. This approach enables a deeper understanding of both systematic and systemic risks and dependencies within the portfolio, ultimately leading to more effective risk management and investment decision-making.

The Adjacency Matrix and the Inverse Covariance Matrix

Thus far, we have utilized the regular covariance matrix for portfolio construction. However, because the adjacency matrix captures mutual relationships between the assets in a network, it is straightforward to use it instead of the well-known variance-covariance matrix in portfolio optimizations. Specifically, because the variance-covariance matrix is used to estimate portfolio risk, we leverage the adjacency matrix to derive portfolio risk based on the distances or connections between the assets. The stronger the links or the shorter the distance between the nodes, the larger the impact on risk. It's important to note that the notion of (risk) flow is central in directed networks, and thus in portfolio management using directed networks as input parameters.

Optimization techniques that use networks as input parameters for the variance-covariance matrix have been successfully implemented in various contexts. Konstantinov et al. (2020) applied these techniques to multi-asset and factor portfolios. Sandhu et al. (2016) focused on equities, specifically for the S&P 500 Index. Clemente et al. (2022) extended this approach to financial and insurer stocks, the S&P 500, and Nikkei-225 index constituents. Additionally, Konstantinov (2022a) utilized it for emerging market bonds allocation. The core idea behind using the adjacency matrix instead of the covariance matrix is that assets with fewer connections are considered less risky.

Using the inverse of the adjacency matrix can be more meaningful than using the regular adjacency matrix, because the information of the eigenvalues of the inverse is more informative and delivers more precision than the regular eigenvalues. Aldridge (2019) showed that this is the case, because the eigenvalues of the regular matrix often explain the largest market factor. Leibowitz (2011) identified that the primary determinant of risk, or the most significant factor influencing asset exposure, is typically linked to the equity market, noting that underlying equity market risk is inherent in every investment and asset. Therefore, market risk is often absorbed by the largest eigenvalue. However, the small eigenvalues of the inverse carry more information about the idiosyncratic risks in a network, which might be more relevant in evaluating portfolios prone to idiosyncratic risks and shocks. It's important to note that the inverse of an adjacency matrix reverses the information network flow between the nodes.[12]

Weighted graphs, characterized by adjacency matrix entries that differ from one in nondiagonal positions, are particularly interesting because they carry more edge information. In a portfolio context, such information might include information on systematic risk, trading volumes, and liquidity, to name a few. Importantly, as highlighted in Chapter 2, in a simple graph there are no self-edges. The main diagonal of a simple graph contains only zeros, but the elements of a graph containing self-edges have nonzeros on the main diagonal. In the case of an adjacency matrix with the main diagonal containing zeros, the assets are not modeled as interacting with themselves. For the example networks shown in this book, the Markov Chain network and the variance-decomposition technique automatically result in graphs containing self-edges. The most significant challenging aspect when directly applying adjacency matrices is the choice of multi-edges or simple graphs.

---

[12] In general, a graph is invertible if its adjacency matrix is invertible. Technical details are provided by Bapat (2014; Ye et al. (2017); and Kelathaya, Bapat, and Karantha (2023).

At this stage, it is necessary to highlight the role of expected returns as an input variable in portfolio management.

Centrality-Weighted Expected Returns

Asset class-based portfolio allocation forms the foundation of traditional portfolio management. While factor-based investing has gained popularity over the years, some studies suggest that portfolio allocation based on asset classes might yield superior results.[13] Generating return expectations at the asset-class level is a crucial aspect of the investment process for many portfolio managers. Typically, one starting point in creating capital market assumptions for various asset classes is to rely on the indexes that broadly track them.

In the preceding section, we focused on risk and how it is assessed through the adjacency matrix. In this section, we will focus on the primary determinant of portfolio allocation: expected returns. Generally, expected returns are determined using econometric or valuation models, and the estimation of these returns is unbiased concerning other asset classes. However, the centrality metrics used to adjust the expected returns serve to incorporate the concept of connectivity into return estimation.

By integrating expected returns with centrality scores, we effectively incorporate the concept of connectedness into expected returns, ensuring they are not treated as isolated elements within the portfolio context. To address the potential negative impact of overlooking returns in centrality-score–based allocation, a return-weighted centrality score is proposed. This integration enables for a more comprehensive assessment of asset attractiveness and portfolio construction, considering both the expected returns and structural importance of assets within the network. This involves a weighted sum of all individual centrality scores and their corresponding expected returns. That is, the centrality-weighted sum of the expected returns is the product of the individual scores and the expected returns for all nodes in the network as shown:[14]

$$E(R_S) = s\,E(r) \tag{10.14}$$

where s is the centrality scores of each node i and $E(r)$ is the expected return of asset i. Note that this is an element-wise multiplication of centrality scores s and the expected returns $E(r)$ of each node.

By simulating various return distributions, we can calculate centrality-weighted returns, effectively blending the concept of network position with financial performance. In the following example, we will utilize random numbers generated according to the student's t-distribution for the asset and factor networks. A similar approach can be applied to any asset networks, such as equity markets, emerging markets, or funds. However, Chopra and Ziemba (1993) emphasized that misestimating expected returns could have a more severe impact on portfolio allocation than errors in risk estimation. Therefore, it is highly desirable to apply theoretically sound concepts to estimate expected returns. Ilmanen (2011) demonstrated various methods to model expected returns across asset classes, including equities and bonds. Meanwhile, Chambers, Anson, Black, and Kazemi (2015) and Kazemi, Black, and Chambers (2016) offer a comprehensive overview of alternative asset classes and discuss the estimation of expected returns in investments like hedge funds, private equity, and real estate. Furthermore, Konstantinov, Fabozzi, and Simonian (2023) proposed detailed tools for computing bond and currency expected returns. It is worthwhile exploring several methods for deriving expected returns.

[13] See, for example, Kritzman (2021).

[14] Expected returns are perhaps the most important input variable in portfolio management and their estimation is central in financial research. The expected returns of each asset class are highly dependent on an underlying model. For example, for an estimation of expected returns in currencies and bonds, see Konstantinov, Fabozzi, and Simonian (2023). For expectation returns of commodities, hedge funds, private equity, and other alternative investments, see Kazemi et al. (2016). For equities, see Ilmanen (2011).

Bond Expected Returns Bond returns can be derived directly from index data.[15] As demonstrated by Konstantinov (2014, 2022a), local currency expected bond returns can be derived using yield curves. Alternatively, the expected bond returns for portfolio-allocation optimization can be based on directly observable market data, such as duration, duration-times-spread (DTS), and yield-to-maturity (YTM). The following approach incorporates maturity into the return estimation formula:

$$E(R)_t^{LC\ Index} = MD_t^{LC\ Index} \Delta y_t^{LC\ Index} + y_t^{LC\ Index} \Delta t \tag{10.15}$$

where MD_t^{Index} is the bond index duration, y_t^{Index} is the index yield-to-maturity, and $E(R)_t^{LC\ Index}$ is the local currency expected return on a bond index level.

An alternative approach to estimating expected bond returns, which considers bond yields and foreign exchange (FX), is based on forward rates or expected spot rates. It's important to note that this approach implies a connection between interest rates and foreign exchange in the market. Integrating currency impact into bond returns has been advocated by Thornton and Valente (2012) and Nucera and Valente (2013), and is formalized as follows:

$$E(R)_t^{BC\ Index} \equiv y_t^{BC\ Index} = \left(1 + y_t^{LC\ Index}\right) \frac{E(S_{t+1})}{S_t} - 1 \tag{10.16}$$

where $y_t^{LC\ Index}$ is the bond yield of the foreign currency bond index, $E(S_{t+1})$ is the expected spot rate at time $t+1$, S_t is the current FX rate, and $E(R)_t^{BC\ Index}$ is the expected bond index return in domestic currency.

Foreign Exchange Returns Pojarliev and Levich (2008) report that currency returns can be decomposed into three currency management strategies: carry, value, and momentum. Here's a brief overview of these three currency return determinants' expected returns, as discussed extensively by Konstantinov, Fabozzi, and Simonian (2023).

Currency Value The relative purchasing power parity (PPP) theory states that the economic relationship between two currencies is governed by the relationship between the inflation rates of their home countries. In other words, if there is a difference in the inflation rates between two countries over a specific time period, the country with the higher inflation rate should depreciate against the currency with the lower inflation rate. Mathematically, the relative PPP can be expressed as:

$$\frac{S_{PPP}}{S_t} = \frac{1 + inf_{BC}}{1 + inf_{qx}} \tag{10.17}$$

where the equilibrium spot currency price is denoted by S_{PPP}, inf_{BC} is the base currency inflation rate, the foreign inflation rate is denoted by inf_{qx}, and the current spot price is S_t. To measure the currency value exchange post return, it is necessarily to compute the fair value (S_{FV}) of a currency pair as follows:[16]

$$R_t^{FX\ Value} = ln(S_{t+1}/S_{PPP}) \text{ if } S_{PPP} > S_t \text{ and } ln(S_{PPP}/S_{t+1}) \text{ if } S_{PPP} > S_t \tag{10.18}$$

---

[15] See Koijen et al. (2018) and Martens et al. (2019). Both studies use index data (and the risk-free rate) to derive bond and currency returns using forward contracts. Koijen et al. (2018) use forward rates, while Martens et al. (2019) use index data of different maturity bucket indexes to show the relevance of yield-curve positioning.

[16] See Kazemi et al. (2016) and Pojarliev and Levich (2012).

where S_{t+1} is the spot rate at the time $t+1$, S_t is the spot rate at time t, S_{PPP} is the fair value of the currency at time t, and $R_t^{FX\ Value}$ is the currency value return.

If the current spot price is below the theoretical price estimated using relative PPP, then the currency is undervalued. Consequently, the currency's expected returns are positive if the foreign exchange price estimated using relative PPP is greater than the current spot price. This suggests that there is an expectation for the currency to appreciate to its theoretical value according to relative PPP.

Currency Carry   The intuition behind the uncovered interest parity (UIP) is found in the relationship between the current spot rate and the unknown expected future spot rate of a currency using the corresponding interest rates given by

$$\frac{E(S_{t+1})}{S_t} = \frac{1 + i_{BC}}{1 + i_{qx}} \tag{10.19}$$

UIP estimates the expected spot future price of a currency $E(S_{t+1})$ using the relationship between the base currency interest rate i_{BC}, the foreign interest rate i_{qx}, and the current spot price S_t. To measure the currency carry profit-and-loss (P&L) of a strategy we use the following formula, adapted from Pojarliev (2009) and Kazemi et al. (2016):

$$R_t^{FX\ Carry} = ln\big(E(S_{t+1})/S_{t+1}\big)\ if\ E(S_{t+1}) > S_t\ and\ ln\big(S_{t+1}/E(S_{t+1})\big)\ if\ E(S_{t+1}) < S_t \tag{10.20}$$

where S_{t+1} is the spot rate at the time $t+1$, S_t is the spot rate at time t, $E(S_{t+1})$ is the forward rate at time t, and $R_t^{FX\ Carry}$ is the currency carry return.

We can calculate the carry return using the forward rates as soon as we exchange the expected spot rate $E(S_{t+1})$ with the forward rate F_t. If the current foreign exchange price is below the theoretical price estimated using the UIP, then the current spot rate is undervalued. As a result, the expected carry return is positive if the expected spot price is higher than the current spot price.

Currency Momentum   The main intuition behind momentum returns is that positive returns in the past are likely to be followed by other positive returns and vice versa. In other words, if an asset's current returns are preceded by other positive returns, it indicates positive momentum. There are two major alternative rules typically applied in currency momentum strategies. The first is to use lagged values over specific previous periods of 1, 2, 3, 6, 9, or 12 months or days, depending on the investment horizon when computing currency momentum returns or entry and exit currency price levels.

The following formula is used to compute the returns from currency momentum trades:

$$R_t^{FX\ Momentum} = ln(S_{t+1}/S_{t-h})\ if\ S_{t-h} - S_t > 0\ and\ ln(S_{t-h}/S_{t+1})\ if\ S_{t-h} - S_t < 0 \tag{10.21}$$

where S_{t+1} is the spot rate at time $t+1$, S_t is the spot rate at time t, S_{t-h} is the spot rate at time t based on h lagged values, and $R_t^{FX\ Carry}$ is the currency momentum return.

Integrated Asset and Factor Returns   Separating asset classes and separate estimation of expected returns has a long tradition in finance. However, because networks provide an integrated, complex, and holistic view of the interacting nodes, a proper model makes sense that helps to estimate all factor and asset class returns. One such model has been proposed by Clarke, de Silva, and Murdock (2005) and Bender et al. (2010), and discussed in detail by Bender et al. (2019). The intuition of this model is to integrate the strategic and tactical asset allocation within a cross-sectional framework for all asset and factor returns. The main advantage of this approach is that it enables portfolio managers and researchers to integrate both time series expected returns and their subjective views. In other words, it enables the integration of pure factor and asset class perspectives in a single, systematic, and consistent investment process for expected returns.

To combine the framework suggested by Bender et al. (2019), a starting point of the model is the arbitrage pricing theory introduced by Ross (1976), a simple decomposition of asset and factor returns as a framework of unobserved factors.[17] In a nutshell, the asset and factor returns can be decomposed to be the product of underlying factors and the sensitivity of the asset and factors to these underlying factors.

$$R_t = B_t F_t + \epsilon_t \tag{10.22}$$

where R_t are the asset and factor return, B_t are the sensitivities of the asset and factor returns to the underlying factors, and F_t is the vector of asset and factors, and ϵ_t is the vector of residual terms. That is,

$$R_t = B_t(\overline{F}_t + \Delta F_t) + \Gamma_t \Theta_t + Z_t + \eta_t \tag{10.23}$$

where F_t is the long-term mean (i.e., strategic), ΔF_t is the vector of the short-term or time-varying factor returns (i.e., tactical), Θ_t is the vector of the within-asset and factor idiosyncratic returns that capture locally predictable residual return patterns, Γ_t is the vector of the exposure to those idiosyncratic factors, Z_t is the vector of the portfolio managers views on the asset and factors, and η_t is the residual term.

Random Expected Returns Return simulation based on an underlying return distribution is one of the most widely used techniques to estimate the impact of expected returns. Historically, much of the financial literature has focused on the Gaussian (i.e., normal) distribution of returns. However, numerous studies advocate for using more realistic return distributions that allow for fat tails.[18]

The most reasonable question that should be raised is how centrality metrics cope with the negative or positive returns of the assets in a network. Both historical and expected returns are not always positive numbers so that return-weighted centrality scores may result in nodes with negative scores. This can be treated as negative node weights in a graph, but graphs with negative weights may not make sense, as negative weights might be associated with negative information or interactions such as hostility in social networks. It is worth discussing how different centrality metrics solve this problem. Determining which centrality metric delivers more precision and intuitive solutions is also interesting. For this purpose, we compute all three of the centrality metrics for the asset and factor graphs and discuss the results.

The reason for applying all three of the centrality metrics – eigen, alpha, and power centrality – is that they measure node importance differently. Therefore, the centrality-weighted expected returns would have different magnitudes, and, most importantly, they will have different relative relationships to each other. For example, alpha centrality takes negative and positive values. Positive alpha centrality node scores (indicating a more central position in the network) and positive returns are automatically associated with

---

[17]The clustering in these four groups has been proposed by Konstantinov, Fabozzi, and Simonian (2023). However, the grouping has been largely investigated by Fama and French (1992, 1993), Carhart (1997), and Asness et al. (2013).

[18]See Bianchi, Tassinari, and Fabozzi (2023) for an explanation of the non-normal distributions. Detailed overviews are provided by Rebonato and Denev (2013), Taleb (1997), and Diebold and Yilmaz (2015). Goldstein and Taleb (2007) offer a critique of using the Gaussian distribution in fat-tailed asset markets.

justification to retain in a portfolio. However, negative returns and positive scores (and vice versa – negative scores and positive returns) neutralize the impact. Multiplying negative scores (indicating a less-central position) and negative returns results in a positive number, and such nodes might appear attractive when they are not. Centrality scores that enable rescaling and normalization are easier to interpret. Therefore, alpha centrality deserves attention and careful implementation in a financial network because return-based attractive nodes might become suddenly unattractive by their centrality score with a positive sign eventually. As a rule of thumb, researchers should prioritize centrality scores over returns in their decision-making process and specify whether they prefer nodes with higher or lower centrality scores.

Figure 10.8 displays the histogram of simulated asset and factor returns, showing fat tails and a leptokurtic distribution. Furthermore, Figure 10.9 captures the eigen centrality-weighted returns for the asset and factor networks using simulated expected returns for all 31 nodes. Alpha centrality-weighted returns for the asset and factor networks using simulated expected returns for all 31 nodes are plotted in Figure 10.10. The results for the Bonacich Centrality (power centrality) scores are plotted in Figure 10.11.

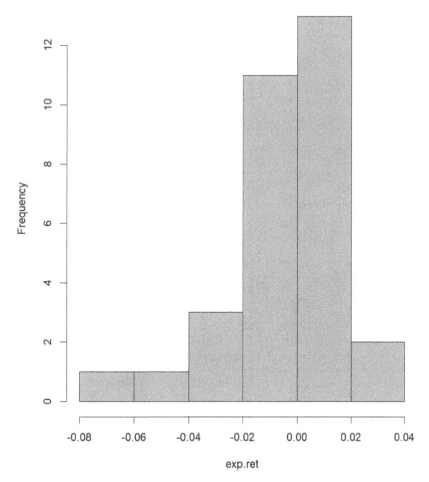

FIGURE 10.8 A Histogram of Simulated Returns for Assets and Factors.

Note: This is a very simplistic simulation of random returns with the purpose of showing the advantages of centrality-weighted returns.

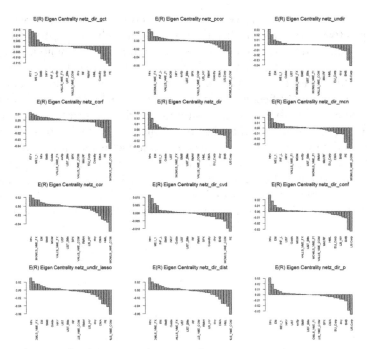

FIGURE 10.9   Eigen Centrality-Weighted Returns of Asset and Factor Networks.

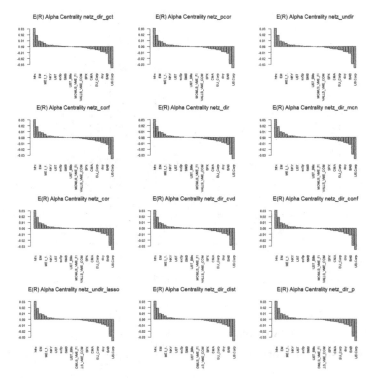

FIGURE 10.10   Alpha Centrality-Weighted Returns of Asset and Factor Networks.

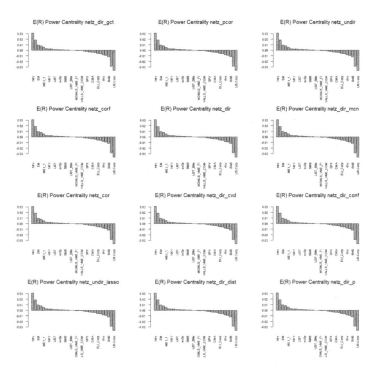

FIGURE 10.11 Power Centrality-Weighted Returns of Asset and Factor Networks.

Note: The Power Centrality enables the centrality scores to be rescaled.

The codes for random expected returns are shown in Box 10.8. Note that this is a simplistic code, which generates random expected returns for all assets and factors without any further differentiation and specification. The expected returns reflect all 31 assets and factors, and the histogram in Figure 10.7 captures the cumulative distribution. In Box 10.9, we show the code that plots all eigen centrality-weighted expected returns. Similarly, the code can be applied to the power and alpha centrality-weighted returns, which are more suitable for asymmetric relationships in a network, in which some nodes might remain unconnected. Note that the script for the power and alpha centrality in R differs from the eigen centrality.

BOX 10.8:   CODE FOR RANDOM EXPECTED RETURNS.

```
#Random Simulated Expected Returns
exp.ret<-rt(31, df=3)/100 #simulate returns
hist(exp.ret) #plot the histogram to ensure it is reasonable
```

BOX 10.9:   CODE FOR RANDOM EXPECTED RETURNS-WEIGHTED CENTRALITIES FOR ALL FACTOR AND ASSET NETWORKS.

```
#Plot different Centralities with Random Expected Returns
allem<-list(netz_dir_gct,netz_pcor,netz_undir,netz_corf, netz_dir,netz_dir_mcn, netz_cor,
netz_dir_cvd, netz_dir_conf, netz_undir_lasso, netz_dir_dist, netz_dir_p)
```

(Continued)

(Continued)

```
all.netz<-c("netz_dir_gct","netz_pcor","netz_undir","netz_corf", "netz_dir","netz_dir_
mcn", "netz_cor", "netz_dir_cvd","netz_dir_conf", "netz_undir_lasso", "netz_dir_dist",
"netz_dir_p")
par(mfrow=c(4,3))

foreach (i=all.netz, j=allem) %do% {

  ranking=eigen_centrality(j)$vector*exp.ret
  #raniking=alpha_centrality(j)*exp.ret
  #raniking=power_centrality(j, rescale=TRUE)*exp.ret

  names(ranking)<-colnames(AssetsFactors)
  barplot(sort(ranking, decreasing=TRUE),lwd=0.5, cex.names=0.7,cex.axis=0.7,las=2,
main=bqote(paste('Expected Returns ', .(i))))

}
```

A Notion on Portfolio Constraints   The network-based nonoptimization approach to portfolio construction is more flexible, yet often numerous constraints including minimum and maximum weights, as well as restrictions related to countries, sectors, or specific securities, are imposed. One of the main advantages of portfolio optimization techniques is that the algorithms enable the implementation of various capital and exposure constraints. Like traditional models for portfolio allocations, network-enhanced approaches enable the implementation of similar restrictions on portfolio exposure. Indeed, a key benefit of network-based portfolio optimization over nonoptimization methods is its ability to mitigate the impact of portfolio constraints on the risk-return profile. This is because the interconnectedness among assets is largely maintained, enabling for a more nuanced management of constraints.

Alternative Allocation Models

In general, leveraging adjacency matrices and centrality metrics can be applied to almost all optimization approaches. A straightforward benchmark could be the nonoptimization approach or the mean-variance framework utilizing adjacency matrices. Alternatively, the Adjusted Sharpe Ratio (ASR), proposed by Pezier and White (2008), incorporates the third (skewness) and fourth (kurtosis) moments of the distribution. The ASR is calculated using the following expression, with the risk being assessed by the adjacency matrix, which serves as an input in the optimization process:

$$ASR = SR\left[1 + \frac{skew}{6}SR - \frac{(kurt - 3)}{24}SR^2\right], \text{ with } SR = \frac{(\mu - r_f)}{\sigma} \tag{10.24}$$

where *skew* is the skewness, *kurt* is the kurtosis, μ is the mean return, σ is the standard deviation, μ is the mean return, and r_f is the the risk-free rate.

The Certainty Equivalent return (CEQ), as defined by Demiguel et al. (2009), considers the risk-free return for an investor with quadratic utility and risk-aversion parameter compared to the risky portfolio. The following equation expresses it:

$$CEQ = (\mu - r_f) - \frac{\lambda}{2}\sigma^2 \tag{10.25}$$

where λ is the risk aversion parameter, with all the other variables defined previously.

KEY TAKEAWAYS

- The underlying assumption behind nonoptimization allocation approaches is that there is an inherent hierarchical structure in the data and economic variables, making it possible to derive structure in a portfolio without the need for optimization.
- The focus of nonoptimization allocation approaches is on risk and how it is assessed through the adjacency matrix.
- Nonoptimization allocation approaches utilize centrality scores to assign weights to the assets.
- The approaches used for nonoptimization-based allocation include hierarchical clustering or centrality-based allocation, which identifies and weights portfolio exposure based on the underlying importance scores and clusters embedded in the network data.
- In nonoptimization-based allocation, the weights in a portfolio are proportional to the normalized centrality scores.
- The main idea behind network-based models for portfolio allocation is to replace the portfolio risk, which is typically gauged by the variance-covariance metric, with the adjacency matrix of interconnected assets of the underlying network.
- The main intuition when applying the adjacency matrix instead of the covariance matrix is that less connected assets are regarded as less risky.
- The main advantage of combining expected returns and centrality scores is that the notion of connectedness to the expected returns is introduced as centrality-weighted expected returns. The centrality-weighted expected returns assure that the connectedness is preserved and considered in the portfolio allocation.
- The integration of network-based metrics, which are applied to connectedness and the tools used to estimate risks and returns in portfolios, enables for a more comprehensive assessment of asset attractiveness and portfolio construction, considering both the expected returns and the structural importance of assets within the network.

## CHAPTER 11

Systematic and Systemic Risk, Spillover, and Contagion

Contents

Risk management is a critical aspect of portfolio management, beginning with the identification of the major risks faced by the portfolio. The investigation of specific risks assumes that network interference exists, meaning that nodes within the network are interconnected. Indeed, portfolio risks are not isolated but interrelated, often causing a cascade effect where the escalation of one risk heightens the likelihood of others. This interconnection can influence other nodes through emerging edges. For instance, an increase in bond yields might lead to wider credit spreads. Similarly, a sustained rise in commodity prices can elevate inflation expectations, subsequently increasing the likelihood of an interest rate hike by a central bank.

In Chapter 1, we described financial market risks and how they are interrelated in network-based portfolio management. Once these risks are measured, the next step in portfolio risk management is to control them to increase the likelihood that the portfolio will accomplish its strategic objectives. This is the task of traditional portfolio risk management.

In this chapter, we will focus on the network approach for dealing with risks. Given the interconnected nature of risks, we will offer tools to assess the overall rise in risk and develop metrics designed to capture these interconnected risks. Furthermore, we will discuss how networks can be applied to measure systematic risk and their role in estimating contagion and spillover effects. We will include several practical examples that demonstrate these concepts using graph theory. However, the main purpose is to provide the economic background and foundation applied to risk management and to highlight the differences between the concepts of risk in financial markets and portfolio management on which investors and portfolio managers should focus.

Network-based approaches differ substantially from traditional tools. The major difference lies in the holistic treatment of interconnectedness and relationships between portfolio assets. Chapter 10 provided examples, codes, and computational frameworks, where we addressed the risk in networks based on the two most fundamental properties of a network – edges and vertices.

THE ROLE OF NETWORKS IN RISK MANAGEMENT

Traditional quantitative financial models trace back to the work of Markowitz (1952), who emphasized the need to assess risks in a portfolio. The initial task was defining risk, with the standard deviation of returns as a prominent measure for decades. Additionally, using correlation coefficients between assets to gauge their association (rather than causation) proved to be an interpretable and statistically robust tool. The statistical properties of the covariance matrix emerged at the right time to capture and represent the pairwise relationships between assets and economic variables. The covariance matrix took center stage in financial risk analysis, with most risk management tools employing notions of volatility, correlation, and covariance to measure and represent risk in financial markets and portfolio management.

Within the traditional risk management framework, risk is often measured by variances or other moments of a distribution, such as kurtosis and skewness. However, the covariance matrix primarily serves as a tool to gauge pairwise relationships, isolating risk factors from one another. In other words, the risk of a portfolio to a specific factor, as captured by the covariance matrix, is treated separately from other risk factors. The total risk of a portfolio is perceived as the sum of these isolated risk factors. However, because of the interactions the whole is more than the sum of its parts, and the risk factors influencing portfolio risk can be separated but also interact with each other. Networks play an essential role in risk management by representing markets as more than just the sum of their individual components.

One significant advantage of network analysis is its ability to investigate the propagation of risk between nodes. Understanding the structure of risk transmission, which occurs over network edges, is crucial for evaluating the spread of systemic risk. Portfolio networks represent just one subset of the broader financial networks that exist. However, in this book, our focus is on asset markets and asset networks. Therefore, we present and discuss risk management tools applicable to asset networks, which are also compatible with a wide range of financial networks.

It's crucial to note that both edge connectivity and node connectivity exist, but they carry different implications when assessing portfolio risk. This distinction is vital because network inference models and corresponding metrics analyze node and edge behavior differently. For example, centrality and degree scores measure connectedness at the node level, reflecting the positioning of each node in the network.

To delve deeper into the systematic risks and how they can potentially become systemic, we will first explore the nature of financial market risk, contagion, and spillover. Once these concepts are understood, we will then shift our focus to the models and metrics used to assess risk. Graph theory, as compared to traditional regression models, offers a holistic approach to examining the various aspects of risk transmission, impact, and separation. This includes understanding how risk affects important nodes and how it is transferred among nodes in a portfolio network. It's important to emphasize once more that every portfolio, and generally the financial markets, can be viewed as a network.

RISK OVERVIEW

To effectively monitor risk and manage portfolio allocation, portfolio managers and analysts require techniques that capture and elucidate connectivity and risk transmission. Network analysis plays a central role in addressing these challenges. Systematic risk is of paramount importance for asset management and the financial industry, but its impact typically extends beyond that of a single entity, asset class, or economic variable, such as equities, bonds, country risk, or a sector-specific risk.

The foundation of network-based risk analysis lies in understanding interconnectedness. In graph-based metrics, assets are not examined in isolation but in their relationships. A key distinction in the financial literature that deals with networks is whether risk is analyzed at the node or edge level. Before delving into the major findings of relevant works, it's essential to differentiate between contagion and spillover risk. A clear definition of these processes is imperative.

Both contagion and spillover are dynamic processes triggered by a risk event that has already emerged. The critical question is how and through which channels this risk will propagate through the network. To assess transmission channels, we explore volatility-based frameworks that focus on modeling edges between nodes. Here, the emphasis is on risk transmission, with less focus on the relative importance of a node (i.e., asset) in the network. This distinction is crucial. When discussing spillover and contagion, the focus is on transmitting already identified risks through the network, highlighting edge connectivity.

Defining contagion is complex, but according to Forbes and Rigobon (2002), Bekaert, Harvey, and Ng (2005), and Li and Kazemi (2007), it involves left-tail events during crises associated with financial shocks that affect economic variables, institutions, and financial markets. Contagion is well-documented and observed in financial markets and often linked to concentration risk measured by correlations.

Expanding on the insights of Sais, Turtle, and Zykaj (2018), contagion can manifest as intermarket or intramarket phenomena. Intermarket contagion relates to left-tail risks propagating within a segment such as the hedge fund industry. Intramarket contagion involves left-tail risks affecting the cross-section of assets. For instance, liquidity risk can spread from hedge fund strategies, with equity exposure to the mutual fund industry, with similar equity market exposure.

From a formal and economic standpoint, network analysis offers a more comprehensive description of the economic effects of contagion compared to traditional methods. Because correlation is used to detect contagion, correlation metrics serve as a valuable informational source when constructing networks. As mentioned, we provided empirical data and formalism behind specific risk management tools in Chapter 10.

SYSTEMATIC AND SYSTEMIC RISK

In today's rapidly evolving financial landscape, the channels through which risks are transmitted and market causality vary, leading to increased interconnectedness and potential intensification of systematic risk. Das (2016) highlights a critical distinction between systematic and systemic risk: systemic risk, characterized by its significant magnitude, widespread impact, and threat to the entire system's existence and functionality, poses a more severe threat. Interconnectedness often catalyzes for systematic risk to escalate into systemic risk.

The focus in assessing systemic risk lies not solely on its origins – often stemming from external factors like macroeconomic shifts, financial distress among key institutions, or sovereign crises – but rather on how it spreads and permeates through the network. Thus, systemic risk analysis centers on the potential failure of individual nodes within the system, as their risk exposure can precipitate broader systemic repercussions. The centrality scores of nodes play a pivotal role here, as they indicate which nodes are most susceptible to impact simultaneously or in a specific sequence.

Diebold and Yilmaz (2015) have identified various contexts where systematic and systemic risk may emerge. These contexts align closely with the risks commonly encountered in broader portfolio management practices. They encompass portfolio concentration risk, model risk, market risk, credit risk, business cycle risk, and macroeconomic risk. A fundamental question arises: why are networks more effective in measuring these risks than traditional quantitative methods? Additionally, why is network theory better suited to elucidate systemic risk than conventional techniques? The answers lie in the distinct advantages offered by graph theory, particularly in its ability to analyze holistic structures comprehensively. Networks enable the measurement of all these financial risks at both the node and edge levels; while financial risk arises from or impacts nodes, it is transmitted across edges.

Portfolio Risk

Consider, for example, a conventional method for analyzing the risk of fund returns using a regression model with independent (i.e., orthogonal) risk factors. A typical linear regression model may effectively identify and elucidate the fund returns' exposure to a set of underlying risk factors. For instance, in the

Fama–French three-factor model (Fama and French, 1992) – market factor, size factor, and value factor – commonly serve as drivers of fund returns, identified by academic research as orthogonal. However, such models tend to assess risk factors in isolation, overlooking their interconnectedness and spread of risk among them. Standard statistical tools, like regression models, fail to discern how risk propagates and affects individual assets, groups of assets or factors, and industry sectors. In the case previously mentioned, the risk analysis remains indifferent to how risk transfers between value and size factors, assuming these factors are orthogonal. However, they might be significantly interconnected, conveying risks undetectable by other regression models. Moreover, the systematic exposure of fund returns to a set of factors might escalate into systemic risk, if not detected using appropriate techniques.

A pertinent question arises: how can systematic risk be measured and evaluated for its potential to become systemic in portfolio management? Combining econometric analysis with graph theory offers a promising solution to this conundrum. The initial step involves devising a suitable model to assess the systematic risk of assets.

One well-established approach in investment management is a returns-based style analysis pioneered by Sharpe (1992). This method employs a linear regression model to express the factors explaining asset returns. The rationale for opting for a linear multifactor model in the literature lies in its ease of interpretation and intuitive representation of asset returns as a linear combination of several explanatory variables. Using the arbitrage pricing model of Ross (1976), financial research has formulated the following model for asset returns R_i:

$$R_i = \alpha + \sum_i \beta_i F_i + \varepsilon \tag{11.1}$$

where R_i is return of an asset (regressed against the factor returns), α is a parameter that measures the idiosyncratic return, β_i is the coefficient or factor loading that measures the sensitivity of the asset return to factor F_i, and ε is the random error term.

Integrating econometric analysis with graph theory, Konstantinov and Rebmann (2019) forged a direct connection between standard econometric models and network analysis, facilitating the monitoring and evaluation of systematic risk.[1] Specifically, they leveraged the benefits of network analysis alongside a factor-based style analysis. By combining risk factor analysis with the implementation of importance scores, they gained insights into investment size, market data, community structure, risk factor exposure, and their interrelationships. As discussed in Chapter 4, eigenvector and alpha centrality yield similar results for symmetric and asymmetric relations when there is a dominant eigenvalue. However, alpha centrality outperforms eigenvector centrality in several scenarios. First, it is well-suited for directed networks with asymmetric relations and disconnected nodes. Second, it enables for the incorporation of exogenous factors into the network and is expressed in matrix form as follows:

$$x = (I - \alpha A^T)^{-1} e \tag{11.2}$$

---

[1] The authors investigated currency funds (pure FX manager) and applied network analysis to measure the relationship between fund size, factor exposure, and manager performance. In addition, they applied factor risks weighting the networks and to see the risk that emerges, based on previous factor exposure, importance score, and connectivity. The authors found that that centrality score is related to fund size. Economically, funds with the highest centrality scores and largest assets under management could significantly influence the entire fund network, especially in the case of financial turmoil.

where matrix I is the identity matrix and the transposed matrix A^T is the adjacency matrix, x is the vector of centrality scores, and vector e reflects the exogenous node effects of status or information importance scores.

Significantly, the parameter α indicates the balance between internal (endogenous) and external (exogenous) influences on centrality within a network. It holds an inverse relationship with the largest eigenvalue (λ) of the adjacency matrix (A), such that $\alpha = 1/\lambda$ This means that as the principal eigenvalue increases, the weight of internal network structures on determining a node's centrality diminishes compared to external factors. Note that a governs the relative importance of exogenous factors relative to the endogenous information incorporated in the adjacency matrix.

Using a vector of ones, denoted as e, implies equal consideration for all nodes during the initial phase of centrality score computation. This approach ensures that each node starts with the same baseline importance, enabling the network's structure to naturally influence the final centrality outcomes without initial bias towards any node.

Konstantinov and Rebmann (2019) set e to reflect risk factor exposure when applied to financial markets. They aim to highlight possible interconnectedness by using significant risk factor exposure as endogenous weights. In other words, exogenous factors, or risk factor exposure, immediately impact the importance score of a node based on the exogenous information assigned by a researcher. Researchers can utilize beta factors to identify systematic risk within a network context. The objective is to detect potential relationships between the largest beta exposures and centrality scores. An additional advantage is the ability to conduct stress tests and simulations of risk factor exposure. By weighting the factor exposure in centrality measures combined with clustering analysis, we can observe communities where risk factor inefficiencies could easily spread through the network.

Figure 11.1 illustrates beta exposure as an exogenous factor in an undirected network (netz_undir).[2] In this example based on the study by Konstantinov and Rebmann (2019), beta coefficients resulting from regressing assets and factors against the US dollar are utilized. The rationale is to evaluate the beta of the assets and factors against the US dollar, assessing how various asset classes respond to changes in the US dollar. Specifically, some assets, such as global and corporate bonds and emerging markets, may be highly vulnerable to fluctuations in the US dollar.

Once the significant beta coefficients of each asset or factor are estimated and evaluated, the network can be plotted, with node sizes determined by alpha centrality using the beta exposure as an exogenous factor. This approach helps identify the riskiest nodes. Visualizing the graph provides valuable insights into the potential interconnectedness of nodes with high centrality scores compared to nodes with lower but different beta loadings. The code for this step is provided in Box 11.1.

A visual examination of Figure 11.1 reveals that US Treasury bills (UST_Bills) are indeed highly vulnerable to fluctuations in the US dollar. Similarly, the US Basket Currency (dxy) exhibits a notable effect. Additionally, the hedge fund index (hfrx), the US High Yield Bond market (US_HY), the S&P 500 Index (SPX), and the Russell 2000 (RTY) are among the asset classes highly vulnerable to changes in the US dollar. Among the factors, FX Value (VALLS_VME_FX), FX Momentum (MOMS_VME_FX), and Betting-Against-Beta (BAB) are the factors with the greatest node USD beta-weighted centrality.

Table 11.1 summarizes the results for the algorithm. The first column summarizes the beta coefficients, and in the second column, we show the p-values. The rescaled alpha centrality scores are plotted in the third column, and the fourth column represents the rescaled alpha centrality scores using the beta vector as exogenous factors.

---

[2]The code for the undirected asset and factor network is provided in Chapter 6.

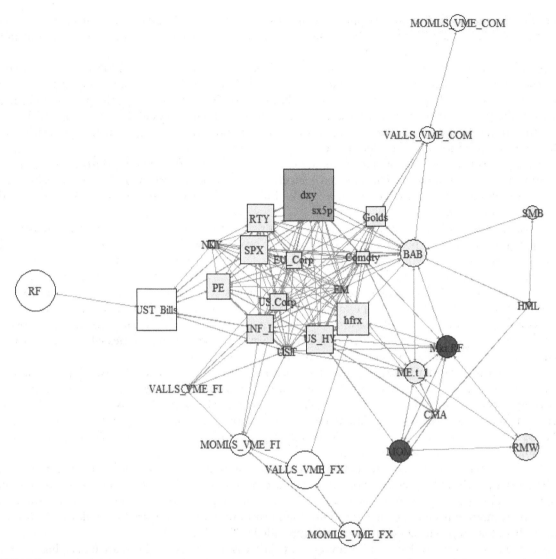

FIGURE 11.1 Exogenous Beta and Alpha Centrality as Node Weights in Undirected Asset and Factor Networks.

BOX 11.1:   CODE FOR BETA EXPOSURE AND ALPHA CENTRALITY.

```
par(mfrow=c(1,1))
beta.c<-matrix(nrow=ncol(AssetsFactors), ncol=1)
beta.p<-matrix(nrow=ncol(AssetsFactors), ncol=1)
#estimate the regression models for each asset against the US Dollar and store the
coefficients and the p-values in vectors
for(i in 1:ncol(AssetsFactors)) {
   beta.c[i]=coef(summary(lm(formula=AssetsFactors[,i]~usd[,1])))[2]
   beta.p[i]=coef(summary(lm(formula=AssetsFactors[,i]~usd[,1])))[8]
```

```
}
beta=cbind(beta.c,abs(beta.p))
rownames(beta)<-colnames(AssetsFactors)
beta #examine the array comprising beta
rev.beta=as.matrix(ifelse(beta[,2]>0.05,0,beta[,1])) #select only significant beta
coefficients and set others to zero

rev.beta #examine the vector with betas
rescale <- function(x) (x-min(x))/(max(x) - min(x)) #reslace function for alpha centrality
E(netz_undir)$arrow.size<-0.1 #sets the Edge arrows to 0.1
#once the vector with beta coefficients is prepared and expected, we use the vector in the
alpha centrality computation formula as exogenous factor and scale it up (multiplying by 20)
plot(netz_undir, vertex.size=rescale(alpha_centrality(netz_undir, exo=(rev.beta)))*20,
layout=layout_with_kk, vertex.label.cex=0.6)
```

TABLE 11.1   Results for the Alpha Centrality-Weighted Network.

Asset/Factor	Short Name	Beta Coefficient	p-Values	Alpha Centrality Score	Alpha Centrality Score with Exogenous Factors
Market Excess Returns	Mkt.RF	−0.009	0.932	0.67	0.44
Size Factor	SMB	−0.039	0.310	0.60	0.27
Value Factor	HML	0.035	0.506	0.46	0.12
Profitability Factor	RMW	−0.013	0.680	0.82	0.4
Investment Factor	CMA	0.038	0.325	0.36	0.09
Risk Free Rate	RF	−0.002	0.592	0.13	0.81
Sx5p	Sx5p	−0.093	0.364	1.00	0.07
S&P 500 Index	SPX	−0.528	0.000	0.61	0.55
Russel 2000	RTY	−0.593	0.00	0.61	0.54
MSCI EM Equity Index	EM	−1.078	0.00	0.66	0.00
HFRX Hedge Fund Global Index	Hfrx	−0.198	0.00	0.91	0.62
US dollar Index	Dxy	0.788	0.00	0.63	1.00
The Gold Price Index	Golds	−0.666	0.00	0.37	0.39
J.P.Morgan U.S. Treasuries Index	UST	−0.055	0.081	0.52	0.16
ICE BofAML U.S. Corporate Bond Index	US_Corp	−0.182	0.00	0.69	0.32
ICE BofAML U.S. High-Yield Bond Index	US_HY	−0.250	0.00	0.43	0.53
ICE BofAML U.S. Inflation-linked Index	INF_L	−0.552	0.00	0.47	0.54
ICE BofAML Euro Corporate Bond Index	EU_Corp	−0.049	0.045	0.76	0.32

(*Continued*)

TABLE 11.1 (*Continued*)

Asset/Factor	Short Name	Beta Coefficient	p-Values	Alpha Centrality Score	Alpha Centrality Score with Exogenous Factors
Goldman Sachs Commodity Index	Comdty	–1.032	0.00	0.61	0.25
The Thomson Reuters Private Equity Index	PE	–0.475	0.00	0.61	0.48
ICE BofAML U.S. Treasury Bills Index	UST_Bills	–0.002	0.448	0.00	0.81
Nikkei-225Index	NKY	–0.312	0.015	0.69	0.14
Betting-Against-Beta Factor	BAB	–0.188	0.005	0.62	0.55
FX Value Factor	VALLS_VME_FX	0.027	0.580	0.75	0.75
FX Momentum Factor	MOMLS_VME_FX	–0.009	0.854	0.48	0.49
Fixed-Income Value Factor	VALLS_VME_FI	0.008	0.614	0.56	0.18
Fixed-Income Momentum Factor	MOMLS_VME_FI	–0.004	0.811	0.48	0.44
Commodity Value Factor	VALLS_VME_COM	0.206	0.115	0.17	0.33
Commodity Momentum Factor	MOMLS_VME_COM	–0.052	0.658	0.31	0.33
Equity Market Liquidity Factor (t-1)	ME.t_1	–0.116	0.367	0.67	0.44
Equity Momentum Factor	MOM	0.013	0.883	0.59	0.45

Model Risk

Model risk encompasses all risks associated with the models utilized in portfolio management. It ranges from issues such as variable estimation (e.g., expected returns) to the specification of variance-covariance matrices, network models, and the accurate estimation of causality, as well as the algorithms used for portfolio allocation. One method to mitigate this risk is to employ vectors instead of single variables when estimating portfolio inputs, as vectors enable the consideration of the interrelationships among input variables.

Another crucial aspect of standard models, as highlighted by Diebold and Yilmaz (2009, 2014) and Baitinger and Maier (2019), is that connectedness is a highly nonlinear phenomenon, and time-varying parameters are crucial for accommodating this nonlinearity. Billio et al. (2012, 2016), Das (2016), Lo and Stein (2016), and Das, Kim, and Ostrov (2019) have demonstrated that graph theory can effectively elucidate interconnectedness and provide tools for understanding, monitoring, and predicting connectedness. From a risk management perspective, it is advantageous to leverage standard analytical frameworks like regression models to monitor factor exposure. Thus, integrating standard econometric tools with network analysis should be a minimum requirement in modern financial analysis.

Market Risk

Under market risk, we comprehend the risk associated with financial market exposure, known as financial market risk. This risk type is the most widely recognized risk that impacts investments, and traditional models are built around managing portfolios with consideration of this risk. However, portfolios represent networks, and the assets within them are interconnected. Traditional analysis attempts to disentangle the effects of risk and explain them individually. Yet, portfolio risk is a function of the interacting risk-contributing entities or factors. Consequently, minimizing the market risk of a portfolio, or the risk of adverse market movements, is both a goal of risk management and a function of portfolio optimization, which aims to minimize the market risk of a portfolio. In other words, attempting to isolate market risk factors when they are constantly interacting is less efficient. It leads to improper estimation of market risk, impacting all portfolios due to the interaction of portfolio factors.

Market risk is not universally defined. While market risk in equities is easily identified and measured in empirical finance, other asset classes like bonds struggle to rigorously measure and define it.[3] This difficulty arises from their uniqueness of market size, which is determined by the utility function of trading agents. In other words, market microstructure, which gauges the tradability and liquidity of a market, is responsible for measuring market size and risk. For instance, bond markets exemplify an asset class in which market risk is not easily defined; the price of a bond depends on the notional amount traded, and therefore, there is no unique price for a bond. If bond prices are not unique because they depend on the notional amount exchanged, then it is impossible to define the market size of a single bond, and subsequently, the overall bond market size and risk. Other illiquid asset classes like private equity, real estate, private debt, and distressed debt face similar challenges.

Microprudential and Macroprudential Risks

The role of microprudential and macroprudential analysis is one of the most compelling and central aspects when applying network analysis. Microprudential analysis focuses on the idiosyncratic risks of financial entities to prevent them from becoming too risky for the entire system and network. These idiosyncratic risks, such as concentrated exposure to risky assets, products with elevated default risk, and market exposure to illiquid assets, impact individual nodes within the network. Consequently, the microprudential approach primarily centers on the vertices in a network.

In contrast, macroprudential analysis monitors and investigates the connections between players in the financial market. This entails examining the interactions between financial organizations and institutions and the feedback loops between the financial market and the real economy. The primary objective of macroprudential analysis is to monitor the edges between financial actors and institutions and the real economic variables through which risks may be transmitted within financial networks.

Regulatory authorities are naturally interested in the interaction between microprudential and macroprudential analytical processes. Furthermore, microprudential analysis may be integrated into the macroprudential toolkit to monitor, prevent, and regulate the financial system as a network. This integrated approach emphasizes financial stability and integration.[4] The integration of real economic development and the financial market depends on the analysis and prediction of the business cycle, which is highly important.

---

[3]See, for example, de Jong and Fabozzi (2020) and Konstantinov, Fabozzi, and Simonian (2023) for the definition of market risk in corporate and global bonds, respectively.
[4]See, for example, Hanson, Kashyap, and Stein (2011), and Kashyap, Berner, and Goodhart (2011) for more information regarding the macroprudential toolkit and its role in the financial stability.

Business Cycle Risk

The business cycle plays a crucial role in financial research, with origins traced back to the early works of Fama and French (1989) and Fama (1990). Gregory, Head, and Reynauld (1997) pioneered the measurement of global business cycles. A business cycle is commonly determined by analyzing the rate of change and the acceleration of changes in a leading economic indicator's time series, which mirrors the economic activity within a country. This estimation reveals four stages of the economic cycle: contraction, expansion, slowdown, and recovery. As economic cycle activity is associated with lagged variables, market reactions often outpace the measured business cycle activity. To smooth the index of business cycle changes, a common approach involves using a rolling time step, typically a six-month interval.

Directed multi-asset networks exhibit interesting properties across different phases of the business cycle. In a study by Konstantinov, Chorus, and Rebmann (2020), a directed multi-asset and factor return-based network (*netz_dir*) was estimated. Comparing network density and reciprocity, applicable to directed networks only across business cycle phases, revealed intriguing patterns. Network density dispersion is highest during contraction, indicating an elevated network interaction during business uncertainty. Conversely, low density suggests fewer links between nodes (assuming a fixed network size of 31 nodes). Generally, during economic slowdowns and expansions, network density increases. However, the information conveyed by reciprocity, which reflects mutual connectedness, is even more compelling. Reciprocity tends to drop during expansion and usually spikes during recovery and slowdown phases. Reciprocity appears closely linked to business cycle leading indicators compared to network density.

The key message from this business cycle analysis is the importance of monitoring the economic cycle and network dynamics from a financial analytical perspective. Increased interconnectedness during economic stress and recovery periods may signal asset market overheating and crowded behavior, often associated with heightened investor exposure to the same asset classes. In a market crash, this elevated exposure can turn negative as investors rush to liquidate their positions, triggering a liquidity spiral. Figure 11.2 illustrates the business cycle and plots network density and reciprocity according to the cycle stage. The business cycle is identified as the level of change and its second derivative (acceleration/deceleration).

Graph theory and the business cycle have yet to be fully integrated as monitoring tools in investment management. Konstantinov and Simonian (2020) explored the impact of single hedge fund connectedness across different business cycle phases: contraction, expansion, slowdown, and recovery. Their study revealed several key insights. First, they observed a significant decrease in the average degree of connectedness during contraction phases. Conversely, during the recovery and expansion phases, they found a notable increase in the average degree, indicating heightened interconnectedness.

One of the most significant findings was that the transition between slowdown and expansion, and vice versa, poses the most significant risk in terms of hedge fund interconnectedness. Overall, they observed that connectedness peaks during slowdowns and declines during recovery phases. While predicting business cycles remains challenging, integrating business cycle analysis with measures of interconnectedness can offer valuable insights for risk measurement and monitoring in investment management. Whereas business cycle predictability is challenging, the predictability of network metrics is promising. Predicting overall connectedness measures like density, reciprocity, and transitivity reveals valuable risk management perspectives related to markets.

Credit Risk

Credit risk is a significant concern that extends beyond individual companies to encompass broad asset markets and countries, with potential repercussions for the global economy. For instance, the US subprime mortgage crisis and Lehman Brothers' collapse serve as stark examples of the severe impact credit events can have, leading to market meltdowns, increased insolvencies, and bailouts. Understanding the causality in financial markets is crucial, particularly when examining network effects, and credit risk is no exception to this scrutiny.

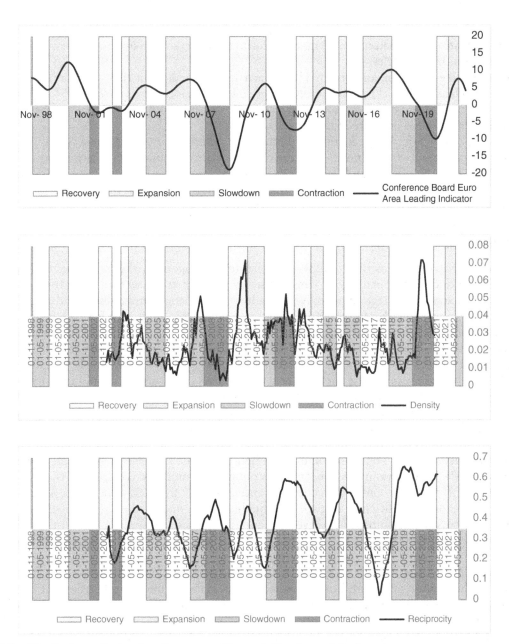

FIGURE 11.2 The Business Cycle of an Economy – Network Density and Reciprocity.
Note: Monthly data for the Conference Board Euro Area Lending Indicator is used (EUCBLIYY Index) as a leading indicator. The rolling moving average window is six-monthly observations. Index data was obtained from Bloomberg, LLC.

Schularick and Taylor (2012) noted that credit risks often precede banking crises. Credit market exposure can diverge from real economic development as economic cycles progress. Defaults are typically interconnected events that spread throughout financial systems, rather than remaining isolated incidents. Consider the scenario of a corporate bond default by an internationally significant issuer, whose securities are held by numerous asset managers. The initial impact extends beyond bondholders to similar securities and can reverberate through international markets due to the issuer's extensive business connections across sectors, industries, and countries.

Researchers like Das, Kim, and Ostrov (2019) have investigated credit risk within a network context, using models such as the model for corporate debt pricing as developed by Merton (1974). They highlight the importance of interconnectedness in risk management, showing how systemic risk can be mitigated by altering the node and edge structure of the network.

Credit risk can be effectively identified and managed within a network framework by isolating and removing vulnerable nodes from a portfolio network. For instance, a bond with deteriorating credit quality or risk of default can be isolated and removed, enabling the estimation of total network risk by assessing the impact on connected assets or securities. Analyzing the edge structure of the affected node is essential for understanding the risk implications for other assets in the portfolio network.

Macroeconomic Risk

Konstantinov, Fabozzi, and Simonian (2023) argue that macroeconomic risks encompass countries' financial operations, including their banking systems and securities markets. These risks differ from country-level risks related to factors, such as economic growth, employment, inflation, and political and geopolitical considerations, which impact market factors. While numerous interconnections exist between financial markets and real economies, they represent distinct sets of risks and are treated separately for analytical purposes.

Developed financial markets are generally considered more investable than emerging financial markets due to factors like robust regulatory institutions and property rights laws. Additionally, developed financial markets tend to be better capitalized, making them more liquid and transparent, and thus, less susceptible to shocks from capital flows. This stability is reflected in the weightings of countries like the United States, European Union (EU), and Japan in international bond indexes, where their bonds denominated in major currencies like the US dollar, euro, and Japanese yen are highly liquid and sought after.

Countries with well-capitalized financial markets and strong regulatory frameworks, such as the United Kingdom and Australia, also boast deep and liquid bond markets. However, reliance on a world reserve currency like the US dollar can amplify global macroeconomic risks and interconnectedness, as Konstantinov and Fabozzi (2022) noted. In contrast, emerging financial markets frequently encounter obstacles, including capital restrictions, insufficient transparency, liquidity issues, and inadequate regulation. These challenges lead to increased fluctuations in interest rates, currency values, and spreads. This justifies the liquidity premium associated with bonds issued in emerging financial markets, reflecting the risks investors face in these markets.

Understanding interest rate dynamics is crucial in bond portfolios, as they impact both bond and currency markets, highlighting their role in interconnectedness. Isolating interest rate risk alone does not provide a comprehensive view of its potential international impact. Ehrmann, Fratscher, and Rigobon (2011) demonstrated the interconnectedness of global assets in shock transmission, suggesting that a graph theoretical approach may offer more effective monitoring of these risks than traditional models.

Aside from macroeconomic risk, countries also present political and institutional risk to investors. Again, the latter risks are generally more significant in emerging market countries. For example, the judicial systems of many emerging market countries are not yet fully formed and often dispense justice in an unreliable and arbitrary way.[5] Moreover, the mechanisms of democracy, such as elections and separation of

---

[5] Lian (2022) discusses the problems and solutions that gave rise to emerging market debt investing, and de Jong and Fabozzi (2022) discuss the rise of emerging market bonds as an asset class, whose risks and returns have changed with improving economic fundamentals, market, and financial integration.

powers, are also often ill-formed in emerging market countries. As a result, the organizational structure of these countries is generally more fragile and prone to failure than that of developed market countries. Nevertheless, although institutional fragility is an important part of assessing the risk associated with emerging financial markets, it is notoriously difficult to quantify.

A common approach for quantifying country-level risk is the production of scores (or indexes) for individual countries. Scores typically represent cumulative values assigned to a country across various sectors, such as political corruption,[6] legal frameworks, and regulatory environments. Consequently, this enables for the inclusion of political risk alongside macroeconomic risk. The individual scores for each category can be thought of as roughly analogous to the credit ratings assigned to corporate and sovereign bonds.[7] Such scoring systems are common among credit rating agencies like Fitch, Standard & Poor's, and Moody's.

SPILLOVER AND CONTAGION

In a rapidly evolving financial landscape, the channels through which risk is transmitted and the causal relationships within financial markets are subject to variation, with interconnectedness on the rise. This heightened interconnectedness increases the likelihood of systematic risk evolving into systemic risk, posing a threat to the broader economic system. A notable example of systemic risk materializing occurred with the collapse of Lehman Brothers, which triggered significant turmoil in financial markets and jeopardized the stability of the entire global financial system. Systemic risk assessment is inherently challenging without considering networks, leading to extensive research on this topic. Notable studies by Forbes and Chinn (2004) and Lo and Stein (2016) delved into systemic risk within financial markets.

Building on the work of Diebold and Yilmaz (2009) and Konstantinov and Fabozzi (2022), spillover effects arise when risks originating from trading activities, market liquidity, political shocks, or aggregate shocks propagate to other asset classes closely intertwined with volatility and returns. Since the turn of the century, globalization and the internationalization of financial and product markets have intensified trading and financial market integration. Research on volatility spillovers primarily focuses on their impact on different asset classes. The drivers of these spillovers may be exogenous, such as macroeconomic factors, fundamental shifts, or changes in central bank policies. However, the core objective remains to understand how these shocks propagate through the network, emphasizing the significance of modeling edge structures.

A crucial distinction lies between systematic and systemic risk and between spillover and contagion. Systematic risk pertains to the risk associated with individual nodes within a financial network, such as assets, factors, financial institutions, banks, and individual investors, all of which may have significant exposure to the market. On the other hand, systemic risk becomes apparent when the importance of single nodes or entities in a financial or portfolio network is emphasized. The risk of failure or default can be examined, and regulatory authorities can address distressed nodes or institutions, particularly considering the pivotal role of interconnectedness, represented by edges between nodes, in risk management.

In contrast, contagion affects the edges in a network, as risk is propagated across nodes through these connections. In contagion scenarios, the focus shifts from the importance of individual nodes to the links or edges through which financial risk spreads in the markets. Density, a metric relating the number of edges to the number of nodes, becomes significant here. A denser network, where the number of edges grows faster than the number of nodes, becomes more vulnerable to transmitting risk between nodes.

---

[6]For example, the Corruption Perceptions Index ranks countries "by their perceived levels of public sector corruption, as determined by expert assessments and opinion surveys."
[7]These points are further discussed in Paserman (2017) and Simonian (2021).

While Diebold and Yilmaz (2015), and Leung (2016) employed traditional econometric analysis to measure and explain spillover effects of monetary policy and information shocks, numerous other studies have investigated spillovers and systemic risk within specific asset classes. For instance, Acemoglu, Ozdaglar, and Tahbaz-Salehi (2015) explored systemic risk and stability in financial networks, while Bollerslev et al. (2018) delved into the spillover effects of realized volatility across various markets, including currency, fixed-income, equity, and commodity markets. Additionally, studies such as those by Hamao et al. (1990) and King and Wadhwani (1990) documented volatility spillover and contagion effects within equity markets, showcasing the directional and time-varying nature of phenomena. Further research by Tiwari et al. (2018) and Barunik et al. (2017) investigated global volatility spillovers across different asset classes, emphasizing the significance of understanding contagion dynamics in financial markets.

Notable contributions investigating contagion and spillover effects include studies by Amini et al. (2013), Acemoglu et al. (2015), Amini and Minca (2016), and Liu and Huang (2022), which explore contagious links and risk propagation in financial markets. These studies typically focus on market indices, stocks, and financial institutions. Furthermore, a body of literature utilizes network theory to elucidate complex market relationships. Glasserman and Young (2015), for example, argue that market interconnectedness creates potential channels for contagion, spillover, and amplification of shocks to the financial system. Levy-Carciente et al. (2015) apply network theory to investigate the vulnerability of the financial system to external shocks and contagion risks.

Pioneering work by Gale and Kariv (2007) demonstrates how network structures influence asset prices, leading to increased connectedness. Merton et al. (2013) propose a novel approach for measuring connectedness and the systemic importance of financial institutions. For instance, Das (2016) investigates risk networks using dynamic pairwise mapping of connectedness to illustrate systemic risk propagation. Understanding network structure is crucial for building models and predicting future values of risk factor exposure.

Khandani and Lo (2011) explore the transmission of systemic risk in financial networks and assess the financial system's resilience to idiosyncratic shocks. Bech and Atalay (2011) investigate the US federal funds market, highlighting the strengths of network analysis in explaining complex behavior. Fernandez-Rodriguez and Sosvilla–Rivero (2020) study volatility spillover effects between stock markets and foreign exchange, while Da Fonseca and Ignatieva (2018) analyze spillover effects between commodity markets before and after the Global Financial Crisis. Recent attention has also been drawn to spillover effects during normal and crisis periods, with Hussain Shahzad et al. (2019) employing rolling estimation models to investigate spillover risk in the Eurozone credit markets.

Network analysis has been applied to investigate interconnectedness at the portfolio level. Several studies have examined the node structure in financial markets and portfolio management. Billio et al. (2012) conducted a study on return-based hedge fund interconnectedness using Granger causality tests, emphasizing the importance of network analysis for hedge funds given the rising systemic risk they pose. More recently, Zareei (2019), Konstantinov et al. (2020), and Raddant and Kenett (2021) have studied portfolio networks from both risk and return perspectives.

By applying volatility analysis and graph theory to examine causal relationships in the financial market, Wang (2010) found that volatility shocks in specific industries contribute most heavily to spillover effects. However, a common issue in these studies is that they primarily focus on the nodes, with less attention given to the edge structure. This means that the risk is seen as inherent in the assets, portfolios, or institutions themselves rather than in their mutual links, which may change over time. However, some studies address this problem from an edge-risk perspective.

In analyses that emphasize the investigation of links such as those conducted by Braverman and Minca (2018), portfolios represent nodes and risks are transmitted over the links between them. Using a similar approach, Konstantinov and Fabozzi (2022) utilized network theory to investigate portfolio spillover across major asset classes, including currencies, equities, bonds, hedge funds, and private equity.

Diebold and Yilmaz (2009, 2014) have extensively analyzed risk networks in finance for both financial markets and financial institutions. De Carvalho and Gupta (2018) applied networks to investigate the comovement and interconnectedness of numerous assets. Similarly, Bostanci and Yilmaz (2020) followed the approach of Diebold and Yilmaz (2009) and demonstrated that the level of connectivity between sovereign and corporate bonds is high.

KEY TAKEAWAYS

- Exogenous or endogenous factors, such as macroeconomic factors, fundamental shifts, or changes in central bank policies, may drive spillovers.
- The core objective, nonetheless, is to comprehend the transmission of these shocks throughout the network, emphasizing the importance of modeling the connections between nodes. The risks associated with systematic and systemic risk include market risk, portfolio risk, credit risk, microprudential and macroprudential risks, model risk, and business cycle risk.
- Compared to traditional regression models, graph theory offers a holistic way to investigate the different aspects of transmission, impact, and separation of risk, subject to how risk impacts important nodes and how risk is transferred among the nodes in a portfolio network.
- Systemic risk arises when the interconnectedness of the financial system becomes large, and fragility threatens the economic system.
- The major difference between systematic and systemic risk is that systemic risk is large, has severe and broad impacts, and threatens the system's existence and functionality.
- A critical consequence of interconnectedness is that systematic risk might become systemic.

Networks in Risk Management

Contents

In this chapter, we will examine the application of networks to risk management, explaining how current financial theories and practices utilize network analysis to understand and reduce portfolio risks. We will describe various risk management indicators at both the node and edge levels, demonstrating the complex interconnections and transmission of risk through financial networks. By integrating systemic, criticality, and fragility indicators with more dynamic methods, such as network entropy and spillover indices, we will provide a comprehensive overview of the methods used to evaluate and control interconnected risk factors within a networked environment. The combination of these indicators provides a deeper comprehension of the sources and the intricate ways these risks are communicated across the network, thus facilitating more informed decision-making in portfolio risk management.

We will begin by discussing how recent applications of network theory have shed light on portfolio allocation networks from a risk and return perspective. Specifically, we will examine how volatility analysis, combined with graph theory, can uncover causal relationships in financial markets. For instance, Wang (2010) highlights how volatility shocks in certain industries predominantly drive spillover effects, emphasizing the significant impact of specific sectors on broader market dynamics. We will then transition to explain how portfolio volatility is traditionally measured using standard deviation, which is synonymous with risk in a financial context. Explaining the composite nature of portfolio return variance, which considers the volatilities of individual assets and their covariances/correlations, will set the stage for a more complex understanding of risk. We will then explain that the complexity of portfolio volatility extends beyond merely summing individual risks. It involves a detailed matrix of variances and covariances that captures portfolio assets' interconnectedness and reciprocal influences. This matrix illustrates how the assets interact with one another, impacting the overall portfolio risk in a way that cannot be understood by looking at the risk of each asset in isolation.

Traditional risk metrics utilizing the mean-variance framework formulated by Markowitz (1952), when complemented by network-based analyses, provide a richer more dynamic view of risk that is consistent with contemporary financial realities. While traditional models give a snapshot of risk at a point in time, network analysis offers a more nuanced perspective that captures the evolving nature of financial markets and the intricate web of relationships that define them.[1] The perspective that we will take in this chapter deepens our understanding of market dynamics and equips portfolio managers with the tools to make more informed decisions in an increasingly complex financial environment.

PORTFOLIO VOLATILITY AND NETWORK ANALYSIS

As explained, the most common measure of risk in portfolio management is standard deviation, which measures deviations from a variable's expected value. In finance, standard deviation is often referred to as volatility. Investors view increased volatility in an asset's return negatively because it signifies greater risk. This applies to both individual financial instruments and portfolios.

A portfolio comprises many assets whose returns generally exhibit some degree of positive and negative comovement. As a result, portfolio variance is not derived solely by summing the variances or volatilities of the assets in the portfolio. It must also consider asset covariances or correlations. This is done formally using a variance-covariance matrix or a correlation matrix. As a practical matter, correlation matrices are more commonly used as they are invariant to scale and are generally considered more intuitive than covariance matrices, which are not invariant to scale. There are challenges when computing the inverse of the covariance matrix of historical volatilities. This matrix is constructed from correlations that require the cosines of the angles between any two vectors of asset returns, forming a fully connected network with an edge density equal to 1. Inverting the covariance matrix requires partial correlations between the portfolio assets. As a result, in a correlation-based network all nodes in the portfolio are connected. This represents a completed graph, and real networks are rather sparse than dense (i.e., completed).

Consequently, using correlation-based networks in finance, while straightforward and practical, can exaggerate the degree of connectedness among assets. This method implies a uniform impact across all assets during market events, which is not always true. In certain crises, some assets may remain largely unaffected and disconnected from others.[2] The standard computation of portfolio variance does not accurately capture these nuances of disconnected regimes or the dynamic nature of risk and volatility, which vary over time.[3] This limitation highlights the need for more nuanced approaches that can adapt to the evolving financial landscape and its complexities.

The mean-variance framework considers only one source of risk: asset variance. However, with many asset types, including factors, other risk types are often the primary drivers of portfolio risk. Whatever set of risks portfolio managers consider in their process, they must also contend that investment risks are not

---

[1] See Peralta and Zareei (2016), Zareei (2019), Konstantinov et al. (2020), Raddant and Kenett (2021), and Ciciretti and Pallota (2024) among others for constructing portfolio networks.

[2] For example, consider an asset that remains disconnected. Such networks might be simulated using the Barabási–Albert model, which we discussed in Chapter 5. The history of financial markets clearly indicates that, in specific periods, there are asset classes that either remain disconnected or are simply weakly affected by risks. This occurred in COVID-19 pandemic where the US dollar was among the very few asset classes that performed positively despite strong connections.

[3] See Kazemi et al. (2016) and Bollerslev et al. (2018) for modeling volatility.

temporally stable but time varying. This time-varying nature of asset price behavior is related to another set of criticisms of the standard mean-variance optimization (MVO) framework. For example, Duarte and Rajagopal (1999) show that the mean-variance framework is not capable of optimizing with respect to different market scenarios as its inputs are only point-in-time estimates. Moreover, regime shifts and time-varying premiums often require more sophisticated rebalancing that is not fixed to a predefined frequency (e.g., monthly, quarterly, or weekly) but based on market thresholds that may be achieved at intermittent points in time. This is where network risk analysis helps to overcome the challenges associated with large connectedness among the portfolio constituents and the assets.

A common issue in the models that investigate network risk is that the focus lies predominately on the nodes and with less attention given to the edge structure.[4] This means that risk is seen as inherent in the assets, portfolios, or institutions themselves rather than in their mutual links, which can change over time. As we shall see in this chapter, several other authors approach the problem from the edge-risk perspective.[5] Network analysis that emphasizes the investigation of links is usually volatility based and requires volatility-based models or sophisticated models like vector-autoregressive models to construct the links between the nodes in a network. The studies of Diebold and Yilmaz (2009, 2014, and 2015) are dedicated to such models.

When the focus is on edge connectivity within a network, the links represent strong mutual relationships and facilitate the transfer of risk between the connected entities. For example, Braverman and Minca (2018) represent networks where portfolios are nodes and risks are transmitted over the links between the nodes. Applying the same reasoning, Konstantinov and Fabozzi (2022) used network theory to investigate portfolio spillover in the major asset classes, including currencies, equities, bonds, hedge funds, and private equity. The study of risk networks, particularly concerning markets and financial institutions, has been analyzed by Diebold and Yilmaz (2009, 2014). Moreover, De Carvalho and Gupta (2018) applied networks to investigate the comovement and, thus, interconnectedness of a large number of assets. Bostanci and Yilmaz (2020) followed the approach of Diebold and Yilmaz (2009) and showed that the level of connectivity among sovereign and corporate bonds is high.

RISK MANAGEMENT INDICATORS

Risk management tools focus on node-level or edge-level connectedness, each serving distinct purposes. Node-level risk management often evaluates factors, such as creditworthiness, default risk, illiquidity, debt levels, systemic risk, trading leverage, and enterprise risk. These elements assess the individual risk associated with specific nodes within the network.[6] Conversely, delving into the edge structure reveals the risk from the perspective of a flow process, or how it propagates through interconnected entities. Various risk

---

[4]In general, financial market studies that incorporate centrality scores focus on investigating node risk. Notable research on financial node risks include Bech and Atalay (2011), Merton et al. (2013), Lo and Stein (2016), Billio et al. (2012), Konstantinov and Simonian (2020), Konstantinov and Rusev (2020), Baitinger and Papenbrock (2017a, 2017b), Baitinger and Flegel (2021), and Ciciretti and Palotta (2024). The financial literature on node connectedness is rather extensive, with network research most broadly discussing the contagion risk – e.g., Rigobon (2003), Ehrman et al. (2011), Elliot et al. (2014), Corsetti et al. (2014), Glasserman and Young (2015), Amini et al. (2013), Acemoglu et al. (2015), and Amini and Minca (2016), Amini et al. (2017), and Levy-Carciente et al. (2015), Barunik et al. (2017), and Barunik et al. (2020).

[5]Chapter 11 discussed the node and edge structure of risk. The most notable studies investigating financial markets edge risk are Forbes and Chinn (2004), Diebold and Yilmaz (2009, 2014, 2015), Da Fonseca and Ignatieva (2018), Tiwari et al. (2018), and Sandhu et al. (2016).

[6]See Battiston et al. (2012) and Battiston et al. (2016) for discussion of the debt as a risk indicator, and Haldane and May (2009) for discussion of the financial markets and the arbitrage pricing theory in node-level risk.

metrics are employed to quantify these risks within a network of assets, highlighting the interconnected nature of risk in complex financial systems.[7]

The distinction is crucial because it provides unique insights into portfolio management within a networked context, broadly categorizing risk metrics into two distinct groups: node-level and edge-level metrics. Node-level metrics focus on identifying and analyzing risks affecting individual network nodes (e.g., specific funds, indices, or asset classes). Traditional risk factor analysis often utilizes regression models to assess the behavior of these individual actors, but this approach typically isolates them, thereby failing to account for their interconnectedness. To deal with this, aggregate funds or asset class returns can be placed in clusters to understand cumulative risk effects better. Alternatively, they might measure the crowdedness of an asset class by applying regression models to individual asset returns, and then aggregating these to form a comprehensive risk exposure index. This method enables for a deeper understanding of how risks are distributed across and influence various components of a portfolio. Unfortunately, this reductionist approach disregards the possible interactions between the various sources of risk.[8]

The second important group refers to spillover and contagion risk. The risk metrics that focus on edge connectivity aim to model risk transmission between the nodes. In this case, the focus is on the edges and their strength rather than the nodes. The common property of these indices is the transmission of risks between the nodes over the edges. They consider (1) the adjacency matrix of the assets, often derived from volatilities, (2) the investigation of the transmission of shocks within the network or endogenously, and (3) the derivation of risk metrics from the network model itself. Prominent studies that investigate risk propagation at the edge level include the research conducted by Diebold and Yilmaz (2009, 2014).

Nevertheless, time-varying analysis is the most compelling idea behind node- and edge-level risk management indicators for portfolio networks. Importantly, many financial networks applied to investment management and portfolio analysis are correlation-based networks.[9] Using a kernel function and setting a threshold level for correlation coefficients typically results in networks that resemble complete graphs. However, most real networks, particularly those in financial markets, are sparse and are usually modeled rather than observed. Therefore, the representation of these networks as complete generally results in low receiver operating characteristic (ROC) and area under the curve (AUC), which may not accurately reflect the true network dynamics. That is, there are better classifier algorithms that apply to sparse portfolio networks. Interconnectedness and edge structure are time-varying and depend on the flow process. To explain network dynamics and edge structure, networks should be estimated and constructed on a rolling basis. Therefore, the risk indices discussed in the upcoming sections are time-varying metrics that gauge network dynamics and can identify risks that might arise on the node or edge level.

Risk metrics are often estimated as static measurements that assess risk at any point in time. However, the main idea of this chapter is to provide a dynamic view on these risk metrics, which is highly valued by portfolio and risk managers. Continuous risk monitoring is of key interest in investment management, and network metrics provide efficient tools to monitor interconnectedness dynamically. The codes and metrics we will discuss enable a dynamic exposition of risk.

---

[7]The authors of this book discussed the new alternatives to measure portfolio risk using graph theory. They used networks to construct both node-based and edge-based risk metrics. Because of the rise in factor investing, Konstantinov (2024) uses the Ilmanen et al. (2021) dataset that reflects factor investing in different asset classes – equities, fixed income, commodities, and currencies and discusses the network-based Ricci curvature meaning in asset management.

[8]The research on crowdedness is very extensive. Notable studies are Pojarliev and Levich (2011) on currency funds, Konstantinov (2017) on global bond funds, Konstantinov and Rebmann (2020) on single hedge funds, Konstantinov and Fabozzi (2022) on European Monetary Union (EMU) bond funds, and Baltas (2019) on alternative risk premia.

[9]For example, see Onella et al. (2003), Baitinger and Papenbrock (2017a, 2017b), Umar et al. (2024), Ciciretti and Pallotta (2024), among others.

RISK INDICATORS ON THE NODE LEVEL

This section's topic is the metrics that investigate risk transmission at the node level. In the next section, we will investigate risk transmission at the edge level.

Das (2016) identified network-based metrics that can be defined as criticality, fragility, and risk increment, collectively referred to as systemic risks. These metrics are risk indicators at the node level. The most common properties of these risk indices or metrics are that they consider the (1) adjacency matrix of the assets or variables, (2) the centrality scores of the nodes, and (3) unified risk score metrics like spreads, volatilities, ratings, among others. In essence, these risk metrics are related to the network's adjacency matrix.

Systemic Risk Score

The systemic risk indicator originated with the work of Das (2016), which sought to gauge the systemic risk within a network of assets. This approach adopts principles of the mean-variance optimization (MVO) model, where the network is evaluated using a weighted sum. Instead of standard weights, however, this model uses specific risk scores known as the compromise index. These scores may encompass a variety of market indicators or variables, such as spreads, credit ratings, maximum drawdowns, or other predictive risk metrics, including volatility, the Sharpe ratio, and dispersion. This comprehensive array of risk indicators helps capture a nuanced view of systemic risk across different market conditions and asset behaviors.

Essentially, the compromise index has the same dimension as the nodes in the network. For example, if the network comprises 31 assets, the compromise nodes have the same vector length ($n \times 1$) as the vector of asset compromise scores.

The systemic risk indicator has the same properties as the minimum variance and can be formally written in matrix notation:

$$S = \sqrt{C^T A C} \tag{12.1}$$

where A is the $n \times n$ adjacency matrix of the network, and C is the $n \times 1$ compromise vector of assets, or the nodes in a network.

Note that the risk score has the same representation as the risk in a portfolio as captured by the Markowitz mean-variance optimization (MVO) framework. Economically, the risk score represents the weighted risk of connected elements as depicted by the adjacency matrix. Like the risk attribution of a portfolio, this approach enables the calculation of how each element within the adjacency matrix contributes to the overall portfolio risk.

Criticality Risk Score Index

As with the systemic risk index, the criticality risk score index traces its origins to the work of Das (2016). We can construct this index using compromise risk scores and a rolling period analysis. The major difference is that the criticality risk score index relies on a risk score metric called compromise scores, which may be independently modeled. The input variables for the criticality risk score index are these compromise risk scores. This metric, known as the compromise index, refers to a set of variables that identify the risk associated with the nodes in the network. To emphasize, the criticality risk score index aims to gauge node properties in a dynamic manner.

However, defining the compromise score is the first task before calculating an index. Compromise scores can encompass different variables, such as volatilities, risk-return ratios, econometric results, or simulation results. The selection of a compromise score is not confined to a specific asset class, enabling a range of metrics tailored to different portfolio needs. For example, in a credit bond portfolio, the risk score might be based on asset volatilities or the inverse of the credit metric known as Altman's Z-score associated with each node in the network.[10] In a global bond portfolio, spreads and inversely related credit ratings could be potential compromise scores. It is crucial that the selected score directly correlates with the node's risk. For instance, a higher spread would indicate a higher score. At the same time, a lower credit rating would also translate to a higher score, both of which are associated with a negative systemic risk impact.

Widely adopted ratios in portfolio management, such as the Sharpe ratio, information ratio, or other similar metrics, are useful for determining the criticality scores of investments and portfolios. Generally, higher Sharpe and information ratio scores are associated with lower risk for a given rate of return.

The criticality index, denoted by C, is computed by the element-wise multiplication of centrality scores and compromise scores and has the following form:

$$C = \sum_i s_i c_i \qquad (12.2)$$

where s_i is the eigenvectors, and c_i is the criticality risk score associated with the risk of each node i.

Note that C can be computed using the individual constituents of an index, or a market portfolio comprising assets, because the dimensionality of s and c is an $(n \times 1)$ vector. We can rewrite as:

$$C = s \times c \qquad (12.3)$$

Clearly, C can be computed using daily, weekly, or monthly data and can provide valuable information for risk and portfolio managers who wish to focus on the most critical parts of the portfolio and market. Different risk indicators used as compromise vectors would yield different criticality scores. Figure 12.1 illustrates the different criticality scores obtained when using the Sharpe ratio, volatility, and maximum drawdown as compromise vectors in asset allocation networks.

It is important to note that the interpretation underlying the compromise scores may vary. While positive Sharpe ratios are favorable, larger drawdowns and higher volatility harm investors. Therefore, in the maximum drawdown example, the risk increment is readily associated with assets whose weaknesses could harm the portfolio. Figure 12.1 displays all criticality scores for the 12 asset and factor networks used throughout this book, estimated using node-specific volatility as a compromise score. The corresponding code is provided in Box 12.1.

BOX 12.1: SORTED CRITICALITY PLOTS FOR THE TWELVE ASSET AND FACTOR NETWORKS.

```
#Sorted Criticality for all Asset and Factor Networks
vola<-apply(AssetsFactors,2,sd)
as.matrix(vola)
volrank=as.matrix(rank(vola))
allem<-list(netz_dir_gct,netz_pcor,netz_undir,netz_corf, netz_dir,netz_dir_mcn, netz_cor,
netz_dir_cvd, netz_dir_conf, netz_undir_lasso, netz_dir_dist, netz_dir_p)
all.netz<-c("netz_dir_gct","netz_pcor","netz_undir","netz_corf", "netz_dir","netz_dir_
mcn", "netz_cor", "netz_dir_cvd","netz_dir_conf", "netz_undir_lasso", "netz_dir_dist",
"netz_dir_p")
par(mfrow=c(4,3))
foreach (i=all.netz, j=allem) %do% {
    ranking=eigen_centrality(j)$vector*volrank/max(volrank)
```

---

[10] Altman (1968).

```
    names(ranking)<-colnames(AssetsFactors)
    barplot(sort(ranking, decreasing=TRUE),lwd=0.5, cex.names=0.7,cex.axis=0.7,las=2,
main=bquote(paste('Criticality ', .(i))))
}
```

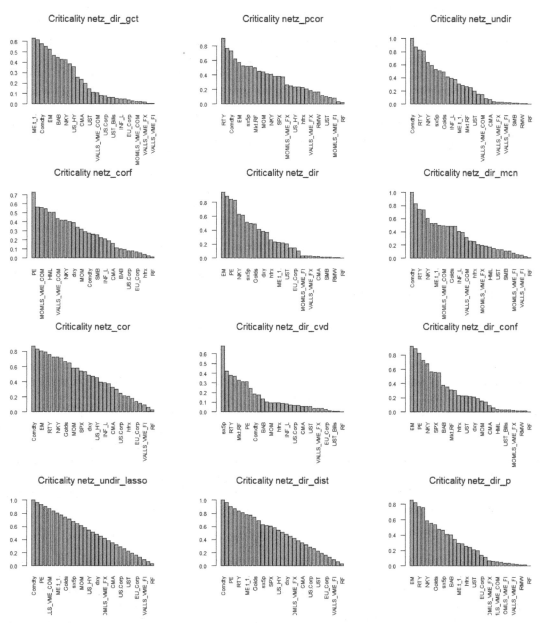

FIGURE 12.1 Criticality Scores Using the Eigenvector Centrality Scores and the Asset Volatilities as a Compromise for the Twelve Networks.

To define a network as critical, it is essential to understand how criticality is measured and what variables are used as input. In Chapter 4, we identified important metrics for measuring centralities. Recall that the most widely used centrality scores in risk management include eigen centrality, alpha centrality, and degree centrality. Importantly, regardless of the centrality metric used, the focus is on node connectedness rather than edge connectedness.[11] The purpose of using centrality scores is to enable construction of a centrality-weighted index that maps interconnected risks. There are two ways to build such criticality indices: a criticality return index and a criticality risk score index. These indices can be constructed as static or dynamic measures, and we will highlight their differences shortly.

The criticality return index, as proposed by Konstantinov (2022b) and applied in a modified form to hedge funds, is a simple weighted metric of centrality scores and historical returns. This approach utilizes time-varying centrality scores of nodes in the network, where the nodes represent assets, and the adjacency matrix gauges systematic risk and interconnectedness among them. Following the principles outlined by Lo (2016), an index using centrality network scores enables asset managers to monitor and respond to changing market and risk transmission conditions.

Intuitively, the criticality return index can be interpreted as a centrality-weighted index of node connectivity. The underlying idea is that an asset with a high centrality score in a network indicates higher systematic risk and, thus, receives a higher weight in the index. The index is a product of the returns and the corresponding centrality scores, as shown:

$$HIC_t = HIC_{t-1} \prod_{i=1}^{13} \left(1 + \frac{R_{i,t}}{R_{i,t-1}} \right) w_{i,t} \tag{12.4}$$

where $R_{i,t}$ and $R_{i,t-1}$ are the returns of an asset i at the times t and $t-1$, respectively. The $w_{i,t}$ are the weights proportional to the normalized centrality scores.

Because risk is time-varying as is connectedness, it is reasonable to compute the weights using the rolling period of $t - m$ monthly observations.

$$w_{i,t} = \frac{s_{i,t}}{\sum_j s_{j,t}} \quad s_{i,t} \propto x_t, \quad \text{with } \lambda x_t = A x_t \tag{12.5}$$

where A is the adjacency matrix, λ are the eigenvalues, x is the set of eigenvectors, and $s_{i,t}$ are the weights associated with centrality scores of the assets at the time t, with each being a multiple of the leading eigenvector, the one corresponding to the largest eigenvalue.

The use of eigenvector centrality scores here is less straightforward. Eigenvector centrality is suitable for both directed and undirected networks, provided all nodes are interconnected. In the following sections, we apply eigenvector centrality to illustrate the intuition behind risk score metrics. However, alpha centrality becomes necessary when nodes, such as the risk-free rate, exist independently, disconnected from other nodes.

The intuition behind the criticality return index is to weight an asset in proportion to its centrality score given by $\lambda x = Ax$.[12] In other words, assets with higher centrality scores receive higher weight in the criticality return index, while those with lower centrality scores receive lower weight.

---

[11] Edge connectedness is the topic in next section where we discuss the spillover framework using approaches that model edge connectivity.

[12] The use of eigenvector centrality for directed networks is not unproblematic, because directed networks are asymmetric and often include nodes not related to other nodes. Correlation networks are symmetric (Newman, 2010). For directed networks, alpha centrality is a better instrument to capture asymmetric relationships. However, in this case, eigenvector centrality still applies, as the directed network is asymmetric, but no individual node is unchosen (Bonacich and Lloyd, 2001). One important factor to consider is the Perron–Frobenius Theorem. An alternative approach might be Katz centrality for directed graphs.

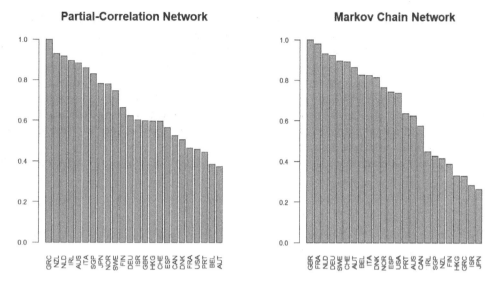

FIGURE 12.2 Eigenvector Centrality for an Undirected, Partial Correlation, and Markov Chain Directed Network for the Global Equity Markets 1994 to 2023.
Note: Daily data was collected to estimate the centralities over the period from January 12, 1994, to September 29, 2023. Adapted from AQR Capital Management, LLC.

Computing a directed Markov chain network and an undirected partial-correlation network for global equity markets provides valuable information about the importance scores of local equity markets worldwide.[13] Unlike orthogonal regressions, the importance score is higher for nodes highly connected to other strongly connected markets. In Figure 12.2, we plot the two global equity market networks using the same algorithms provided in Chapters 6 and 7.

Centrality scores are influenced by both the type of network and underlying estimation methods, including correlations, regression models with confounders, or simple Pearson pairwise correlations. These variations in the analytical framework led to differences in the resulting risk metrics. We will investigate further in the next section.

Fragility Indicator

The fragility indicator assesses the likelihood of risk spreading throughout a network. Various types of fragility indicators aim to assess a network's fragility, differing primarily in how they measure node and edge fragility. Another key distinction lies in whether the entire system is considered fragile when a node fails, or whether the focus is on how systemic risk may affect individual nodes as it spreads throughout the network. In this section, we will present an indicator that reflects fragility based on both nodes and edges.

For the criticality risk indicator, we utilized centrality (specifically eigenvector centrality), which identifies central nodes highly connected to other nodes in the network. In contrast, Das (2016) proposed using degree centrality for the fragility indicator. In Chapter 4, we examined the roles and differences between degree centrality and eigenvector centrality. Degree centrality, as defined by Newman (2010), measures the immediate impact of changes in node connections within the network and is considered a fundamental network property.

---

[13]We use the AQR Capital Management, LLC, data for 18 global equity markets based on the work of Frazzini and Pedersen (2014).

The main advantage of degree centrality is its direct measurement of the degree of each node in the network, assessing the immediate impact of risk at the node level. Fragility assesses the network's degree as a simple metric representing each node's connections. When risk emerges, its spread immediately affects each node based on its degree, which is why we use node degree rather than eigenvector centrality.

However, fragility varies significantly depending on the network type – whether directed or undirected – a distinction previously highlighted in Chapter 2 when discussing node degree. In undirected networks, both the number of incoming and outgoing connections to a node are identical, whereas in directed networks they can differ. For example, in a banking system, a bank may lend more than it borrows, impacting how risks originating from other nodes affect its position in the network.

The overall degree in undirected networks, including correlation networks, is expressed as follows:

$$k_i = k_j = \sum_i A_{ij} = \sum_j A_{ji} = \frac{2m}{n} \tag{12.6}$$

where m is the number of links, n is the number of nodes, and A_{ji} is the adjacency matrix that contains a value of 1 if node i and node j have a link, and zero otherwise.

The in- and out-degree has the following expression for directed networks:

$$k_i = k_j = \sum_i A_{ij} = \sum_j A_{ji} = \frac{m}{n} \tag{12.7}$$

Das (2016) employed the Herfindahl–Hirschman Index (HHI) as a concentration indicator. Widely used in asset management, the HHI measures the diversification of a portfolio based on the weights of its assets. It ranges from 0 (indicating a highly diversified portfolio) to 1 (suggesting a highly concentrated portfolio). Lower HHI values are desirable when diversification is sought after. Diversified portfolios tend to have HHI values close to zero, whereas concentrated portfolios have HHI values close to 1.

To adapt the HHI concept to network analysis, an appropriate metric is needed because the HHI in portfolios is based on asset weights. In network settings, these weights correspond to node weights, which determine the HHI. Therefore, the graph metric that closely behaves like the HHI index should primarily focus on nodes.

The density of a network, as defined in Chapter 2, indicates how competitive the network is. A network has a high density when its values are close to 1, indicating many connections among nodes. Conversely, a sparse network has values close to 0, indicating few connections relative to the number of nodes. Density is a ratio of the actual number of links relative to the maximum possible links among nodes.

The relationship between density and the HHI can be understood as follows: mathematically, as the number of nodes n increases ($n \rightarrow \infty$), the density of the network becomes smaller and approaches 0 given a fixed number of edges. This implies that larger networks tend to be sparser. Assuming n equals the number of assets in a portfolio, computing the limit as $n \rightarrow \infty$ shows that the HHI decreases towards 0. Therefore, the following inverse relationship exists between density and the HHI index:

$$HHI = \tilde{n}^{-1} \tag{12.8}$$

In a network context, density serves a similar purpose to portfolio analysis. A higher density indicates more connections relative to the number of nodes, making the network more interconnected. Das (2016) applied the HHI alongside the average degree of nodes in networks. We use the density of a network. Note that density and degree are related.

To define a fragility metric using density and average degree in an undirected network, we sought a metric that increases when the density is low, relative to the average connectivity. This means a network with fewer connections relative to its potential (given its average degree) would have a higher fragility metric. The fragility metric estimates the relationship between the network size (i.e., nodes) and the squared number of links as follows:

$$F^u = \frac{\tilde{n}^{-1}}{k} = \frac{n(n-1)}{2m}\frac{n}{m} = \frac{n^2(n-1)}{2m^2} \approx \frac{n^3}{2m^2} \tag{12.9}$$

where F^d is the fragility of an undirected network, m is the number of links, and n is the number of nodes in the network.

This ratio given by equation (12.9) ensures that a larger network with fewer links is more fragile than a network with numerous connections but lower concentration. In the context of finance, where modeling a directed graph may offer more insight, each link is counted twice due to the directed nature of the graph. Consequently, the equivalent ratio, when considering the average node degree, is $k = m/n$ and takes the following form:

$$F^d = \frac{\tilde{n}^{-1}}{k} = \frac{n(n-1)}{m}\frac{n}{m} = \frac{n^2(n-1)}{m^2} \approx \frac{n^3}{m^2} \tag{12.10}$$

where F^d is the fragility of a directed network, $\tilde{n}$ is the network density, and all variables are as defined previously.

It is worthwhile to examine the behavior of the ratio involving network metrics. Increasing the number of links decreases the ratio given by equation (12.10), while increasing the number of nodes relative to the number of links increases the ratio. However, in a random network, the number of nodes remains constant in the short term. Thus, as the number of links in the denominator m approaches infinity, the fragility metric decreases. Conversely, a decrease in the number of links as m approaches zero increases the fragility metric.

Using the code provided in Box 12.2 for a directed asset and factor network, we can estimate the fragility indicator for assets and factors as a time-varying index that captures market behavior. Figure 12.3 illustrates the computed dynamic fragility indicator. This index would increase when there are fewer links and a constant number of nodes and decrease as the network density increases.

It is important to note that, all else being equal, with a relatively constant number of nodes, a network with fewer edges may exhibit greater fragility compared to a network with more links. The code that computes the time-varying fragility index for a directed network (netz_dir) is provided in Box 12.2.

BOX 12.2: A ROLLING FRAGILITY INDEX FOR THE ASSET AND FACTOR NETWORKS.

```
mtx_dir<-matrix(nrow=ncol(AssetsFactors), ncol=ncol(AssetsFactors))
rollstep=36
p.t=0.05/6
periods=nrow(AssetsFactors)-rollstep
y<-seq(from=1, to=periods, by=1)
fragil_d<-foreach(a=y) %do% {
    return_step=AssetsFactors[a:(a+rollstep),]
    for(i in 1:ncol(return_step)) {
        for(j in 1:ncol(return_step)) {

mtx_dir[i,j]=coef(summary(lm(formula=return_step[,i]~return_step[,j]+I(return_
step[,j]^2))))[11]
```

(Continued)

(*Continued*)

```
        netz_dir=as.matrix(abs(mtx_dir))
        netz_dir=ifelse(netz_dir[,]<p.t,1,0)
        diag(netz_dir)<-0
        g=graph_from_adjacency_matrix(netz_dir)
      }
    }
    vcount(g)^3/ecount(g)^2


}
fragil_d<-as.matrix(fragil_d)
datebreaks<-seq(as.Date("2004-02-01"), as.Date("2021-03-31"), by = "1 month")
plot(datebreaks, fragil_d, type="l", ylab="", xlab="")
```

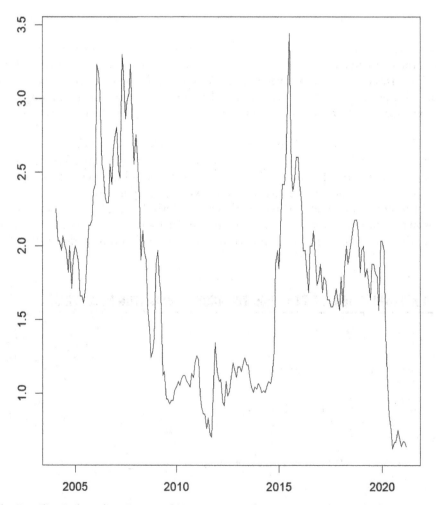

FIGURE 12.3 The Fragility Index of an Asset and Factor Network.

Risk Increment

Portfolio and risk managers are often interested in understanding how a particular node could impact the entire asset or portfolio network if it becomes highly compromised or fragile. The risk increment identifies the portfolio's vulnerability to shocks associated with specific nodes based on their risk score. This metric informs us about the change in the network's aggregate risk score when the compromise score of an asset changes.

Mathematically, the risk increment (denoted as RI) represents the first derivative of the systemic risk indicator and is estimated using the adjacency matrix and the criticality index:

$$RI = \frac{1}{2S}[AC + A^T C] \tag{12.11}$$

where A is the adjacency matrix, C is the criticality index, and S is the systemic risk defined previously.

Note that the risk increment as given by equation (12.11) varies, depending on the network type (i.e., directed, undirected, complete, or multigraph) and the compromise score index, which captures the compromise score of each node in consistent units. These variations stem from differences in eigen centrality scores, influenced by network characteristics, such as connectivity, edge count, and the underlying criticality scores used for computing compromise vectors.

It's important to note that for networks where nodes may have missing links between them, alpha centrality is typically applied. However, in the case of the 12 networks discussed, none of them have nodes with missing edges, thus eigen centrality is applicable. Figure 12.4 illustrates the risk increment for the 12 asset and factor networks.

The risk increment varies significantly depending on the network structure. In networks such as the correlation network (netz_cor) and the variance-decomposition network (netz_dir_cvd), which exhibit high cross-sectional eigenvector centrality values, the risk increments for all nodes tend to be high. A complete graph, in contrast, offers less informative insights compared to sparse directed or undirected networks.

We utilize the code provided in Box 12.3 to compute the risk increment for these networks using a volatility compromise vector for the asset and factor dataset.

BOX 12.3:   RISK INCREMENT SCORES FOR THE 12 ASSET AND FACTOR NETWORKS.

```
vola<-apply(AssetsFactors,2,sd) #estimate standard deviation of the time series
as.matrix(vola)
volrank=as.matrix(rank(vola)) # rank the volatility
allem<-list(netz_dir_gct,netz_pcor,netz_undir,netz_corf, netz_dir,netz_dir_mcn, netz_cor,
netz_dir_cvd, netz_dir_conf, netz_undir_lasso, netz_dir_dist, netz_dir_p)
all.netz<-c("netz_dir_gct","netz_pcor","netz_undir","netz_corf", "netz_dir","netz_dir_
mcn", "netz_cor", "netz_dir_cvd","netz_dir_conf", "netz_undir_lasso", "netz_dir_dist",
"netz_dir_p")
par(mfrow=c(4,3))
foreach (i=all.netz, j=allem) %do% {
    ranking=eigen_centrality(j)$vector*volrank/max(volrank) #compute the raking
    adj_matrix_j<-as.matrix(as_adjacency_matrix(j)) #estimates the adjacency matrix
    es_j<-sqrt(t(volrank)%*%adj_matrix_j%*%volrank) #computes the risk score
    risk_increment_j=0.5*(adj_matrix_j%*%volrank+t(adj_matrix_j)%*%volrank) #computes the
risk increment given risk score and compromise vector
    risk_increment_j=0.5*risk_increment_j%*%(1/es_j)
    names(risk_increment_j)<-colnames(AssetsFactors)
    barplot(sort(risk_increment_j, decreasing=TRUE),lwd=0.5, cex.names=0.7,cex.
axis=0.7,las=2, main=bquote(paste('Risk Increment ', .(i))))
}
```

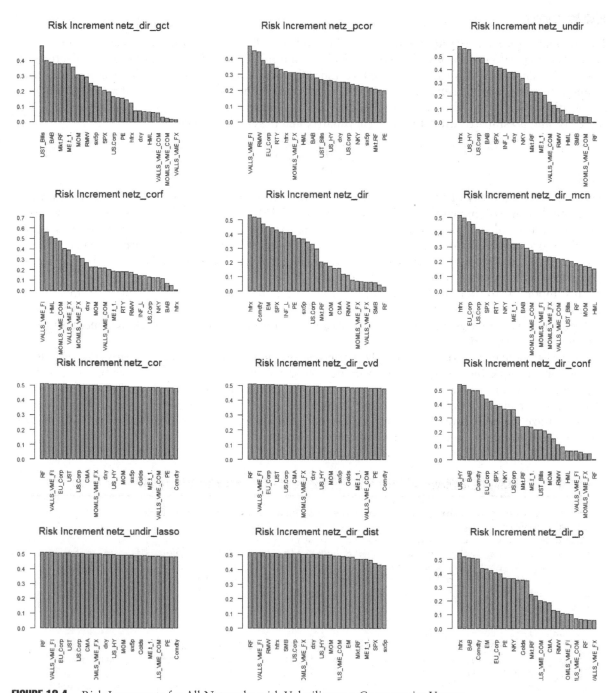

FIGURE 12.4 Risk Increments for All Networks with Volatility as a Compromise Vector.

Normalized Risk Score

We previously defined the systemic risk score. The normalized risk score shares a similar intuition to the Sharpe ratio and enables researchers to compare portfolios with their networks of assets. This risk score is normalized using the L-2 norm of the vectors containing the compromise scores, as shown:

$$\overline{S} = \frac{\sqrt{C^T A C}}{\sqrt{C^T C}}, \; with \; C = s \times c \qquad (12.12)$$

where all variables have been defined previously.

Exploring the concept of the normalized risk score is insightful for understanding network dynamics. This score is based on the premise where the adjacency matrix A equals the identity matrix I (i.e., $A = I$). In such cases, the network exhibits no risk, indicating a subcritical state with no connections between the nodes, and the average network degree approaches zero.[14] The off-diagonal entries in the adjacency matrix are zeros when $A = I$. In a more fragile network, the normalized score of a portfolio tends to be higher.

The normalized risk score is a valuable source of information for analyzing and testing different portfolio strategies. It adds value to the portfolio research process by aiding in evaluating and testing trading strategies. After evaluating successful strategies and deriving specific portfolio asset allocations, estimating the normalized risk score can help compare the risk among statistically significant portfolio strategies.[15] It's important to note that the normalized risk score (NRS) varies, depending on the underlying network structure (whether directed, undirected, or multigraph). These variations can be significant, necessitating economic reasoning when evaluating the NRS. Combining it with other network-based risk metrics can enhance the robustness and depth of the analyses.

The score can be computed as a static metric on a daily, weekly, or monthly basis. However, adopting a dynamic approach to computation provides more insightful and actionable information for portfolio management. Figure 12.5 illustrates the NRS estimation for an undirected network (netz_undir) using volatility as a risk-score indicator, with a rolling window estimation over 36 monthly observations. Consequently, higher volatility over the rolling period corresponds to a higher risk score for the network.

Visual examination of the NRS index reveals important characteristics of market interconnectedness. For instance, NRS decreased prior to the 2007 to 2008 Global Financial Crisis (GFC) but surged immediately afterward due to the financial turmoil triggered by events like the subprime crisis and Lehman Brothers' bankruptcy in Fall 2008. The NSR index remained elevated and even increased slightly during the onset of the European debt crisis in 2011. Following a period of declining risk as markets stabilized, the index peaked again in 2015 amid the third European debt crisis. It surged once more following the outbreak of the COVID-19 pandemic in early 2020.

In Chapter 6, we introduced the Wasserstein distance. The code that estimates the W_2-Wasserstein distance-based undirected network and calculates the rolling NRS using time-series data is provided in Box 12.4.[16] It's important to note the distinction in the W_2-Wasserstein distance network estimation methods. The first approach involves a weighted graph where the entries are the actual W_2-Wasserstein distance metrics. In contrast, the second method sets all entries in the adjacency matrix that are less than a specified threshold level to 1, and zero otherwise, resulting in an unweighted network. The difference between these approaches can be substantial.

---

[14] See Chapter 4 for the Erdös–Renyi simulation of a random network.
[15] In evaluating trading strategies, Bailey and López de Prado (2014), Harvey and Liu (2014), and Fabozzi and López de Prado (2018) stressed the use of the Probabilistic Sharpe ratio.
[16] Different NRS indices depend on the network construction

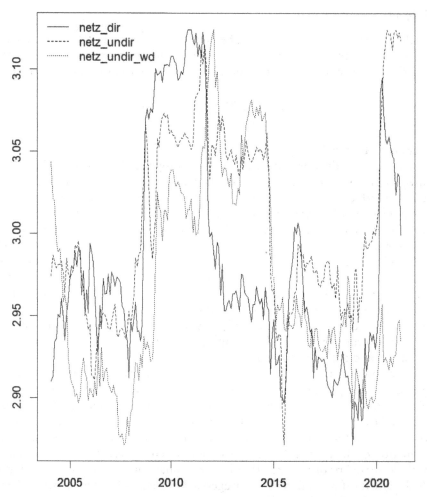

FIGURE 12.5 A Normalized Risk Score for a Directed, Undirected, and the Undirected W_2-Wasserstein Distance Asset and Factor Network.
Note: we use netz_undir, netz_undir_wd, and netz_dir for the computation of the NRS indices.

BOX 12.4:   NORMALIZED RISK SCORES FOR AN UNDIRECTED, UNDIRECTED W_2-WASSERSTEIN DISTANCE, AND AN UNDIRECTED ASSET AND FACTOR NETWORKS.

```
mtx_undir_wd<-matrix(nrow=ncol(AssetsFactors), ncol=ncol(AssetsFactors))
return_step<-as.matrix(AssetsFactors)
rollstep=36
periods=nrow(AssetsFactors)-rollstep
y<-seq(from=1, to=periods, by=1)
nrs_wd<-foreach(a=y) %do% {
  return_step=AssetsFactors[a:(a+rollstep),]
  for(i in 1:ncol(return_step)) {
     for(j in 1:ncol(return_step)) {
```

```
            mtx_undir_wd[i,j]=wasserstein1d(return_step[,i], return_step[,j], p=2)
            mtx_undir_wd=as.matrix(abs(mtx_undir_wd))
#allowing for the next line of code makes the adjacency matrix an unweighted graph with
elements 1 and 0.
#disallowing the line makes a weighted adjacency matrix with raw estimations
        #mtx_undir_wd1=ifelse(mtx_undir_wd[,]<mean(mtx_undir_wd),1,0)
        g<-graph_from_adjacency_matrix(mtx_undir_wd1, weighted=TRUE)
    }
  }

    ecs_undir<-as.matrix(eigen_centrality(g)$vector)
    vola<-apply(return_step,2,sd)
  as.matrix(vola)
  volrank=as.matrix(rank(vola))

  #Risk Score
  adj_matrix_<-as.matrix(as_adjacency_matrix(g))
  es_undir=sqrt(t(volrank)%*%adj_matrix_%*%volrank)

  #Normalized Risk Score
  norm_crit_undir=sqrt(t(volrank)%*%volrank)
  es_undir/norm_crit_undir

}
nrs_wd<-as.matrix(nrs_wd)
datebreaks<-seq(as.Date("2004-02-01"), as.Date("2021-03-31"), by = "1 month")
plot(datebreaks, nrs_wd, type="o", ylab="", xlab="")
```

Network Entropy

Financial markets can be viewed as systems where complexity naturally increases over time. This concept of increasing complexity can be attributed to the works of Weaver (1948) and Simon (1962), who highlighted that the development of social and economic relationships tends towards greater complexity. Similarly, portfolios composed of diverse assets also exhibit evolving systems. Entropy means evolution, and Prigogine (1997) argues that entropy only remains constant in equilibrium or isolated systems without information flow. Applied to financial markets that are in nonequilibrium states with constant information flow and steady volatility fluctuations, the entropy-generation process never ceases. The description of financial markets as dynamic systems requires the formulation of deterministic processes, which occur during periods of stable conditions and the formulation of probabilistic processes that model the transition phases.

Shannon entropy is a widely adopted measure for assessing the dynamics of such evolving systems, quantifying the degree of uncertainty. In investment management, applying entropy at the portfolio level can be traced to the contributions of Bera and Park (2008) and Meucci (2009), who suggested that higher entropy, as a measure of independent sources of risk in a portfolio, signifies greater diversification benefits.[17] In essence, while a diversified portfolio benefits from higher independent risk sources, this perspective shifts in the context of network analysis, where assets or nodes interact. According to Rebonato and Denev (2013), entropy serves as a measure of structure: higher entropy signifies better diversification and node independence within this context.

---

[17] See Poddig and Unger (2012).

Following the ideas of evolutionary development and adaptation, Demetrius and Manke (2005) expanded on the analyses of Bornholdt and Sneppen (2000) and Albert and Barabási (2002), asserting that entropy reflects changing robustness at the node level. This concept was further supported by López de Prado (2018) who demonstrated entropy's suitability for measuring diversity in portfolios. Fiedor (2014a, 2014b, 2014c) also showed that asset prices respond to changes in entropy, indicating that higher entropy states are preferable due to their robustness against financial market uncertainty.

In network analysis, Shannon entropy has been utilized to quantify information gain between assets by Sandhu et al. (2016), Billio et al. (2016), and Baitinger and Papenbrock (2017a, 2017b). However, the primary application of Shannon entropy in risk management is to gauge fragility, or deviation states among nodes. Greater deviations correspond to higher uncertainty. To apply Shannon nodal entropy in a network context, the Markov chain approach, described in Chapter 7, is necessary. Here, nodal entropy measures transition rates between nodes while disregarding direct links.

This is achieved by converting the distance matrix into transition probabilities, typically facilitated by a kernel function. Various distance kernels are used in finance, leveraging correlation coefficients, such as those proposed by Prim (1957), Onella et al. (2003), Phoa (2013), and Konstantinov (2022b) as follows:

$$d_{ij}^{Mantegna} = \sqrt{2\left(1 - \rho_{ij}\right)} \tag{12.13}$$

$$d_{ij}^{Phoa} = 1 + \rho_{ij} \tag{12.14}$$

$$d_{ij}^{K} = 1 + |\rho_{ij}| \tag{12.15}$$

Using the distance metrics that are the entries in the distance matrix $D(n \times n)$, we can compute the transition rates in the adjacency matrix. These transition probabilities are calculated by dividing each entry in $D(n \times n)$ by the sum of the corresponding row. The result is a matrix of transition probabilities $\eta_i(n)$ describing Markov chain transition rates from node i to node $j(i \rightarrow j)$, with probability $\eta_{ij} \geq 0$ and $\sum \eta_{ij} = 1$. Then the network entropy on the node level may be defined as:

$$H_i^G = -\sum_j \eta_{ij} \log \eta_{ij} \tag{12.16}$$

where η_{ij} are the transition probabilities from node i to node j.

The higher the entropy, the greater the risk at the node level, indicating increased node-based fragility. Network entropy, computed using methods such as the Granger causality test or applying a proper distance metric for directed weighted networks, serves to quantify this risk. Although many network types can be used to estimate entropy, the probabilistic Markov chain network is especially common.

Figure 12.6 illustrates the entropy of a W_2-Wasserstein undirected asset and factor network, capturing the uncertainty and complexity within the network structure. Following is an outline of the approach used, with its implementation details provided in Box 12.5.

In the multi-asset and factor landscape, isolating entropy computations can offer deeper insights into the drivers of risk. For instance, computing entropy for a directed weighted network, using the variance decomposition technique, illustrates this concept clearly.

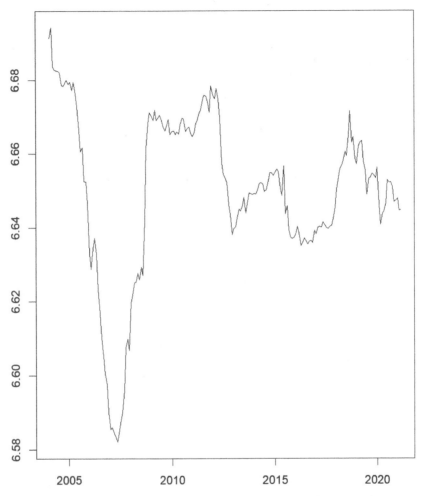

FIGURE 12.6 Nodal Entropy for a W_2-Wasserstein Distance-Based Undirected Asset and Factor Network.

BOX 12.5: ENTROPY FOR AN UNDIRECTED W_2-WASSERSTEIN DISTANCE ASSET AND FACTOR NETWORKS.

```
mtx_undir_wd<-matrix(nrow=ncol(AssetsFactors),ncol=ncol(AssetsFactors))
return_step<-as.matrix(AssetsFactors)
rollstep=36
periods=nrow(AssetsFactors)-rollstep
y<-seq(from=1, to=periods, by=1)
ent_wd<-foreach(a=y) %dopar% {
  return_step=ts(AssetsFactors[a:(a+rollstep),])
  for(i in 1:ncol(return_step)) {
     for(j in 1:ncol(return_step)) {
```

(Continued)

(*Continued*)

```
        mtx_undir_wd[i,j]=wasserstein1d(return_step[,i], return_step[,j], p=2)
        mtx_undir_wd=as.matrix(abs(mtx_undir_wd))
        netz_undir_wd<-graph_from_adjacency_matrix(mtx_undir_wd, weighted=TRUE)
    }
  }
  entropy(mtx_undir_wd)
}
ent_wd<-as.matrix(ent_wd)
datebreaks<-seq(as.Date("2004-02-01"), as.Date("2021-03-31"), by = "1 month")

plot(datebreaks,ent_wd, type="l", col="black", cex.lab=1, ylab="", xlab="")
```

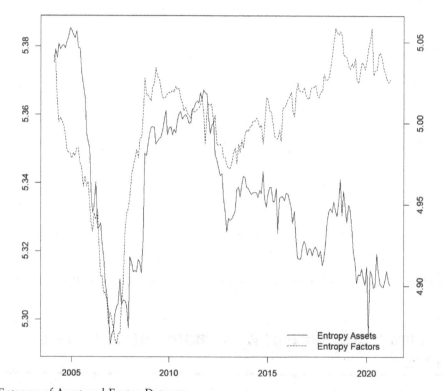

FIGURE 12.7   Entropy of Asset and Factor Datasets.
Note: The entropy for the factors is shown on the left-hand side of the figure, while the entropy for the assets is displayed on the right-hand side.

Applying the same code to separate sets of factors and assets provides valuable insights into the nodal structure of asset and factor portfolios. Figure 12.7 illustrates a significant difference in entropy between assets and factors. Higher entropy in factors suggests a potential diversification advantage. This analysis enables portfolio managers to monitor these variances over time, providing a dynamic view of portfolio structure. Significantly, the gap in entropy widened post-2011, aligning with the onset of the European debt crisis, highlighting the method's utility in capturing shifts in market dynamics.

Portfolio and risk managers can derive several important insights from such analyses. The entropy of the factor subgraph differs from that of the asset subgraph. Uncertainty at the node level is higher for factors but exhibits less volatility compared to assets. Visual inspection reveals that assets reacted more swiftly to market turmoil preceding the COVID-19 pandemic, while factors showed a more pronounced reaction, indicating higher node-based uncertainty associated with factors than with assets.

A significant drawback of network entropy is its inherent information loss due to neglecting links and aggregating sums across nonadjacent nodes. Sandhu et al. (2016) noted that this information loss stems from the weighted contraction of link dependencies. To mitigate this, edge-level risk and fragility indicators preserve information geometry by considering the links between nodes, which we will discuss next.

EDGE CONNECTIVITY AND SPILLOVER INDICATORS

In earlier sections, we examined risk indicators at the node level using centrality metrics. This section shifts the book's focus to risk transmission through edge-level indicators. Unlike the static indicators previously discussed, we will now expand the framework to introduce dynamic risk metrics. These metrics aim to capture the evolving nature of financial markets and provide insights into risk dynamics over time.

As discussed in Chapter 4, one approach to explore edge centrality involves reversing the network structure using a method known as the line graph transformation. This transformation converts nodes into edges and edges into nodes, enabling a deeper analysis of edge importance.[18]

In financial networks, edge connectivity refers to the strength of mutual relationships where risk is transmitted through these links. Network analysis provides tools to measure how portfolios are embedded in relationship contexts and analyze the spread of systematic risk. Edge connectivity differs from node-level risk, focusing instead on how risk propagates through mutual links between nodes.

To illustrate this, it's essential to outline various network models and approaches used to model edge connectivity. For instance, Braverman and Minca (2018) constructed networks where portfolios are nodes, and risks are transmitted across the links between these nodes. Their primary focus is on contagion and spillover risk.

Diebold and Yilmaz (2009, 2014) and Konstantinov and Fabozzi (2022) propose a prominent metric for measuring risk propagation in portfolio management. These models aim to develop indices that capture risk connectivity at the edge level, often utilizing volatility networks as indicators of spillover.

Volatility Networks for Risk Management

Risk networks aim to demonstrate the existence of portfolio spillover across assets, factors, countries, sectors, or other portfolio components. This technique is particularly applicable to asset and factor returns, using volatility networks for computation. Andersen et al. (2003) and Diebold and Yilmaz (2009, 2015) highlighted the utility of volatility in constructing such networks. Volatility, a widely accepted risk indicator in financial markets, represents the square root of portfolio asset variances and covariances.

Volatility-based networks are well-suited for examining edge-level connectedness and spillover risk because volatility captures risk through its measure of price fluctuations. Volatility shocks in specific markets can propagate to affect other assets, reflecting directional and return-based interactions. These shocks go beyond common movements driven by economic fundamentals, influencing the returns of other asset classes.

---

[18]See Chapter 11 for a detailed explanation of the edge connectivity and the information that can be extracted from edge connectivity and network metrics that describe edge properties.

The significance of volatility in network analysis lies in its role in low-volatility strategies aimed at reducing overall portfolio risk.[19] Volatility, being non-negative, reflects stress in financial portfolios (high volatility) with positive or zero energy but never negative. Bevilacqua et al. (2019) discussed positive and negative volatility shocks, where negative shocks indicate deteriorating market conditions and increased contagion risk across financial markets.

Echoing the findings by Ehrmann et al. (2011), Bekaert et al. (2011), and Morales and Andreosso-O'Callaghan (2014), which identified interconnectivity among interest rates, government bonds, equity markets, and exchange rates, Konstantinov and Fabozzi (2022) observed that portfolio spillover affects diverse asset classes. Unlike orthogonal shocks, volatility shocks persist longer, transmitting across portfolios due to their strong interconnectedness.

The variance decomposition network differs from other networks by representing a complete graph in its adjacency matrix. Shocks in this network are not orthogonal; they affect all nodes simultaneously. This approach enables for estimating how each node (asset or factor) responds to shocks, providing insights into cascading effects propagated through network links.

In summary, variance decomposition networks are instrumental in analyzing return-based and directional risk flow across portfolios. They reveal how risks from trading activities, market liquidity, political events, and aggregate shocks transmit across asset classes, tightly intertwined with volatility dynamics.

Spillover Index

Our focus here is on understanding how spillover risk impacts portfolios and propagates through interconnected assets and factors, reflecting market integration. While drivers of spillovers can be exogenous (e.g., macroeconomic factors and policy shifts by central banks), our interest lies in examining how spillovers are transmitted among assets within portfolios. Financial history has shown that disparities in economic variables, expectations, and fundamentals can amplify risk, propagating through interconnected markets.

De Grawe and Ji (2013) argue that cascading risk effects can become self-fulfilling prophecies driven by irrationality and fear, spreading through market edges. Combining econometric analysis with graph theory demonstrates that volatility spillover is directional and can be decomposed into contributions to and from other portfolios. The variance-decomposition technique, particularly Cholesky factorization as suggested by Diebold and Yilmaz (2009, 2011), is pivotal in constructing volatility networks that emphasize edge connectivity.

In Chapter 7, we detailed the construction of volatility networks using a VAR model and Cholesky variance decomposition. This approach splits the forecast error variance of the adjacency matrix A ($n \times n$) into components attributed to different shocks. Notably, this adjacency matrix forms a complete graph where the main diagonal represents the variances of individual nodes, not zero.

Specifically, the spillover index quantifies the proportion or contribution of forecast-error variance of node i originating from shocks to node j. The column sums of off-diagonal elements in the adjacency matrix are computed across all nodes, while the row-sums (including the diagonal) provide the denominator of the spillover index.[20] Using the notation of Diebold and Yilmaz (2009, 2015) and Konstantinov and Fabozzi (2022), the spillover index at time t is given by:

$$S_t^* = \frac{C_t'}{C_t^{total}} = \frac{\sum_{i,j=1}^{n} a_{ij}^2}{tr(A)} \tag{12.17}$$

---

[19] For the definition of low-volatility strategies and their construction, intuition, and relevance in portfolio management, see Alighanbari et al. (2016), Blitz (2016), and Alonso and Nusinzon (2020).

[20] See Diebold and Yilmaz (2009) for more details on the estimation of spillover indexes.

where $C_t^{total} = tr(A)$ is equivalent to the trace of the matrix A comprising all nodes, and the numerator of the spillover index C_t' represents the total connectedness represented by the adjacency matrix.[21]

To explore the potential of constructing VAR networks across different asset classes and datasets, akin to the approach by Diebold and Yilmaz (2015), we compute the spillover index using VAR Cholesky Decomposition Networks for various datasets. These include Emerging Markets Bond Index (EMBI) country returns, asset and factor returns, global equity market data, and hedge fund index returns.[22] To illustrate the spillover index in different asset classes in Figure 12.8, we provide several spillover indices computed for the datasets used in this book. We plot the spillover index for the hedge fund index returns, EMBI, asset and factors, and global equity markets. The code is provided in Box 12.6

An important question in financial research concerns whether there are meaningful differences between portfolios comprising assets and factors versus those composed solely of factors. Kritzman (2021) emphasizes that asset classes should typically be the focus in portfolio construction, while factors are valuable for enhancing returns. To explore this, we compute the spillover index and compare results between the entire set of assets and factors versus portfolios consisting exclusively of factors. Similarly, we analyze the spillover index for portfolios consisting exclusively of assets. This comparison provides insights into how spillover risk differs between assets and factors during periods of market stress. Figure 12.9 illustrates these differences using a split of asset and factor sets from our original data.

BOX 12.6: SPILLOVER INDEX FOR THE DIRECTED VARIANCE-DECOMPOSITION ASSET AND FACTOR NETWORKS.

```
mtrx<-matrix(nrow=ncol(AssetsFactors), ncol=ncol(AssetsFactors))
return_step<-as.matrix(AssetsFactors)
rollstep=72
periods=nrow(AssetsFactors)-rollstep
y<-seq(from=1, to=periods, by=1)
spill<-foreach(a=y) %dopar% {
  return_step=ts(AssetsFactors[a:(a+rollstep),])

  info.bv<-VARselect(return_step,lag.max=12, type="const")
  bv.est<-VAR(return_step, p=1,type="const", season=NULL,exog=NULL)
  bv.vardec<-fevd(bv.est,n.ahead = 12)
  proba<-do.call("rbind", lapply(bv.vardec, "[", 3, ))
  proba<-as.matrix(proba)
  mreja<-graph_from_adjacency_matrix(proba, weighted=TRUE)
  trace.mat<-diag(proba)
  sum(proba)/sum(trace.mat)
}
spillover<-as.matrix(spill)
datebreaks<-seq(as.Date("2007-02-01"), as.Date("2021-03-31"), by = "1 month")

plot(datebreaks,spillover, type="l", col="black" , main="Spillover", cex.lab=1, ylab="",
xlab="")
```

---

[21] The trace of a square matrix is simply the sum of the elements on the main diagonal of the square (adjacency) matrix.
[22] Data from the studies by Konstantinov (2022a), Konstantinov et al. (2020), Konstantinov and Fabozzi (2021), and Konstantinov (2022b).

FIGURE 12.8   A Spillover Index for Different Asset Classes.
Note: The data time-series diverge, and the spillover indices are not directly comparable.

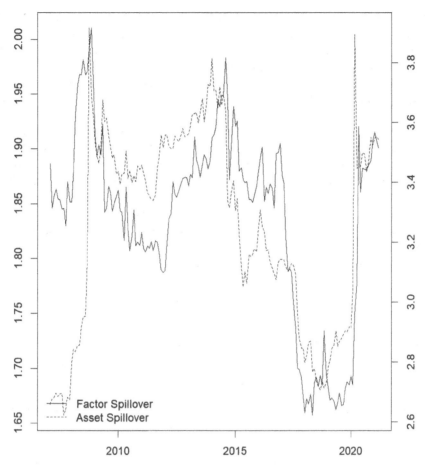

FIGURE 12.9   A Spillover Index for the Assets and Factors and the Multi-Asset Factor Data Sets.
Note: We use the asset and factor data set from Konstantinov et al. (2020). Factors spillover values are on the
left-hand side of the chart. Asset spillover values are on the right-hand side of the chart.

The findings reveal distinct responses of factors and assets to variance shocks, which, despite their high correlation, vary greatly in magnitude. This variation warrants further investigation within the investment process.

Ricci Curvature

To consider how curvature and markets relate to networks, let's first consider a simple (i.e., geodesic) triangle with edge points (ABC) and a median m_C that connects C with the middle point of AB.[23] A triangle lying on a planar surface exhibits zero curvature, with its sides connecting points A, B, and C being straight lines. Curvature, whether positive or negative, can be vividly illustrated using a torus[24] and a sphere. On a

---

[23]In a geodesic triangle, the points are connected by edges, which represent the shortest distance between the points. All point where all medians are intersected is the mass point of the triangle. This is the important intuition behind applying the Wasserstein distance to networks and the computation of Ricci curvature.

[24]A torus is a doughnut-shaped geometric figure formed by rotating a circle around an axis that lies in the same plane as the circle.

spherical surface, the sides of a triangle have positive curvature, where the path distance for m_C is longer compared to a planar surface. Conversely, on the inner side of a torus, the sides of a triangle display negative curvature, resulting in a shorter path distance for m_C compared to a planar surface. Thus, the median m_C between triangle points has a shorter path length on the torus.

Translating this concept to financial markets, shorter distances imply higher information transmission between nodes. The absolute level of curvature is less crucial than its change from lower to higher or vice versa. In financial terms, changing curvature suggests faster risk transmission that impacts nodes.

Ricci curvature is a compelling indicator for assessing fragility both at the edge and at the node level of networks, focusing on how tightly nodes are connected rather than their individual characteristics. It employs geodesics – shortest paths between nodes – based on probability measures using the Markov probability matrix. The Ricci curvature utilizes Wasserstein-1 (W_1) or Wasserstein-2 (W_2) distances, approximated by the Manhattan W_1 and Euclidean W_2 metrics of the discrete transition probability matrix, as discussed by Rachev and Rüschendorf (1998) and adapted from Ollivier (2007, 2009) and Sandhu et al. (2016).[25] The W_1 distance is also known as earth mover's' distance (EMD). We discussed the Wasserstein distance in Chapter 6.

According to Aktas et al. (2019), the p-th Wasserstein W_p distance is given by:

$$W_p(\mu_p, \mu_q) = \inf_{\gamma:\mu_p \to \mu_q} \left(\sum_{x \in \mu_1} \|x - \gamma(x)\|_\infty^p \right)^{\frac{1}{p}} \tag{12.18}$$

where γ ranges over all matchings from μ_1 to μ_2 and the p-th order is given by

$$\|\mu_p - \mu_q\|_p = \left(|\mu_1 - \mu_1|^p + |\mu_2 - \mu_2|^p \right)^{1/p} \tag{12.19}$$

Once the Wasserstein distance is defined, the compuation of the Ricci curvature is 1 minus the ratio of the Wasserstein distance divided by the node distance measure.

$$Ric_{ij}^O = 1 - \frac{W_1(\mu_i, \mu_j)}{d_{ij}} \tag{12.20}$$

where d_{ij} is the geodesic (i.e., mean) distance between nodes i and j, and $W_1(\mu_i, \mu_j)$ is the distance that considers the probabilistic distance and the distribution of the point masses μ_i and μ_j of the nodes. Note that the point masses are computed using the discrete probabilistic matrix $P(n \times n)$, estimated using the correlation kernel distance matrix $D(n \times n)$.[26] This Markov chain describes the transition rates from node i to node j with probability $\eta_{ij} \geq 0$ and $\sum \eta_{ij} = 1$. This results in a directed, weighted graph.

The W_1 distance is approximated by the earth mover's distance (EMD). This distance is subject to a specific order parameter p order, which defines the order of the distance. The second order of the Wasserstein distance W_2 is used with respect to the Euclidean norm. The Manhattan distance metric is used when p is equal to 1, taking the absolute value of differences between components, while the Euclidean distance metric is applied when p is equal to 2; that is:

$$W_p(\mu_i, \mu_j) = \|\mu_i - \mu_j\|_p^p \tag{12.21}$$

---

[25] Note that the Wasserstein distance measures the distance between clusters and distribution of clusters. Similarly, it can be used to compare networks using the point masses.

[26] Here, n is the number of nodes or assets in a network.

where p is a parameter that usually takes values of 1 or 2. In the case of $p = 1$, we obtain the Manhattan distance. With $p = 2$, we can apply the Euclidean distance already explained in Chapter 6. In the computations, we use the W_2-Wasserstein distance, which is a proxy for the Euclidean distance between the portfolio constituents in the network.

The algorithm to compute the Wasserstein distance using financial time series data is as follows:

1. Convert nominal data to ordinal data.
2. Sum up the elements by vectors, and for each vector, divide each element by the respective sum.
3. Compute the differences of each pair of vectors: $d_{ij,t+1} = v_{i,t} + d_{ij,t} - v_{j,t}$, setting the first $d_{ij,t+0} = 0$.
4. The W_1 Wasserstein metric, or the EMD in this case, is then the sum of all $W_1 = \sum_{i=0}^{n} |d_i|$.

Note that the methodology and approach suggested by Lott and Villani (2009) and applied to financial markets by Sandhu et al. (2016) can be extended to other networks. To compare the Ricci–Olivier curvature for asset and factors, we compute the metric using the Wasserstein distances for a directed, Granger causality network. We plot the Ricci curvature with the W_2-Wasserstein distance network in Figure 12.10 and provide the code in Box 12.7. Alternatively, we can use the Markov chain algorithm and compute the Ricci curvature using the Markov chain procedure in Figure 12.11. The corresponding code is in Box 12.8.

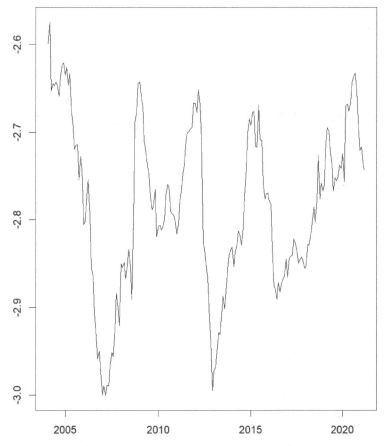

FIGURE 12.10 The Ricci Curvature for a W_2-Wasserstein Distance Asset and Factor Network.

BOX 12.7:   A RICCI CURVATURE FOR A W_2-WASSERSTEIN DISTANCE ASSET AND FACTOR NETWORK.

```
mtx_undir_wd<-matrix(nrow=ncol(AssetsFactors),ncol=ncol(AssetsFactors))
return_step<-as.matrix(AssetsFactors)
rollstep=36
periods=nrow(AssetsFactors)-rollstep
y<-seq(from=1, to=periods, by=1)
ricci_wd<-foreach(a=y) %dopar% {
   return_step=ts(AssetsFactors[a:(a+rollstep),])
   for(i in 1:ncol(return_step)) {
      for(j in 1:ncol(return_step)) {

         mtx_undir_wd[i,j]=wasserstein1d(return_step[,i], return_step[,j], p=2)
         mtx_undir_wd=as.matrix(abs(mtx_undir_wd))
         netz_undir_wd<-graph_from_adjacency_matrix(mtx_undir_wd, weighted=TRUE)
      }
   }

      1-(mean(dist(mtx_undir_wd,method="euclidean"))/mean_distance(netz_undir_wd))
}
ricci_wd<-as.matrix(ricci_wd)
datebreaks<-seq(as.Date("2004-02-01"), as.Date("2021-03-31"), by = "1 month")

plot(datebreaks,ricci_wd, type="l", col="black" , cex.lab=1, ylab="", xlab="")
```

BOX 12.8:   A RICCI CURVATURE FOR A MARKOV CHAIN PROBABILISTIC ASSET AND FACTOR NETWORK.

```
mtrx<-matrix(nrow=ncol(AssetsFactors), ncol=ncol(AssetsFactors))
return_step<-as.matrix(AssetsFactors)
rollstep=36
periods=nrow(AssetsFactors)-rollstep
y<-seq(from=1, to=periods, by=1)
ricci<-foreach(a=y) %dopar% {
   return_step=AssetsFactors[a:(a+rollstep),]

   mtrx=sqrt(2*(1+cor(return_step)))
   mtrx_markov<-t(apply(mtrx,1,function(x) x/sum(x)))
   mreja=as.matrix(abs(mtrx_markov))
   g=graph_from_adjacency_matrix(mtrx_markov, weighted=TRUE)

   1-(mean(dist(mtrx_markov,method="euclidean"))/mean_distance(g))
}
ricci<-as.matrix(ricci)
datebreaks<-seq(as.Date("2004-02-01"), as.Date("2021-03-31"), by = "1 month")
plot(datebreaks,ricci, type="l", xlab="",ylab="")
```

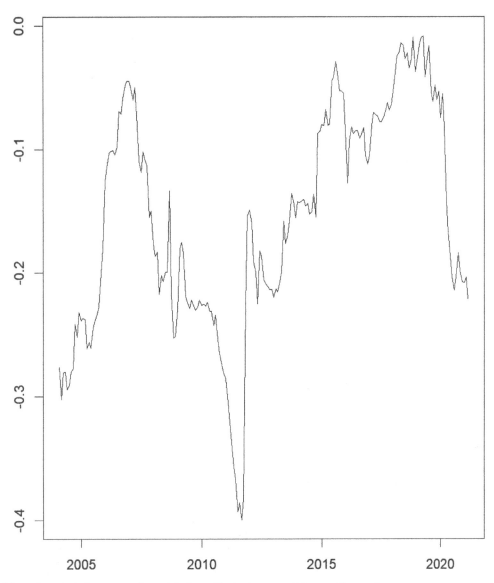

FIGURE 12.11　The Ricci Curvature for a Markov Chain Asset and Factor Network.

Figure 12.12 shows the Ricci curvature indices for different markets. The metrics are applied as follows: assets and factors according to the study by Konstantinov et al. (2020); the EMBI as studied by Konstantinov (2022a); EMU assets and factors, according to the study by Konstantinov (2021, 2023); foreign exchange markets from a EUR-investor perspective as documented by Konstantinov (2016); and hedge funds according to the study by Konstantinov (2022b).

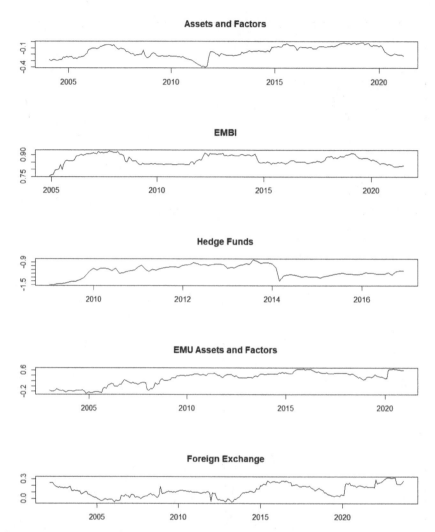

FIGURE 12.12 The Ricci Curvature Indices for Different Markets.
Note: We used the datasets from different studies to compute the indices. The sample ranges are not equal for all indicators.

COMPARING RISK METRICS

Comparing the risk metrics enables a natural assessment of the value added by the metrics presented in this chapter. We categorize these metrics into three groups: node-based, edge-based, and combined. To ensure meaningful comparisons, we separately evaluate node-level metrics, such as entropy and normalized risk score, and edge-level metrics, such as Ricci curvature, fragility, and spillover index.

It's important to note that these indicators are computed using different underlying statistical models. For instance, the VAR network employs variance-decomposition techniques, while the Ricci curvature is computed using an undirected correlation-test network. This section aims to provide a comprehensive overview of the versatility of network models, rather than advocating for a preferred network construction method in portfolio and risk management analysis.

Comparing Risk Metrics on the Edge and Node Level

In this book, we have described various methods for constructing portfolio networks, yet many other approaches also exist, complicating the comparison of risk indicators. To maintain consistency in model implementation and ensure meaningful comparisons, choosing methods that match the specific goals and traits of the financial and portfolio networks under study is crucial. Given the absence of a one-size-fits-all financial or portfolio network model, we recommend that practitioners continually implement and test different network construction methods. This practice helps to represent the interactions among financial market instruments over time accurately.

Risk measures at the node level are typically represented by characteristics that describe node behavior, such as degree centrality, eigen centrality, and alpha centrality scores. Centralization and average node degree are robust metrics applicable to most networks, excluding complete networks. Additionally, computing nodal entropy provides insights into the structural diversification of asset nodes. For example, following Konstantinov (2024), a comparison can be made between two fragility indices: one estimated using nodes and edges, and another derived from nodal entropy and Ricci curvature.

The correlation between Ricci curvature and fragility indicators is 0.53, highlighting their moderate relationship in capturing network dynamics. Recall that the code for computing the fragility index is provided in Box 12.2, while Box 12.8 contains the code for Ricci curvature estimation using a Markov chain approach. Figure 12.13 captures the plots of the fragility index and the Ricci curvature for a directed asset and factor network.

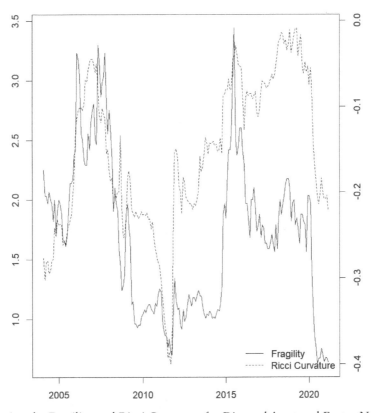

FIGURE 12.13 Comparing the Fragility and Ricci Curvature for Directed Asset and Factor Networks.
Note: We use the netz_dir algorithm, based on the squared regression equation provided in Chapter 7.

Comparing Node and Edge-Based Risk Measures

In this section, we will compare nodal and edge connectedness measures to understand the sources of risk – whether they originate from impaired nodes, such as a bankrupt financial institution or a defaulting issuer, or from the interconnected financial market where leverage and increased transfer of information and money cause financial risk to spread across many nodes. It is crucial to discern whether risk arises from individual nodes with a focus on node analysis, or is transmitted through the network with a focus on link investigation.

We specifically examine network entropy, which assesses node fragility resulting from fluctuations and Ricci curvature, which measures how information spreads and dissipates across edges. Our analysis reveals a correlation between Ricci curvature and nodal entropy, highlighting their interrelated dynamics. Visual examination of Figure 12.14 illustrates distinct reactions in nodal and edge properties. Significant drops or spikes in these measures often indicate heightened risk.

For instance, prior to the Global Financial Crisis (GFC), both entropy and Ricci curvature exhibited a sharp decline starting in 2006, suggesting elevated risk at both the node and edge levels. However, during the European debt crisis, characterized by divergences in core and periphery country fundamentals and

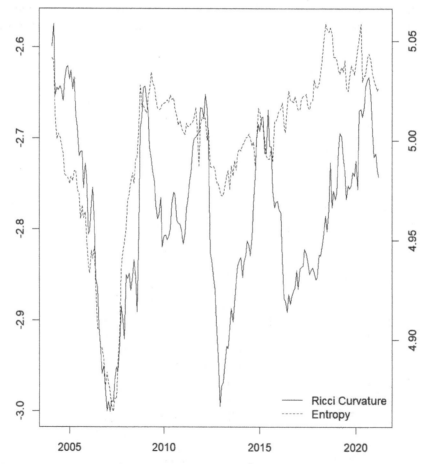

FIGURE 12.14   Comparing Entropy and Ricci Curvature for the W_2-Wasserstein Distance Undirected Asset and Factor Network.
Note: Ricci curvature values are on the left-hand side of the chart. Entropy values are on the right-hand side of the chart.

financial metrics (such as spreads, yields, and default rates), nodal entropy remained relatively stable. This stability indicates that edge-level factors primarily drive risk dynamics, intensifying propagation between nodes. Similarly, during the onset of the COVID-19 pandemic, both entropy and Ricci curvature spiked sharply, reflecting increased risk transmission, followed by a subsequent decline as markets recovered by late 2020. This comparative analysis of nodal and edge measures provides a nuanced understanding of risk origins and transmission in financial networks.

The code for the plot in Figure 12.14 has been provided in the corresponding sections and in Box 12.9. We show the code for a combined plot.

In investigating equity markets, we apply the algorithm based on the Wasserstein distance to estimate a weighted network, presenting nodal and edge risk indicators in Figure 12.15. Visual inspection reveals both entropy and Ricci curvature for global equity markets, exhibiting a high correlation of 0.96.

Figure 12.16 plots the spillover, Ricci curvature, and entropy estimated using a variance decomposition network. Inspecting this figure highlights the importance of these three measures in explaining interconnectedness risk through the differing dynamics of nodal and edge fragility. Directly plotting these measures suggests the potential sources of risk and which index might best capture and represent portfolio risk. There may be situations where one metric reacts more intensely than the others. Spikes or sharp decreases in all risk indicators might signal worrisome news.

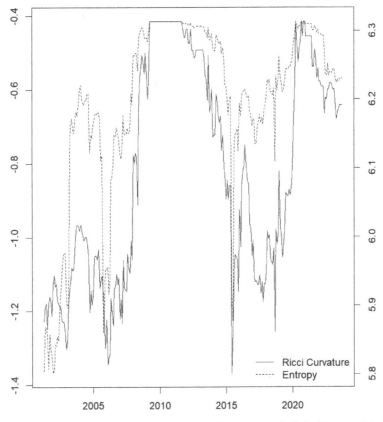

FIGURE 12.15 The Combined Plot for the Ricci Curvature and Entropy of Global Equity Markets.
Note: Ricci curvature values are on the left-hand side of the chart. Entropy values are on the right-hand side of the chart. Data was obtained by the authors from AQR Capital Management, Ltd.

BOX 12.9: PLOTS FOR THE RICCI CURVATURE AND THE ENTROPY OF THE W_2-WASSERSTEIN DISTANCE-BASED ASSET AND FACTOR NETWORK.

```
plot(datebreaks,ricci_wd, type="l", col="black" , cex.lab=1, ylab="", xlab="")
par(new=TRUE)
plot(datebreaks,ent_wd, type="l", col="black" , lay=2,axes=FALSE, cex.lab=1, ylab="",
xlab="")
axis(4)
legend("bottom right", by="n",legend = c("Ricci Curvature", "Entropy"),
    lay= c(1,2))
```

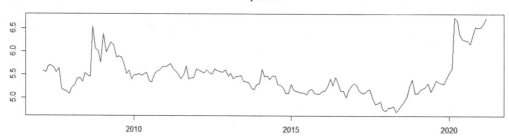

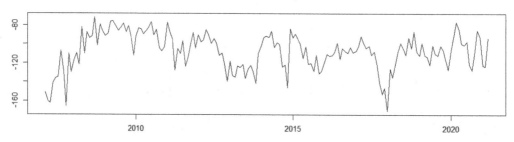

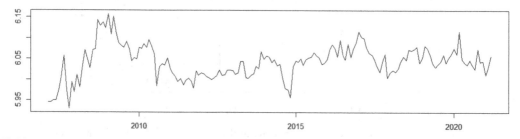

FIGURE 12.16   Spillover Index, Ricci Curvature, and Entropy for the Asset and Factor Directed Variance Decomposition Network.

Observing the three figures, the immediate conclusion that can be drawn is that spillover risk intensified in early 2020, as the Ricci curvature spiked. Notably, the nodal risk measured by entropy remained relatively calm. Because the financial market risk in 2020 stemmed from the global COVID-19 outbreak, it is clear that it did not have a nodal origin but was caused by edge transmission in the markets, leading to turmoil. Returning to the GFC, we can see node and edge connectivity spikes, accompanied by a constant decrease in curvature. The spread over edges was immediate and severe because the GFC impact was driven by nodal risk. Both entropy and curvature increased and spillover spiked. Cause and effect are difficult to measure, but the simultaneous spikes in entropy and Ricci curvature suggest that combined metrics clearly indicate serious financial market turmoil.

Risk arises and spreads for various reasons. It may originate at the node level or result from edge connectivity and increased edge flow between nodes. Generally, it is in the best interest of portfolio managers to monitor and predict using statistical learning models a representative set of several risk indices rather than focusing on just one. To that end, rolling estimations of network density, reciprocity (in the case of directed networks), mean degree, diameter, transitivity, and assortativity provide valuable information on the dynamics of network nodes and edges.

As previously mentioned, the information gained from edge and nodal risk measures like entropy and Ricci curvature lies in their differences. Konstantinov (2024) demonstrated that both negative and positive spikes in Ricci curvature indicate changes in the CBOE Volatility Index. The changes in Ricci curvature and entropy for the asset and factor W_2-Wasserstein distance network are plotted in Figure 12.17. The mean values are negative, indicating a lack of connectedness, as opposed to flatness. In other words, changes in Ricci curvature (i.e., becoming positive) signal financial market stress. This phenomenon is clearly observed in Figure 12.17, where Ricci curvature spikes during the GFC, the European debt crisis in 2011, and the COVID-19 outbreak in early 2020.

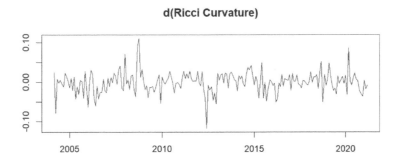

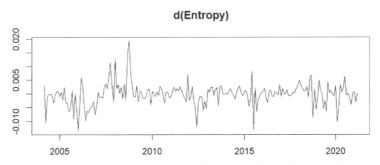

FIGURE 12.17 Differences of Ricci Curvature and Entropy for an Undirected Asset and Factor Network.

KEY TAKEAWAYS

- Risk management strategies that leverage network analysis depend on understanding the interconnected relationships between assets. Constructing networks is crucial as it shapes these relationships and enables the application of various network metrics. There are three major types of network risk metrics: node-level risk management tools, edge-level risk management tools, and combined measures that gauge both node and edge behavior and risk transmission.
- Node-level risk management tools focus on node behavior, identifying risks associated with nodes. In finance, such risks might include default, liquidity, enterprise, issuer, and credit risk. The critical question is where the risk arises and the impact of individual nodes.
- Edge-level risk metrics focus on the transmission of risk within the network. The edge structure plays a vital role, with sparser networks considered riskier compared to denser networks. Understanding the distances or probabilistic modeling of edges is essential for grasping edge risk transmission.
- Important node-level risk measures include entropy and node centralization (both degree and eigen centrality), which determine the centrality of nodes in a network.
- Important edge-level risk measures include the Ricci curvature and spillover indices. These focus on the distance between nodes, with shorter distances indicating a higher risk of spillover and contagion.
- Metrics that combine edges and nodes include fragility, risk increment, and normalized risk scores. These metrics might incorporate exogenous criticality inputs that directly influence node behavior but spread through the entire network, affecting edges as well.

References

Acemoglu, D., Ozdaglar, A. and Tahbaz-Salehi, A. (2015) Systemic risk and stability in financial networks, *American Economic Review*, 105(2), pp. 564–608.

Akaike H. (1973) Information theory and an extension of the maximum likelihood principle, in Petrov, B. N. and Csáki, F. (eds.) *Proceedings of the 2nd International symposium on information theory*. Budapest: Akadémia Kiadó, pp. 267–281.

Aked, M. R., Arnott, R., Bouchey, P., Li, T. and Shakernia, O. (2019) Tactical and tax aware GTAA, *Journal of Portfolio Management*, 45(2), pp. 23–37.

Aktas, M. E., Akbas, E. and Fatmaoui, A. E. (2019) Persistence homology of networks: Methods and applications, *Applied Network Science*, 4, pp. 61.

Albert, R., and Barabási, A.-L. (2000) Topology of evolving networks: Local events and universality, *Physical Review Letters*, 85(24), pp. 5234–5237.

Albert, R., and Barabási, A.-L. (2002) Statistical mechanics of complex networks, *Reviews of Modern Physics*, 74(1), pp. 47–98.

Albert, R., Jeong, H. and Barabási, A.-L. (1999) Diameter of the world-wide web, *Nature*, 401(6749), pp. 130–131.

Aldous, A. D. (1985) Exchangeability and related topics, in Hennequin, P. L. (ed.) Ecole d'Été de probabilités de Saint-Flour, XIII—1983, *Lecture Notes in Math*, 1117, Springer: Berlin, 1985, pp. 1–198.

Aldridge, I. (2019) Big Data in portfolio allocation: A new approach to successful portfolio optimization, *Journal of Financial Data Science*, 1(1), pp. 45–63.

Alighanbari, M., Doole, S. and Shankar, D. (2016) Designing low-volatility strategies, *Journal of Index Investing*, 7(3), pp. 21–33.

Allez, R. and Bouchaud, J-P. (2012) Eigenvector dynamics: General theory and some applications, *Physical Review E*, 86(4): 46202, doi: 0.48550/arXiv.1203.6228

Almaas, E., Kulkarni, R. V. and Stroud, D. (2002) Characterizing the structure of small-world networks, *Physical Review Letters*, 88(9):098101, doi: 10.1103/PhysRevLett.88.098101.

Alonso, N. and Nusinzon, O. (2020) The devil is in the details: The risks often ignored in low-volatility investing, *Journal of Portfolio Management*, 46(7), pp. 58–70.

Altman, E. I. (1968) Financial ratios, discriminant analysis and the prediction of corporate bankruptcy, *Journal of Finance*, 23(4), pp. 589–609.

Amaral, L. A. N. A., Scala, A., Barthelemy, M. and Stanley, H. E. (2000) Classes of small-world networks, *Proceedings of the National Academy of Sciences of the United States of America*, 97(21), pp. 11149–11152.

Amini, H., Minca, A. and Sulem, A. (2017) Optimal equity infusions in interbank networks, *Journal of Financial Stability*, 31, pp. 1–17.

Amini, H. and Minca, A. (2016) Inhomogeneous financial networks and contagious links, *Operations Research*, 64(5), pp. 1109–1120.

Amini, H., Cont, R. and Minca, A. (2013) Resilience to contagion in financial networks, *Mathematical Finance*, 26(2), pp. 329–365.

Andersen, T. G., Bollerslev, T., Diebold, F. X. and Labys, P. (2003) Modeling and Forecasting Realized Volatility, *Econometrica*, 71(2), pp. 579–625.

Aral, S. and Walker, D. (2011) Creating social contagion through viral product design: A randomized trial of peer influence in network, *Management Science*, 57(9), pp. 1623–1639.

Aronow, P. M. and Samii, C. (2017) Estimating average causal effects under general interference with application to a social network experiment, *The Annals of Applied Statistics*, 11(4), pp. 1912–1947.

Asness, C., Moskowitz, T. J. and Pedersen, L. H. (2013) Value and momentum everywhere, *Journal of Finance*, 68(3), pp. 929–985.

Avallaneda, M. and Lee, J. H. (2010) Statistical arbitrage in the US equities market, *Quantitative Finance*. 10(7), pp. 761–782.

Bacidore, J., Berkow, K., Polidore and Saraiya, N. (2012) Cluster analysis for evaluating trading strategies, *Journal of Trading*, 7(3), pp. 6–11.

Bailey, D. H. and Lopez de Prado, M. (2019) The Deflated Sharpe Ratio: Correcting for Selection Bias, Backtest Overfitting, and Non-Normality, *Journal of Portfolio Management*, 40(5), pp. 94–107.

Baitinger, E. (2021) Forecasting asset returns with network-based metrics: A statistical and economic analysis, *Journal of Forecasting*, 40(7), pp. 1342–1375.

Baitinger, E. and Papenbrock, J. (2017a) Interconnectedness risk and active portfolio management: The information-theoretic perspective, *Journal of Network Theory in Finance*, 3(4), pp. 25–47.

Baitinger, E. and Papenbrock, J. (2017b) Interconnectedness risk and active portfolio management, *Journal of Investment Strategies*, 6(2), pp. 63–90.

Baitinger, E. and Flegel, S. (2021) The better turbulence index? Forecasting adverse financial markets regimes with persistent homology, *Financial Markets and Portfolio Management*, 35(3), pp. 277–308.

Baitinger, E. and Maier, T. (2019) The (Mis)behaviour of hedge fund strategies: A network-based analysis, *Journal of Alternative Investments*, 22(1), pp. 57–74.

Baltas, N. (2019) The impact of crowding in alternative risk premia investing, *Financial Analysts Journal*, 75(3), pp. 89–104.

Bapat, R. B. (2014) *Graphs and Matrices*. New York: Springer.

Barabási, A.-L. (2016) *Network Science*. Cambridge: Cambridge University Press.

Barabási, A.-L. and Albert, R. (1999) Emergence of scaling in random networks, *Science*, 286(5439), pp. 509–512.

Barigozzi, M. and Brownlees, C. (2018) NETS: Network estimation for time series. *Journal of Applied Econometrics*, 34(3), pp. 347–364.

Barrat, A., Barthelemy, M., Pastor-Satorras, R. and Vespignani, A. (2004) The Architecture of Complex Weighted Networks, *Proceedings of the National Academy of Sciences*, 101(11), pp. 3747–3752.

Barunik, J., Kocenda, E. and Vacha, L. (2017) Asymmetric volatility connectedness on the forex market, *Journal of International Money and Finance*, 77, pp. 39–56.

Barunik, J., Bevilacqua, M. and Tunaru, R. (2020) Asymmetric network connectedness of fears, *Review of Economics and Statistics*, 104(6), pp. 1–41.

Battiston, S., Puliga, M., Kaushik, R., Tasca, P. and Caldarelli, G. (2012) DebtRank: Too central to fail? Financial networks, the Fed and systemic risk, *Scientific Reports*, 2, p. 541.

Battiston, S., D'Errico, M. and Gurciullo, S. (2016) DebtRank and the Network of Leverage, *Journal of Alternative Investments*, 18(4), pp. 68–81.

Battiston, F., Cencetti, G., Iacopini, I., Latora, V., Lucas, M., Patania, A., Young, J.-G. and Petri, G. (2020) Networks beyond pairwise interactions: Structure and dynamics, *Physics Reports*, 874, pp.1–92.

Bayraktar, M., Doole, S., Kassam, A. and Radchenko S. (2015) Lost in the crowd – Identifying and measuring crowded strategies and trades, *MSCI Research Insight*.

Bech, M. L. and Atalay, E. (2011) The topology of the federal funds market, *Physica A: Statistical Mechanics and its Applications*, 389(22), pp. 5223–5246.

Beirne, J. and Fratscher, M. (2013) The pricing of sovereign risk and contagion during the European sovereign debt crisis, *Journal of International Money and Finance*, 34, pp. 60–82.

Bekaert, G., Ehrmann, M. and Fratzscher, M. (2011) Global crises and equity market contagion, Working Paper 1381. European Central Bank.

Bekaert, G., Harvey, C. H. and Ng, A. (2005) Market integration and contagion, *The Journal of Business*, 78(1), pp. 39–69.

Bender, J., Sun, J. L. and Thomas, R. (2019) Asset allocation vs. factor allocation – Can we build a unified method? *Journal of Portfolio Management*, 45(2), pp. 9–22.

Bender, J., Briand, R., Nielsen, F. and Stefek, D. (2010) Portfolio of risk premia: A new approach, *Journal of Portfolio Management*, 36(2), pp. 17–25.

Benzi, M, Estrada, E. and Klymko, C. (2013) Ranking hubs and authorities using matrix functions, *Linear Algebra and Its Applications*, 438(5), pp. 2447–2474.

Bera, A. K. and Park, S. Y. (2008) Optimal portfolio diversification using maximum entropy, *Economic Review*, 27(4–6), pp. 485–512.

Bevilacqua, M., Morelli, D. and Tunaru, R. (2019) The determinants of the model-free positive and negative volatilities, *Journal of International Money and Finance*, 92, pp. 1–94.

Bhatia, R., Jain, T. and Lim, Y. (2019) On the bures – Wasserstein distance between positive definite matrices, *Expositiones Mathematicae*, 37(2), pp. 165–191.

Bianchi, M. L., Tassinari, G. L. and Fabozzi, F. J. (2023) Fat and heavy tails in asset management, *Journal of Portfolio Management*, 49(7), pp. 236–263.

Billio, M., Getmansky, M., Lo, A. W. and L. Pelizzon. (2012) Econometric measures of connectedness and systemic risk in the finance and insurance sectors. *Journal of Financial Economics*, 104(3), pp. 535–559.

Billio, M., Casarin, R. Costola, M. and Pasqualini, A. (2016) An entropy-based early warning indicator for systemic risk, *Journal of International Financial Markets, Institutions and Money*, 45, pp. 42–59.

Black, F. and Litterman, R. (1992) Global portfolio optimization, *Financial Analysts Journal*, 48(5), pp. 28–43.

Blitz, D. (2016) The value of low volatility, *Journal of Portfolio Management*, 42(3), pp. 94–100.

Blitz, D. 2018. Are hedge funds on the other side of the low-volatility trade? *Journal of Alternative Investments*, 21 (1), pp. 17–26.

Blondel, V. D., Guillaume, J-L., Lambiotte, R. and E. Lefebvre. (2008) Fast unfolding of communities in large networks, *Journal of Statistical Mechanics*, 2008(10): P10008, doi: 10.1088/1742-5468/2008/10/P10008.

Bollerslev, T., Hood, B. and Huss, J. (2018) Risk everywhere: Modeling and managing volatility, *Review of Financial Studies*, 31(7), pp. 2729–2773.

Bonacich, P. and Lloyd, P. (2001) Eigenvector-like measures of centrality for asymmetric relations, *Social Networks*, 23(3), pp. 191–201.

Bonacich, P. B. (1972) Factoring and weighing approaches to status scores and clique identification, *Journal of Mathematical Sociology*, 2(1), pp. 113–120.

Bonacich, P. B. (1987) Power and centrality: A family of measures, *American Journal of Sociology*, 92(5), pp. 1170–1182.

Bonanno, G., Caldarelli, G., Lillo, S., Micciche, Vanderwalle, N. and Mantegna, R. N. 2004. Networks of Equities in Financial Markets, *The European Physical Journal B*, 38 (2): 363–371.

Bonne, G., Lo, A.W., Prabhakaran, A., Siah, K. W., Singh, M., Wang, X., Zangari, P. and Zhang, H. (2022) An artificial intelligence-based industry peer grouping system, *Journal of Financial Data Science*, 4(2), pp. 9–36.

Borgatti, S. P. (2005) Centrality and network flow, *Social Networks*, 27(1), pp. 55–71.

Borgatti, S. P., Everett, M. G., Johnson, J. C. and F. Agneessens. (2022) *Analyzing Social Networks Using R*. Los Angeles: SAGE Publishing Inc.

Borgatti, S. P. and Everett, M. G. (2006) A graph-theoretic perspective on centrality, *Social Networks*, 28(4), pp. 466–484.

Bornholdt, S. and Ebel, H. (2001) World wide web scaling exponent from Simon's 1955 model, *Physical Review E*, 64(3):035104, doi: 10.1103/PhysRevE.64.035104.

Bornholdt, S. and Sneppen, K. (2000) Robustness as an evolutionary principle, *Proceedings of the Royal Society*, B267(1459), pp. 2281–2286.

Bostanci, G. and Yilmaz, K. (2020) How connected is the global sovereign credit risk network? *Journal of Banking and Finance*, 113(2), pp. 105761.

Bouchaud, J.-P. and Potters, M. (2000) *Theory of Financial Risk: From Statistical Physics to Risk Management*. Cambridge: Cambridge University Press.

Bramoulle, Y., Djebbari, H. and Fortin, B. (2009) Identification of peer effects through social networks, *Journal of Econometrics*, 150(1), pp. 41–55.

Braverman, A. and Minca, A. (2018) Networks of common asset holdings: Aggregation and measures of vulnerability, *Journal of Network Theory in Finance*, 4(3), pp. 53–78.

Broder, A., Kumar, R., Maghoul, F., Broder, P., Raghavan, P., Rajagopalan, S., Stata, R., Tomkins, A. and Wiener, J. L. (2000) Graph structure in the web, *Computer Networks*, 33(1–6), pp. 309–320.

Brooks, J., Palhares, D. and Richardson, S. (2018) Style investing in fixed income, *Journal of Portfolio Management*, 44(4), pp. 127–139.

Brooks, J., Richardson, S. and Xu, Z. (2020) (Systematic) investing in emerging market debt, *Journal of Fixed Income*, 30(2), pp. 44–61.

Burt, R. S. (1980) Models of network structure, *Annual Review of Sociology*, 6, pp. 79–141.

Burt, R. S. (1988) Some properties of structural equivalence measures derived from sociometric choice data, *Social Networks*, 10(1), pp. 1–28.

Bussiere, M., Hoerova, M., and Klaus, B. (2014) Commonality in Hedge Funds Returns: Driving Factors and Implications. Frankfurt: ECB Working Article Series No. 1658 (March).

Cahan, R. and Luo, Y. (2013) Standing out from the crowd: Measuring crowding in quantitative strategies, *Journal of Portfolio Management*, 39(4), pp. 14–23.

Cajas, D. (2023) *A Graph Theory Approach to Portfolio Optimization*. Rochester: SSRN Electronic Journal.

Carhart, M. M. (1997) On persistence in mutual fund performance, *Journal of Finance*, 52(1), pp. 57–82.

Carvalho, E. C., Nickenig Vissoci, J. R., de Andrade, L., de Lara Machado, W., Cabrera Paraiso, E. and Nievola, J. C. (2021) BNPA: An R package to learn path analysis input models from a data set semi-automatically using Bayesian networks, *Knowledge-Based Systems*, 223, pp.1–15.

Chakrabarti, A. S., Pichl, L. and Kaizoji, T. (2019) *Network Theory and Agent-Based Modeling in Economics and Finance*. New York: Springer.

Chambers, D. R., Anson, M. J. P., Black, K. H., and Kazemi, H. (2015) *Alternative Investments: U.S.: CAIA Level, Third Edition*. Hoboken, New Jersey: John Wiley & Sons.

Chiang, K. C. H., Wisen, C. H. and Zhou, T. (2007) Emerging market bonds as an asset class, *Journal of Investing*, 16(3), pp. 104–110.

Chopra, V. and Ziemba, W. (1993) The effect of errors in means, variances, and covariances on optimal portfolio choice, *Journal of Portfolio Management*, 19, pp. 6–12.

Chow, G., Jacquer, E., Kritzman, M. and Lowry, K. (1999) Optimal portfolios in good times and bad, *Financial Analysts Journal*, 55(3), pp. 65–73.

Ciciretti, V. and Pallotta, A. (2024) Network risk parity: Graph theory-based portfolio construction, *Journal of Asset Management*, 25(2), pp. 136–146.

Clarke, R. G., de Silva, H. and Murdock, R. (2005) A factor approach to asset allocation, *Journal of Portfolio Management*, 32(1), pp. 10–21.

Clauset, A., Newman, M. E. J. and Moore, C. (2004) Finding community structure in very large networks, *Physical Review E*, 70(6), pp. 6–11.

Clemente, G. P., Grassi, R. and Hitaj, A. (2022) Smart network based portfolios, *Annals of Operations Research*, 316, pp. 1519–1541.

Cleveland, W. (1993) *Visualizing Data*. Wallingford, United Kingdom: Hobart Press.

Cohen-Steiner, D., Edelsbrunner, H. and Harer, J. (2007) Stability of persistence diagrams, *Discrete and Computational Geometry*, 37, pp. 103–120.

Corsetti, G., Pericoli, M. and Sbracia, M. (2005) Some contagion, some interdependence: More pitfalls of financial contagion, *Journal of International Money and Finance*, 24, pp. 1177–1199.

Czasonis, M., Pamir, B. and Turkington, D. (2019) Carry on, *Journal of Alternative Investments*, 22(2), pp. 100–111.

Da Fonseca, J. and Ignatieva, K. (2018) Volatility spillovers and connectedness among credit default swap sector indexes, *Applied Economics*, 50(36), pp. 3923–3936.

Das, S. R., Kim, S. and Ostrov, D. (2019) Dynamic systemic risk: Networks in data science, *Journal of Financial Data Science*, 1(1), pp. 141–158.

Das, S. R. (2016) Matrix metrics: Network-based systemic risk scoring, *Journal of Alternative Investments*, 18(4), pp. 33–51.

Das, S. R. and Sisk, J. (2005) Financial communities, *Journal of Portfolio Management*, 31(4), pp. 112–123.

De Carvalho, P. J. C. and Gupta, A. (2018) A network approach to unravel asset price comovement using minimal dependence structure, *Journal of Banking and Finance*, 91, pp. 119–132.

De Grauwe, P. and Ji, Y. (2013) Self-fulfilling crises in the Eurozone: An empirical test, *Journal of International Money and Finance*, 34, pp. 15–36.

De Haan, L., Hessel, J. and van den End, J. W. (2014) Are European sovereign bonds fairly priced? The role of modelling uncertainty, *Journal of International Money and Finance*, 47, pp. 239–267.

De Jong, M. and Fabozzi, F. J. (2020) The market risk of corporate bonds, *Journal of Portfolio Management*, 46 (2), pp. 92–105.

De Jong, M. and Fabozzi, F.J. (2022) Emerging markets debt securities: A literature review, Journal of Portfolio Management 48(8), pp. 113–126.

DeMarzo, P., Vayanos, D. and Zwiebel, J. (2003) Persuasion bias, social influence, and unidimentional opinions, *Quarterly Journal of Economics*, 118, pp. 909–968.

Demetrius, L. and Manke, T. (2005) Robustness and network evolution – An entropic principle, *Physica A*, 346(3–4), pp. 682–696.

DeMiguel, V., Garlappi, L. and Uppal, R. (2009) Optimal versus naïve diversification: How inefficient is the 1/n portfolio strategy? *Review of Financial Studies*, 22(5), pp. 1915–1953.

di Battista, G., Eades, P., Tamassia, R., and Tollis, I. (1999) *Graph Drawing*. Englewood Cliffs: Prentice Hall.

Diebold, F. X. and Yilmaz, K. (2012) Better to give than to receive: Predictive directional measurement of volatility spillovers, *International Journal of Forecasting*, 28(1), pp. 57–66.

Diebold, F. X. and Yilmaz, K. (2014) On the network topology of variance decompositions: Measuring the connectedness of financial firms, *Journal of Econometrics*, 182(1), pp. 119–134.

Diebold, F. X. and Yilmaz, K. (2015) *Financial and Macroeconomic Connectedness: A Network Approach to Measurement and Monitoring*. New York: Oxford University Press.

Diebold, F. X. and Yilmaz, K. (2009) Measuring financial asset return and volatility spillovers, with application to global equity markets, *The Economic Journal*, 119(534), pp. 158–171.

Do Carmo, M. P. (2016) *Differential Geometry of Curves and Surfaces*. New York: Courier dover Publications.

Dorogovtsev, S. N. and Mendes, J .F. F. (2002) Evolution of networks, *Advances in Physics*, 51, pp. 1079–1187.

Duarte, A. M. and Rajagopal, R. (1999) A scenario-based approach to optimal currency overlay, *Journal of Portfolio Management*, 25(4), pp. 51–59.

Easley, D. and Kleinberg, J. (2010) *Networks, Crowds, and Markets: Reasoning about a Highly Connected World*. Cambridge: Cambridge University Press.

Edelsbrunner H. and Morozovy, D. (2014) *Persistent Homology: Theory and Practice*. European Mathematical Society Publishing House: Helsinki, pp. 31–50.

Edelsbrunner, H. D. and Mücke, E. P. (1994) Three-dimensional alpha shapes, *ACM Transactions on Graphics (TOG)*, 13(1), pp. 43–72.

Edelsbrunner, H., Letscher, D. and Zamorodian, A. (2002) A topological persistence and simplification, *Discrete & Computational Geometry*, 28, pp. 511–533.

Edelsbrunner H., Kirkpatrick, D. and Seidel, R. (1983) On the shape of a set of points in the plane, *IEEE Transactions on Information Theory*, 29(4), pp. 551–559.

Ehrmann, M., Fratzscher, M. and Rigobon, R. (2011) Stocks, bonds, money markets, and exchange rates: Measuring international financial transmission, *Journal of Applied Econometrics*, 26, pp. 948–974.

Elkamhi, R., Lee, J. S. H. and Salerno, M. (2024) Enhancing the inverse volatility portfolio through clustering, *Journal of Financial Data Science*, 6(1), pp. 43–60.

Elliot, M., Golub, B. and Jackson, M. O. (2014) Financial networks and contagion, *American Economic Review*, 104(10), pp. 3115–3153.

Erb, C. B., Harvey, C. R. and Viskanta, T. E. (1999) New perspectives on emerging market bonds, *Journal of Portfolio Management*, 25(2), pp. 83–92.

Erdos, P. and Renyi, A. (1959) On random graphs, *Publicationes Mathematicae*, 6, pp. 290–297.

Erdos, P. and Renyi, A. (1960) On the evolution of random graphs, *Publications of the Mathematical Institute of the Hungarian Academy of Sciences*, 5, pp. 17–61.

Erdos, P. and Renyi, A. (1961) On the strength of connectedness of a random graph, *Acta Mathematica Scientia Hungary*, 12, pp. 261–267.

Fabozzi, F. J., and Lopez de Prado, M. (2018) Being honest in backtest reporting: A template for disclosing multiple tests, *Journal of Portfolio Management*, 45(1), pp. 141–147.

Fagiolo, G. (2007) Clustering in complex directed networks, *Physics Review E*, 76: 026107.

Fama, E. F. (1990) Stock returns, expected returns, and real activity, *Journal of Finance*, 45, pp. 1089–1108.

Fama, E. F. and French, K. R. (1989) Business conditions and expected returns on stocks and bonds, *Journal of Financial Economics*, 25, pp. 23–49.

Fama, E. F. and French, K. R. (1992) The cross-section of expected stock returns, *Journal of Finance*, 47(2), pp. 427–465.

Fama, E. F. and French, K. R. (1993) Common risk factors in the returns on stocks and bonds, *Journal of Financial Economics*, 33(1), pp. 3–56.

Fama, E. F. and French, K. R. (2015) A five-factor asset pricing model, *Journal of Financial Economics*, 116, pp. 1–22.

Fatemi, Z. and Zheleva, E. (2023) Network experiment designs for inferring causal effects under interference, *Frontiers in Big Data*, 6:1128649, doi: 10.3389/fdata.2023.1128649.

Fath, B. D. and B. Hannon. (2007) Ecological network analysis: Network construction, *Ecological Modelling*, 208, pp. 49–55.

Fell, D. A. and Wagner, A. (2000) The small world of metabolism, *Nature Biotechnology*, 18, pp. 1121–1122.

Feragen, A., Lauze, F. and Hauberg, S. (2015) *Geodesic exponential kernels: When curvature and linearity conflict*, IEEE Conference on Computer Vision and Pattern Recognition (CVPR). Boston: IEEE, pp. 3032–3042.

Fernandez-Rodriguez, F. and Sosvilla-Rivero, S. (2020) Volatility transmission between stock and foreign exchange markets: A connectedness analysis, *Applied Economics*, 52(19), pp. 2096–2108.

Fiedler, M. (1973) Algebraic connectivity of graphs, *Czechoslovak Mathematical Journal*, 23, pp. 298–305.

Fiedor, P. (2014a) Networks in financial markets based on the mutual information rate, *Physical Review E*, 89, pp. 052801.

Fiedor, P. (2014b) Information-theoretic approach to lead-lag effect on financial markets, Working Paper, arXiv, pp. 1402.3820.

Fiedor, P. (2014c) Causal non-linear financial networks. Working Paper, arXiv, pp. 1407.5020.

Focardi, S. M. and Fabozzi, F. J. (2012) What's wrong with today's economics? The current crisis calls for an approach to economics rooted more on data than on rationality, *Journal of Portfolio Management*, 38(3), pp. 104–119.

Forbes, K. J. and Chinn, M. D. (2004) A decomposition of global linkages in financial markets over time, *Review of Economics and Statistics*, 86(3), pp. 705–722.

Forbes, K. J. and Rigobon, R. (2002) No contagion, only interdependence: Measuring stock market comovements, *Journal of Finance*, 57(5), pp. 2223–2261.

Frank, O. and Strauss, D. (1986) Markov graphs, *Journal of the American Statistical Association*, 81(395), pp. 832–842.

Frazzini, A. and Pedersen, L. (2014) Betting against beta, *Journal of Financial Economics*, 111(1), pp. 1–25.

Freeman, L .C. (1978) Centrality in social networks conceptual clarification, *Social Networks*, 1(3), pp. 215–239.

Freeman, L. C. (1979). Centrality in Social Networks I: Conceptual clarification, *Social Networks*, 1(3), pp. 215–239.

Freeman, L .C. (1996) Some antecedents of social network analysis, Connections 19(1), pp. 39–42.

Froot, K. A. and Thaler, R. H. (1990) Anomalies: Foreign exchange, *Journal of Economic Perspectives*, 4(3), pp. 179–192.

Fruchterman, T. M. J. and Reingold, E. M. (1991) Graph drawing by force-directed placement. *Software: Practice and Experience*, 21(11), pp. 1129–1164.

Fung, W. and Hsieh, D. (1997) Empirical characteristics of dynamic trading strategies: The case of hedge funds, *Review of Financial Studies*, 10(2), pp. 275–302.

Fung, W. and Hsieh, D. (2002) Asset-based style factors for hedge funds, *Financial Analysts Journal*, 58(5), pp. 16–27.

Fung, W. and Hsieh, D. (2003) The risk in hedge fund strategies: Alternative alphas and alternative betas, in J. Lars (ed.) *The New Generation of Risk Management for Hedge Funds and Private Equity Investments*. London: Euromoney Books, pp. 72–87.

Galaskiewicz, J. and Marsden, P. V. (1978) Interorganizational resource networks: Formal patterns of overlap, *Social Science Research*, 7, pp. 89–107.

Gale, D. M. and Kariv, S. (2007) Financial networks, *American Economic Review*, 97(2), pp. 99–103.

Garvey, G. and Madhavan, A. (2019) Reconstructing emerging and developed markets using hierarchical clustering, *Journal of Financial Data Science*, 4(1), pp. 84–102.

Gilbert, E. N. (1959) Random graphs, *Annals of Mathematical Statistics*, 30(4), pp. 1141–1144.

Girvan, M. and Newman, M. E. J. (2002) Community structure in social and biological networks, *Proceedings of the National Academy of Sciences of the United States of America*, 99 (12), pp. 8271–8276.

Glasserman, P. and Young, P. H. (2015) How likely is contagion in financial networks? *Journal of Banking and Finance*, 50, pp. 383–399.

Goldstein, D. G. and Taleb, N. N. (2007) We don't quite know what we are talking about, *Journal of Portfolio Management*, 33 (4), pp. 84–86.

Granovetter, M. S. (1973) The strength of weak ties, *The American Journal of Sociology*, 78, pp. 1360–1380.

Gregory, A. W., Head, A .C. and Reynauld, J. (1997) Measuring world business cycles, *International Economic Review*, 38, pp. 677–701.

Grossman, S. and Stiglitz, J. (1980) On the impossibility of informationally efficient markets, *American Economic Review*, 70(3), pp. 393–408.

Hahn, P. R., Murray, J. S., and Carvalho, C. M. (2020) Bayesian regression tree models for causal inference: Regularization, confounding, and heterogeneous effects, *Bayesian Analysis*, 15(3), pp.1–33.

Haken, H. (1978) Synergetics. An introduction. Nonequilibrium phase transitions and self-organization in physics, chemistry, and biology, *Synergetics*, 1. Berlin: Springer.

Haldane, A. G. and May, R .M. (2009) Systemic risk in banking ecosystems, *Nature*, 469, pp. 451–455.

Hamao, Y., Masulis, R. W. and Ng, V. (1990) Correlations in price changes and volatility across international stock markets, *Review of Financial Studies*, 3(2), pp. 281–307.

Hamming, R. W. (1950) Error detecting and error correcting codes, *Bell System Technical Journal*, 29(2), pp.147–160.

Handcock, M. S. (2003) Assessing degeneracy in statistical models of social networks, *Journal of the American Statistical Association*, 76, pp. 33–50

Hanson, S., Kashyap, A. and Stein, J. (2011) A macro-prudential approach to financial regulation, *Journal of Economic Perspectives*, 25(1), pp. 3–28.

Harary, F. (1953) On the notion of balance of a signed graph, *Michigan Mathematical Journal*, 2, pp. 143–146.

Hage, P., and Harary, F. (1995) Eccentricity and centrality in networks, *Social Networks*, 17(1), pp. 57–63.

Harris, J. K. (2013) *An Introduction to Exponential Random Graph Modeling.* Thousand Oaks: SAGE Publications Inc.

Harvey, C. R. and Liu, Y. (2014) Evaluating trading strategies, *Journal of Portfolio Management*, 40(5), pp. 110–118.

Harvey, C. R., Liu, Y. and Zhu, H. (2016) ...and the cross-section of expected returns, *Review of Financial Studies*, 29(1), pp. 5–68.

Harvey, C. R. and Liu, Y. (2015) Backtesting, *Journal of Portfolio Management*, 42(1), pp. 13–28.

Heckel, T., Amghar, Z., Haik, I, Laplénie, O. and de Carvalho, R. L. (2020) Factor investing in corporate bond markets: Enhancing efficacy through diversification and purification! *Journal of Fixed Income*, 29(3), pp. 6–21.

Hoff, P. D., Raftery, A. E. and Handcock, M. S. (2002) Latent space approaches to social network analysis, *Journal of the American Statistical Association*, 97(460), pp. 1090–1098.

Hoff, P. (2007) Modeling homophily and stochastic equivalence in symmetric relational data, *Proceedings of the 20th International Conference on Neural Information Processing Systems*, pp. 657–664.

Holland, J. (2012) *Signals and Boundaries: Building Blocks for Complex Adaptive Systems.* Cambridge: The MIT Press.

Hoover, D. N. (1982) Low-column exchangeability and a generalized model for probability, In *Exchangeability in Probability and Statistics*. North Holland: Amsterdam, pp. 281–291

Horvitz, D. G. and Thompson, D. J. (1952). A generalization of sampling without replacement from a finite universe, *Journal American Statistical Association*, 47, pp. 663–685.

Howell, M. J. (2018) What does the yield-curve slope really tell us? *Journal of Fixed Income*, 27(4), pp. 22–33.

Hudgens, M. and M. Halloran (2008) Toward causal inference with interference, *Journal of the American Statistical Association*, 103(482), pp. 832–842.

Hunter, D .R., Goodreau, S. M. and Handcock, M. S. (2008) Goodness of fit of social network models, *Journal of the American Statistical Association*, 103(481), pp. 248–258.

Hussain Shahzad, S. J., Bouri, E., Arreola-Hernandez, J., Roubaud, D., & Bekiros, S. (2019). Spillover across Eurozone credit market sectors and determinants, *Applied Economics*, 51(59), pp. 6333–6349.

Huxham, M., Beaney, S. and Raffaelli, D. (1996) Do parasites reduce the chances of triangulation in a real food web? *Oikos*, 76, pp. 284–300.

Ilmanen, A. (2011) *Expected Returns: An Investor's Guide to Harvesting Market Rewards.* New Jersey: Wiley.

Ilmanen, A., Israel, R., Lee, R., Moskowitz, T. J. and Thapar, A. (2021) How do factor premia vary over time? A century of evidence, *Journal of Investment Management*, 19(4), pp. 15–57.

Ito, T., Chiba, T. Ozawa, R., Yoshida, M., Hattori, M. and Sakaki, Y. (2001) A comprehensive two-hybrid analysis to explore the yeast protein interactome, *Proceedings of the National Academy of Sciences of the United States of America*, 98, pp. 4569–4574.

Jagadeesh, N. and Titman, S. (1993) Returns to buying winners and selling losers: Implications for stock market efficiency, *Journal of Finance*, 48, pp. 65–91.

James, G., Witten, D. Hastie, T. and Tibshirani, R. (2013) *An Introduction to Statistical Learning: With Applications in R.* New York: Springer Science+Business Media.

Jensen, F. V. (2001). Causal and Bayesian networks, in *Bayesian Networks and Decision Graphs. Statistics for Engineering and Information Science*. Springer, New York.

Jeong, H. R., Oltvai, Z. N. and Barabasi, A.-L. (2000) The large-scale organization of metabolic networks, *Nature*, 407, pp. 651–654.

Jeong, H., Mason, S. P., Barabási, A. L. and Oltvai, Z. N. (2001) Lethality and centrality in protein networks, *Nature*, 411, pp. 41–42.

Johnson, S. C. (1967) Hierarchical clustering schemes, *Psychometrica*, 2, pp. 241–254.

Kalyagin, A. V., Pardalos, P. M. and Rassias, T. M. (2014) *Network Models in Economics and Finance*. New York: Springer.

Kamada, T. and Kawai, S. (1989) An algorithm for drawing general undirected graphs, *Information Processing Letters*, 31(1), pp. 7–15.

Kanas, A. (2025) Pricing factors and causal networks for U.S. industry portfolios, *Journal of Portfolio Management*, 51.

Kara, G., Tian, M. H. and Yellen, M. (2015) Taxonomy of studies on interconnectedness, *FEDS Notes*. Washington: Board of Governors of the Federal Reserve System. Available at: https, pp.//doi.org/10.17016/2380-7172.1569 (Accessed:31 July 2015).

Kashyap, A., Berner, R. and Goodhart, C. (2011) The macro-prudential toolkit, *IMF Economic Review*, 59, pp. 145–161.

Katz, L. (1953) A new status index derived from sociometric analysis, *Psychometrika*, 18, pp. 39–43.

Kauffman, S. A. (1993) *The Origins of Order*. Oxford: Oxford University Press.

Kaufmann, M. and Wagner, D. (1998) *Drawing Graphs*. Berlin: Springer.

Kaya, H. (2015) Eccentricity in asset management, *The Journal of Network Theory in Finance*, 1(3), pp. 1–32.

Kazemi, H., Black, K. H. and Chambers, R. D. (2016) *Alternative Investments: CAIA Level II, Third edition*. Hoboken: John Wiley & Sons.

Kelathaya, U., Bapat, R. B. and Karantha, M. P. (2023) Generalized inverses in graph theory, *AKCE International Journal of Graphs and Combinatorics*, 20(2), pp. 108–114.

Khandani, A. E. and Lo, A. (2011) What happened to the quants in August 2007? Evidence from factors and transactions data, *Journal of Financial Markets*, 14(1), pp. 1–46.

King, M. A, and Wadhwani, S. (1990) Transmission of volatility between stock markets, *Review of Financial Studies*, 3(1), pp. 5–33.

Kinlaw, W., Kritzman, M. and Turkington, D. (2012) Toward determining systemic importance, *The Journal of Portfolio Management*, 38(4), pp. 100–111.

Kleinberg, J. and Lawrence, S. (2001) The structure of the web, *Science*, 294, pp. 1849–1850.

Klir, G. (2006) *Uncertainty and Information. Foundations of Generalized Information Theory*. Hooboken: Wiley Interscience.

Kickerbocker, D. (2023) *Network Science with Python: Explore the Networks Around Us Using Network Science, Social Network Analysis, and Machine Learning*. Birmingham, UK: Packt Publishing.

Koijen, R., Moskowitz, T.J., Pedersen, L. and Vrugt, E. (2018) Carry, *Journal of Financial Economics*, 127(2), pp. 197–225.

Kolaczyk, E. D. (2017). *Topics at the Frontier of Statistics and Network Analysis: (Re)Visiting the Foundations*. Cambridge: Cambridge University Press.

Kolaczyk, E. D. and Csardi, G. (2020) *Statistical Analysis of Network Data with R, Second Edition*. New York: Springer.

König, F. (2014) Reciprocal social influence on investment decisions: Behavioral evidence from a group of mutual fund managers, *Financial Markets and Portfolio Management*, 28(3), pp. 233–262.

Konstantinov, G. (2014) Active currency management of international bond portfolios, *Financial Markets and Portfolio Management*, 28 (1), pp. 63–94.

Konstantinov, G. (2017) Currency crowdedness generated by global bond funds, *Journal of Portfolio Management*, 43(2), pp. 123–135.

Konstantinov, G. S. (2021) What portfolio in Europe makes sense? *Journal of Portfolio Management*, 47(7): 79–94.

Konstantinov, G. S. (2023) Errors and challenges associated with investing in EMU government bonds, *Journal of Portfolio Management*, 49(6), pp. 132–143.

Konstantinov, G. (2024) A network look at risk management. Working Paper. Frankfurt, Germany.

Konstantinov, G. S. (2022a) Emerging market bonds: Expected returns and currency impact, *Journal of Portfolio Management*, 48(8), pp. 139–158.

Konstantinov, G. S. (2022b) Hedge fund networks, *Journal of Alternative Investments*, 25(2), pp. 14–32.

Konstantinov, G. S., Fabozzi, F. J. and Simonian, J. (2023) *Quantitative Global Bond Portfolio Management*. Singapore: World Scientific Press.

Konstantinov, G. S. and Fabozzi, F. J. (2022) Portfolio volatility spillover, *International Journal of Theoretical and Applied Finance*, 25(4/5): 2250019, doi: 10.1142/S0219024922500194.

Konstantinov, G. S. and Fabozzi, F. J. (2021) Carry strategies and the US dollar risk of US and global bonds, *Journal of Fixed Income*, 30(3), pp. 26–46.

Konstantinov, G. S. and Fabozzi, F. J. (2021) Towers a dead end? EMU bond market exposure and manager performance, *Journal of International Money and Finance*, 116:102433, doi: 10.1016/j.jimonfin.2021.102433.

Konstantinov, G. S. and Simonian, J. (2020) A network approach to analyzing hedge fund connectivity, *Journal of Financial Data Science*, 2(3), pp. 55–72.

Konstantinov, G. S., Aldridge, I. and Kazemi, H. (2023) Financial networks and portfolio management, *Journal of Portfolio Management*, 49(9), pp. 190–216.

Konstantinov, G., Chorus, A. and Rebmann, J. (2020) A network and machine learning approach to factor, asset, and blended allocation, *Journal of Portfolio Management*, 46(6), pp. 54–71.

Konstantinov, G. and Rebmann, J. (2019) From risk factors to networks: A case study on interconnectedness using currency funds, *Journal of Financial Data Science*, 3(1), pp. 108–123.

Konstantinov, G, and Rebmann, J. (2020) Different in nature, common in style: View commonality of single hedge funds and funds of hedge funds, *Journal of Alternative Investments*, 23(2), pp. 49–66.

Konstantinov, G. and Rusev, M. (2020) The bond-equity fund relation using the Fama–French–Carhart factors: A practical network approach, *Journal of Financial Data Science*, 2(1), pp. 22–44.

Krapivsky, P. L. and Redner, S. (2002) Finiteness and fluctuations in growing networks, *Journal of Physics A*, 35, pp. 9517–9534.

Krautz, S. and Fuerst, F. (2015) Size signals success: Evidence from real estate private equity, *Journal of Portfolio Management*, 41(6), pp. 73–81.

Kritzman, M. (2021) The role of factors in asset allocation, *Journal of Portfolio Management*, 47(5), pp. 58–64.

Kritzman, M. and Li, Y. (2010) Skills, financial turbulence, and risk management, *Financial Analysts Journal*, 66(5), pp. 30–41.

Laloux, L., Bouchaud, J.-P. and Potters, M. (1999) Noise dressing of financial correlation matrices, *Physical Review Letters*, 83(7), p. 1467.

Lance, G. and Williams, W. T. (1967) A general theory of classification sorting strategies: Hierarchical systems, *The Computer Journal*, 9(4), pp. 373–380.

Laudy, O, Denev, A., and Ginsberg, A. (2022) Building probabilistic causal models using collective intelligence, *Journal of Financial Data Science*, 4(2) pp. 83–109.

Laughlin, R. (2005) *A Different Universe: Reinventing Physics from the Bottom Down*. New York: Basic Books.

Lee, L-F., Liu, X. and Lin, X. (2010) Specification and estimation of social interaction models with network structures, *Econometrics Journal*, 13(2), pp. 145–176.

Lefcheck, J. S. (2015) piecewiseSEM: Piecewise structural equation modelling in R for ecology, evolution, and systematics, *Methods in Ecology and Evolution*, 7(5), pp. 573–579.

Leibowitz, M. L. (2011) Alpha orbits, *Financial Analysts Journal*, 67(4), pp. 6–7.

Leung, M. P. (2016) Treatment and spillover effects under network interference, *Review of Economics and Statistics*, 102(2), pp. 1–42.

Levy-Carciente, S., Kenett, D. Y., Avakian, A., Stanley, E. H., and Havlin, S. (2015) Dynamical macroprudential stress testing using network theory, *Journal of Banking and Finance*, 59, pp. 164–181.

Li, Y. and Kazemi, H. (2007) Conditional properties of hedge funds: Evidence from daily returns, *European Financial Management*, 13(2), pp. 211–238.

Lian, C. L. (2022) Evolution of emerging markets debt investing, *Journal of Portfolio Management*, 48(8), pp. 109–112.

Liljeros, F., Edling, C. and Amaral, L. (2001) The web of human sexual contacts, *Nature*, 411, pp. 907–908.

Liu, L. and M. Hudgens (2014) Large sample randomization inference of causal effects in the presence of interference, *Journal of the American Statistical Association*, 109(505), pp. 288–301.

Liu, P., and W-P. Huang (2008) Modelling international sovereign risk information spillovers: A multilayer network approach, *The Nort American Journal of Economics and Finance*, 63, 101794

Lo, A. W. (2010) *Hedge Funds: An Analytic Perspective (New Edition). Advances in Financial Engineering.* New Jersey: Princeton University Press.

Lo, A. W. (2017) *Adaptive Markets: Financial Evolution at the Speed of Thought.* Princeton, New Jersey: Princeton University Press.

Lo, A. W. (2016) What is an index? *Journal of Portfolio Management*, 42(2), pp. 21–36.

Lo, A. W. and Stein, R. M. (2016) Tree networks and systemic risk, *Journal of Alternative Investments*, 18(4), pp. 52–67.

Loistl, O. and Landes T. (eds) (1989) *The Dynamic Pricing of Financial Assets.* Hamburg: McGraw-Hill.

Loistl, O. and Konstantinov, G. (2020) Interactions and interconnectedness shape financial market research, *Journal of Financial Data Science*, 2(2), pp. 51–63.

López de Prado, M. (2016) Building diversified portfolios that outperform out of sample, *Journal of Portfolio Management*, 42(4), pp. 59–69.

López de Prado, M. (2018) The 10 reasons most machine learning funds fail, *Journal of Portfolio Management*, 44(5), pp. 120–133.

López de Prado, M. (2019) A data science solution to the multiple-testing crisis in financial research, *Journal of Financial Data Science*, 1(1), pp. 99–110.

López de Prado, M. (2023) Where are the factors in factor investing? *Journal of Portfolio Management*, 49(5), pp.6–20.

López de Prado, M. and Fabozzi, F. J. (2017) Who needs Newtonian finance? *Journal of Portfolio Management*, 44(1), pp.1–3.

Lorrain, F. and White, H. C. (1971) Structural equivalence of individuals in social networks, *Journal of Mathematical Sociology*, 1, pp. 49–80.

Lott, J. and Villani, C. (2009) Ricci curvature for metric-measure spaces via optimal transport, *Annals of Mathematics*, 169, pp. 903–991.

Luke, D. A. (2015) *A User's Guide to Network Analysis in R.* New York: Springer.

Lütkepohl, H. (2005) *New Introduction to Multiple Time Series Analysis.* New York: Springer.

Machalanobis, P. C. (1936) On the generalized distance in statistics, *Proc. Natl. Inst. Sci. India*, 2(1), pp. 49–55.

Mackay, C. (2003). *Extraordinary Popular Delusions and the Madness of Crowds*, Hampshire, UK: Harriman House Classics.

Mandelbrot, B. B. and Hudson, R. L. (2004) *The (Mis)behaviour of Markets.* New York: Basic Books.

Mantegna, R. N. (1999) Hierarchical structure in financial markets, *European Physical Journal B: Condensed Matter and Complex Systems*, 11(1), pp. 60–70.

Mariolis, P. (1975) Interlocking directorates and control of corporations: The theory of bank control, *Social Science Quarterly*, 56, pp. 425–439.

Markowitz, H. 1952. Portfolio selection, *Journal of Finance*, 7(1), pp.77–91.

Marmer, H. S. (2015) Fire! Fire! Is U.S. Low volatility a crowded trade? *Journal of Investing*, 24(3), pp. 17–37.

Martellini, L. and Milhau, V. (2018) Proverbial baskets are uncorrelated risk factors! A factor-based framework for measuring and managing diversification in multi-asset investment solutions, *Journal of Portfolio Management*, 44(2), pp. 8–22.

Martens, M., Beekhuizen, P., Duyvesteyn, J. and Zomerdijk, C. (2019) Carry investing on the yield curve, *Financial Analysts Journal*, 75 (4), pp. 51–63.

Martin, S., Brown, W., Klavans, R. and Boyack, K. (2008) DrL: Distributed Recursive (graph) Layout report, Sandia Tech. Rep. 2936.

Maslov, S. and Sneppen, K. (2002) Specificity and stability in topology of protein networks, *Science*, 296, pp. 910–913.

Mayoral, S., Moreno, D. and Zareei, A. (2022) Using a hedging network to minimize portfolio risk, *Finance Research Letters*, 44: 102044

Mendelson, B. (1990) *Introduction to Topology, Third Edition.* New York: Dover Publications Inc.

Merton, R. K. (1968) The Matthew effect in science, *Science*, 159, pp. 56–63.

Merton, R. C. (1974) On the pricing of corporate debt: The risk structure of interest rates, *Journal of Finance*, 29(2), pp. 449–470.

Merton, R. C., Billio, M., Getmansky, M., Gray, M. D., Lo, A. W. and Pelizzon, L. (2013) On a new approach for analyzing and managing microfinancial risks, *Financial Analysts Journal*, 69(2), pp. 22–33.

Meucci, A. (2009) Managing diversification, *Risk*, 22(5), pp. 74–79.

Mezzeti, A., Maillart, D., David, D. P., Maillart, T., and Mermoud, A. (2024). TechRank, *Journal of Alternative Investments*, 26(3), pp. 57–83.

Milgram, S. (1967) The small world problem, *Psychology Today*, 2, pp. 60–67.

Mizruchi, M. S. (1982) *The American Corporate Network 1904–1974*. New York: Sage.

Molyboga, M. (2020) A modified hierarchical risk parity framework for portfolio management, *Journal of Financial Data Science*, 2(3), pp. 128–139.

Monk, A., Prins, M. and Rook, D. (2019) Rethinking alternative data in institutional investment, *Journal of Financial Data Science*, 1(1), pp. 14–31.

Morales, L. and Andreosso-O'Callaghan, B. (2014) The global financial crisis: World market or regional contagion effects? *International Review of Economics and Finance*, 29, pp. 108–131.

Morris, M., Handcock, M. S. and Hunter, D. R. (2008) Specification of exponential-family random graph models, *Journal of Statistical Software*, 24(4), pp. 1–24.

Moskowitz, T., Ooi, Y. H. and Pedersen, L. (2012) Time series momentum, *Journal of Financial Economics*, 104(2), pp. 228–250.

Nagarajan, R., Scutari, M. and Lebre, S. (2013) *Bayesian Networks in R: With Applications in Systems Biology*. New York: Springer.

Newman, M. E. J. (2000) Models of the small world, *Journal of Statistical Physics*, 101, pp. 819–841.

Newman, M. E. J. (2001) The structure of scientific collaboration networks, *Proceedings of the National Academy of Sciences of the United States of America*, 98, pp. 404–409.

Newman, M. E. J. (2002a) Assortative mixing in networks, Physical Review Letters 89,20870, doi: 10.1103/PhysRevLett.89.208701.

Newman, M. E. J. (2002b) The structure and function of networks, *Computer Physics Communications*, 147, pp. 40–45.

Newman, M. E. J. (2003) Mixing patterns in networks, *Physical Review E*, 67:026126, doi: 10.1103/PhysRevE.67.026126.

Newman, M. E. J. (2006): Finding community structure using the eigenvectors of matrices, *Physical Review E*, 74:036104, doi: 10.1103/PhysRevE.74.036104.

Newman, M. E. J. (2010) *Networks: An Introduction*. Oxford: Oxford University Press.

Newman, M. E. J., Barabási, A-L. and Watts, D. J. (2006) *The Structure and Dynamics of Networks*. New Jersey: Princeton University Press.

Newman, M. E. J., Strogatz, S. H. and Watts, D. J. (2001) Random graphs with arbitrary degree distributions and their applications, *Physical Review E*, 64:026118, doi: 10.1103/PhysRevE.64.026118.

Nofsinger, J. and Sias, R. (1999) Herding and feedback trading by institutional and individual investors, *Journal of Finance*, 54(6), pp. 2263–2295.

Nowicki, K. and Snijders, T. (2001) Estimation and prediction for stochastic block structures. *Journal of the American Statistical Association*, 96(455), pp. 2077–1087.

Nucera, F., and G. Valente (2013) Carry trades and the performance of currency hedge funds, *Journal of International Money and Finance*, 33, pp. 407–425.

Nystrup, P., Hansen, B. W., Larsen, H. O., Madsen, H., and Lindström, E. (2018) Dynamic allocation or diversification: A regime-based approach to multiple assets, *Journal of Portfolio Management*, 44(2), pp. 62–73.

O'Shea, D. (2007) *The Poincare Conjecture: In Search of the Shape of the Universe*. New York: Walker Publishing Company, Ltd.

Ollivier, Y. (2007) Ricci curvature of metric spaces, *Compte Rendus Mathematique*, 345 (11), pp. 643–646.

Ollivier, Y. (2009) Ricci curvature of Markov chains on metric spaces, *Journal of Functional Analysis*, 256(3), pp. 810–864.

Onnela, J-P., Chakraborti, A., Kaski, K., Kertesz, V. J. and Kanto, A. (2003) Dynamics of market correlations: Taxonomy and portfolio analysis, *Physical Review E*, 68:056110, doi: 10.1103/PhysRevE.68.056110.

Otter, N., Porter, M. A. and Tillmann, U. (2017) A roadmap for the computation of persistent homology, *EPJ Data Science*, 6, pp. 17.

Papenbrock, J. and Schwendner, P. (2015) Handling risk-on/risk-off dynamics with correlation regimes and correlation networks, *Financial Markets and Portfolio Management*, 29(2), pp. 125–148.

Paserman, M. (2017) Comovement or safe haven? The effect of corruption on the market risk of sovereign bonds of emerging economies during financial crises, *Journal of International Money and Finance*, 76, pp. 106–132.

Pearl, J. (2000) *Causality: Models, Reasoning, and Inference*. New York: Cambridge University Press.

Pearl, J. (2009) Causal inference in statistics: An overview, *Statistics Surveys*, 3, pp. 96–146

Peralta, G. and Zareei, A. (2016) A network approach to portfolio selection, *Journal of Empirical Finance*, 38, pp. 158–180.

Perea, J. A. and Harer, J. (2015) Sliding windows and persistence: An application of topological methods to signal analysis, *Foundation of Computational Mathematics*, 15 (3): 799–838.

Pesaran, H. H. and Shin, Y. (1998) Generalized impulse response analysis in linear multivariate models, *Economic Letters*, 58, pp. 17–29.

Pezier, J. and White, A. (2008) The relative merits of alternative investments in passive portfolios, *Journal of Alternative Investments*, 10 (4), pp. 37–49.

Pfaff, B. (2008) VAR, SVAR, and SVEC Models: Implementation within R package VARS, *Journal of Statistical Software*, 27 (4), pp. 1–32.

Phoa, W. (2013) Portfolio concentration and the geometry of co-movement, *Journal of Portfolio Management*, 39 (4), pp. 142–151.

Poddig, T. and Unger, A. (2012) On the robustness of risk-based asset allocation, *Financial Markets and Portfolio Management*, 26(3), pp. 369–402.

Pojarliev, M. (2009) Trading the forward rate puzzle, *Journal of Alternative Investments*, 11(3), pp. 26–36.

Pojarliev, M. and Levich, R. M. (2008) Do professional currency managers beat the benchmark? *Financial Analysts Journal*, 64(5), pp. 18–32.

Pojarliev, M. and Levich, R. M. (2011) Detecting crowded trades in currency funds, *Financial Analysts Journal*, 67(1), pp. 26–39.

Pojarliev, M. and Levich, R. M. (2012) *A New Look at Currency Investing*. New York: Research Foundation of CFA Institute.

Pons, P. and Latapy, M. (2005) *Computing communities in large networks using random walks*, in Yolum, P., Güngör, T., Gürgen, F., and Özturan, C. (eds.) *Computer and Information Sciences – ISCIS 2005. ISCIS 2005. Lecture Notes in Computer Science*, 3733. Berlin, Heidelberg: Springer.

Pozzi F., Matteo, T. Di and Aste, T. (2013) Spread of risk across financial markets: Better to invest in the peripheries, *Scientific Reports*, 3, p. 1665.

Price, D. J. de S. (1965) Networks of scientific papers, *Science*, 149, pp. 510–515.

Prigogine, I. V. (1997) *End of Certainty: Time, Chaos, and the New Laws of Nature*. Washington, D.C.: Free Press.

Prim. R. C. (1957) Shortest connection networks and some generalizations, *Bell System Technical Journal*, 37, pp. 1389–1401.

Provost, F. and Fawcett, T. (2013) *Data Science for Business*. California: O'Reilly Media Inc.

Rabemananjara, R., and Zakoian, J. M. (1993) Threshold arch models and asymmetries in volatility, *Journal of Applied Econometrics*, 8(1), pp. 31–49.

Rachev, S. T. (1991) *Probability Metrics and the Stability of Stochastic Models*. New York: Wiley.

Rachev, S. T. and Rüschendorf, L. (1998) *Mass Transportation Problems*. New York: Springer-Verlag.

Raddant, M. and Kenett, D. Y. (2021) Interconnectedness in the global financial market, *Journal of International Money and Finance*, 110:102280, doi: 10.1016/j.jimonfin.2020.102280.

Raffinot, T. (2018) Hierarchical clustering-based asset allocation, *Journal of Portfolio Management*, 44(2), pp. 89–99.

Raghavan, U. N., Albert, R. and Kumara, S. (2007) Near linear time algorithm to detect community structures in large-scale networks, *Physical Review E*, 76:036106, doi: 10.1103/PhysRevE.76.036106.

Rapoport, A. (1957) Contribution to the theory of random and biased nets, *Bulletin of Mathematical Biophysics*, 19, pp. 257–277.

Rapoport, A. (1968) Cycle distribution in random nets, *Bulletin of Mathematical Biophysics*, 10, pp. 145–157.

Rebonato, R. and Denev, A. (2013) *Portfolio Management Under Stress: A Bayesian-Net Approach to Coherent Asset Allocation*. Cambridge: Cambridge University Press.

Redner, S. (1998) How popular is your paper? An empirical study of the citation distribution, *European Physical Journal B*, 4, pp. 131–134.

Reichardt, J. and Bornholdt, S. (2006) Statistical mechanics of community detection, *Physical Review E*, 74 (1):016110, doi: 10.1103/PhysRevE.74.016110.

Ricca, F. and Scozzari, A. (2024) Portfolio optimization through a network approach: Network assortative mixing and portfolio diversification, *European Journal of Operational Research*, 312(2), pp. 700–717.

Rigobon, R. (2003) On the measurement of the international propagation of shocks: Is the transmission stable? *Journal of International Economics*, 61(2), pp. 261–283.

Robins, G. L. and Morris, M. (2007) Advances in exponential random graph (p*) models, *Social Networks*, 29(2), pp. 169–172.

Robins, G. L., Woolcock, J. and Pattison, P. (2005) Small and other worlds: Global network structures from local processes, *American Journal of Sociology*, 110, pp. 894–936.

Robins, G. L., Snijders, T., Wang, T., Handcock, P. M. and Pattison, P. (2007) Recent developments in exponential random graph (p*) models for social networks, *Social Networks*, 29, pp. 192–215.

Rosenbaum, P. (1999) Reduced sensitivity to hidden bias at upper quantiles in observational studies with dilated treatment effects, *Biometrics*, 5(2), pp. 560–564.

Ross, S. A. (1976) The arbitrage theory of capital asset pricing, *Journal of Economic Theory*, 13(3), pp. 341–360.

Rosvall, M., Axelsson, D. and Bergstrom, C. T. (2009) The map equation, *European Physical Journal Special Topics*, 178, pp. 13–23.

Sabidussi, G. (1966) The centrality index of a graph, *Psychometrika*, 31(4), pp. 581–603.

Sais, R., Turtle, H. J. and Zykaj, B. (2018) Reconsidering hedge fund contagion. *Journal of Alternative Investments*, 21(1), pp. 27–38.

Sandhu, R. S., Georgiou, T. T. and Tannenbaum. A. R. (2016) Ricci curvature: An economic indicator for market fragility and systemic risk, *Science Advances*, 2(5), pp. e1501495, doi: 10.1126/sciadv.1501495.

Schwarz, G. E. (1978) Estimating the dimension of a model, *Annals of Statistics*, 6(2), pp. 461–464.

Schwendner, P., Papenbrock, J., Jaeger, M. and S. Krügel. (2021) Adaptive seriational risk parity and other extensions for heuristic portfolio construction using machine learning and graph theory, *Journal of Financial Data Science*, 3(4), pp. 65–83.

Schularick, M., and Taylor, A. M.(2012) Credit booms gone bust: Monetary policy, leverage cycles, and financial crises, 1870–2008, *American Economic Review*, 102(2), pp. 1021–1061.

Scutari M (2010). Learning Bayesian networks with the bnlearn R package, *Journal of Statistical Software*, 35(3):1–22.

Scutari M (2017). Bayesian network constraint-based structure learning algorithms: Parallel and optimized implementations in the bnlearn R package, *Journal of Statistical Software*, 77(2), 1–20.

Seglen, P. O. (1992) The skewness of science, *Journal of the American Society for Information Science*, 43(9), pp. 628–638.

Shannon, C. E. (1948) A mathematical theory of communication, *Bell System Technical Journal*, 27, pp. 79–423.

Sharpe, W. (1992) Asset allocation: Management style and performance measurement, *Journal of Portfolio Management*, 18(2), pp. 7–19.

Shearer, C. (2000) The CRISP-DM model: The new blueprint for data mining, Journal of Data Warehousing, 5, pp. 13–22.

Shimada, Y., Hirata, Y., Ikeguchi, T. and Aihara, K. (2016) Graph distance for complex networks, *Scientific Reports*, 6, p. 34944.

Simon, H. A. (1955) On a class of skew distribution functions, *Biometrika*, 42, pp. 425–440.

Simon, H. A. (1962) The architecture of complexity, *Proceedings of the American Philosophical Society*, 106, pp. 467–482.

Simonian, J. (2021) Geopolitical risk in investment research: Allies, adversaries, and algorithms, *Journal of Portfolio Management*, 47(9), pp. 92–109.

Simonian, J. (2024) *Investment Model Validation: A Guide for Practitioners*. New York: CFA Institute Research Foundation.

Snijders. T. A. B. (2002) Markov chain Monte Carlo estimation of exponential random graph models, *Journal of Social Structure*, 3(2), pp. 1–40.

Snijders. T. A. B., Pattison, P., Robins, G.L. and Handcock, M. (2006) New specifications for exponential random graph models, *Sociological Methodology*, 36(1), pp. 99–153.

Sole, R. V. and Pastor-Satorras, R. (2003) Complex networks in genomics and proteomics, in S. Bornholdt and H. G. Schuster (eds.) *Handbook of Graphs and Networks*. Berlin: Wiley-VCH, pp. 145–167.

Soramäki, K. R. J. Glass, and W. E. Beyeler. (2006) The topology of interbank payment flows, *Physica A*, 379(1), pp. 317–333.

Strogatz, S. H. (2001) Exploring complex networks, *Nature*, 410, pp. 268–276.

Suhonen, A. and Vatanen, K. (2024) Do alternative risk premia diversify? New evidence from the post-pandemic era, *Journal of Portfolio Management*, 50(5), pp. 218–236.

Surowiecki, J. (2005) *The Wisdom of Crowds*: Peterborough, UK: Anchor Books.

Taleb, N. N. (1997) *Dynamic Hedging*. Hoboken, New Jersey: John Wiley & Sons.

Tantardini, T., Ieva, F., Tajoli, L. and Piccardi, C. (2019) Comparing methods for comparing networks, *Scientific Reports*, 9, p. 17557.

Thornton, D. L. and G. Valente (2012). Out-of-Sample predictions of bond excess returns with forward rates: An asset-allocation perspective, *Review of Financial Studies*, 25, pp. 3141–3168.

Tiwari, A. K., Gupta, R. and Wohar, M. (2018) Volatility spillovers across global asset classes: Evidence from time and frequency domains, *Quarterly Review of Economics and Finance*, 70, pp. 194–202.

Tobin, J. (1958) Liquidity preference as behavior towards risk, *The Review of Economic Studies*, 25(2) pp. 65–86.

Tse, C. K., Liu, J., and Lau, F. C. M. (2010) A network perspective of the stock market, Journal of Empirical Finance, 17(4), pp. 659–667.

Tumminello M., Di Matteo, T., Aste, T. and Mantegna, R. N. (2006) Correlation based networks of equity returns sampled at different time horizons, *European Physics Journal B*, 55, pp. 209–217.

Umar, Z., Zaremba, A., Umutlu, M. and Mercik, A. (2024) Interaction effects in the cross-section of country and industry returns, *Journal of Banking and Finance*, 165, p. 107200.

Vandewalle, N., Brisbois, F. and Tordoir, X. (2001) Nonrandom topology of stock markets, *Quantitative Finance*, 1(3), pp. 372–374.

Výrost, T., Lyócsa, Š. and Baumöhl, E. (2019) Network-based asset allocation strategies, *The North American Journal of Economics and Finance*, 47, pp. 516–536.

Wang, G.-J., Huai, H., Zhu, Y., Xie, C. and Uddin, G. S. (2024) Portfolio optimization based on network centralities: Which centrality is better for asset selection during global crises? *Journal of Management Science and Engineering*, 9, pp. 348–375.

Wang, Z. (2010) Dynamics and causality in industry-specific volatility, *Journal of Banking and Finance*, 34(7), pp. 1688–1699.

Wasserman, S. and Faust, K. (1994) *Social Network Analysis: Methods and Applications*. New York: Cambridge University Press.

Watts, D. J. (1999) Networks, dynamics, and the small world phenomenon, *American Journal of Sociology*, 105, pp. 493–592.

Watts, D. J. (1999) *Small Worlds*. Princeton: Princeton University Press.

Watts, D. J. (2003) *Six Degrees: The Science of a Connected Age*. New York: Norton.

Watts, D. J., and Strogatz, S. H. (1998) Collective dynamics of "small-world" networks, *Nature*, 393, pp. 409–410.

Weaver, W. (1948) Science and complexity, *American Scientist*, 36, pp. 536–544.

Yang, S., Keller, F. B., and Zheng, L. (2016) *Social Network Analysis: Methods and Examples*. New York: SAGE Publications, Inc.

Yang, Z., Algesheimer, R. and Tessone, C. J. (2016) A comparative analysis of community detection algorithms on artificial networks, *Scientific Reports*, 6:30750, doi: 10.1038/srep30750.

Ye, D., Yang, Y., Mandal, B. and Klein D. J. (2017) Graph invertibility and median eigenvalues, *Linear Algebra and its Applications*, 513, pp. 304–323.

Zareei, A. (2019) Network origins of portfolio risk, *Journal of Banking and Finance*, 109: 105663, doi: https://doi.org/10.1016/j.jbankfin.2019.105663.

Zuckerman, G. (2023) The Man Who Solved the Market: How Jim Simons Launched the Quant Revolution. New York: Penguin.

Index